WINGED
CRUSADERS

WINGED CRUSADERS

The Exploits of 14 Squadron RFC & RAF 1915–1945

Michael Napier

Pen & Sword
AVIATION

First published in Great Britain in 2012 by
PEN AND SWORD AVIATION
an imprint of
Pen and Sword Books Ltd
47 Church Street
Barnsley
South Yorkshire S70 2AS

ISBN 978 1 78159 059 1

A CIP record for this book is available from the British Library.

Printed and bound in India by
Replika Press Pvt. Ltd.

Typeset in Plantin by Chic Graphics

Pen & Sword Books Ltd incorporates the imprints of
Pen & Sword Aviation, Pen & Sword Family History, Pen & Sword Maritime,
Pen & Sword Military, Pen & Sword Discovery, Wharncliffe Local History,
Wharncliffe True Crime, Wharncliffe Transport, Pen & Sword Select,
Pen & Sword Military Classics, Leo Cooper, Remember When,
The Praetorian Press, Seaforth Publishing and Frontline Publishing

For a complete list of Pen and Sword titles please contact
Pen and Sword Books Limited
47 Church Street, Barnsley, South Yorkshire, S70 2AS, England
E-mail: enquiries@pen-and-sword.co.uk
Website: www.pen-and-sword.co.uk

Contents

Foreword

by

Air Marshal T M Anderson CB DSO RAF

As a former Crusader accorded the singular honour of joining the list of its Commanding Officers it is my great delight to offer a Foreword to this latest, definitive, chapter in the Squadron's recorded history. I have had the pleasure and great privilege of meeting and getting to know some of my predecessors from bygone years and to talk in a corner of a noisy bar with men who can describe in passionate detail, with a clarity of memory I can only ever witness in awe, what they experienced in the service of their country, is a pleasure to be savoured. Men like the late Dick Maydwell, charismatic squadron commander and spellbinding raconteur; Brian Dutton, who broke the news of the German retreat from Sicily having flown at wave-top height in appalling weather through the Straits of Messina and described the event to me as if he had popped out to the shops to buy a newspaper; Joe Lowder, whose passion for the Squadron is matched only by his commitment to keeping its history living over the decades since; and Deryck Stapleton, a true gentleman, the unassuming yet undisputed leader of the Old Guard, who as a 23 year-old commanded the Squadron through the bleak days of 1941. Their generosity with their time and their patience with my unending questions have provided me with personal memories that I cherish dearly and greater understanding than I could ever have hoped for of the motivations, contributions, emotions and sense of duty and honour that characterized the generation of their day. And, in turn, I like to think that their bequest served in some way to both guide me and strengthen me in my own leadership of their Squadron.

But, no matter how clear the minds and memories, how vibrant the stories, there is still the need for a framework on which to hang such priceless gems and, more than this, a framework which is worthy of its role. Mike Napier, a former Executive Officer on 14 Squadron and, over many years, peerless steward of the Squadron's moral component, has crafted just such a framework; an unsurpassable canvas upon which he has delicately and expertly applied the colours of the period to depict what is, and always will be, a very human story. That story is expertly underpinned by a plethora of technical detail and primary research that gives the accompanying anecdotes and recollections relief, light and shadow and communicates to the reader not just a history, but the very terrain of that period in the Squadron's life. From his exceptional

FOREWORD

research into the Squadron's aircraft and their contemporary appearances, to his conscientious analysis of German and Greek records to tell the fullest story of the Melos Harbour raid, to his cataloguing for the first time of all of the combat losses in WWII, his expertise and significant commitment are a most fitting tribute in themselves to the men he describes in his book. And a tribute this book unashamedly is – a tribute to a most successful Squadron and to its people, who have operated with commitment and pride at the epicentre of the Royal Air Force's own illustrious history for longer than most and who, to their great credit, continue to do so.

London 2011

Introduction

Formed in 1915 and still operational today, 14 Squadron is one of the RAF's longest serving and most senior squadrons. Its longevity is largely due to its service in the Middle East for most of the first thirty years of its existence; this service has endowed the Squadron with a uniquely rich and fascinating, but paradoxically poorly recorded, history. "Winged Crusaders," which is part of a wider campaign to record the first hundred years of 14 Squadron's exploits, represents the first serious attempt to pull together the diaspora of records, documents and photographs to tell the story of 14 Squadron between 1915 and 1945. Of course it is a story of aeroplanes and military campaigns, but above anything else it is the story of people: it tells of the endeavours and the achievements, the setbacks and the sacrifices of the people who were 14 Squadron.

Notes on Nomenclature

Names of People
On first mention individuals are identified by rank (at the time) initials and surname with very brief (footnoted) biographical notes; thereafter rank and surname are used. I have tried to mention by name as many people as I can, but in the case of wartime losses of multi-crew aircraft I have (in general) only mentioned the aircraft captain's name. All the names of those involved in the aircraft losses are given in Appendix 1 which lists, by serial number, every one of the aircraft operated by the Squadron.

Names of Places
The names of many places in the Middle East, North Africa and the Balkans have changed as political circumstances altered since the 1920s, 30s and 40s. I have tried to use the spelling which will make it easiest for the reader to find in a modern atlas if they wish to investigate further – except that I have retained "traditional" spellings of places where these are still best known in this country at least by those spellings – eg Alexandria and Tobruk. There is also a problem with transliteration of Arabic names in that many Arabic sounds do not match exactly with English; so vowels are often interchangeable, as are throaty sounds can be rendered equally as "G" "H" "K" or "Q". Thus the exact English spelling of Arabic names is still open to some debate. The sketch maps which accompany the text reflect the spelling which I have used in this book.

Empire and Dominion Forces
For simplicity the term "British" is used as a general adjective to cover the armed

forces from the UK, Australia, Canada, New Zealand, South Africa, India and the rest of the Empire. During the Second World War most of 14 Squadron's aircrew came from the Dominions, with the vast majority from Australia..

Times
Times are given in 24 hour clock with the suffix "hrs." In most cases the time zone (i.e. local time or Greenwich Mean Time) is not specified because the original records do not specify which time zone is used. However it seems likely that most of these timings are in local time, which in the Levant and Egypt would have been two hours earlier than GMT.

Acknowledgements

This history of 14 Squadron is very much a collaborative effort and I have been greatly helped by the enthusiastic support of many wartime members of the Squadron (many of whom are now sadly deceased) who have over the years patiently answered many questions about the Squadron and have provided photographs, logbooks and reminiscences. Relatives of former squadron members have also been extremely supportive and I have received a great deal of material from relatives who are keen to see the efforts of their loved ones properly recorded. I have also been greatly helped by a number of other researchers who have gladly shared their work with us in order to get the story of 14 Squadron told.

Firstly I need to acknowledge the tremendous support of my good friend, neighbour and ex-colleague from 14 Squadron days, Dougie Roxburgh. Dougie has been a major collaborator in this project, who has helped me in so many ways: from spending many hours over cups of coffee "brainstorming" almost every aspect of the project to researching numerous matters of detail. Dougie also drafted the chapter covering operations with the Blenheim from 1941-42 with characteristic thoroughness and precision.

Secondly I must single out Mike O'Connor, ex-Concorde pilot and World War One guru, whose help and support made the first three chapters of this book possible. Mike's encyclopedic knowledge of First World War aviation, particularly in the Middle East theatre and his encouragement and advice on writing up this period have been invaluable. Perhaps more important still was Mike's kindness in allowing me full access to his extensive collection of photographs and in loaning me his copies of the entire 14 Squadron and 5 Wing RFC war diaries. A series of articles by myself and Mike for the journal "Cross and Cockade" were the drafts for the first three chapters of this book.

I am grateful to the following wartime veterans of the Squadron for their support and help: Colin Campbell (Marauder and Wellington pilot), Bill Cavanagh (wireless operator and air gunner on Blenheims and Marauders), Wally Clarke-Hall (Blenheim and Marauder pilot), Ron Dawson (MT section throughout the North African campaign), Lord Deramore (Blenheim, Marauder and Wellington navigator), Don Francis (engine fitter on Wellesleys, Blenheims and Marauders), Bob Fagan (Marauder pilot), Dick Froom (Wellington wireless operator), Arthur Galilee (Wellington pilot), Gil Graham (Marauder gunner), Jim Hanson (engine fitter on Wellesleys, Blenheims and Marauders), Peter Henry (Marauder and Wellington pilot), Norman Hooker (wireless section throughout the North African campaign), Joe Lowder (Marauder and Wellington wireless operator), Dick Maydwell (Blenheim and Marauder pilot who commanded the squadron from 1942-1943), Ron Page (engine

ACKNOWLEDGEMENTS

fitter on Blenheims and Marauders), John Robertson (Marauder and Wellington pilot), Deryck Stapleton (Gordon, Wellesley and Blenheim pilot who commanded the Squadron from 1940-41), Frank Slack (Engine fitter on Marauders), Richard Slatcher (Marauder wireless operator), Alex Thomson (Marauder gunner). Sadly many of those mentioned here are no longer with us, but I hope that this book will ensure that their efforts and accomplishments will no be forgotten.

The following relatives of ex-Squadron members have also been generous in their support: Ruth Allen (who provided photos and biographical information about her uncle "Jimmy" Chick), Linda Aiton (who provided a copy of her book and also copies of the logbook of her father "Joe" Tait), Vince Ashworth (who provided a copy of his book about his brother Corran Ashworth and copies of pages from his logbook), Tim Bates (who provided a copy of his father Hugh Bates' logbook), Mike Ball (who provided photographs and biographical information about his father Ray Ball), David Barnes (who provided photographs and biographical information about his father Harry Barnes), John Blake (who kindly gave copies of his father's photographs), Dianne Bowes (who very kindly furnished a copy of Gil Graham's logbook), Marie Buckland (who gave permission to quote from her father John Buckland's book), Malcolm Bullock (who provided his brother Tom Bullock's logbook and photographs), John Bullock (who provided photos of his father Peter Bullock), Christine Dean (who shared her research about her uncle Maurice German), John Divall (who provided photos and information about family friend Douglas Mackie), Howard Gibbins (who provided numerous photos and the logbook of his father Ivor Gibbins), Phillip Hall (who gave details of his uncle Jean Hall), Mike Hallett (who gave photographs and biographic details of his grandfather Harold Blackburn), Jamie Hetherington (who kindly shared the large collection of photos taken by his grandfather Jack Bury), Lee Hogg (who shared a wealth of material including photos about his uncle Mervin Hogg), Sue Holmes (who provided her father Alan Cadell's photos), Martin Hooker (who provided much material from his father Norman Hooker), Dave Lapthorne (who provided some memoirs of his grandfather Rod Lapthorne), Mike Lofthouse (who provided numerous photographs from his wife's grandfather Walter Showell), Ian Macfadyen (who provided photos and logbooks of his father Douglas Macfadyen), Cliff Mark (who let me have photographs from his great Uncle Jack's album from the 1920s), Alan Parker (who provided photos and biograhical information about his brother Freddie Parker), Anthea Perry (who provided diaries of her father Joe Lowder), Patrick O'Connor (who provided photos and the logbook of his father Neil O'Connor as well as much other information about former Squadron members), Mim Regan (who provided copies of her father Ken Turner's logbook), Natalie Ward (who provided letters and photos of her grandfather Frank Carberry), Matt Wethered (who provided photos taken before the war by his father Sydney Wethered).

I am extremely grateful for the generosity of the following researchers who shared the fruits of their work with us: Nicholas Vasilatos (who provided much material about Melos including reports from the German Archives), Dimitris Galon (who also provided photos and more extracts from the German Archives), Fiona McKay (who kindly translated some of the German reports from Melos) Roger Haywood (whose expertise on torpedoes and mines was most useful), Pel Temple (whose detailed work on RAF aircraft losses was invaluable in compiling the aircraft list), Ray Sturtivant (who also did much of the original research on the list of aircraft operated by the Squadron in the Inter-War years), Joe Baugher (whose comprehensive listing of USAAF aircraft serial numbers was very helpful in completing the list of Marauder aircraft operated by the Squadron), Roger Bragger (who provided Tom Henderson's account and photographs of the Hejaz expedition), Peter Dawson (whose friend Ron Lanham perished at Mataro in 1944 and who has done an incredible amount of research into that loss), Pedro Argila (from the Fundación Parque Aeronáutico de Cataluña who did some fantastic research into the Mataro incident), David Kennedy (who provided some photos of Amman and also a biography of Rees VC), Elimor Makevit (who kindly provided much detail about 14 Squadron's activities at Petah Tiqva and Hadera in 1921 and whose advice about the historical context of the Arab/Jewish friction in Pre-War Palestine was invaluable), Dov Gavish (who generously provided a copy of Henry Hanmer's papers and also patiently answered a number of questions about RAF landing grounds in Palestine), Christopher Mattheson (who was able to give some information about T E Lawrence's connections to the Squadron), Tony O'Toole (whose support and enthusiasm for the project has been invaluable), Andy Thomas (who kindly provided a number of photos of aircraft), John Cilio (who provided some photos of Marauders), Alessandro Ragatzu (who provided the photograph of Lovelace and Cowie), Drew Harrison (who provided Martin Johnson's photos of Blenheims and Marauders), GS Leslie (who provided photos of InterWar aircraft), Mark Postlethwaite (who provided some photos of aircraft via ww2 images), Malcolm Barrass (whose excellent website Air of Authority is a must for anyone with an interest in RAF history).

Thanks are due, too, to the following from various institutions who helped us greatly: Susan Dearing at the FAA Museum (for photos), Peter Elliott at the RAF Museum for his great support and for making documents available for research and providing copies of photographs, Andrew Renwick also at the RAF Museum for photos, Sandra Rogers of the War Graves Photographic Project who provided details of headstones at Ramleh Cemetery, Flt Lt Gareth Austin of 14 Squadron for copies of a number of photographs held by 14 Squadron.

Thank you to Pete West for the artwork in Appendix 2 and finally, many thanks to my son Tom Napier for drawing up the maps.

Mike Napier
Great Rollright 2012

Chapter 1

1915–1916
Egypt and Sinai

Beginning

By late 1914 it was apparent that the War would not be "over by Christmas" as the British people had somewhat overconfidently predicted when it all started in August. Lord Kitchener was appointed Secretary of State for War and plans were made for a massive increase in the size of the British Army. The bigger army would require a bigger Royal Flying Corps, and it was clear that the RFC would need to be enlarged from its seven squadrons. The question was: how big should it be? At HQ RFC the staff officers did their calculations and, with some trepidation, put forward a tentative suggestion of 50 squadrons. Their proposal was returned with a note in red ink scrawled in the margin "Double this – K"

The problem facing the RFC staff was how to manage this expansion when they had neither pilots nor aeroplanes with which to do it. Their answer was to form the new squadrons as cadres of semi-trained pilots around a nucleus of experienced pilots and to build up to full operational strength slowly as aeroplanes became available. In this way nearly ten new squadrons were formed in the four months from December 1914. As part of that expansion, Capt A Ross Hume[1] formed 14 Squadron RFC on 3 February 1915 at the airfield at Shoreham near Brighton. This unit consisted of three qualified pilots (Capt R O Abercrombie, Lt R E Lewis and 2Lt H C Barber) and two trainees (2Lts F H Jenkins[2] and D S Jillings[3] MC) from 3 Reserve Aeroplane Squadron using aircraft from the RFC school at Shoreham. At the end of March, Maj GE Todd[4], Ross Hume's successor as OC 3 RAS, arrived to assume command of the Squadron.

On 11 May 14 Squadron moved to Hounslow Heath just to the west of London where it began to receive its own aircraft. There was an assortment of eight aeroplanes on the Squadron strength by the end of the month, including a number of Martinsyde and BE2c scouts as well as Avro and Blériot training aircraft. In June the Unit received a number of "pusher" training aircraft such as Caudrons and Maurice Farman Longhorns, reflecting the Squadron's growing training task. As one might expect with primitive aeroplanes and inexperienced pilots, Flt Sgt W G Stafford[5] and his ground crews were kept busy maintaining both aircraft and engines in flyable state and it was not unusual for only half of the aeroplanes on the Squadron strength to be actually serviceable. The Unit was operating much like a training school with typically about seven officers under training with the Squadron at any one time. Some of those trainee

1

pilots were posted away to different squadrons once they had gained sufficient skills. One such was Lt W S Douglas[6] who joined 14 Squadron in July for training as a pilot after he had gained operational experience as an observer on the Western Front with 2 Squadron. Douglas thoroughly enjoyed his short time with 14 Squadron, which was chiefly memorable to him for Hounslow's proximity to the social life of London and for the number of aeroplanes which he crashed! However by the end of the month he was deemed competent enough to be sent back to France.

In early August the Squadron moved from Hounslow to Gosport where it joined 17 Squadron as part of the newly-formed 5 Wing, under the command of Lt Col W G H Salmond[7]. Both squadrons continued their operational work-up in the expectation of being sent to France in the autumn. Equipment was by now being standardised with the BE2c aeroplane. These "tractor" biplanes were the mainstay of the front line squadrons in France, so pilots were able to gain experience on the very aeroplanes that they would be using operationally. By now the Squadron's training included practical exercises such as artillery co-operation with the Royal Artillery units at nearby Cosham. Pilots were also detached to airfields further afield in order to gain experience of night flying. On 13 October Lt J C Slessor[8] was sent up[9] from Gravesend at 2130 hrs to patrol against Zeppelins on their way to bomb London. Despite the darkness of the night, Slessor spotted a Zeppelin as he patrolled at 3,000 feet. Unfortunately, what might have been 14 Squadron's first operational success was thwarted when Slessor lost contact with the raider amongst the clouds as he climbed to intercept it.

New pilots continued to be posted in, and typical of these new pilots was Lt C W Hill, an Australian, who joined the unit in November. Hill had sailed from Australia earlier in the year with the intention of joining the RFC but when he reached Britain he found that he would not be considered until he had gained his Aviator's Certificate at his own expense. This he did, along with many other would-be military pilots, at Brooklands before being accepted by the RFC and receiving his posting to 14 Squadron. Meanwhile, command of 14 Squadron had passed to Major G B Stopford[10].

To Egypt

On the strategic front it had become apparent that Turkey's entry into the war in November 1914 threatened the critically important link with the Empire by way of the Suez Canal. Ottoman Turkish troops, who controlled the Sinai Desert, had already attempted to raid the Canal. That raid on 3 February 1915 had been detected by a Flight of aircraft (later re-numbered 30 Squadron) based at Kantara which was able to give advance warning to the army. Indeed this event served to show how aerial reconnaissance could play a major role in the defence of the Canal and could cover a much greater area than would be possible by cavalry reconnaissance alone. So it was that on 7 November, the personnel of HQ 5 Wing and 14 Squadron, along with "X" Aeroplane Park embarked on the Blue Funnel Liner RMS *Anchises* at Southampton and headed not for France but for Egypt.

The *Anchises* reached Alexandria ten days later. The equipment and transport followed in the SS *Hunsgrove* some days behind – giving personnel the chance for some sight-seeing as they acclimatised to relative warmth of the Egyptian winter. Many enjoyed the opportunity to be tourists for a week or so, but others were impatient to get flying again. When *Hunsgrove* eventually docked at Alexandria she was unloaded and the aeroplanes she carried were transported, still in their crates, by rail to Heliopolis, just outside Cairo. Here an airfield complete with canvas hangars had been laid out in the desert and the aeroplanes were erected.

Meanwhile "A" Flight, comprising nine officers and forty-seven airmen under the command of Capt J B T Leighton[11] , had deployed to Ismailia where they took over the BE2c aeroplanes and wooden hangars left behind by 30 Squadron. The Flight also inherited five observers from 30 Squadron – who would prove invaluable for their knowledge of the area and of operating in the harsh conditions of the desert. Amongst these was Maj A J Ross[12] of the Royal Engineers, who, according to TE Lawrence "spoke Arabic so adeptly and was so splendid a leader that there could be no two minds as to the wise direction of his help"[13]. "A" Flight's task was to patrol the desert to the east of the Canal in order to detect any advance by Turkish troops, and also to start a photographic survey of the Sinai so that accurate maps of the region could be produced. The first of these patrols was flown on the morning of 26 November by 2Lt H I F Yates[14] and Maj Ross who reconnoitred the area of Qatiya and Bir El Mageibra. Another patrol resulted in the award of a MC to both pilot Capt Leighton and observer 2Lt V A Stookes[15]: under heavy ground fire Leighton descended to two hundred feet in order to photograph enemy positions, while Stookes gave covering fire armed only with his rifle. Meanwhile, aircraft were urgently required to help counter a threat which had sprung up in the Western Desert of Egypt.

THE SENUSSI CAMPAIGN

During the summer of 1915 German and Turkish agents had agitated Arab and Berber tribes in Libya and western Egypt against the British. Their main success was among the Senussi, a religious sect based in the deserts of Egypt, Libya and Sudan. In November the Senussi started their campaign against the British and raided the British coastal outposts at Sollum and Sidi Barani, occupying the latter on 17 November. The small garrisons at these posts were quickly overwhelmed and withdrew eastwards along the coast to Mersa Matruh. British commanders in Egypt recognised that they were now facing a substantial threat from the west along two axes: firstly along the Mediterranean coast from Sidi Barani towards Alexandria, and secondly from Sudan towards Fayoum and Cairo. As a result, the Western Frontier Force (WFF), a scratch force of assorted yeomanry regiments with infantry and artillery support was dispatched to Mersa Matruh on 23 November, under the command of Maj Gen A Wallace, to deal with the coastal threat.

Maj Ross was dispatched with Sgt C R King and seven mechanics to Mersa

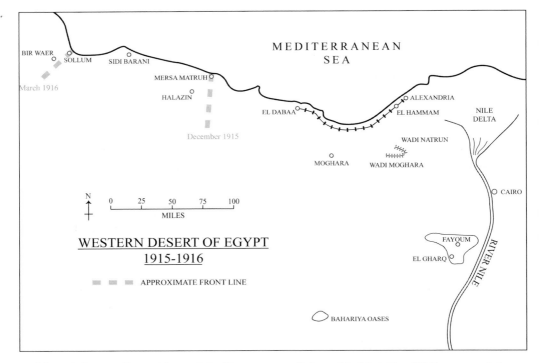

MEDITERRANEAN
SEA

BIR WAER
SOLLUM SIDI BARANI
MERSA MATRUH
March 1916
HALAZIN
ALEXANDRIA
EL DABAA EL HAMMAM NILE DELTA
December 1915
WADI NATRUN
MOGHARA WADI MOGHARA
CAIRO

N

0   25   50   75   100
MILES

WESTERN DESERT OF EGYPT
1915-1916

FAYOUM
EL GHARQ

RIVER NILE

APPROXIMATE FRONT LINE

BAHARIYA OASES

Matruh by sea from Alexandria. Ross was to liaise with Maj Gen Wallace to advise how the WFF could make best use of aeroplanes, while the groundcrew were to set up an aerodrome at Mersa Matruh. Since the harbour at Mersa Matruh was too shallow to allow unloading of large items such as aeroplanes, two BE2c aircraft were dismantled and sent in packing cases by train to the rail head at El Dabaa. With them went two aircrews from "A" Flight and an erection party of eight mechanics under the leadership of Capt C H Awcock[16]. The first aeroplane[17] was flown the 75 miles to Mersa Matruh on 4 December by Capt A G Moore[18] and Lt R C Gill[19]. Moore flew the aeroplane on its first reconnaissance flight the following morning with Ross as the observer and they were immediately able to locate Senussi encampments in the area. Until then, the Senussi had used their knowledge of the desert to camp just beyond sight of British positions, enabling them to strike swiftly and unexpectedly before disappearing back into the desert; the advent of the aeroplane now denied them this tactic.

Battle of Mersa Matruh
On 11 December, the WFF made its first sortie from Mersa Matruh. That afternoon the Independent Cavalry supported by armoured cars came up against a small force of Senussi camelmen in the Wadi Haruba. Moore and Gill, airborne just after midday, maintained a watch over the skirmish. They were able to drop messages to the

4

Independent Cavalry commander and to the commander of the main column during the engagement with details of the action as it unfolded. Two days later a large force of some 1,200 Senussi with field artillery and machine guns, counter-attacked the WFF column in the early afternoon in the Wadi Shaifa. The attack was vigorously repulsed, but much of the credit for the success of the WFF in this action must go to Moore and Gill who were able to forewarn the column commander of the impending attack and who, despite coming under continuous ground fire, remained on station overhead the engagement for two hours to give tactical information to the GOC.

The number of aeroplanes at the call of the WFF doubled on 12 December when Lt C R Rowden[20] and 2Lt Stookes flew the newly-erected machine[21] to Mersah Matruh from Dabaa. Reconnaissance sorties continued over the desert to the south of Mersa Matruh: various small Senussi camps were located and details were added to maps of the area. On 17 December Rowden and Capt L V A Royle[22] found[23] the main body of up to 3,000 Senussi troops where they had regrouped at Wadi Majid, immediately to the southwest of Mersa Matruh. During this sortie the aircraft came under accurate ground fire and received a number of hits. Rowden and Royle retaliated by dropping three bombs on the camp, though they did not hit anything. Further sorties by Rowden, accompanied by Ross on 22 December and by Stookes on the afternoon of 24 December confirmed the enemy dispositions and estimated their numbers to have risen to 5,000. The observers on these flights produced accurate drawings depicting the exact locations of the enemy forces: these were used by the army commanders to plan their attack. On Christmas day, the WFF advanced from Mersa Matruh in two columns with artillery support from the sloop HMS *Clematis*. Moore and Ross took off[24] at 0728 hrs for a two-hour flight, with the job of directing the guns of *Clematis* and providing tactical reconnaissance for the Force Commander. This sortie was successful, and included thirty-five minutes directing *Clematis'* guns over a range of 10,000 yards and the dropping of numerous tactical reports to Maj Gen Wallace; however, another reconnaissance flight in the afternoon by Rowden and

A BE2c seen at El Dabaa during the Senussi campaign. (JMB/GSL)

5

Stookes[25] was abandoned because of engine failure. By the end of the day the WFF had routed the Senussi, who lost around 450 killed or captured. However despite the success of this action and the heavy losses inflicted upon them, the bulk of the Senussi managed to escape destruction and fled inland.

Meanwhile, on 5 December, two aircraft of "B" Flight under the leadership of Lt R J Tipton had deployed to El Gharaq near Fayoum (on the Nile about 50 miles south of Cairo) to cover the approaches to Moghara and Bahariya Oases. The first patrol from Fayoum was flown[26] without incident on 11 December by Tipton and Lt E A Floyer[27]. However six days later 2Lt H I F Yates had a more eventful patrol. Having taken off[28] at 0910 hrs he headed towards Bahariya but by 1030 hrs his engine was running very roughly. He soldiered on for another half an hour, but was eventually forced to land on top of cliffs to the east of Bahariya, puncturing a tyre on the rocky ground in the process. After overhauling the engine, Yates filled up with spare fuel and oil and then cleared a path through the rocks to make a runway. Having successfully repaired his engine Yates took off once more and completed his patrol, eventually returning to the aerodrome at Fayoum six hours after he had left it. For the remainder of the month daily patrols were made from Fayoum. Then, on 28 December a 17 Squadron aeroplane patrolling from El Hammam apparently reported that a force of some 300 men had left Moghara. The following day a special reconnaissance was ordered by GHQ Cairo from Fayoum to check Moghara and the area to the southeast to attempt to locate the force. Tipton and Floyer took off at 0755 hrs[29] and flew to Wadi Natrun to refuel before continuing to Moghara. At Moghara they carried out a through search of the area, descending to low level on occasions to ensure that they missed nothing. On their return to Wadi Natrun they met with the "B" Flight commander, Capt F H Jenkins, who had flown there from Heliopolis[30] with Lt J A Barton[31]. They gave the report of their reconnaissance to Jenkins, who took it straight back to GHQ. Tipton and Floyer landed back at Fayoum at 1620 hrs. It was only two days later that GHQ Cairo realised that the mission had been a wild goose chase: the original report from 17 Squadron had said "no change at Moghara" but this had been reported up the line of command as "nothing at Moghara" which in turn had been interpreted as meaning that the previously reported tents were no longer there!

Battle of Halazin
On 1 January 1916 a reconnaissance sortie by Moore and Gill from Mersah Matruh reported the return of the Senussi with 80 tents at Jebel Howimil, but heavy rain on the coastal plain brought the campaign there to a temporary halt. The aerodrome at Mersa Matruh became completely waterlogged and the canvas hangars were soaked. It was not until the morning of 19 January that conditions improved sufficiently for flying operations to resume and on that day Rowden and Royle discovered the main enemy encampment at Halazin some 25 miles southwest of Mersa Martruh. Royle reported seeing over 250 Bedouin tents including that of the Grand Senussi himself, as well as 100 European tents. The following day Moore and Gill set out for another reconnaissance of Halazin, but they suffered an engine failure soon after take-off.

With the shoreline crowded with troops and equipment, Moore could not find space to make a forced landing and his only option was to ditch into the sea in Matruh harbour. Happily both officers were rescued immediately by sailors from the boats in the harbour.

At this stage the pilots who had been operating from Mersa Matruh through December and January were relieved by members of "B" Flight. Among the replacement pilots was Capt C R S Bradley[32] who flew his first patrol[33] with Maj Ross in the early afternoon of 22 January. Bradley and Ross confirmed Rowden and Royle's sightings and armed with this information the WFF set out from Mersa Matruh to attack the Senussi the following morning. In a large set-piece battle they inflicted a heavy defeat on the Senussi, killing or wounding over 700 of them. Unfortunately the glutinous mud resulting from the previous three weeks' heavy rain prevented the WFF from achieving a full encirclement the Senussi army and once again a large number of them were able to disengage and retreat into the desert. The battle continued the next morning with the WFF column harrying the retreating force, however the flat terrain made it difficult for the column commander to see what was happening at the points of engagement: Lt G deL Wooldridge[34] and Stookes located the main body of Senussi and remained over the area for two hours[35] dropping smoke bombs to mark it. A second machine, armed with bombs and Lewis gun, was to have joined them to harass the enemy, but that aeroplane remained unserviceable all day. Bradley and Ross took over the serviceable aeroplane in the afternoon for another two hour patrol during which they provided tactical information for the WFF column and confirmed the westward flight of the Senussi. That night heavy rain once more brought operations to a halt and the Senussi were able to melt away into the western desert.

Four days later Wooldridge and Ross made a reconnaissance of the area to the southwest of Mersa Matruh and found it completely clear of Senussi. However, on returning to the aerodrome at 1610 hrs Wooldridge side-slipped from a height of about seventy feet and crashed[36]. Both men were heavily bruised and suffered from shock, but they were otherwise uninjured.

The half Flight at Fayoum moved north to El Hammam (20 miles west of Alexandria) on 9 February to cover the Moghara Oasis, swapping places with a detachment from 17 Squadron which had been patrolling this area. This redeployment gave "B" Flight 14 Squadron responsibility for the whole of the coastal area and 17 Squadron responsibility for the southern areas. Unfortunately tragedy struck the Squadron three days later when a BE2c broke up in mid-air 25 miles south of El Hammam killing the crew Lt R Yates[37] of 14 Squadron and his observer Lt T G Hakewill from 17 Squadron. Thus Richard Yates became 14 Squadron's first casualty of war.

On 15 February 2Lt L F Hursthouse[38] and Royle mounted a long-range reconnaissance from Mersah Matruh via an advanced landing ground located a large Senussi camp at Agagiya 14 miles to the southeast of Sidi Barrani. They dropped three bombs on the camp before returning to report their find. The WFF moved to engage the enemy and in the morning of 26 February the Senussi were again defeated in a battle which included a full cavalry charge by the Dorset Yeomanry. The action was supported by tactical aerial reconnaissance by Rowden and Gill in the morning and Hursthouse and Barton in the afternoon.

Re-occupation of Sollum

The campaign now moved its focus westwards to Sollum and how the town might be recaptured. Sollum lies at the bottom of a steep escarpment and it was clear that detailed knowledge was needed of the condition of each pass and the positions of Senussi forces covering them. Two flights, one on 3 March by Rowden and Royle [39]and the second two days later by Hursthouse and Ross[40], made detailed the inspections the passes and were able to locate the Senussi positions accurately. By now all four of "B" Flight's aeroplanes were at Sidi Barani – the first time that all the whole Flight was available to support of the WFF directly. On 13 March a final check of the passes[41] was made by Rowden with Lt Gill to determine which ones would be most suitable for armoured cars. Rowden and Gill flew two sorties and then reported directly to Maj-Gen Wallace at Bir El Algerin. Thanks to "B" Flight's preparatory work, the advance through the passes was unhindered and Sollum itself was reoccupied the next day. That afternoon aerial reconnaissance by Hursthouse and Ross revealed the Senussi survivors fleeing from Bir Waer; these were subsequently intercepted and engaged by armoured cars of the Cheshire Yeomanry led by the Duke of Westminster. This action marked the end of the organised campaign by the Senussi in western Egypt, but aircraft and troops were maintained in the area as a precaution against the small bands of renegades who still roamed free.

One half of "B" Flight was permanently based at Sollum, while the other half remained at Sidi Barani. From these landing grounds, the aeroplanes were used over the next two months to mount patrols along the coastal roads, both towards Tripoli and between Sollum and Mersah Matruh, and into the hinterland, to ensure that the area was clear of renegade Senussi bands. They also carried out searches for U-boats in the coastal waters. As the summer drew on, both aeroplanes and personnel became exposed to the harsh conditions of the desert. During day time temperatures rocketed, and the air became turbulent with thermals, restricting flying to early mornings and late evenings. Sunglasses had to be sent from Alexandria to protect eyes from the glare of the sun and from reflections from the white desert sand around Sollum. Flying operations were also affected by the Khamsin – a strong gale of wind thick with sand – which could stop all operations for several days, as men battled in the choking dust to keep the aeroplanes from being blown away and wrecked.

In May 1916 the two aircraft[42] at Sollum were crewed by Capt Jenkins and Lts W D Long[43], H L Lascelles[44], J Wedgwood[45] and J A Williamson[46]. By this stage of the campaign the Western Desert was quiet, but the crews took the opportunity to hone their skills by participating in artillery direction exercises with ground artillery and the naval monitor M3. There was a major scare at the beginning of June when reports were received that a force of 3-4,000 German troops had landed at Benghazi. This information was found to be incorrect, but nevertheless they tied up British forces in the Sollum area for a little longer.

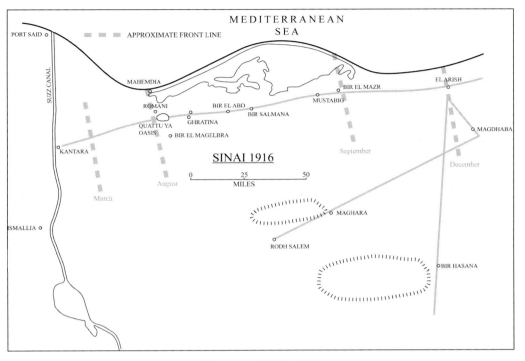

SINAI CAMPAIGN

While one detachment was busy in the Western Desert, the remainder of the Squadron had settled into the routine of the defence of the Suez Canal. By March 1916 "A" Flight was commanded by Capt Lord Lucas[47] and remained at Ismailia, near Lake Timeseh at the mid-point, and immediately west, of the Canal; "C" Flight commanded by Capt H Blackburn[48] was about 30 miles north of them at Kantara just to east of the Canal. Major W R Freeman MC[49] had taken command of the Squadron and each Flight was up to strength with five BE2c aircraft, a Martinsyde and a Bristol Scout for operational use and a couple of Maurice Farmans for continuation training. All of these aircraft types were by now obsolescent, but whereas the squadrons in France could expect more modern types, the RFC units in Egypt would continue to be equipped with the "cast offs" from the Western Front throughout the War. The BE2c aircraft were modified to carry bombs, with one bomb rack under each wing and another under the fuselage each capable of carrying four 20-pound "Hales" or "Cooper" bombs or one 100-pounder. In addition, "C" Flight had been equipped to be fully mobile, with a train of 80 camels and sufficient fuel, oil and ammunition to keep two aircraft operating in the field for twenty hours' flying.

Daily reconnaissance patrols set out to ensure that the desert beyond the canal was clear of enemy troops. In addition to this duty, survey flights were flown to

9

produce an overlapping photo-mosaic from which accurate maps of the area could be printed. Most flights routine patrols covered the area sixty miles out into the Sinai. However there were occasional forays further afield. One such, by Lts Yates and H H James[50] on 26 January 1916 went as far as Nakhl, 100 miles east of the Suez Canal and. This particular sortie, which lasted for 5¾ hours in appalling weather conditions, illustrated the perils of that dangerous mix of low cloud and mountains: Yates only narrowly missed hitting a mountain peak which he had not seen amongst the cloud. On 21 March Capt J E Dixon-Spain[51] and Lt Stookes also learnt a valuable lesson about navigation and meteorology. "A beautiful morning, but a strong west wind," wrote Dixon-Spain in his journal later that day, "very misty outside a radius of four or five miles. We both lost our way but by sticking to a compass bearing [we] came again to Lake Temseh."

Sporadically, bombs were dropped on "suspicious activity" – but they were very ineffective (on 18 December 1915 none of the bombs dropped by Lts Hursthouse and H V Stammers[52] either hit anything or even exploded!) and there was no organised offensive action. This policy changed in February 1916 when a change in command at the Egyptian Expeditionary Force brought a new strategy of "active defence" and the RFC started a campaign of weekly bombing attacks against Turkish strong-points.

The Sinai Desert provided Egypt with a buffer zone against the main body of Turkish troops in Palestine; it was a wilderness which was essentially impassable except by three distinct routes. The routes which led from the main Turkish base at Beersheba in southern Palestine all ran through El Arish on the coast before fanning out across the desert. The northerly, or coastal, route followed the coast through the Qatiya oases to Kantara. The central route ran to Bir Hasana and over a barren plateau 2,000 feet above sea level towards Ismailia, while the southern route ran to Nakhl and thence through the Mitla Pass towards Suez. The movement of any large numbers along any of these routes was dependent on the availability of water, and the Turkish strong-points commanded the watering places along them. Thus, at the beginning of 1916 it was the Turks who controlled all movement within the Sinai peninsular.

Bir Hasana Raids

The bombing raids carried out by the RFC were directed mainly at the Turkish installations on the central and coastal routes. Since these flights covered the relatively long range of nearly 200 miles there and back, the aircraft were modified to carry an extra fuel tank in the front cockpit instead of the observer. The first raid was carried out in mid-February, when 2Lt Yates from "A" Flight was ordered to attack the water pumping station at Bir Hasana, some 90 miles east of Ismailia. In preparation for this operation, he spent a day carrying out practice runs at 600 feet over Ismailia. The following morning Yates set out across the Sinai armed with a 100-pound bomb. As he dived onto his target he attracted heavy machine gun and rifle fire, but he pressed his attack to 600 feet and dropped his bomb directly onto the station, completely destroying it. Yates earned a MC for his actions and he also inspired 2Lt Hill of "C"

Lt C W Hill's attack at Bir Hasana on 27 February 1916, showing the direct hit scored on the rectangular water reservoir in the centre of the picture. The plume of water from the explosion is seen as a white circle in the reservoir and in the low morning sun it casts a long shadow to the left. (IWM HU54536)

Flight to try and better his feat using a bombsight developed by his Flight Commander, Capt Blackburn.

Blackburn was something of an innovator: an early experiment had been to mount "bullet deflectors" on the propeller of a Bristol Scout so that he could fire a machine gun through the propeller arc. Alas this experiment had ended in failure when the gun shot through the propeller during a ground test! However Blackburn's bombsight proved to be more successful. Hill spent a few days practising bombing using the sight along with some home-made canvas-and-sand practice bombs, on an area of wet sand alongside the Canal. According to Col Salmond who was taking great interest in Hill's efforts, his first attempts were "hopeless but he got better and better." At 0630 hrs, just as dawn was breaking on 27 February, Hill set out for Bir Hasana, his BE2c loaded with two 20-pound bombs and one 100-pound bomb. "It was beautiful flying at this time in the morning," wrote Hill[53], "As the light gradually increased towards the east the horizon turned pink and objects took on shape. Then

A line up of 14 Squadron's BE2c aircraft preparing to take off to attack the Turkish forces at Qatiya on 24 April 1916. (Walter Showell via Mike Lofthouse)

a little later the sun broke free making long shadows across the desert... I had not flown over this bit of country before except for about the first fifty miles or so which I knew well, but I had seen photographs of the reservoir and it showed up quite clearly at about two miles ahead as I approached at 3000 feet... The Turks had several anti-aircraft guns located about the area and these opened up as soon as I was within a mile of the reservoir, but they were not terribly accurate at first. There was also lots of rifle fire and occasionally a rifle bullet could be heard hitting the plane." Hill approached the reservoir from directly up wind, released one of his 20-pound bombs and watched its fall; the bomb overshot by twenty yards and exploded beyond the reservoir. After making adjustments to his sight Hill returned for a second attack, this time selecting the 100-pounder. This second release was perfect: "I watched it descending slowly and following underneath me at about the same forward speed, then increasing in a downward and slightly forward curve. Keeping the aircraft straight and level I concentrated on the photograph and, as I saw the bomb hit and a great column of water rise, I pressed the button." His third attack was less successful, and with the anti-aircraft fire getting closer, Hill turned and headed back to Kantara. His photograph of the second bomb confirmed the direct hit, and a subsequent reconnaissance the next day also showed that the reservoir had been seriously damaged and was leaking water.

Bir Hasana was raided again on 24 March by six aircraft. This time, four BE2c machines from 14 Squadron left Ismailia at 0530 hrs and headed south towards Suez. Here two 17 Squadron aircraft joined them and all six then headed for Bir Hasana. As usual, all the machines were flown in single seat configuration to allow maximum weapon load of 20-pound bombs; the brief was to drop their bombs on the tents and buildings in the camps surrounding the reservoir from 2,000 feet. The four aircraft from 14 Squadron were to lead the attack and the 17 Squadron aircraft were to approach the target from a different axis of attack after the first aircraft had dropped

12

their bombs. In all, forty 20-pound bombs were dropped and hits were obtained on six tents, and various buildings within the complex. One observer was quoted in the Daily Telegraph as saying that the camp resembled "a volcano in eruption." During the attack, the redoubtable Yates noticed a body of infantry firing at the aircraft; realising the threat to others, he immediately dived on them, descending to 200 feet as he opened up with his machine gun. All six aeroplanes returned safely from the operation. Salmond reported that the C-in-C was extremely gratified by the success of this attack.

The Qatiya Affair

Gen Sir Archibald Murray, who had replaced Maxwell as C-in-C Egyptian Expeditionary Force in March 1916, started to advance along the coastal route with a view to driving the Turks out of Sinai. His solution to the perennial problem of water supply was to build a twelve-inch water pipeline as he went and to extend the railway eastwards from Kantara at the same time. The initial advance was to Romani, some thirty miles east of Kantara, with a light mounted brigade of yeomanry regiments tasked with covering the flank of the main advance. The brigade deployed into a defensive screen at the oases round Qatiya, just to the south of Romani.

During the middle of April the Squadron's daily reconnaissance sorties were bringing reports of Turkish troop movements towards Qatiya. This information, which included sightings of enemy aircraft operating in the area, led Salmond to believe that the Turks were moving in strength against the yeomanry positions. However this interpretation was not shared at GHQ and so no action was taken. Unfortunately Salmond was proved correct and on 23 April the Yeomany were ejected from Qatiya by a strong Turkish force who attacked under cover of thick fog. With the cavalry driven off, the ground forces had no means of knowing where the enemy troops were deployed, so it fell to the RFC to locate the Turkish positions amongst the palm trees. In the afternoon of 23 April, Lt F F Minchin[54] and 2Lt W Baillie[55] of "C" Flight discovered the main body of the enemy at Qatiya and reported back. A plan was hastily devised by Freeman and Blackburn to attack the Turks at first light the next day. Starting at 0455 hrs the following morning, three aircraft from "A" Flight (flown by Capts Tipton, G A C Cowper[56] and S Grant-Dalton[57]) took off from Ismailia at three minute intervals. They flew at low level towards Kantara where five more aircraft (with Minchin, 2Lt C E Wardle[58], Hill and 2Lt A S C Maclaren[59] from "C" Flight, plus Rowden of "A" Flight) were waiting for them. The combined formation of eight BE2cs then followed Minchin in a loose gaggle at 2,000 feet for the forty minute flight to Qatiya. When he reached Qatiya, Minchin was able to locate the Turkish positions once again; he dropped a smoke ball as a signal to start the attack before peeling off to the right and diving towards his target. He released his ten bombs from 700 feet. The rest of the formation followed him down and Tipton, Wardle and Rowden dropped all their bombs on the camp. The others decided that further bombing was unnecessary at the camp and found other targets. After dropping their bombs, Rowden, Hill, Tipton, Cowper and Grant-Dalton came down below 200 feet and strafed troops with Lewis guns. The camp was completely destroyed and the troops were dispersed. Hill then flew further east, looking for more Turks and found another body of some 1,000 troops at Bir El Abd, which he also attacked with bombs and machine gun fire. A follow-up raid that afternoon by eight more aircraft was called off when no enemy troops could be found .

At 0700 hrs the next morning, the same eight pilots, this time led by Wardle, set out to attack the Bir El Abd positions, dropping seventy bombs. On this occasion, however, they themselves were attacked by an enemy aeroplane. Capt Grant-Dalton was strafing troops with his Lewis gun after he had dropped his bombs when he heard the rattle of machine guns and splinters started flying from the floor of his aircraft. He glanced round and discovered that he was under attack from a "pusher" type machine[60]. Grant-Dalton tried giving chase, but the enemy was able to use its superior speed to disengage and run away from him. One BE2c was also damaged by ground fire: Lt Rowden was wounded in the left knee and the force of the impact put the aircraft into a spin. Recovering from the spin, Rowden aimed his remaining four bombs at the camp and headed for home at best speed, flying with his right foot on the rudder bar and his hand on the left rudder wire. Despite losing a lot of blood he, along with the rest of the aircraft, returned safely. The "C" Flight aircraft were rearmed and were launched again from Kantara at 1035 hrs. This time twenty six bombs were dropped on densely-packed groups of men and camels. In all, nine separate attacks were made by the RFC against the Turkish forces in the Qatiya area over three days before the Turks finally withdrew.

14 Sqn Officers early 1916 – Lt H I F Yates, 2Lt C Mills, 2Lt G deL Wooldridge, Lt C W Hill, Lt C F Pitman (Equipment officer), 2Lt W Baillie. (Ray Vann-Mike O'Connor 22-24)

El Arish: Counter-Air Campaign

The appearance of the German air service in late April 1916 marked a change in the dynamics of air operations over the Sinai where the RFC had hitherto had free reign. The first priority for the RFC was to locate the enemy aerodrome, which was thought to be near El Arish. The Squadron's first combat loss occurred on the morning of 3 May when Cedric Hill[61] was shot down by rifle fire during a photographic reconnaissance of El Arish. Hill, flying[62] in the single-seat configuration should have been in company of another aircraft flown by Minchin and Baillie. "It was pitch dark when we left," wrote Hill, "and about half an hour later when it was light enough to see there was no sign of Minchin, so I carried on to El Arish. When I arrived there was a good deal of cloud about, the cloudbase being about 1,000 feet above sea level. Assuming I was well ahead of Minchin I decided to hang around for a while... after ten or fifteen minutes there was still no sign of the other aircraft and the clouds were just the same, so I went in under them to get odd photographs of anything worth taking. Before I had been many minutes over the town the whole Turkish Army as it seemed by the noise, turned out with rifles and kept up a continuous fire." Hill flew back and forth taking his photographs for about a quarter of an hour, during which time he "heard several bullets hit the machine [but] the only noticeable damage was one control cable shot through." Unbeknown to him, however, one round had penetrated the oil sump. On the return leg Hill's engine seized; he managed to force-land successfully but was taken prisoner by local Arabs, who turned him over to the Turks.

The German aircraft now started making their presence felt with bombing attacks on British positions and facilities in Egypt. Ain Sudr (about forty miles east of Suez) was attacked on 6, 9 and 11 May and Port Said on the night of 20/21 May. The British response was two-fold: firstly to mount retaliatory attacks against Turkish positions and secondly concentrate efforts to locate and neutralise the enemy aerodrome. El Arish was revisited by six aircraft on 18 May. The attack was carefully planned: routing to the target was at 6000 feet, following the coast one mile out to sea to achieve maximum surprise. Three naval trawlers were stationed along the coast to provide rescue services in the event of engine failure and the attack was to open at 0500 hrs with a naval bombardment. Five of the aircraft (flown by Maj Freeman, accompanied by Tipton, Grant-Dalton, Yates and MacLaren) were to be in single-seat configuration armed with bombs, while the sixth flown by Minchin with Baillie as the observer armed with a Lewis gun was to remain overhead at 6,000 feet to look out for enemy aircraft. The idea was that the German machine would be lured into the air by the either the naval attack or the sight of the bombers so that it could be ambushed by the two-seater. In fact the priority for all aircraft was to attack enemy aircraft and the bombers were instructed that if they saw a German aircraft they should drop their bombs and then engage it. The aircraft arrived over the Turkish camp at El Arish at 0553 hrs, diving to 2,000 feet to release their bombs and in the complete absence of enemy aircraft they attacked the Turkish camp and returned to Kantara[63]. Yates dropped three of his bombs amongst a column of 1,000 men marching westwards.

15

Four days later, raids were ordered against Turkish troop concentrations and facilities in Sinai in retaliation for the bombing of Port Said. Two aircraft from Kantara visited Bir Bayud, Bir Salmana and Bir El Mazr (which was believed to be the Turkish regional HQ) and two aircraft from Ismailia attacked Rodh Salem and El Hamma. In all forty bombs were dropped in these locations. The "C" Flight aircraft, flown by Capt Tipton and Lt Hursthouse arrived over Rodh Salem at 0545 hrs and dropped five bombs on the camp before flying on to El Hamma. However things nearly went horribly wrong here for Tipton when his machine was hit by a bullet after he had dropped only two of his bombs. The engine stopped completely and only recovered at 100 feet above the ground. With his engine running again, Tipton climbed back up and returned to El Hamma to drop four more bombs on the camp buildings. The two aircraft then flew to Rodh Salem where Tipton bombed the large reservoir. By now his aircraft was losing fuel so he forced landed at Wadi Muksheib. He was able to repair the engine and returned to Ismailia at 1100 hrs. However in the meantime Hursthouse had already returned, reporting that he had lost sight of Tipton in the clouds over the target. Yates was dispatched to search for Tipton and although he could not find him, Yates was able to confirm the damage done at El Hamma and Rodh Salem, Bir El Hamma.

Henry Yates also decided to try out some modifications to three aeroplanes to make the more effective as fighter aircraft. In an attempt to streamline them, he added "Fokker" style propeller bosses to two BE2cs[64]; more radically, he cut out and removed the centre section of the upper wing of another[65] and added a gun-mounting in the space. This allowed an observer to stand with head and shoulders above the upper wing surface and fire his gun forwards over the propeller. Capt Dixon-Spain declared that this last modification made the aircraft "a really good fighting machine."

In another move to counter the new threat of enemy air raids, a DH1a and a Bristol Scout were detached to Port Said to act as interceptors. The "pusher" configuration of the two-seat DH1a at least gave the observer a clear field of fire forwards – something that no other British aircraft in the Middle East could offer at that time. An early warning station was established at Romani with a telephone and wireless link directly to Port Said. In theory at least, a call from Romani would give sufficient time for the scout aircraft to scramble from Port Said to meet the intruder and do battle with it. However, despite this measure, German air raids continued virtually unmolested into June 1916. An effective high altitude bombing raid by a German aeroplane on Romani on the first of the month was countered with a retaliatory raid by five 14 Squadron aircraft on Maghara the next day .

Another attack ten days later, this time on Kantara itself, was less effective. An aeroplane was scrambled from Kantara to try and intercept the raider, but could not catch it; instead another retaliatory raid was ordered on El Arish for 13 June. This, too, was an attempt to entrap the elusive German aeroplane as well as an attempt to locate the exact position of the aerodrome which was still uncertain. Three aircraft left Kantara at around 0400 hrs: one was tasked with bombing Bir El Mazar ten minutes before two others flown by Minchin and Maclaren approached El Arish. The intention was that the bombing of Bir El Mazar would induce the German aircraft from its hangar at El Arish and that the other two would then find it defenceless on the ground where they would destroy it. However, the Germans were quicker off the mark than the raid's planners had anticipated and their aeroplane had already left the ground when the bombers arrived overhead El Arish. As they were leaving having dropped their bombs, Lt Maclaren and James noticed a "Fokker" (actually a Pfalz E II[66]) climbing rapidly towards them. The German monoplane looked brand new, its white fabric gleaming in the morning sun with black Maltese crosses clearly visible on the wings and fuselage. Maclaren headed towards the coast climbing as hard as he could, but the Pfalz kept closing on him. By the time he was five miles west of El Arish, Maclaren had made it to 7,000 feet, but by this stage the Pfalz had closed to within 500 yards range. It opened fire and immediately scored hits on the BE2c. Maclaren turned sharply towards the Pfalz – leaving both aircraft on opposite sides of the circle in a turning fight within fifty feet of each other. James was able to fire across the circle almost continuously with his Lewis gun, and despite turning steeply, the German could not bring his guns to bear. After a few minutes of hard manoeuvring, the German disengaged by diving steeply away back towards El Arish. Maclaren tried to follow, but the superior performance of the Pfalz enabled it to escape from the BE2c with ease. While Maclaren had been busy with the Pfalz, Minchin had bombed the camp from 4,000 feet. He had also located and photographed the aerodrome, which comprised an area of wadi used as a landing ground and, immediately to the north of it two lines of hangars (one of four hangars and another of six hangars) facing each other and running north-south.

Lt A S C MacLaren and Maj H Blackburn. – Archibald "Mac" MacLaren won two MCs while serving with 14 Sqn, the first for his destruction of a German aircraft during the raid on El Arish on 18 June 1916 and the second for shooting down a Fokker on 2 August 1916. He remained in the RAF after the war and retired as a Sqn Ldr in 1931 having added an OBE, DFC and AFC to his decorations. A pre-War test pilot, Harold Blackburn went on to command the Aeroplane & Armaments Experimental Establishment at Martlesham Heath in the late 1920s. He retired to Jersey in 1929. (Mike Hallett)

Capt J E Dixon-Spain in BE2c with Lt D C Beck about to set off in BE2c 2118 for El Arish in June 1916. (Ray Vann-Mike O'Connor 233-8A)

With the location of the aerodrome at El Arish now known, the RFC mounted a major raid on 18 June in an effort to neutralise it. Like the raids before it, this raid was planned with a route over the sea and navy trawlers on station to provide rescue cover. Eleven aircraft participated in the raid: eight single-seater bombers (Tipton and Hursthouse of "A" Flight, Minchin, W R S Humphreys[67] and Maclaren of "C" Flight and Capt H A Van Ryneveld[68], Lt ER Pretyman[69] and 2Lt M Minter of 17 Squadron) and three two-seaters (Grant-Dalton with 2Lt D K Paris[70] and Capt Dixon-Spain with Lt D C Beck[71] from "A" Flight , and Wardle with James from "C" Flight) to provide top cover against enemy aircraft. After a delayed start, due to a heavy surface and an unfavourable wind at Kantara the aircraft took off between 0623 hrs and 0637 hrs and climbed in an extended trail to 7,000 feet. The flight to El Arish took just over an hour and a half, following the coast about a mile out to sea and extending eastwards past El Arish to hook back and attack from a south-easterly direction from out of the sun. The first aircraft over the target at 0800 hrs was Maclaren. As he dived towards the hangars, he noticed that a Rumpler biplane was starting up just outside its hangar. Pressing on down to 100 feet to ensure that he didn't miss this target, Maclaren released a stick of three bombs. The centre bomb in the stick hit the enemy aircraft squarely, blowing it to pieces and although the pilot Leutnant Ditmar miraculously escaped injury, the seven ground crew in attendance were all wounded. Pulling up from his dive, Maclaren turned and dropped bombs on one of the westerly hangars before completing two more circuits dropping bombs on the hangars. While Maclaren struck the aerodrome, Tipton was attacking[72] the camp to the northwest of the aerodrome. His 100 pounder was seen to explode, but Tipton[73] was shot down by the heavy ground fire now boiling up from the defenders. Tipton crash landed to the north of El Arish and was taken prisoner.

At 0810 hrs, Minchin arrived over the aerodrome just as Maclaren was departing. He saw the biplane which Maclaren had left aflame and dropped his 100 pounder on the camp buildings – however it did not explode. Turning to the right, by now under heavy fire, he bombed two wooden sheds in the camp complex, before making another circuit of the aerodrome. This time he saw another biplane marked with large black crosses in the wadi just to the southwest of the hangars[74]. He dropped two bombs on this target and saw his bombs fall close by. Van Ryneveld was close behind Minchin and he, too, bracketed the Rumpler with a stick of bombs from about 300 feet. However shortly afterwards he was hit by heavy machine gun fire and anti-aircraft fire which caused huge damage to his aircraft. Van Ryneveld coaxed his machine towards the coast where he managed to forced land close to the shoreline. Minter, following Van Ryneveld was also hit by the ground fire. After bombing the western hangars from 600 feet, he turned back to the left to attack the biplane which Minchin and Van Ryneveld had bombed. But by then his aeroplane was so badly damaged that it was struggling to stay in the air: even with full power on he was still descending. Minter turned away from the airfield and nursed his machine away towards the coast, eventually ditching close to a trawler.

Dixon-Spain, who made two circuits of the aerodrome at about 0820 hrs thought that the second enemy biplane looked undamaged, though he attacked the hangars on the western side of the aerodrome. However, Pretyman of 17 Squadron, considered that the southern biplane looked badly damaged, and he, too, dropped his bombs on

BE2c 2116 starting up – Lt Richard Tipton was shot down while flying this machine during the raid on El Arish on 18 June 1916.

the hangars just behind Dixon-Spain. The last two aircraft over the target were Humphreys at 0830 hrs and Hursthouse at 0855 hrs. Humphreys dropped four bombs from 100 feet on the hangars to the west of the aerodrome; he then turned his attention to the easterly hangars but of his remaining four bombs, two dropped but did not explode and the other two hung up on the bomb racks. Hursthouse was similarly unlucky with his bomb release gear and despite three circuits of the aerodrome he only managed to drop four bombs.

The two-seaters flown by Wardle and James, and Grant-Dalton and Paris had remained in the overhead at 7,000 feet in case enemy aircraft attempted to interfere with the attackers. They remained on station from 0820 hrs until the last attackers left the area at 0900 hrs before leaving for home. Wardle and James (who had already dropped bombs on the camp at El Arish from high level) had been tasked with making a reconnaissance of the coastal route; Grant Dalton and Paris were due to retrace their route over the sea, but as they neared the coast Paris sent a note back to Grant-Dalton suggesting that they should follow the coastline instead in case any of the others had forced landed. It turned out to be an inspired idea: very soon Grant-Dalton and Paris came across the wreck of van Ryneveld's machine. Grant-Dalton decided to land next to van Ryneveld to see if he could assist. It was decided the best course of action was to burn van Ryneveld's BE2c[75] and for all three officers to return to base in Grant-Dalton's aircraft[76]. However on starting his machine Grant-Dalton found that he was bogged down and couldn't move. By clearing away some of the sand and putting the aluminium cowls from van Ryneveld's aircraft in front of the wheels they could get Grant-Dalton's moving again – but not with all three of them on board. At this, Paris and van Ryneveld decided to walk inland to try and find some firmer ground. This they did after a mile-and-a-half, and after struggling to get off himself, Grant-Dalton flew the short hop to pick them up. With the three officers on board, the overloaded BE2c finally staggered airborne after a very long take-off run.

The raid was considered to be a great success with one enemy aircraft destroyed and one damaged[77] plus six of the ten hangars on the aerodrome badly damaged. However, the success had been at the relatively high cost of three aircraft and one pilot lost.

The Battle of Romani

Command of the Squadron passed to Maj E J Bannatyne[78] MC in the middle of July, coinciding with an end to 14 Squadron's direct offensive action in Sinai, and a change in emphasis to reconnaissance operations, and to air defence patrols. Daily reconnaissance sorties checked the area ahead of the front line at Romani, while survey flights gathered photographs for the overlap mosaic which would be used to produce accurate maps of the area. The ground forces had found that the available maps of the country to the east of Romani were extremely inaccurate; the area is covered by numerous "hods" or depressions filled with palm trees, which provided good cover for enemy forces, and many hods were unmarked or mapped incorrectly.

17 Squadron had been dispatched to Salonika, and their place was taken by the newly-formed 67 (Australian) Squadron. 14 Squadron had been closely involved with

setting up this unit, which was manned entirely by Australian personnel, and as a result there was a special bond between the squadrons. It was a bond which was strengthened as the units worked closely together over the next two years.

Despite the success of the raid on El Arish, German aircraft continued to be a threat to British aircraft operating in Sinai. On the morning of 18 July 2Lts Humphreys and James were in one of two aircraft[79] carrying out a photographic task over El Arish. As they left the area they were attacked from above by an Rumpler. After delivering a burst of fire which damaged the BE2c's throttle and severed a control wire, the Rumpler repositioned for another attack, this time hitting James in the leg and shoulder. The wounds rendered James unconscious for a while, but he recovered and fired four drums at the Rumpler which was eventually driven off. Humphreys recovered the aircraft to Kantara, but their box of photographic plates had been damaged in the combat.

On the following day the morning reconnaissance brought reports of a large Turkish force numbering 7-8,000 moving westwards along the coastal route towards Qatiya. This was clearly the prelude to a major offensive by the Turks and all available RFC aircraft were concentrated at Ismailia, Port Said and Kantara in order to mount continuous reconnaissance over the Turks over the next days. The Turkish forces were by now well supported by anti-aircraft guns and British machines over flying Turkish

A DH1a – 14 Squadron was the only unit to use this type operationally. The Squadron's first aerial victory was achieved on 2 August 1916 in DH1a 4609 by Lts MacLaren and West, thereby earning MacLaren his second MC. (Walter Showell via Mike Lofthouse)

forces were subjected to heavy and accurate barrages. As German aircraft continued to pose a threat to the reconnaissance aircraft, the latter were provided with a fighter escort. On 23, 24 and 25 July the DH1a escorts engaged German Pfalzs and Rumplers. None of these combats were decisive, but Lts R P Willock[80] and T J West[81] were wounded in the first engagement[82] and heavy damage was inflicted on their DH1a[83] in the second.

Over the next week, RFC aircraft monitored the build up of troops and their supplies. By the end of the month, Turkish forces were deployed along a fortified line which stretched from Oghratina to Mageibra, outflanking the British positions at Romani. On 29 July the morning reconnaissance[84] over Mageibra by Lt W R S Wilberforce[85] and Lt J Brown was attacked by an Aviatik at 5,000 feet. The Aviatik was driven off, but not before it had caused enough damage to the BE2c to prevent it continuing its reconnaissance. On the same day two BE2cs carried out a bombing attack on Turkish camel lines at Bir el Mazar, but one of the aircraft crewed by 2Lts R L H Laye[86] and Lord Glentworth[87] was hit by anti-aircraft fire and forced-landed south of Lake Bardawil about 12 miles west of the British lines. The crew burnt the aircraft and then managed to walk back to friendly positions.

14 Squadron scored its first aerial victory on the afternoon of 2 August. 2Lt Maclaren and 2Lt West had left Port Said[88] to escort a BE2c carrying out a reconnaissance of Oghratina. Overhead Salmana they noticed an enemy biplane[89] stalking the reconnaissance aircraft. They attacked and after a short engagement during which West fired two drums of ammunition at point blank range, the enemy aircraft was seen to fall out of control, eventually crashing at Salmana. On the following days, the results were less successful: Lt Hursthouse (3 August) and Lt E H Pullinger[90] (4 August) both suffered machine gun stoppages in Bristol scouts as they engaged enemy aircraft, and Pullinger was wounded twice. Hursthouse was airborne in a Bristol again on 5 August, this time thwarted by the Bristol's lack of performance when he attempted to engage. On the same day Capt Grant-Dalton's Bristol was badly shot up and he was severely wounded, when he was bounced by an unseen Rumpler[91] as he engaged two others.

Meanwhile, the Turkish offensive had opened on the morning of 3 August. Throughout the ensuing battle, 14 Squadron aircraft remained over the enemy forces, providing tactical reconnaissance for the force commander. In attacking the southerly British flank, the Turkish commander had chosen poor ground for offensive action. The Turkish attack quickly became bogged down in heavy sand and lost its momentum; the British were able to seize the initiative and drive them back. As the battle continued on 4 August, one 14 Squadron aircraft directed the fire of the Monitor M15, and managed to achieve hits on the Turkish headquarters unit at Hod um Ugba.

Two days after it had started the Battle of Romani was over with Turkish troops in full retreat. Aircraft were used to track the progress of the enemy and to harass them with bombs and machine gun fire. The retreat continued during the next week and by 11 August the Turks had fallen back as far as Bir El Abd. On that day the

Bristol Scout 4684 – photographed at Kantara in summer 1916. The Scouts were used for hostile aircraft patrols with little success, for although a small and manoeuvrable aeroplane, the Scout did not have sufficient margin of performance to catch high-flying German raiders. (Ray Vann-Mike O'Connor 228-24A)

Squadron suffered its second combat fatality. 2Lts E W Edwards[92] and Brown were carrying out the morning reconnaissance along the coastal road in a BE2c. As they returned towards Bir el Abd they were under heavy anti-aircraft fire; however, the barrage lifted and two Rumplers[93] dived onto the BE2c, raking it with machine gun fire. One bullet smashed Edwards' jaw and he was shot through his shoulder, left hand and left leg. He lost consciousness, but came round just 500 feet above the ground and was able to make a landing near the British lines. Brown was also severely wounded with bullets through his chest and shoulder. John Brown was bleeding profusely as he was lifted from the aircraft, but despite his wounds he insisted in making his full report before he received treatment for his wounds, and having given his report he lost consciousness and died shortly afterwards[94]. The whole episode was witnessed by Brig-Gen E W C Chaytor commanding the New Zealand Mounted Rifles, who was greatly moved by Brown's bravery and devotion to duty.

The Turkish retreat continued and British troops occupied Salmana on 13 August; here they paused to consolidate. During the days after Romani all the available crews and aircraft had been utilised and between them 14 Squadron and 67 Squadron mounted an average of 23 hours of reconnaissance each day. Many crews were flying two or three times a day, always under accurate anti-aircraft fire.

The Advance to Gaza

A German air attack on Port Said on 1 September provoked a retaliation against Maghara the next day. The plan was for eight BE2cs, Including two from 67 Australian Squadron to carry out an early morning attack, but fog and low cloud delayed the take off until 0955 hrs. Eight BE2cs took off from Ismailia, but one was forced to return because of engine trouble. The remaining seven aircraft flown by Capt Minchin, Lts Floyer, H A Fordham[95], T Henderson[96], Maclaren, W J Y Guilfoyle[97] (from 67 Squadron) and 2Lt W E L Seward[98] continued towards the pumping facilities at the two reservoirs at Maghara. En-route, MacLaren's BE2c suffered a camshaft failure and he forced-landed. The others found their targets and bombed with some success. On his return leg Minchin landed[99] next to MacLaren to offer assistance, but his aircraft wrecked its undercarriage on boulders as he landed. However Guilfoyle and Fordham managed to land successfully[100]and once MacLaren's and Minchin's aircraft had been burnt, all four officers returned in the two remaining aircraft.

Minchin and Fordham were in action again four days later when they carried out a small-scale raid on El Arish. Unfortunately the DH1a which was to be their fighter escort suffered a forced-landing and they pressed on without it. Minchin, in a single-seater BE2c had been given the task of with taking photographs of the area after he had dropped his bombs. However, as he started doing so he came under attack from an enemy aircraft. Remaining over El Arish as long as he dared, Minchin finished his photography before setting off westwards with the German in hot pursuit. Fortunately, Fordham and his observer 2Lt S S Hume had seen his plight and they manoeuvred to engage the enemy, managing to drive it off.

On the ground, after the Turkish retreat from Romani, the front lines had stabilised near Bir El Mazar. The British were unable to capitalise fully on their victory at Romani because of the lack of water. A period of consolidation was needed while the railway and water pipe could be extended to support a further advance. Some small-scale bombing raids were made on Bir El Mazar: Lts R H Freeman[101] and West dropped four bombs and Lt S K Muir[102] (from 67 Squadron) ten bombs on 4 September. Three days later Lt Freeman revisited Bir El Mazar and took a mosaic of fifteen photographs of the camp. Freeman's photographs were the basis for accurate maps of the area which would be put to good use a week later.

It was decided to mount a cavalry raid on Bir El Mazar over 15-17 September in order to maintain pressure on the Turks. The task of the 14 Squadron would be to mount a continuous air patrol over Bir El Mazar to ensure that no enemy aircraft could observe the approach and subsequent withdrawal of the cavalry. Eight aircraft were detached to a forward landing ground at Mahemdia for the operation. In the early hours of 16 September a night bombing raid was flown against El Arish with the intention of destroying or damaging enemy aircraft in their hangars. Capts Jenkins and Minchin left Mahemdia at around 0245 hrs and followed the coast line to El Arish. Jenkins was to attack six hangars[103]. He arrived over the target at 0415 hrs and found four of the hangars which he attacked from 500 feet, dropping six bombs and achieving near-misses with them. However despite circling the area twice he could not locate the other two hangars in the darkness so he decided instead to drop them on muzzle flashes nearby. As Minchin arrived over El Arish he saw Jenkins' bombs exploding and the smoke was still visible as he pressed his attack on the sheds which were his target. He carried out two bombing runs and scored a direct hit on his second pass before dropping the rest of his bombs on sheds in the camp to the north of the airfield. Minchin commented afterwards that the still air had helped him drop more accurately than he had managed previously.

During the day, pairs of aircraft patrolled Bir El Mazar at 7,000 feet continuously in relays from 0530 hrs to 1800 hrs. Each pair, comprising a Bristol Scout and either a DH1a or a Martinsyde or two BE2cs, remained on station for two-and-a-half hours. However, the air blockade was not entirely successful: just before 0730 hrs Maj Bannatyne in a Martinsyde accompanied by a DH1a came on station to relieve a Bristol Scout and a DH1a which then returned to Mahemdia. Almost at once Bannatyne's wingman suffered an engine failure and had to forced-land; unfortunately it was just at this moment that two German aircraft appeared over Salmana. Bannatyne engaged them and succeeded in turning one back, but the other managed to get a lucky long-range shot into the Martinsyde's radiator and Bannatyne had to forced land himself, leaving the way open for the German machine to get through to Romani. However, it was chased off by other aircraft and it seems that the crew did not notice the cavalry force poised to attack Bir El Mazar. The attack went ahead on 17 September when, once again, 14 Squadron aircraft were in the air from dawn until 1730 hrs covering the ground engagement and the withdrawal. Four days later the Turks evacuated Bir El Mazar.

On 18 September there was a general redeployment of the RFC units in Egypt, reflecting the end of the Sennussi threat in the west and the strategic focus in the east on the advance across the Sinai. As a result, 14 Squadron concentrated with its HQ and two Flights at Ismailia and one Flight at Suez.

Two days later the newly arrived 2Lt S G Kingsley[104] set off with Lt A B Jarvis[105] to reconnoitre[106] advanced Turkish positions in the hills beyond Ain Sudr. As he reached the area near Sudr el Heitan he started to suffer magneto problems. With his engine running roughly Kingsley managed to forced land on a small ledge on the eastern side of the hills and then set about repairing the magneto. Unfortunately he had chosen an area which was close to Turkish troops, who started to advance along a pass to capture the crew. With Jarvis providing covering fire with the machine gun, Kingsley managed to complete the repairs just in time. He succeeded in restarting the engine and then, since the ledge was so small, he taxied at high speed over the edge, gaining flying speed as the aircraft fell away.

In late September the RFC was ordered to prepare a Flight to move to Arabia for operations in support of the Arab revolt. By the end of the month "C" Flight at Suez, under Capt V A Albrecht[107] MC, was ready to embark and Maj Bannatyne had already visited Yenbo and Rabegh to select suitable landing grounds . "C" Flight sailed for Arabia aboard HMT *Georgia* in early October but diplomatic problems – based largely on the unwillingness of the Sharif of Mecca to allow non-Muslims into his territory – meant that they were recalled and found themselves back in Suez by 21 October. However a second attempt, this time under Maj Ross a month later was successful and the Flight eventually arrived at Rabegh with personnel aboard the HMT *El Kahira* and equipment aboard HMT *Elele* on 16 November.

Back at Ismailia, 14 Squadron's ground crews had been busy modifying the wireless installations on the BE2c aircraft. Each one was now fitted with the wireless and accumulators located behind the pilot's cockpit. The hard work of the Squadron's groundcrew had been recognised by the awards during the year of a DCM to Flt Sgt Stafford and a MSM to Sgt Maj G Felstead[108]. Although many of the groundcrew had experienced the harshness of working in the desert during the Sennussi campaign, all of the Squadron's personnel were now getting used to living under canvas in the desert. The lack of water – sometimes just a teacupful a day for ablutions – made for a miserable existence. Nevertheless the groundcrews continued to maintain the aircraft with great care.

With wireless equipment now fitted to all the BE2c aircraft, crews carried out wireless training and artillery co-operation with ground batteries from 267 Brigade and also the naval Monitors *Ladybird*, *Scarab* and *Bee*. A "smoke puff" range was set up at Ismailia to help train observers in the art of artillery co-operation. Despite the wireless equipment there remained a problem as to how to communicate with aircraft in flight and in particular how ground force commanders could pass orders to aircraft in the air. While it was easy enough for aircraft to drop messages containing tactical information, there was no way to send messages the other way. Maj Bannatyne and Col Salmond carried out an interesting experiment on 22 October to test the feasibility of picking up messages from the ground using a hook attached to the wireless aerial. The message was picked up on the first attempt, but it would be another year before this technique was perfected and used on a routine basis.

With the stagnation of ground operations, flying became restricted to daily the reconnaissance sorties and the occasional small raid on Turkish camps. However aircraft from 67 Squadron was dispatched to Mahemdia support a mobile column operating near Maghara on 15 October. Fog and low clouds disrupted air operations, but two aircraft from 14 Squadron, Lt Floyer in a BE2c and Capt Minchin in a Martinsyde carried out a successful bombing raid on Maghara in the morning, re-arming at Mahemdia for another raid before returning to Ismailia.

14 Squadron's "A" Flight moved to a forward landing ground at Salmana on 4 November leaving "B" Flight at Ismailia. Routine reconnaissance sorties by both RFC squadrons continued throughout the end of October and the beginning of November, including some long-range missions ranging as far as Khan Yunis in Palestine. Additionally Maghara was visited frequently, with a small number of bombs dropped on each occasion to harass the troops there. On 11 November 67 Squadron mounted a large raid on Beersheba and on the same day five BE2c aircraft from 14 Squadron attacked the Turkish encampments at Bir Lahfan and Magdhaba. Lts E H Grant[109],

Willock and James dropped twenty six 20-pound bombs and a 100-pounder on a new camp at Bir Lahfan and Lts W R S Wilberforce and Kingsley obtained several hits on the camp at Magdhaba with the twenty-two 20-pound and single 100-pound bombs which they dropped there. A similar raid on Turkish positions was carried out four days later by Minchin, Wilberforce and Grant on Maghara and by Lt V D Siddons[110] on Hama. On 16 November Freeman, now a Capt, was co-operating with a brigade-strength infantry column attacking a Turkish position in the hills near Bir Um Gurf. He located the enemy position and bombed it with a 20-pound and a 100-pound bomb before descending to 800 feet and strafing the troops with his machine gun. He then dropped a message to the column's field gun battery with the co-ordinates of the Turkish strongpoint. By the time Freeman landed back at Ismailia he had been airborne for four hours and twenty minutes.

The following day the presence of a German aircraft over Suez caused as retaliatory strike by four RFC aircraft on the camp at Masa'id. Two of these aircraft, flown by Lts Wilberforce and Siddons with Capt H R Coningsby[111], were provided by 14 Squadron[112].

As the Arab revolt gathered momentum, the RFC decided to mount a long-range attack on the Hedjaz railway to demonstrate the capability of air power to the Arab leadership. On 24 November two Martinsydes flown by Capt Freeman and Lt Muir set off to attack facilities on the railway, over 150 miles away on the far side of the Dead Sea. Freeman was armed with two 100-pound bombs, each with a 39 second delay fuse, and four 20-pounders. His target was the railway bridge four miles south of Qal'at El Hasa, while his wingman was to attack the railway station at Jauf El Derwish. The weather was perfect for the operation, with almost unlimited visibility: during this flight the pilots could see the entire length of the Dead Sea on one side and the Red Sea on the other, while at the same time the Mediterranean Sea was clearly visible to the west. Freeman found his target and dropped his 100-pound bombs from a height of only twenty feet – a tactic made possible by the delayed-action fuse. Thanks to the low bombing height he managed to achieve great accuracy and scored a direct hit with one bomb which shattered the bridge structure and displaced the tracks. On his return, Freeman dropped his 20-pounders on a military camp at Asluj, destroying a building there. The two aircraft landed after five-and-a-half hours' flying time. The same day saw "A" Flight move further forward to Mustabig, where it was joined in early December by "B" Flight and the three Flights of 67 Squadron.

On 2 December, Freeman and Minchin were on a photo-reconnaissance mission[113] at 9,500 feet over Beersheba. Just after 1000 hrs Freeman was attacked by a Rumpler[114]. He managed to manoeuvre behind it and opened fire, but suffered a temporary stoppage. As the enemy aircraft turned, Freeman stuck to its tail and on his second attempt managed to fire off a whole drum of ammunition from a range of about 100 yards. Meanwhile Minchin had also seen the Rumpler and turned to engage it: while Freeman disengaged and tried to change drums, Minchin closed to 100 yards and he, too, fired off a whole drum at it. Minchin was now so busy trying to follow the Rumpler while simultaneously changing his drum, that he failed to notice a second enemy aircraft, a Fokker, which had closed on his tail. The Fokker opened fire, immediately scoring hits which punctured his fuel and oil tanks. By this time Freeman had reloaded and he rejoined the fray, attacking the Fokker and driving it off. But Minchin was already gliding down to carry out a forced landing five miles south of Rafah. Freeman landed alongside him and after setting fire to his own machine, Minchin clambered aboard Freeman's aircraft, riding on the engine cowling of the single-seater, for a lift home.

From mid-December, the daily reconnaissance sorties began to report major reductions in the strengths of the Turkish garrisons. On 15 December it was noticed that the enemy strength at Masaid was greatly reduced and five days later both Masaid and El Arish had apparently been evacuated. British cavalry captured El Arish on 22 December and the following day ground forces were moving to surround the Turkish positions at Magdhaba. A major bombing raid in which over 120 bombs were dropped was carried out against Magdhaba by thirteen BE2cs – ten from 67 Squadron and three more (flown by James, Grant and Siddons) from 14 Squadron. On the same morning five Martinsydes each armed with two 100-pound bombs took off from Mustabig to attack the bridge at Tel Es Sharia and carry out a reconnaissance of Beersheba. Three of the Martinsydes (flown by Lts Muir, Guilfoyle and A Murray-Jones) were provided by 67 Squadron with the remaining two (flown by Freeman and Wilberforce) from 14 Squadron. Wilberforce had to return soon after take-off with engine trouble, leaving Freeman[115] as the only representative of 14 Squadron. The attack on the bridge was carried out successfully with accurate bombing – but alas the results were disappointing with minimal damage caused. The aircraft moved on to Beersheba, about a hundred miles behind enemy lines, where they were engaged by three enemy aircraft. A Fokker closed on Freeman, who evaded it and managed to fire half a drum; meanwhile, Muir and Murray Jones also attacked it and Muir emptied two drums of ammunition from close range before it crashed. The other two aircraft were driven off and all four Martinsydes returned safely to Mustabig.

The jaws of the trap closed round the Turkish forces in Maghara on the morning of 23 December. As the ground forces advanced into position Capt Albrecht with Lts James and Seward in three Bristol Scouts strafed Turkish positions in the Wadi El Arish to the south of Maghara. The enemy troops were difficult targets in small widely scattered groups, but there is little doubt that the morale effect of the air attack greatly outweighed its limited physical success. The shooting was not all one way, however, and a BE2c was shot down leaving 2Lt G C Gardiner[116] wounded in the arm. The British attack was pressed with great determination and by 1630 hrs the Turkish garrison of nearly 1,300 had surrendered. With the fate of Maghara sealed, the remaining Turkish forces in Sinai hastily withdrew to Palestine, leaving the entire Sinai peninsular in British hands by the end of 1916.

Notes

1 Lt Col Alexander Ross Hume OBE retired from the RAF in 1920; apart from founding 14 Squadron, his major contribution to the RFC was in running the RFC's recruiting campaign in Canada.
2 Frederick Jenkins had been a civil engineer in Florida before the war. He gained his Royal Aero Club Certificate at the end of February 1915 and remained with 14 Squadron until November 1916, commanding "B" Flight. He ended the war as a Lt Col and after demobilisation he returned to Florida.
3 David Jillings was the first British soldier to be wounded in an aeroplane, while serving as a Sergeant-Major observer with 2 Sqn in France. The remainder of his service was mainly in administrative appointments and he retired from the RAF as a Sqn Ldr in 1926.
4 George Todd was one of the original RFC pilots on 2 Squadron who had deployed to France at the outbreak of war. He ended the war with the rank of Lt Col.
5 Interestingly William Stafford (a founder member of the RFC with the regimental number "22") was himself a qualified pilot, having gained his "wings" in 1913. He died in 1928 aged just 40.
6 MRAF Lord Douglas of Kirtleside (1893-1969), commanded 43 and 84 Squadrons during WW1 and was AOC-in-C Coastal Command 1944-45.
7 ACM Sir Geoffrey Salmond (1878-1933), died in while serving as CAS.
8 MRAF Sir John Slessor (1897-1979) enjoyed a distinguished RAF career eventually serving as CAS. After this incident he moved to 17 Squadron with which he served until late 1916.
9 in BE2c 2065.
10 Commissioned into the Royal Artillery in 1906, George Stopford gained Aviator's Certificate 300 in 1912. He commanded the Experimental Flight at CFS and ended the War as Lt Col Chief Instructor at the School of Military Aeronautics. At the end of the War he rejoined the Royal Artillery, retiring in 1937 but rejoining for service during WW2.
11 John Leighton was promoted to command 23 Squadron in France in 1917, and died in May 1917 from injuries sustained in a flying accident. His younger brother Richard served as a pilot with 56 Squadron.
12 Arthur Ross DSO & bar, a classics scholar at Malvern College, was born in Allahabad India in 1881 and was killed in a flying accident in East Anglia in Aug 1917.
13 "Seven Pillars of Wisdom" – TE Lawrence, Jonathan Cape 1935.
14 Henry Yates (1884-1976) had served in the army during the South African War and gained a French flying licence in 1913. He left 14 Squadron in mid-1916, and after finishing the war as a Lieutenant Colonel he resumed his career as a mining engineer.
15 After serving as an observer with 14 Squadron and a pilot with 60 Squadron, Valentine Stookes was released to resume his medical studies in October 1917.
16 Sqn Ldr Charles Awcock OBE retired from the RAF in 1934 and died in 1944. After his tour with 14 Squadron he transferred to the Technical Branch.
17 BE2c 1757.
18 A veteran of the South African War, Alfred Moore later served with 34 and 24 Squadrons. He survived the war having won two MCs and was twice Mentioned in Dispatches.
19 Brigadier Rockingham Conyers Gill (1895-1970) late Royal Artillery retired from the Army in 1946
20 At this time Cuthbert Rowden was only 18 years old; he was killed in a flying accident in April 1918 at the age of 20, while an Acting Major commanding 78 Squadron.
21 BE2c 4711.
22 33 year old Leopold Royle later trained as a pilot and was killed in April 1918 while serving with 111 Squadron when his aircraft broke up in flight. He had been awarded the MC and was also Mentioned in Dispatches 5 times.
23 flying BE2c 4711.
24 in BE2c 1757.
25 in BE2c 4711.
26 in BE2c 4712.
27 Ernest Floyer retrained as a pilot and rejoined 14 Squadron, winning the MC in 1917; after the War he lived in Kenya.
28 also in BE2c 4712.

29 in BE2c 4356.

30 in BE2c 4552.

31 A medical student before the war, John Barton also flew with 40 Squadron; he was demobbed in 1919.

32 After serving with 14 Squadron, Charles Bradley went on to command 31 Squadron in India. He retired from the RAF as a Gp Capt in 1932.

33 in BE2c 4711.

34 Gilbert Wooldridge ended the War as a Major with an OBE, the Order of the Crown from the King of Italy and the Order of the Rising Sun from the Emperor of Japan

35 in BE2c 4711.

36 BE2c 4711.

37 Educated at Blundell's School 22-year old Richard Yates had qualified as a pilot in July 1915

38 Leonard Hursthouse subsequently served with 108 Sqn in Italy and lived in Jamaica after the war.

39 in BE2c 4552.

40 in BE2c 4315.

41 in BE2c 4552.

42 BE2cs 4356 and 4552.

43 After the War, William Long (1894-1978) by then a Major, remained in Egypt and was seconded to the Egyptian Government He was Comptroller General of Egyptian Civil Aviation when he retired in 1932.

44 Harold Lascelles returned to UK for pilot training but was killed in a flying accident in March 1917.

45 The son of a Norfolk vicar, Josiah Wedgwood trained as a pilot and was seriously wounded in France in March 1918.

46 John Williamson was killed in a flying accident in April 1917.

47 Auberon Thomas Herbert, Baron Lucas and Dindwall, was killed on 3 November 1916 while serving with 22 Sqn in France.

48 37-year old Harold Blackburn had qualified as a pilot in 1911. After the war he remained in the RAF, retiring in 1929 with the rank of Wg Cdr.

49 Later one of the most important and influential senior officers at the outbreak of the second World War, ACM Sir Wilfred Freeman (1888-1953) retired as VCAS and became Chief Executive of the Ministry of Aircraft Production in 1942.

50 Harold Hindle James later qualified as a pilot and flew with 14 Sqn in Palestine and 66 Sqn in Italy.

51 "Ted" Dixon-Spain (1878-1955) had fought in the Boer War and was an architect by profession. After flying with 14 Sqn he founded 3 School of Aeronautics in Cairo during 1916. Immediately after WW2 he was a member of the Monuments, Fine Arts & Archives Commission tasked with locating looted works of art in Europe and returning them to their owners.

52 Victor Stammers commanded 15 Squadron during 1918 earning a DFC and a Croix de Guerre; he retired from the RAF as a Flt Lt in 1929 but rejoined in the Administrative Branch in 1939 reaching the rank of Sqn Ldr during WW2.

53 "The Spook and the Commandant" – CW Hill, William Kimber & Co 1975.

54 Frederick Minchin left 14 Squadron to take command of 47 Squadron at the end of 1916. After the war he joined Imperial Airways, and was lost during an attempt to cross the Atlantic in September 1927.

55 After leaving 14 Squadron William Baillie qualified as a pilot and served with 11 Squadron. He was killed in a motor accident in April 1919.

56 After serving with 14 Squadron, Gerald Cowper transferred to the Australian Flying Corps, ending the war as a Major commanding 8 Training Squadron AFC.

57 Stuart Grant-Dalton ended the war as a Lt Col; after resigning from the RAF in 1929 he joined the RNZAF as Director of Air Services.

58 Charles Wardle served for much of the War as a staff officer and was an Acting Lt Col in 1919; however he reverted to the rank of Flt Lt the following year and retired at that rank in 1926.

59 Archibald MacLaren ended the war with an OBE, two MCs and an AFC. He remained in the RAF and amongst his post-war exploits was an attempt in 1924 to circumnavigate the world in an Avro Vulture amphibian.

60 Grant-Dalton was attacked by a Rumpler C I flown by Oberleutnant Richard Euringer with observer Oberleutnat Fritz Berthold.

61 Hill was taken PoW and managed to get himself repatriated in late 1918 by feigning madness. After the

war he rejoined the RAF and served again with 14 Squadron in the early 1920s. He died in 1975.

62 BE2c 4419.

63 Although they did not realise it, one aircraft had in fact achieved a direct hit on a Rumpler C I on the aerodrome.

64 BE2cs 2118 and 2016.

65 BE2c 2007.

66 flown by Leutnant Walter von Bülow.

67 William Humphreys AFC served with the RAF Reserve during the 1920s and was recalled to the RAF with the rank of Sqn Ldr in 1939 to serve in the Admin Branch.

68 Later Brig Gen Sir Pierre van Ryneveld became Director of the SAAF; he died in 1972.

69 One of two brothers in the RFC, Pretyman resigned from the RAF due to ill health in 1937, but rejoined the service from 1939-42.

70 Darrell Paris later trained as a pilot and was shot down and captured while flying with 15 Sqn in April 1917. He survived the War.

71 Donald Beck started pilot training in July 1916 but was killed in a flying accident two months later.

72 in BE2c 2116.

73 Richard Tipton later escaped from captivity and returned to the UK via Russia, but subsequently died of wounds received while serving with 40 Sqn in France.

74 this was a Rumpler flown by Unteroffizier Otto Kahnt and Oberleutnant Schumburg, who had just landed.

75 BE2c 2691.

76 BE2c 2700.

77 In fact the raid had resulted in the destruction the two Rumplers and also severe damage to a Pfalz which was also on the ground. Two German pilots were wounded: Uunteroffiziers Kahnt and Heinrich Ande (the Pfalz pilot).

78 After his service with 14 Squadron Edgar Bannatyne was seriously injured in an aircraft accident at Cirencester in 1917 when his aircraft caught fire in flight and he jumped from it; he subsequently died from his injuries.

79 BE2c 4152.

80 AVM Robert Willock (1893-1973) retired from the RAF in 1947; he was Civil Aviation Advisor to the High Commissioner of Australia from 1949-1959.

81 An Australian, Theodore West subsequently trained as a pilot and served with 63 Squadron; he survived the war.

82 The Rumpler was flown by Leutnant Hans Henkel and Oberleutnant Karl Stalter.

83 DH1a 4607.

84 in BE2c 4135.

85 The youngest son of the Bishop of Chichester, William Wilberforce won a MC during his tour with 14 Squadron; he was subsequently posted to instruct at CFS Upavon and was killed in a flying accident there on 2 June 1918.

86 Rupert Laye rejoined the Gordon Highlanders reserve in 1919; however he was called up for the RAF in 1939 in the Administration Branch ending WW2 as a Wg Cdr. He died in 1955.

87 Edmund William Claude Gerard de Vere Pery, Viscount Glentworth subsequently served with 32 Sqn on the Western Front and was posted Missing in Action in May 1918.

88 in DH1a 4609.

89 This was Leutnant Hans Henkel's and Oberleutnant Karl Stalter's Rumpler. Neither of the crew was injured and the aircraft was repaired the following day.

90 Ernest Pullinger was attached to the French Air Service in 1918. He left the RAF in 1919.

91 Probably Henkel and Stalter's aircraft.

92 Ernest Edwards joined the Ministry of Labour in 1919.

93 von Bülow is credited with this victory.

94 21-year old John Brown was Mentioned in Dispatches for his bravery.

95 Educated at Harrow and Trinity College Cambridge, Hugh Fordham subsequently served in staff posts for the remainder of the War. He retired from the RAF in 1919 with the rank of Major.

96 Originally from Tynemouth, Thomas Henderson MC AFC (1894-1945) had seen service in France as

an observer with 10 Squadron; later he was a Flight Commander on 58 Squadron. He left the RAF in 1927 and married into the Deuchars brewing family.

97 Later Air Cdre William Guilfoyle, died in 1948.

98 Eric Seward (1891-1975) later transferred to the Technical Branch and ended the War as a Major.

99 BE2c 2118.

100 Guilfoyle in BE2c 4454 and Fordham in BE2c 4354.

101 Russell Freeman was the younger brother of Wilfred Freeman who had commanded 14 Squadron earlier in the year. He was killed in action in April 1918 while commanding 73 Squadron.

102 Stanley Muir was killed in a flying accident while instructing at Harlaxton in September 1917.

103 in BE2c 4216.

104 Shirley Kingsley (1895-1971) had spent some years before the war in South America and was fluent in both French and Spanish. He finished the war as a Major and returned to Argentina where he was involved in early air transport services.

105 Alan Jarvis subsequently trained as a pilot and was killed while serving with 1 Squadron in Flanders in 1917.

106 in BE2c 4390.

107 A pre-War regular officer, Maj Vaudrey Albrecht OBE MC (1888-1944) from Manchester later commanded 97 Squadron. He retired from the Army in Dec 1926 but served in the Admin & Special Duties Branch of the RAFVR during WW2.

108 George Felstead was commissioned in the field as a Lieutenant in 1917 in recognition of his ability. He retired from the RAF in 1921.

109 Edward Grant also served with 31 Squadron in India; he retired from the Army in 1919.

110 The Rev Victor Siddons MBE DFC commanded X Flight in Arabia working closely with Col TE Lawrence. After the war he returned to his theological studies and became a Methodist Minister. During WW2 he served as a chaplain in the 8th Army.

111 Originally from Capetown, Harry Coningsby served with the British Army during the South African War. He trained as a pilot during 1917 and rejoined 14 Squadron in that role later in the year. After the War he returned to South Africa and was the founding Chairman of the South African Aero Club.

112 Siddons and Conginsby were in BE2c 4152.

113 Freeman in Martinsyde 7473 and Minchin in Martinsyde 7474.

114 Flown by Haptman Helmuth Felmy and Leutnant Kurt Jeschonnek; Felmy was wounded in the feet during this engagement.

115 in Martinsyde 7473.

116 Group Captain George Gardiner DSO DFC (1892-1940) served with 17, 47 and 150 Squadrons and achieved 6 aerial victories. He died in Helwan, Egypt.

Chapter 2

1917
Advance into Palestine

Action at Rafah

At the beginning of 1917 both of 5 Wing RFC's squadrons, 14 and 67, were based at Mustabig. The campaign to clear the Turkish from Sinai had been successful, but in the last days of 1916 a large Turkish force had been identified in fortified positions near Rafah. Despite the challenges of poor weather in the first week of January, 5 Wing reconnaissance aircraft monitored the Turkish positions closely. From this surveillance it seemed that the force at Rafah was not directly supported and it was therefore vulnerable to a raid by mounted forces – in the same way that Magdhaba had been captured the previous month. With just such a plan, the Desert Column under Lt Gen P W Chetwode advanced on Rafah on 9 January. The RFC support of the Desert Column's operations was twofold: firstly it provided a continuous artillery direction patrol over the troops, and secondly it carried out a bombing raid against the aerodrome at Beersheba in order to keep German aircraft away from the action.

A forward landing ground was established a mile east of Sheikh Zawaid for the artillery direction task. Major Bannatyne landed there at 0700 hrs to set up the operations centre; petrol and mechanics' tools arrived by camel train under Air Mechanic Pendrons shortly afterwards. Each squadron provided two aircraft which would operate in relays to ensure that two aircraft, operating on a different wireless frequency, were continuously overhead the troops. 14 Squadron's aircraft[1] were flown by Lt A J L Barlow[2] with Capt C H Williamson MC[3], and Capt J A D Dempsey[4] with Lt H J Buchanan-Wollaston[5] and between them they remained airborne from 0700 hrs until 1630 hrs. Four sledge-mounted wireless sets had been issued to the Royal Horse Artillery batteries and Capt Coningsby had also established a wireless reporting station at the GHQ. The arrangement worked well: although the artillery shooting was indifferent in the morning, it became very effective in the afternoon as aerial observers and artillerymen got used to working together.

The raid on Beersheba aerodrome was carried out in the afternoon by two Martinsydes, escorted by three Bristol Scouts, from 67 Squadron. A 14 Squadron Martinsyde which was to have accompanied them was delayed, and took off fifteen minutes later. Lt Kingsley[6] was five miles from Beersheba when he met three Fokkers[7]. He engaged one of them, but the other two aircraft carried out a co-ordinated attack, firing at him simultaneously. The Martinsyde's engine, petrol tank and radiator were

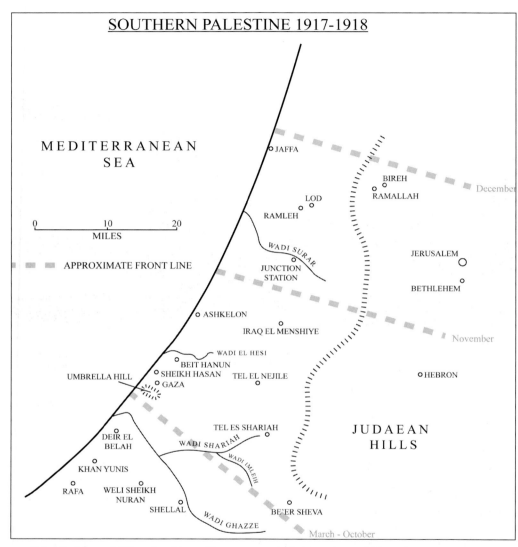

all badly hit and Kingsley himself was wounded three times. With his engine running on three cylinders, Kingsley managed to escape their attentions and headed for the coast, pausing only to drop his bombs on the camp at Sheikh Nuran as he passed it. The engine then failed completely and he ditched the aircraft in the sea just to the west of Khan Yunis. After making sure that the aircraft sank, he swam ashore where he was immediately captured by five Bedouins. Luckily for Kingsley he was also spotted by a patrol of New Zealand Mounted Rifles who rescued him and took him back to the British lines at Rafah[8].

BE2c 4395 was flown by Capt J A D Dempsey and Lt H J Buchanan-Wollaston in support of the Desert Column's operations against Rafah on 9 January 1917. (RAFM PC73-4-069)

Meanwhile the British assault at Rafah had been successful and the garrison surrendered just after 1630 hrs, leaving over 1,600 Turks as Prisoners of War.

The Aerodrome at Beersheba

The bombing raid on Beersheba aerodrome on 9 January confirmed that there were at least nine enemy aircraft based there, representing a potentially great threat to British ground and air forces. The aerodrome and the supporting facilities therefore became the focus of RFC offensive operations over the next week. At 2200 hrs on the night of 11 January two Martinsydes from 14 Squadron took off from Mustabig, each armed with two 100-pound delayed-action bombs for a moonlight bombing raid on the aircraft sheds at Beersheba. Unfortunately it was a cloudy night and the weather prevented Capt Albrecht from reaching Beersheba so he returned at 0120 hrs. However Capt Freeman managed to find a way through the clouds and reached Beersheba where he dropped his bombs on his target from 100 feet, scoring a direct hit on one of the sheds. The weather the following day precluded a follow-up attack, and in the next few days operational flying was limited by weather and by the forward deployment of "A" Flight to a new landing ground at Kilo 143, eight miles west of El

35

Arish on 14 January. Here they joined 67 Squadron who had moved there a few days previously; "B" Flight followed a week later.

Albrecht was able to try another night raid on Beersheba in the early hours of 15 January. Flying a BE2c he accompanied Lts A M Jones[9] and L J Wackett[10] from 67 Squadron for an attack on the aerodrome and the railway station. This attack was followed later in the day by six aircraft from 67 Squadron, and the following day by eleven aircraft in a mixed formation from both squadrons. The 14 Squadron participation in the latter operation was by Capt Dempsey and Lts Barlow, J M Batting[11] and Siddons with 2Lt I Cullen[12], each armed with two 100-pound bombs[13]. Barlow was one of six pilots who attacked Beersheba again on 28 January. There was heavy anti-aircraft fire over the target and Barlow[14] was hit by a shell splinter which blew off his goggles. Unfortunately Barlow was slightly short-sighted and the blast also blew off the spectacles he was wearing under the goggles. With eyes streaming from slipstream and exhaust fumes Barlow made it home, but crashed while attempting to land. Happily he escaped unhurt from the inverted wreckage.

On 19 and 29 January, 5 Wing aircraft mounted long-range reconnaissance missions over Palestine, covering the area from Junction Station to Jerusalem, Jericho and Bethlehem. On the second of these sorties, a new enemy aerodrome was discovered at Er Ramleh near Junction Station. The new landing ground was visited on 1 February by Capts Albrecht and Wilberforce in Martinsydes accompanied by Freeman and 2Lt Cullen in a BE2c and three others from 67 Squadron, but no hits were obtained. Shortly afterwards the RFC was instructed to cease offensive action in order not to provoke reprisal raids against the Egyptian Labour Corps who were making good progress extending the railway line and water pipeline eastwards. Instead the squadrons concentrated on artillery co-operation and photographic duties. The artillery co-operation was becoming much more effective with the establishment of RFC wireless operators attached to artillery units. By February ten airmen from 14 Squadron were attached to five batteries. Aerial photography was providing the basis for new maps of southern Palestine and a

Lt A J L Barlow was short-sighted and lost both goggles and spectacles when struck on the head by a shell splinter while attacking Beersheba on 28 Jan 1917. He crashed on landing, writing off Martinsyde A7476, which was not a popular machine: Russell Freeman's view that the accident was "good riddance of bad rubbish".

The first recorded occasion of a British aircraft being used to evacuate a wounded soldier from the battlefield on 19 February 1917. A member of the Camel Corps with a serious leg injury is lifted into BE2c 4442 flown by Capt J A D Dempsey at Bir Hasana. (IWM HU 97906)

detailed map of Gaza town was produced in February. In the same month new photo-reconnaissance equipment was introduced: the "Aerocam" was designed specifically for the Palestine theatre because of the large distances that needed to be covered. Instead of the single glass plate used by the standard cameras of the day, the Aerocam used film and a motorised drive so that it could take a sequence of photos as the aircraft was flown in a single pass along a line feature. In one early sortie a successful series of prints was obtained along the Gaza to Jaffa road, from an altitude of around 6,000 feet – a completely overlapping set covering thirty-five miles of road taken in just one flight.

The embargo on offensive action was lifted on 15 February for another attack on Beersheba. Four aircraft from 14 Squadron[15] flown by Capt A Clear[16], Dempsey, Lt Barlow and Capt Freeman took off from Kilo 143 in the morning with five aircraft from 67 Squadron. They reached Beersheba at around 0745 hrs finding it under low cloud in rain. The aircraft were armed with 20-pound bombs and the mission was not particularly successful for the 14 Squadron aircraft: a number of bombs either hung up on the aircraft or did not explode, and the bombing accuracy was not particularly good. On the way back from bombing, Barlow's BE2e suffered an engine failure and he forced landed in enemy territory. He managed to set fire to his aircraft, but was taken prisoner before he could escape. Unaware of his fate, the Squadron mounted a number of searches for Barlow, but were hampered by poor weather, and all attempts to find him were suspended after a couple of days.

14 Squadron pioneered a new humanitarian use of aircraft on 19 February when

On 19 February 1917 Capt R H Freeman, in Martinsyde A1576, was escorting the afternoon reconnaissance aircraft at 6,000 feet over Weli Sheikh Nuran when he was attacked by an enemy biplane. However he managed to drive it off by turning towards it, and firing two drums into it at close range. The enemy aircraft dived into a cloud and escaped from him. (Ray Vann-Mike O'Connor 204-11A)

the morning reconnaissance sortie[17] flown by Capt Dempsey and Lt Cullen landed near a column of troops near Bir Hassana to make their report to the column commander. The latter asked for their assistance in evacuating a man of the Imperial Camel Corps, who had been seriously wounded in the leg. In the Medical Officer's opinion, saving 24 hours of travelling by camel-ambulance might mean saving the man's leg, so he was put aboard the aircraft and Dempsey flew him to Kilo 143. This was the first recorded aerial evacuation by a RFC aircraft. Meanwhile Capt Clear was dispatched[18] to pick up Cullen and continue with the reconnaissance. That afternoon, the German air service demonstrated that they were still very active despite the RFC's harassment of the aerodrome at Beersheba: Freeman[19] was escorting the afternoon reconnaissance aircraft at 6,000 feet over Weli Sheikh Nuran when he was attacked by an enemy biplane. However he managed to drive it off by turning towards it, and firing two drums into it at close range. The enemy aircraft dived into a cloud and escaped from him.

First Battle of Gaza
March of 1917 was notable for its appalling weather, but by good fortune two periods of good flying weather coincided with major ground operations. In the first one, from 5 to 9 March, 5 Wing carried out a continuous offensive against Turkish troops withdrawing from Weli Sheikh Nuran. The first clue that a major withdrawal was in progress came on 5 March when the early reconnaissance[20] by Lt Floyer and 2Lt CV Palmer[21] failed to return. Search flights found the wreckage of the aircraft Tel el Jemmi, but no sign of the crew. It was later learnt that they had been shot down by the

German Ace Hauptman G Felmy[22] and had been taken Prisoner of War; however, the search flights also noted that the Turks were drawing back from the positions at Weli Sheikh Nuran. Aircraft were immediately launched to harass the retreating Turks – 67 Squadron operated against Tel el Sharia while Capts Dempsey, Clear, Freeman and 2Lts Seward and GC Dell-Clarke[23] of 14 Squadron were sent against the wooden bridge over Wadi Imleih. Attacks against enemy lines of communication continued through the day. Four separate attacks were made on 6 March against rolling stock and stations from Tel el Sharia to Junction Station by both squadrons. 14 Squadron was also tasked to bomb the new camp at Tel el Nejileh in the afternoon. During this attack Dell-Clarke's aircraft was hit by rifle fire and one of the rounds struck the Verey cartridges stored in a locker behind the cockpit; one of the them ignited, setting the rear fuselage of the aircraft ablaze and the other cartridges then exploded in turn, adding to the inferno. Despite getting burnt and being in great pain, Dell-Clarke managed to recover his aircraft to Rafah, where he doused the flames with his water bottle, and then flew the badly-damaged machine back to Kilo 143 in darkness to make his report.

The air offensive continued and on the night of 7/8 March five attacks were made on Tel el Sharia by single aircraft at one-hourly intervals from 2100 hrs onwards. A mixed formation of six aircraft attacked Junction Station in the following afternoon achieving eight direct hits on buildings, rolling stock and rails; however the attack was not unopposed and five hostile aircraft were sent up against the attackers. The BE2e bombers escaped unscathed and the Martinsyde escorts, including Freeman[24] were able to fend off the enemy.

On 18 Mar Capts Clear, Dempsey and F H V Bevan[25] with 2Lt Seward were part of a mixed formation with 67 Squadron which attacked the aerodrome at Ramleh. The following day during an attack on the railway line near Wadi el Hesi using 100-pound delayed-action bombs one of the Martinsyde escorts, a 14 Squadron machine[26] flown by 2Lt H Kirby[27], suffered an engine failure and forced landed close to the target area. The pilot set fire to the aircraft but burned himself badly in the process. Despite the dangers of advancing enemy troops and of the two 100-pound bombs still on the burning aeroplane, Lt Bailleau[28] and Lt Ross-Smith[29], of 67 Australian Squadron, landed their aircraft[30] alongside to rescue Kirby. Ross-Smith held off the approaching troops with his revolver while the badly burnt Kirby ran towards them. The BE2e struggled off under heavy fire and Bailleau flew to the forward landing ground at Sheikh Zowaid.

On 24 March the Squadron was tasked to reconnoitre Ludd in order to locate the Turkish 53 Division. The reconnaissance aircraft was escorted by 2Lt Seward flying Martinsyde A1590. Both aircraft came under anti-aircraft fire near Ramleh and Seward's machine was hit in the fuel tank. He headed out to sea and ditched just off the coast some four miles north of Ashkelon. Unfortunately he had chosen a point within two hundred yards of a Turkish position on the shoreline and he came under heavy rifle fire. In order to escape the attention of the Turks, he struck out to sea, removing his heavy clothing to make it easier as he went. An accomplished swimmer who had participated in the 1908 Olympics, Seward swum southwards for four hours, but then cold and exhausted he came ashore just before dusk and hid until nightfall. He then continued working his way along the coast in the dark, walking where he could but taking to the sea on five occasions to avoid enemy patrols. He managed to cover some thirteen miles barefoot through the night reaching Wadi Ghazze before once more cold and exhaustion forced him to rest. After digging a hole in the ground he rested until dawn when he was able to make his way along the sand hills where he eventually met a British patrol.

The Battle of Gaza opened on 26 March but thick fog prevented air operations until 0830 hrs. Of the first two aircraft to take-off, one crashed on take-off when the engine failed, while the other flown by Capt Dempsey was wrecked when he hit a sand dune while attempting to land again in the fog. When the weather improved sufficiently, 14 Squadron provided aircraft for contact patrols to locate friendly and enemy forces so that the General Staff could be updated with the progress of individual units; artillery co-operation sorties were also flown with twenty-four targets engaged on 26 March and fifteen the following day. Most of the co-operation was with the heavy 60-pounder batteries and the targets included trench systems (particularly "the Labyrinth" complex) and counter-battery work against Turkish artillery. At least one enemy gun was destroyed and an ammunition dump near another battery was also blown up. Two enemy four-gun batteries were located by air and successfully engaged. Reconnaissance sorties were also flown to locate Turkish reinforcements to the east of Gaza, and interdiction missions were flown to neutralise those reinforcements. All of this aerial activity was flown under heavy anti-aircraft fire.

In the afternoon of 26 March, 2Lt Dell-Clarke was flying a Martinsyde escorting the reconnaissance aircraft near Hareira when he engaged two enemy aircraft. He pursued the first towards Beersheba and emptied a drum into it from close range, which caused the enemy to nose-dive steeply; before he could check whether it actually crashed, Dell-Clarke found himself engaged by a second aircraft. He closed on it from underneath and fired from point blank range, following his victim down as it fell out of control and crashed. Dell-Clarke was in action again the following day on a Hostile Aircraft Patrol when he intercepted a German aircraft armed with twelve bombs. Although the enemy aircraft was superior in speed and performance to Dell-Clarke's Martinsyde, he still managed to block its approach and prevented it from attacking British troops. On 28 March, in his third action in as many days, Dell-Clarke engaged an aircraft over Gaza but this time he took several hits, damaging the Martinsyde's engine and wounding him. He ditched in the sea off Gaza and was rescued by a cavalry patrol.

Unfortunately 14 Squadron suffered a sad loss on 27 March when Lt C C Gibbs[31] and Capt Williamson were killed in an accident. They had just taken off for a reconnaissance sortie when they suffered an engine failure and their aircraft nose-dived into the ground from 100 feet, bursting into flames on impact.

The first Battle of Gaza ended in failure for the British on 28 March. Forewarned by their own aerial reconnaissance, the Turkish had reinforced their positions just in time and, unable to deliver the *coup de main* before nightfall, the British withdrew from the attack. At the end of the month 14 Squadron moved to join 67 Squadron at a new aerodrome at Rafah.

Second Battle of Gaza

The first Battle of Gaza had been intended by Gen Murray to apply pressure on the Turks, but he had been expressly told that there would be no follow-on offensive in southern Palestine in 1917. However, British policy changed in late March and Murray was instructed to renew his attack on Gaza with a view to opening an offensive to drive the Turks out of Palestine. Thus was born the plan for the second Battle of Gaza. For 5 Wing RFC the first half of April was taken in routine tasks of preparation for an assault. On 2 April "B" Flight moved permanently to the forward landing ground at Deir El Belah, close to the Gaza front lines. The major task was to update the maps of Gaza, particularly the new Turkish defensive positions there and of southern Palestine. Artillery co-operation was another priority. By now eighteen airmen wireless operators from 14 Squadron were embedded with nine artillery batteries and a similar number of batteries had personnel from 67 Squadron. The terrain round Gaza led itself much more easily to artillery direction than did the featureless open desert of the Sinai, and the static positions of both batteries and targets in the forthcoming battle would help, too. The improved mapping of the area made it possible for aircraft to send co-ordinates of new targets by wireless, where previously it had sometimes been necessary to drop smoke bombs to mark them.

Meanwhile the German air service carried out a number of small-scale, but nonetheless effective, harassing attacks on British forces. One of these against the lines of communication on 6 April provoked retaliation by the RFC at dawn the following morning. Six aircraft, including two 14 Squadron machines flown by Lts G R A Deacon[32] and R C Steele[33] bombed camps at Tel El Sharia. However, this did not deter another raid on Kilo 143 on 12 April. The first German aircraft came over the aerodrome at 0500 hrs dropping three bombs from below the 1200 foot cloudbase. It was joined ten minutes later by two others who dropped bombs and then strafed the aerodrome with machine-gun fire. Two 14 Squadron Martinsydes scrambled to engage the attackers, but by then the German aircraft had departed as swiftly as they had arrived. Ten aircraft from 67 Squadron were launched for retaliatory attacks at 0915 hrs, but German aeroplanes reappeared after the last of them had left and dropped another sixteen bombs most of which fell in the 14 Squadron camp. Four airmen, Privates J Wilson, W Smith and J Burton were wounded in the attack, and two more, Pte Roland Rodger and Air Mechanic 2nd Class William O'Connor were killed. This second raid provoked more retaliation during the day including the bombing of Turkish camps in the Huj by Capt R O Skinner[34], Lts K G Sclanders[35], Steele, James, Deacon and C D Fellowes[36]. Enemy aircraft also continued to engage reconnaissance and artillery aircraft. On 16 April Lts James and I J Gardiner[37] were attacked in BE2e A2775 while taking photographs northeast of Gaza as, two days later, were Lts M C Crerar[38] and R C Jenkins[39] MC during an artillery co-operation sortie[40] at 7,000 feet over Gaza. In both cases the attacker was a Rumpler which used its superior speed to make a single pass attack before disengaging. Although both aircraft were damaged, they were able to recover safely to Deir El Belah.

The Second Battle of Gaza began on 17 April. The plan was a two phase attack: in the first phase the ground forces would advance to positions beyond the Wadi Ghuzze and in the second two days later, a frontal assault by three divisions, would follow after an artillery barrage. The initial assault on the Mansura and Sheikh Abbas ridges was successful. The first aeroplane was overhead at 0600 hrs and reported troops advancing supported by two tanks and shells landing on the Turkish trenches. In all twelve artillery co-operation sorties were flown by 5 Wing aircraft and seventeen targets were engaged, including nine enemy batteries. The following day the tempo of the artillery fire increased and despite poor weather conditions twenty-three targets were engaged. Once again nine enemy batteries were targeted and one gun was destroyed. The aircraft were forced to fly at low level in order to remain clear of the low clouds, which limited their vision and also made them more vulnerable to ground fire. The weather was no better the next day, 19 April, but fourteen artillery co-operation flights were still made. Throughout the battle it was found that four aircraft could operate simultaneously, each with their own wireless frequency. In addition to ground-based artillery, naval monitors and the battleship *Requin* were also used to bombard Turkish positions.

There were a number of aerial engagements on 19 April including the now-familiar pattern of a single-pass attack by a Rumpler on an artillery co-operation aircraft (flown by Lts Sclanders and Wollaston). However there was a more involved combat by Capt Francis Bevan flying[41] on Hostile Aircraft patrol, who engaged an enemy aircraft east of Gaza. Unfortunately as he manoeuvred to engage the Rumpler[42], Bevan's aircraft broke up and he was seen by observers on the ground clinging to a wing strut as the wreckage fell to earth.

Early on 20 April Lt Seward was conducting a Hostile Aircraft patrol when, through a gap in the clouds, he saw 2-3,000 men bivouacked in a wadi near Hareira. He reported his findings and a reconnaissance aircraft accompanied by four bombers was launched by 67 Squadron. They discovered a force of 2,000 infantry and 800 cavalry in the Wadi El Hareira deploying to attack the British flank and successfully scattered them before their counter-attack could develop.

Meanwhile, on the ground, the British offensive had stalled and the assault was called off on 21 April. There followed a long period of consolidation by both sides, each fortifying their positions in much the same style as on the Western Front in Europe. The war in Palestine had stagnated into trench warfare at least until the British could gather the firepower for another assault on Gaza.

Trench Warfare and Air Combat

In the immediate aftermath of the Second Battle of Gaza, 5 Wing was kept busy with artillery co-operation work, registering targets with British batteries for subsequent engagement. One of the priorities was counter-battery work and a number of enemy positions were neutralised in the last few days of April. Strategic reconnaissance flights were also mounted further afield to Junction Station, Auja, Hebron and Bethlehem. At the end of the month "A" Flight moved to join "B" Flight at Deir El Belah . The Germans made a number of night bombing raids on British airfields, which caused retaliatory attacks, and – perhaps more practically – made the RFC introduce the tactic of dispersing the aircraft in the desert overnight away from the airfields. A more permanent solution was found at the end of June when a new aerodrome was set out at Deir El Belah, amongst fig groves. The tents and hangars were set up under the trees so that they were invisible to German aircraft. The drawback was that the aerodrome itself was surrounded on three sides by trees and by a steep sand bank, making it tricky for take-off in a heavily-laden BE2. Lt G C Gardiner, a former observer who returned to the Squadron after completing his pilot training, managed to crash[43] into a fig tree and the hangar underneath it when he stalled on take-off, trying to clear the obstructions, on 13 July. But apart from the challenges of taking off, the aerodrome was otherwise a pleasant enough home: the shade of the trees provided welcome protection from the heat of the sun and the enticing sea was only two hundred yards away.

The summer months were spent in routine reconnaissance and artillery co-operation. Each day, there was a fixed routine of a morning and an evening tactical reconnaissance covering the front line area. The longer-range strategic sorties also continued, though by their nature they were less of a routine task. Additionally, since no maps of southern Palestine existed, photographic reconnaissance sorties were flown to provide the coverage needed to produce accurate 1:40,000 and 1:20,000 maps of the tactical area. During all these various sorties propaganda leaflets were dropped for the benefit of the Turkish troops. Artillery shoots also featured on the daily flying programme. Since these sorties involved three or four hours flying, the aircraft were fully fuelled, and when this was added to that of the wireless equipment and aerial, plus rations, water and personal weapons which also had to be carried in case of forced landing, the result was a very pedestrian performance from the lumbering BE2. It would take up to an hour to reach 5,000 feet altitude – which was about as high as the aeroplane could manage in the heat at such high operating weights. As a result pilots were very loath to lose any height if they were forced to take evasive action because of anti-aircraft fire, resorting instead to a two-dimensional weave. Despite the notable accuracy of the Turkish gunners, this tactic seemed to be effective; however it did not save Capt R N Thomas[44] and 2Lt J W Howells[45] who were killed when their BE2c[46] was shot down by anti-aircraft fire into the sea near Sheikh Hasan while on an artillery shoot on 23 July.

Enemy aircraft also posed a threat to artillery aircraft. On 12 May Capt N C Riddell[47] and Lt J H Muller[48] in BE2e A2825 were co-operating with 10 Heavy Battery, a 60-pounder unit attached to the Desert Column. The target was Turkish camps and redoubts in the Wadi El Hareira. On the ground Air Mechanic 1st Class A Chalmers and Air Mechanic 2nd Class L Andrews relayed Muller's corrections to the battery commander. At about 1620 hrs the BE2e was attacked by a Rumpler. Although Riddell and Muller had seen the aircraft they were not sure that it was hostile until it opened fire on them. Riddell turned towards the Rumpler and got directly beneath it, enabling Muller to fire at it. The Rumpler turned left to bring its observer's gun to bear, and Riddell mirrored the manoeuvre; however Muller's gun jammed and Riddell was forced to fly in a steeply banked turn while his observer attempted to fix the Lewis gun. All the while the Rumpler was able to circle them flying much faster than the BE and slightly above it, firing continuously. After numerous attempts, all of which resulted in a jam after the first round, Muller finally gave the signal that his gun was unserviceable and Riddell dived out of the action to return home. At this the Rumpler sped away – and so, to the great admiration of the Desert Column troops who had been watching the duel – Riddell and Muller returned to continue with the shoot.

During May 14 Squadron began to receive single-seater DH2 scouts. The DH2s were first used in action on 28 May – the day after Maj AC Boddam-Whetham[49] took command of the Squadron. Capt Riddell in A2629 and Lt Deacon in A2628 were at readiness at Deir El Belah when the alarm was raised that an enemy aircraft was flying east from El Arish. Riddell climbed to 8,500, with Deacon a thousand feet below him when they saw anti-aircraft fire over Rafah. This led them to a Rumpler flying towards them at about the same level. Riddell climbed hard as the Rumpler closed on him and had the advantage of height as the two aircraft passed. He was then able to dive vertically onto the Rumpler firing a burst into it; recovering from the dive, Riddell pulled into steep turn to the right and positioned himself just behind and below the enemy, firing the rest of his double drum into it. The Rumpler meanwhile was S-turning trying to get the observer's gun to bear. The observer also threw a small black bomb at Riddell, which he was able to dodge. Eventually the Rumpler was able to draw away from the engagement and with neither Riddell nor Deacon able to close the range, they returned to base.

The DH2s were joined by Vickers FB Scouts and Bristol M1 Monoplanes during the following month. These, plus the other scout-types were collected into "A" Flight which became the Squadron's scout flight, leaving "B" Flight with the BE2s for reconnaissance and artillery duties. The presence of high speed scouts forced the German air service into being more cautious. German reconnaissance aircraft began to be escorted and missions were flown at heights between 10,000 and 15,000 feet, which greatly reduced their effectiveness. On 22 June Capt Clear and 2Lt Steele[50] in brought down a Rumpler, and four days later Lt Fellowes in a Bristol Monoplane[51] would have accounted for an Albatros had his gun not jammed a number of times. Fellowes commented that his aircraft had the advantage of speed and manoeuvrability over the enemy aircraft – an advantage which up until mid-1917 had been very much the other way round. The Scout Flight was able to experiment using aircraft working in formation rather than as singletons and on 29 June three aircraft[52] engaged an enemy biplane, but the ensuing combat during which Fellowes early collided with the enemy aircraft, ended indecisively with no claims made.

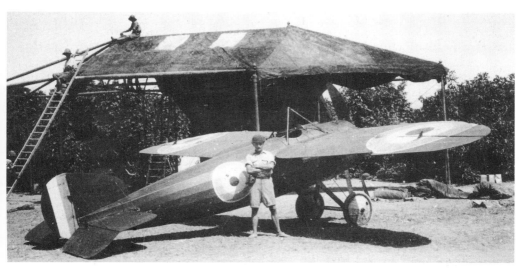

Lt C D Fellowes and Bristol M1B Monoplane A5141 at Deir El Belah June 1917. 14 Squadron was the first unit to fly this type in combat, but despite the aircraft's excellent performance it only saw limited operational service. Both Fellowes and the M1B were transferred to 111 Squadron the following month. (Ray Vann-Mike O'Connor 205/23A)

Crerar and Kingsley were unlucky again[53] on 5 July when they attacked an LVG at 10,000 feet near Shellal and both suffered gun stoppages. But Crerar managed to claim a kill two days later. He was over Khan Younis in a Vickers Scout[54] at 12,000 feet on a Hostile Aircraft Patrol when he saw a Rumpler fighter 3,000 feet below him. Diving to attack from the from the enemy's starboard beam, Crerar fired a long burst at it from 100 yards, at which the Rumpler started to dive steeply towards Shellal. As he turned in pursuit, Crerar's engine faltered and the Rumpler extended away from him. Crerar frantically operated the fuel pressure hand-pump and got his engine back again, closing the range and firing bursts into the enemy. The Rumpler made no attempt to manoeuvre and eventually landed heavily just short of the Turkish front line. The observer crawled out of the wreck, but the pilot remained there inert.

It was not just the scouts who were able to score against enemy aircraft and even the lowly artillery co-operation aircraft carried a sting in the tail: on the afternoon of 16 June a Rumpler attacked Lt Sclanders and Lt R J Morton[55] while they were on an artillery co-operation sortie[56]. Sclanders desperately manoeuvred to avoid the Rumpler's gunfire and to give his observer a clear shot at it, but Morton's gun jammed. With the advantage in performance the Rumpler was able to close the range, and attempted to get under the BE's tail. But at this very moment Morton freed the jam and fired three-quarters of a drum into the enemy at fifty yards range. The Rumpler immediately disengaged and later reports from a prisoner indicated that the enemy observer[57] had been severely wounded in the action. Five days later Sclanders and Morton were in action again[58] when they were attacked by a Fokker biplane. This time Sclanders had seen the enemy coming and warned Morton, who fired a drum at the Fokker which sheared off after just one pass.

The increased number of high performance scouts meant that more of these aircraft were available to escort the vulnerable artillery and reconnaissance aircraft. On the afternoon of 1 August Lts F A Bates[59] and Morton were on an artillery patrol[60] near Sheikh Abbas when a yellow Albatros dived to attack them. Lt Crerar, one of two escorts[61], was able to intervene and stop the Albatros from getting any closer than 200 yards and drive it off them. Unfortunately Malcolm Crerar was killed two days later in a flying accident in a Bristol Monoplane[62].

A hazard of a very different nature faced Lts Fellowes and J W Mitchell[63] on 4 July when they landed next to 3rd Australian Light Horse Brigade four miles west of Beersheba to make their report to the brigade commander. Unfortunately Fellowes had landed in no-man's land in front of the ALH lines and his aeroplane attracted the attention of a concealed Turkish battery which proceeded to shell them with considerable accuracy. The aircraft was badly damaged and would soon be completely destroyed. Demonstrating admirable quick-thinking, Fellowes crawled over 300 yards back to the aeroplane and in full view of the enemy he started up the engine. Lying flat, he allowed the aircraft to taxi over him and then ran after it and jumped aboard. He became airborne, but as all the controls except the rudder had been smashed, he shut off the engine and landed with sufficient speed to taxi over the hill and back to safety.

Another artillery co-operation flight with a difference was flown on 27 July: it was flown in darkness with only the light of the quarter-moon. The darkness enabled the observer, Capt F E Williams[64], to locate eight enemy batteries by their muzzle flashes. He was then able to direct three heavy artillery batteries to engage five of these targets; the remainder were engaged in the subsequent few days. Williams had already had some success against anti-aircraft guns on 17 July when he located three which were shelling him heavily while he was on an artillery shoot. He exacted his revenge by directing a 60-pounder and an 8-inch howitzer battery onto the anti-aircraft position, scoring six direct hits and exploding the ammunition there. Not content with that, he then descended to 2,000 feet and machine-gunned the position.

Arabian Detachment
The Arab Revolt had started in May 1916 with Sharif Hussein ibn Ali's declaration of independence from the Ottomans. Sharif Ali and his sons the Emirs Abdullah and Feisal quickly took control of Mecca before leading their forces northwards along the Red Sea coast to capture Jeddah, Rabegh (a hundred miles away) and Yenbo (a further hundred and fifty miles along the coast). However, by autumn their campaign had come to a halt, with Sharif Ali's army camped at Rabegh, Emir Feisal's forces at Yenbo and facing them, on the other side of the mountain range which separated the coastal plain from the desert plateau of the Nejd, the Ottoman garrison at Medina.

"C" Flight, comprising twelve officers and forty-seven men under command of

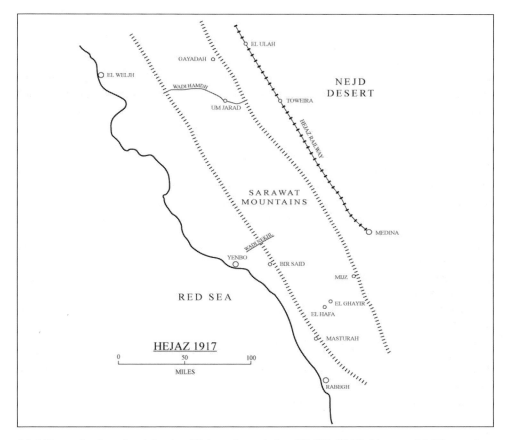

Maj Ross, had arrived in the Hejaz aboard the HMT *El Kahira* on 16 November 1916. They set up their aerodrome just inland from the coast at Rabegh near to Sharif Ali's camp. Cpl W L Showell[65] recorded that the "natives are a very wild looking lot [with] flowing robes, rifles, dum dums and knives. [They] seem very interested in our boats and motors. This country is regarded as holy land by the Mohamedans so we have to be careful. Turks said to be fifty miles away – what hope. [We are] very busy indeed getting things ashore [and] the Navy helps us considerably. The temperature is 100° in the shade." A week after they had arrived, two of the Flight's six aircraft were ready to fly. The first sortie, a photo reconnaissance of Mastura was flown on 24 November. Four days later two more aircraft had been erected. As with earlier campaigns, there were no accurate maps of the area: so most of the Flight's flying in early December was spent surveying the area to produce their own maps. The operating area comprised a coastal strip about twenty miles wide giving way inland to a rugged range of hills and mountains, reaching up to 7,000 feet in places, riven by a maze of wadis.

On 8 December one aeroplane was flown up to Yenbo after reports of Ottoman forces advancing from Medina. The aircraft made a reconnaissance northwards to Bir Said, where a small Turkish force was located and photographed. It then refuelled at Yenbo before returning to Rabegh. This arrangement was repeated on 16 December at the request of Capt T E Lawrence, and on the second occasion the reconnaissance revealed two Turkish columns converging towards Yenbo, one along the Wadi Nekhl and one south of Bir Said.

Unfortunately poor weather set in and heavy rain made the aerodrome at Rabegh unusable for the rest of December. Early in the New Year, Sharif Ali's forces reported the presence of Turkish positions at El Hafa, among the southern foot-hills of the Jebel Ashayer. On 6 January 1917 three aircraft took off to bomb the Turkish camp. Lt Floyer reached the target area at 0730 hrs[66] and dropped eight 20-pounder bombs on the camp from 600 feet; he was followed by Maj Ross half an hour later[67], who dropped a similar number. Unfortunately Lt T Henderson[68] in the third aircraft[69] suffered a technical problem and had to jettison his bombs. Although Floyer and Ross had dropped their weapons with great accuracy they were disappointed to see that a large proportion of them did not explode.

The failure of the bombs to explode was put down to the explosive, so for the next raid the TNT was removed from the bombs and replaced with gelignite. Meanwhile, the Turks had fallen back from El Hafa to a larger and more strongly held cliff-top post at El Ghayir just a few miles away. This new stronghold was well defended from attack by ground forces, but it was an ideal target for air attack. On the morning of 25 January Capt Bevan and Lt Henderson between them[70] dropped sixteen 20-pound gelignite bombs on El Ghayir, doing considerable damage. A week later the Turkish position was revisited by Maj Ross, who dropped the remaining seven gelignite bombs. A third raid on El Ghayir was made by three aircraft, flown by Capt Bevan, Lt H H James[71] and H A Fordham[72] on 7 February.

The *coup de grace* was delivered to Turkish forces around El Ghayir on 15 February by Maj Ross, Capt Bevan and Lt Henderson when they bombed the camp[73] at Khunagut al Rim, a few miles to the rear of El Ghayir. A week later all the Turkish forces had withdrawn from the El Ghayir area.

Sharif Ali's forces had by now taken Mijz, about fifty miles south of Medina, where they prepared an advanced landing ground. Although the landing ground itself was excellent, it was situated in a small basin and the hills surrounding it made it very tricky to use. Nevertheless it was successfully used on several occasions, including a reconnaissance to Medina by two aircraft on 5 March. During this sortie three enemy aircraft were seen in the air, but they made no attempt to engage the British aircraft.

By now the novelty of Arabia had worn off on the detachment. Cpl Showell wrote that over "the last week or so things have been fairly quiet. The Turks have gone so we have less work; altogether we are utterly fed up and want civilisation." On 15 March the Flight was ordered to El Wejh, a hundred and fifty miles along the coast beyond Yenbo; the aircraft were flown via Yenbo and the rest of the men and equipment travelled on the El Kahira. With the new location came a new objective: to harass the Hejaz railway. Now that the Turks had lost their access to the Red Sea, the railway which had become their only line of communication in the region took on a new strategic importance. Cutting the railway would isolate the garrison at Medina leaving it vulnerable to the Sharif's forces.

The country around El Wejh was more mountainous than that between Medina and Rabegh, but a large wadi, the Wadi Hamdh, ran south-eastwards from El Wejh directly to the railway about a hundred and fifty miles away at Toweira. This was on the limits of range for a BE2c carrying any useful payload, so it was decided to establish an advanced landing ground further along the Wadi Hamdh. Maj Ross set out from El Wejh on 21 March by tender for a ground reconnaissance, and he found a suitable landing ground at Um Jarad about a hundred miles along the Wadi.

The first reconnaissance of the railway was made by two aircraft on 30 March, using the new forward landing ground at Um Jarad with success. On his return from the reconnaissance[74] the pilot got lost in a sandstorm and had to forced land near the Jebel Raal when he ran out of fuel. Luckily he was found by a search aircraft the next day. The first attempt to attack the railway was made ten days later, but when the aircraft reached Um Jarad they found that the petrol, which had been sent via camel a few days previously had not yet reached the landing ground, so the raid had to be called off.

Maj Ross was recalled to Egypt and on 22 April he handed command of the Flight to Capt F W Stent[75]. "The new CO is 'some' pilot" wrote Cpl Showell approvingly. By now the harsh conditions were taking their toll of both men and machines. A number of men, including Cpl Showell, had been evacuated because of sickness, mainly typhoid, and the aircraft were suffering from cracked cylinders and a general deterioration of the wood and fabric. One aircraft[76] was by now beyond repair and it was written off. It is a mark of the extraordinary ability of Lt Stafford and his mechanics that the remaining aircraft were kept operational in such difficult conditions.

The second attempt to attack the railway was only a little more successful than the first. On 25 April two aircraft[77], flown by Capt Stent with Air Mech 1st Class Pound and 2Lt Siddons with Lt J A B Lane[78] deployed to Um Jarad. The next day they set off for El Ulah, a large station on the railway, which also served as a refuelling depot for engines. Although the sortie was intended mainly for reconnaissance, Stent took the opportunity to drop two bombs on the station, but observed no effect. On the return leg, Stent's aircraft blew an engine cylinder and he had to forced land in the Wadi Hamdh. The aircraft was eventually recovered eight days later, after much to-ing and fro-ing during which a spare engine was driven out from El Wejh. During this operation also, Stent managed to crash another aeroplane[79]; fortunately he was uninjured, but the accident left the Flight with only four aircraft. On 6 May a party led by Lt Henderson accompanied by Capt Lawrence himself, with Lt Stafford, Sgt Wright and Air Mech 1st Class Warr left Wehj with a Crossley tender and a Ford car to recover the wreckage.

Because of the efforts in recovering aircraft in the Wadi Hamdh it was not until

Stafford (on left) and T E Lawrence (on right), with the tender during the expedition to recover the wreckage of BE2c 4483 from the Wadi Hamdh. (Roger Bragger)

16 May that operational flying could resume, and an attack could be mounted against the railway. On this day Capt Stent with Air Mech 1st Class Shaw and 2Lt Batting with Sgt Courtnadge left Um Jarad bound for El Ula[80]. Batting's machine blew another engine cylinder and Stent carried on alone to El Ula where he dropped eight bombs, scoring two direct hits on station buildings. He then returned to Wejh to pick up a new cylinder before going back to where Batting had landed. This time the engine was easily repaired and both aircraft arrived back at El Weijh that evening.

There followed an interlude during which the Flight practised artillery co-operation with a battery of Egyptian army of 5-inch howitzers in preparation for an attack on El Ulah by British-led forces. Although the exercise was a great success, the planned attack was cancelled when it became apparent that it would be impossible to transport the guns through the rough terrain. Instead a new plan was devised for an attack by the Sharif's forces. The chosen form up point for the attack was Gayadah, a small oasis in a narrow gorge about twenty miles due west of El Ulah. With no detailed information about Gayadah, Stent dispatched an aeroplane to carry out a reconnaissance of the area on 30 May. A ground party in a Crossley tender and armoured car which set out the next day was recalled by aeroplane when it was thought that the Turks were also preparing Gayadah for a raid on El Wejh. Stent tried again on 6 June, returning two days later having found a potential landing ground on a plateau about 3,000 feet above sea level. Two aircraft were dispatched there on 8 June, but found that the landing ground was too small; however Arab troops subsequently enlarged the landing ground to a useable size by clearing bushes and moving rocks away.

Two aircraft set off from El Weijh on 12 June to photograph the defences at El Ulah prior to the attack, but when they reached Um Jarad to refuel the crews discovered that the cache of fuel and rations at the advanced landing ground had been removed by local tribesmen. The reconnaissance was flown five days later after the dump had been resupplied. Meanwhile a working party under Lt Stafford had set out by car and tender to mark out the route through the hills to Gayadah for the armoured cars and artillery which were to be used in the attack. Having done this successfully, Stafford and Air Mech 1st Class W Porter set off back to El Wejh, but they lost their way and soon ran out of water in the searing heat. Having drunk the water from the car's radiator they had to subsist on their own urine for two days, while "C" Flight's aircraft and vehicles carried out a desperate search to find them. Luckily both men were found by Bedouin who returned them to El Weijh on 23 June.

At this stage the attack on El Ulah by ground forces was cancelled for a second time when it transpired that there was insufficient water at Gayadah and the neighbouring wadis to sustain a large attacking force, but it was decided that the bombing raids planned for "C" Flight should go ahead anyway. Petrol and bombs were positioned at Gayadah and the aircraft were flown to the landing ground on 8 July.

The first raid from Gayadah was flown on 11 July by Capt Stent and Lts Henderson and Batting. Batting's BE2c[81] hit a bush after take off and crashed, but Stent and Henderson successfully dropped fourteen bombs on the camp at El Ulah,

Lt Thomas Henderson and BE2c 4488 at the advanced Landing Ground in the Wadi Hamdh. The difficult terrain is apparent from this shot. (Roger Bragger)

causing a stampede amongst the mules and camels. The next day's follow-up attack[82] by Lts Henderson and Siddons was met by stiff resistance from the Turks, who opened fire with four high anti-aircraft guns. However the pilots managed to achieve two direct hits on the railway line and also damaged all four guns. The pace of operations was then disrupted by two factors: firstly a shortage of fuel caused by the loss or damage of petrol tins in transit and evaporation in the severe heat, and secondly the damage to the aircraft caused by the extreme heat in daytime alternating with heavy dew at night, plus the effects of numerous sandstorms. These latter were described by Henderson: "…at about noon daily we were attacked by "sand devils" – a whirlwind of sand and small stones – which very often carried the machines bodily about fifty feet. Luckily they gave one warning as the large whirling tower of sand would appear somewhere down the Wadi bearing down on the camp and machines. Everyone would stand to and hang on to the machines. The tents went down every time, sometimes they went up. Afterwards all was chaos and the noise of the sandstorm was only equalled by expressions of discontent by the RFC personnel and the wailing of the Arabs."

What was to be the final raid on El Ulah[83] was led on 16 July by Lt Henderson, accompanied by Lts Siddons and W L Fenwick[84]. This raid was a great success and the twenty-four bombs caused damage to the water tanks, to the HQ building and also the station buildings. However, the following day a large sandstorm hit Gayadah and damaged the aircraft so severely that further operations were no longer possible. The pilots managed to nurse their machines back to El Wejh. Three days later Lt Siddons flew Capt Lawrence from Wejh to Gayadah and back[85] after which the aircraft were all dismantled. This marked the end of "C" Flight's expedition to the Hejaz; everyone boarded the El Kahira and returned to Egypt.

Third Battle of Gaza
At the end of June Gen Murray was replaced as the C-in-C in Egypt by Gen Sir Edmund Allenby, who brought a completely different style of leadership to that of his predecessor. While Murray's appreciation of detail had been well-suited to organising the logistic infrastructure of the Sinai campaign, he was a distant figure both literally (he remained at his headquarters in Cairo throughout the campaign) and figuratively. Allenby, on the other hand, had great charisma and was often seen at the front where he inspired his troops through his personal example and his approachable manner. He re-organised the army on the Palestine Front into two Corps, XX and XXI Corps, and the RFC was also re-organised to mirror this new arrangement. 14 Squadron and a new unit, 113 Squadron, would become "Corps" squadrons, each attached to one of the two army Corps for tactical reconnaissance and artillery co-operation, while 67 Squadron and a newly formed 111 Squadron would by "Army" squadrons taking the fighter role. 113 Squadron would be formed from reserve units in Egypt, while 111 Squadron was formed as a single flight at the beginning of August from the scout aircraft and their pilots of "A" Flight of 14 Squadron.

With the removal of "A" Flight to become 111 Squadron, a new "A" Flight under the command of Capt Seward MC was formed from drafts of new aircrew from Egypt. Command of "B" Flight was given to Capt C E H Medhurst[86] who was posted to the Squadron from Aboukir; both Flights were now equipped with the BE2e.

Meanwhile, Capt Stent's "C" Flight which had just returned from Arabia was based at Kilo 143 . On 26 August "C" Flight was tasked with a special operation against the Turkish facilities at Ma'an. For this mission, which had been planned in collaboration with Capt Lawrence, Stent chose four aircraft: two BE12s and two BE2es flown by himself and Lts W L Fenwick, Batting and 2Lt Siddons. The four of them, plus two mechanics carried in the BE2es set off for an advanced landing ground at El Kuntilla (about forty miles northwest of Aqaba) where petrol and bombs had been pre-positioned. The six men took the rest of the day man-handling petrol cans and bombs from the dump to the landing ground (a distance of nearly a kilometre) in the intense heat of the desert afternoon.

The following day at 0800 hrs they set off towards Ma'an. The two BE2es lost their way and Lt Batting returned to El Kuntilla; but Siddons continued[87], attacking another station to the south of Ma'an with ten 20-pound bombs. Stent and Fenwick managed to find Ma'an[88] where they dropped thirty-two bombs. Of these, there were only two "duds" and the remaining thirty weapons found their mark on the railway station buildings including eight hits on the engine sheds. Stent also managed to register a direct hit on the Inspector's House, which was being used by the Turkish General commanding the Hejaz. Throughout the attack the aircraft were subjected to heavy gunfire, made all the worse for them by the fact that the target was 3,500 feet above sea level so the BE12 could only manage a bombing height of about 1,000 feet above the ground. After they had dropped their bombs, Stent and Fenwick noticed an enemy aeroplane on the ground, but although they waited in the area for another twenty minutes it did not take off.

The following morning Stent led his Flight to attack the Turkish camps at Fuweila and Abu Lisan. Unfortunately Batting's aircraft did not get off the ground, but the other three successfully found the camp and bombed it, causing mayhem on the ground. Once again the high ground meant low bombing height – resulting in great accuracy both for bombing (one bomb scored a direct hit on a field battery) but also for anti-aircraft fire. All three aircraft were hit. Unfortunately over a quarter of the petrol tins at El Kuntilla were found to be empty through leakage, and the shortage of fuel meant that only the two BE12s could be re-armed for another attack on Fuweila in the afternoon. Stent and Fenwick dropped another thirty-two bombs there to good effect. All four aircraft then returned to Kilo 143 on 30 August.

As summer turned to autumn, things remained relatively quiet on the ground as the army prepared the coming offensive. Nevertheless, routine flying patrols continued and small tragedies still occurred, such as the death in a flying accident of 2Lt R A Davey on 8 August – just two days after he had arrived on the unit. The occasional attack was still made on artillery co-operation aircraft: on 12 August 2Lt W S Jamieson was wounded in the ankle when he and 2Lt J H Maingot[89] were attacked[90] over "Tank Redoubt" to the southeast of Gaza by an Albatros. Four days later Lt Bates and Lt T C Stewart[91] were subjected to a prolonged attack[92], but managed to fight off the enemy aircraft and continue the shoot, earning congratulations from the ground troops for their conduct. In fact Bates earned a reputation (and the respect of his peers) for being steady under fire and was often seen to be seemingly oblivious to heavy anti-aircraft barrages aimed at him.

An unexpected benefit of being at Deir El Belah was the abundance of quail during the month of September. By putting long nets up among the coastal dunes, Squadron personnel found that they could catch between fifty and two hundred quail each night – so quail became, for a while, a regular menu item. Deir El Belah was visited by Gen Allenby on 4 September and the Squadron personnel, both fliers and ground-crew alike, were very impressed with their new C-in-C. The month also brought major changes to the organisation of the Squadron. Maj Boddam-Whetham was promoted to take over 5 Wing and in turn he arranged for Capt Medhurst to take over as OC 14 Squadron. This latter appointment was extremely popular as "Med" was well respected and well-liked by all ranks. Unfortunately the RFC Headquarters had already appointed Capt S G Hodges[93] to command the Squadron; however the Squadron personnel refused to take Hodges and the stage was set for an unpleasant showdown. It is perhaps an indication of Hodges' fine character that he accepted with good grace that the Squadron personnel preferred to keep Medhurst and he found another posting, leaving Medhurst in charge of 14 Squadron. The Squadron had by now made up the loss of parts of the original "A" Flight which had become 111 Squadron and also parts of the original "C" Flight which had now become "X" Flight, an independent unit for further operations in Arabia. The Squadron boasted three Flights of BE2es and new personalities now led them: "A" Flight was commanded by Capt H I Hanmer[94], "B" Flight by Capt Sclanders and "C" Flight by Capt Bates.

As an illustration of the scale of the routine work by the Squadron, over three hundred photographs of the Turkish positions around Gaza during October alone. By the end of the month the Unit was also fully trained at Contact Patrols and had built up an excellent

Lt H I Hanmer originally joined 14 Squadron in mid 1916 as an observer, and rejoined as a pilot, commanding "A" Flight the following year. He won a DFC while serving with 142 Squadron during the final advance to Damascus in 1918. This photograph was taken during his post-War service with the RAF during which he commanded 503 (County of Lincoln) Squadron. (Dov Gavish)

working relationship with the XXI Corps artillery units. All this skill would be put to good effect during the Third Battle of Gaza. This time, Allenby's plan was in four phases. Firstly a barrage on Gaza itself would lead the Turks to expect another frontal attack there, but in fact the attack would be delivered by XX Corps on the eastern flank at Beersheba. Once they had taken Beersheba, XX Corps would start rolling along the front line drawing Turkish troops away from Gaza itself. Then the final *coup de grace* would be a frontal assault on Gaza by XXI Corps.

The British barrage on Gaza opened on 27 October and 14 Squadron aircraft operated in support of XXI Corps' artillery throughout the next few days. On the night of 1 November an attack was made by 52 Division on the Turkish strongpoint on Umbrella Hill, just in front of Gaza. Two wireless-equipped aircraft from 14 Squadron, led by Medhurst himself[95], attacked active batteries with bombs and machine gun. His observer, 2Lt A G Hopkins[96] won a MC for his accurate direction of artillery batteries that night during a four hour sortie in marginal weather under heavy enemy fire. The night was brightly lit by the full moon and the operation was a great success with the aircraft causing the batteries to cease fire. During the rest of the day 14 Squadron aircraft were able to use a pre-arranged shoot to bombard a large Turkish force which had started to deploy at Sheikh Hassan. Capt Bates was airborne in the dark twice on consecutive days. Late on the afternoon of 2 November an urgent call was received about a Turkish counter-attack in the area of Sheikh Hassan. Bates and Lt C E V Graham[97] rushed airborne[98] into the dusk sky. Poor light forced them to fly low so they were vulnerable to ground fire and were badly shot up, but they were able to direct artillery fire onto Turkish troops massed in their trenches. When it became too dark to continue, Bates returned to Deir El Belah, landing by the light of flares. However he was back in action at dawn the following morning in the same aeroplane, this time accompanied by Lt Maingot. This time it was difficult to distinguish who was who, but Bates was able to direct some counter battery shooting successfully. At one stage he became impatient with the length of time it was taking for the guns to reach an anti-aircraft battery which was harassing him, so he dived on the anti-aircraft battery with his machine gun causing it to cease fire.

In the days after the successful capture of Beersheba, the artillery assault on Gaza continued, reaching a peak on 6 November when 14 Squadron flew nine artillery observation patrols, including observing for naval monitors carrying out counter-battery work. The following day, Capts Hanmer and R H Brewis[99] carried out the first Contact Patrol of the day at dawn. "I will never forget leaving Belah aerodrome on that first Contact Patrol Flight," recalled Hanmer, "no-one had had previous experience of the work before in Palestine and from all the reports from France it was a nasty job and there was sure to be lots of 'dirt' flying about. However we proceeded in the grey dawn – not waiting to climb now over the aerodrome as 1,000 or 1,500 feet was all we required for the work – and as we approached the line a few flashes became visible from time to time. Gaza itself appeared to be enveloped in smoke … a battlefield it certainly was. Not far out to see lay the French cruiser *Requin* and a number of torpedo boats and two or three monitors. The artillery fie had died down for the time being, neither side knowing exactly where the front line was – that was our job to find out… Down the line we went sounding the klaxon horn in a succession of 'A's – the signal to the infantry to light their flares. They worked like clock-work: the red flares appeared in the bottom of the trenches which formed the new front line and as soon as we were satisfied that we knew the positions of all the advanced troops back we went to drop maps with the positions marked thereon to Divisional and Corps Headquarters. That done, back again to observe what was going on and what the Turks were doing, until relieved by the next Contact Patrol machine an hour or so later."

However, the Turks were already beaten and began drawing back from Gaza early on 7 November. Nevertheless, enemy aircraft were still active and 2Lt F C Wood[100] and Lt Graham were attacked by two aircraft while on an artillery patrol[101] that afternoon. Graham managed to get two drums of ammunition into one them which retired, followed a little later by other .

As the Turkish retreat started, aircraft were used to harass the troops. Six aircraft attacked the enemy rearguard at Beit Hanum in the afternoon of 7 November. The aircraft were flown by Capts Hanmer, Sclanders and Bates and Lts Batting, P G Wells DCM[102] and Steele on this two hour flight. The following day Lts H L C McConnell and Steele attacked Iraq El Menshiyeh aerodrome; later in the day McConnell was back in action accompanied by Lts A L Bartlett[103] and E S Sawtell[104] to bomb retreating cavalry troops. Another attack was made by two aircraft (flown by Lts Steele and D B Cumming[105]) on 9 November and on the same day six aircraft from the Squadron were part of a force of twenty-two aircraft which bombed the aerodrome at El Tine. For all these missions, the aircraft were flown solo to allow the maximum bomb load of 20-pound and 16-pound bombs. The number of artillery observation sorties dropped dramatically as the Turks outpaced the advance of the British artillery, as there were no targets within range.

On 10 November an ill-considered task was issued for an attack by two aircraft on the bridge over the Wadi Surar just north of Junction Station. Freeman's epic attack on the Hejaz railway bridge had taken place almost exactly a year beforehand and in the intervening twelve months the expertise on fusing and arming the delayed-action 100-pound bombs had been lost. With very short notice, two aircraft were hastily prepared and the bomb fuses were set by an ex-artillery officer who thought he could remember how to do it. At 1430 hrs, Capt Hanmer and Lt McConnell set off for the Wadi Surar each armed with two 100-pound bombs. Flying at 2,000 feet they found El Tine and then followed the railway line up to Junction Station. As they arrived over the wadi and located the single span cantilever, it all seemed very quiet; however as Hanmer dived to make his first bombing pass he "suddenly realised the whole wadi was black with Turks… and sure enough they were stirred up. It was a veritable hornets' nest."

As he descended through 200 feet he came under extremely heavy rifle fire. He dropped his first bomb and pulled away, turning sharply to the right. After counting slowly to three he expected to hear an explosion, but he heard nothing: the bomb had

On 10 November 1917 two aircraft flown by Capt H I Hanmer and Lt H L C MacConnell were ordered to carry out an ill-conceived attack on the bridge over the Wadi Surar. McConnell was shot down and captured, and the wreckage of his BE2e A1811 was found by British troops when they advanced through the area a few days later. (Ray Vann-Mike O'Connor 205-29A)

not exploded. McConnell's first attack similarly ended with an unexploded bomb. Hanmer tipped in for his second pass, all the while taking hits from the ground fire: "I felt the machine being hit and saw little holes appearing in the wing fabric and then when about fifty yards from the bridge there was a crash in my cockpit, splinters of wood flew up by my left side, my coat was ripped up and I felt as if I had been hit by about fifty sledgehammers in the neighbourhood of my heart. There was no stopping though, unless the machine fell to bits or one was no longer able to steer it – so on to the bridge. Again as I thought at the right moment I released the second and last of my bombs and pulled out to see the result – again nothing."

Hanmer stayed in the area for another five minutes, searching for McConnell, but he was nowhere to be seen. Returning to Deir El Belah in some pain Hanmer landed just before sunset. "Medhurst was there on my arrival and in getting out of the machine and telling him I'd been hit – which by the way was pretty obvious seeing the state of my coat – we proceeded to examine the state of the injury ... The bullet which had first gone through the left hand top longeron of the machine had struck the metal crosspiece of my belt and in doing so had bent it pretty considerably. It then glanced off my brandy flask – giving it a small dent – and into my cigarette case. The other side of the cigarette case was drilled through, but the side next to my skin had bulged and opened, but only enough to let splinters of the bullet through. These splinters and the bulge had embedded themselves into me to a depth of about half an inch!"

Horace McConnell had been less lucky – he was brought down by ground fire and had been captured. Although he was only lightly wounded, he died in captivity when his wounds became infected. Thus this raid, which had achieved absolutely nothing had cost the Squadron an aeroplane and a pilot.

Advance to Jerusalem

The Turkish retreat continued northwards, pausing at Junction Station where a battle, which included the last major charge by British cavalry, was fought on 13 November. Then the withdrawal continued, stabilising by the middle of November along a line running from just north of Jaffa on the coast towards Jerusalem, which remained in Turkish hands. 14 Squadron aircraft carried out artillery observation and contact patrols during the action at Junction Station and four aircraft were also involved in a ten-aircraft bombing raid on Junction Station itself on 12 November.

Heavy rainstorms intervened a few days later, giving the Squadron personnel a taste of things to come and causing great difficulty in moving to the new advanced landing ground at Julis. The rough tracks were turned into a sea of mud and vehicles became bogged down, needing to be manhandled almost continuously. The storms also caused two aircraft from "A" Flight to forced-land ten miles from Julis while returning from a patrol. Hanmer took Flt Sgt Etheridge with him to render assistance: the first aircraft was easily dealt with and started up to fly back to Julis, but the second, crewed by 2Lt W J Beer[106] and Lt Graham proved more difficult. By now it was getting dark and raining again and Hanmer was aware that he was short of observers for the next day's flying, so taking Etheridge and Graham with him, he returned to Julis leaving Beer alone in the cold, sodden plain of Palestine. Beer was rescued the next day apparently none the worse for his ordeal. A similar fate befell Lts A G Kay[107] and Morton, who were forced down near Hatteh by a storm on 20 November and spent the night awaiting rescue which eventually came the following day.

By 20 November the whole Squadron had moved to join "A" Flight at Julis and from here attacks were made on troop and transport concentrations at Bireh and Beit Nebala. The two aircraft which attacked Beit Neballa late in the morning of 24 November were flown by Bates and Hanmer; their mission was in support of an assault by 52 Division on Et Tib. Unfortunately Hanmer misread his map while following Bates and dropped his weapons short on Nebi Samwil instead, but no harm was done.

After an absence of enemy aircraft during the Turks' headlong retreat from Gaza, they made an unwelcome return on 28 November. 2Lts C M Hallett[108] and A C Roxburgh[109] were carrying out an artillery patrol[110] northeast of Junction Station at around 0900 hrs when a two-seater dived on their tail. Hallett banked steeply trying to avoid the German's fire and to allow Roxburgh a clear shot at the enemy. Throughout a series of hard manoeuvres, Roxburgh managed to fire off two drums of ammunition, but he was also hit and seriously wounded in the combat. Hallett had noticed a field ambulance unit near Ramleh and landed alongside it so that his unconscious observer could receive medical attention. However by the time Hallett had landed, Alan Roxburgh had already died from his wounds. Another less serious casualty that day was Lt Mitchell, who was hit in the neck while he and Bates carried out a reconnaissance[111] of the area of Beir Sira, Suffa and Tahta while under heavy rifle and machine gun fire.

At the end of November the whole Squadron moved to a new aerodrome at Junction Station. The flats of the Wadi Surar were a perfect landing ground and the tents for the Squadron personnel were pitched on the sloped banks of the wadi. At this time 14 Squadron swapped over to become the XX Corps unit, and 113 Squadron took their place with XXI Corps. The Judean hills brought new challenges to the Squadron which had by now grown used to operations on the coastal plains of Sinai and southern Palestine. The indifferent performance of a fully-loaded BE2e became even more telling as they operated over high ground. Firstly it became more difficult for aircraft to operate in poor weather because the clouds frequently lay on the hills themselves and secondly the reduced terrain clearance made the aircraft more vulnerable to ground fire. The remedy for this latter problem would come soon with the introduction of the more powerful RE8 aircraft. The first of these[112] was collected by Capt Bates on 5 December, but it would be a while before the whole Squadron converted to the new type. Another tactical challenge was of spotting the fall of artillery shot in undulating terrain. But at least the airborne observer had a much better chance of spotting shots than did the ground-based observer, which made the aircraft ever more important in artillery work.

During the first few days of December 14 Squadron aircraft carried out daily reconnaissance of the enemy positions at Bireh, Ramallah, Nebu Samweil and Beitan. In addition, enemy artillery batteries were engaged and photo missions were flown on 3 and 4 December over the Turkish defences to the west of Jerusalem and the south of Bethlehem. Five aircraft carried out a raid on the station and aerodrome at Tul Keram on the afternoon of 3 December, dropping forty

Brought up in Jamaica, 2Lt Alan Roxburgh was killed during an engagement with a German two-seater on 28 Nov 1917 northeast of Junction Station. After the action, his pilot 2Lt Charles Hallett landed BE2e A1365 close to a Field Hospital near Ramleh, but Roxburgh was already dead. (Ray Vann-Mike O'Connor 220-21)

bombs on the targets. The weather broke on 5 December, and torrential rain fell for the next week, hampering flying operations. Hanmer and Williams had landed at the Divisional HQ near Hebron to report in person to the GOC. Hanmer managed to land in a tricky area, but then found when he tried to return home that, try as he might, he couldn't get the engine re-started. In the end his only option was to signal the Squadron by wireless for help. After a night in the open, during which pilfering by locals had to be dissuaded by the occasional revolver shot, help arrived the following day in the persons of Bates with Sgt Cox. Cox was able to start the engine easily and Hanmer and Williams returned to Junction Station while Bates and Cox turned their attention to Capt Hodges who had forced landed about a mile away because of a loose inlet cage nut.

Despite the appalling weather, XX Corps' assault on Jerusalem started on 7 December and 14 Squadron aircraft were able to fly a number of contact patrols in support during the day. However the next day all the aerodromes in Palestine were washed out and unusable. This situation lent itself to some lateral thinking on the part of the pilots in an attempt to find a solution. OC 113 Squadron tried laying tarpaulins over his landing ground at Khirbet Deiran, but although he managed to get airborne for a short flight this method did not prove successful and 113 Squadron was unable to fly for the next two days. At Junction Station Capt Bates attempted to take off in the Wadi[113] but smashed the propeller in the process. He then noticed that although the wadi was waterlogged, the bank on which the tents were pitched was still dry. Bates "…thought of pulling a machine up the slope with ropes and trying to start from there. I did so and glided perilously down a steep incline, reaching the mud of the aerodrome with just sufficient speed to unstuck and fly away." It took about thirty labourers from the Egyptian Labour Corps to manhandle an aeroplane[114] up to the top of the hill, while others cleared a runway through the scrub and stone. With Lt C M Manson[115] in the observer's seat, Bates had hit upon a method which enabled 14 Squadron to continue flying. In this way, 14 Squadron was the only unit to operate on 8 and 9 December, the critical days of the capture of Jerusalem. Apart from mounting contact patrols, 14 Squadron crews attacked Turkish troops and transport in rear areas. Three aircraft dropped twenty-six bombs on troops on the Jerusalem to Bireh road on 8 December (the day Bethlehem was captured) and in two attacks, each by six aircraft, the following day troops and transport were bombed and strafed on the Jerusalem to Jericho road and on the Bireh to Jericho and Jerusalem roads.

The Squadron continued to use its downhill runway on 10 December to keep harassing the Turkish troops: four aircraft attacked transport north of Bireh and three aircraft dropped twenty-seven bombs on troops and transport at Jufna Um Saffa. During these attacks Lt Steele, who had had a narrow escape when his aircraft was badly shot up two days earlier, was wounded. The next day, the weather improved and flying operations continued apace. This was the day of Allenby's triumphal entry into Jerusalem, an event witnessed by Bates and Lt P C Taylor[116]. After carrying out the early reconnaissance[117] of the Jericho-Jordan road they landed at 0845 hrs on a small field near Jerusalem Station, the first aircraft to land at Jerusalem. After

BE2d A3093 towed up hill at Wadi Surar, December 1917. Capt Bates' first attempt to get airborne in this aircraft on 7 December resulted in a smashed propeller. After repairing the prop the aircraft was used over the following two months using the downhill runway from the wadi banks. (Ray Vann-Mike O'Connor 205-34A)

borrowing horses from a nearby unit, they rode into the city. Eight artillery co-operation sorties were flown over the next three days, during which eight enemy batteries were engaged; in addition two raids were flown against troops and transport north of Bireh on 11 and 12 December. However, the Turkish troops fought back with heavy rifle fire and after the raid on 11 December, 2Lt A T Essex[118] counted twenty bullet holes through his aircraft. Another attack on troops[119] on the Bireh road was made on 16 December by 2Lts Essex, E Bell and Lt Hallett.

Bad weather returned on 19 December and flying operations practically ceased for the next week. The break at least allowed Squadron personnel to celebrate Christmas 1917 in style, with the satisfaction of knowing that Jerusalem was in British hands. Christmas Day itself had started inauspiciously when the whole camp was roused in the midst of a storm, to hold down tents and aircraft. The whole squadron was out for most of the day, battling against gale force winds and teeming rain. However spirits rose when the Mess tent was erected and the Christmas meal was served. A few days beforehand, Lt D M Finlayson[120] had been dispatched to Cairo to collect the necessary provisions; although the Squadron personnel knew that Finlayson had got as far as Gaza on his return journey, everyone suspected that he might be stuck there because of the foul weather. However Finlayson rose to the challenge magnificently and reappeared at Junction Station laden with turkeys and chickens, which in a flash of genius he'd had half-cooked so that they just needed re-heating on the day. At 1800 hrs the two hundred and fifty ground crew sat down to their feast of turkey, plum pudding and beer. Two hours later it was the turn of sixty officers to enjoy a similar menu, though in their case it was washed down with copious bottles of champagne. After the meal Lt A T Thompson[121], the Squadron's Wireless Officer led the singing and the sergeants were invited to join the festivities and to enjoy a double whisky or two!

Flying resumed on 27 December. Once again 14 Squadron were able to use the downhill launching technique and mounted a full flying programme when other units were unable to do so. Seven artillery co-operation sorties were flown on 27 December and three other aircraft attacked troops at Jedeira and Kolundia. Counter-battery work and interdiction attacks against troops retreating from Bireh continued for the next two days . Unfortunately on 30 December the Squadron suffered the loss of Frederick Bates[122] who, with Lt D J Aitcheson[123], was badly injured when he crashed on take-off. Thus ended a year which had started with the disappointment of two abortive assaults on Gaza, followed by the breakthrough and the headlong advance through Palestine and then the capture of Jerusalem itself.

Notes

1 BE2cs 4152 and 4395.

2 Educated at Harrow, Arthur Lazarus-Barlow relinquished his commission in the East Kent Yeomanry in 1921. After the War he settled in Essex and was an accomplished yachtsman. Barlow committed suicide at the age of 39 in 1936; his brother Ernest also served in the RAF and was killed in action in 1940 while commanding 40 Squadron.

3 A pre-War TA officer, 29-year old Charles Williamson from Eccles had won a MC while serving with the 7th Bn Manchester Regiment at Gallipoli.

4 James Dempsey, was a rather colourful Irishman. He had served with the French Foreign Legion before joining the Royal Irish Fusiliers at the beginning of the war. In 1920 he was cashiered from the Army and the award of a MC which he had won during service with 14 Squadron was cancelled by order of the King. Later he was also involved in an adulterous divorce case in 1931.

5 Hugo Buchanan-Wollaston (1883-1970) became the Principal Naturalist at the Ministry of Agriculture Farming & Fisheries, retiring from the post in 1944.

6 in Martinsyde A7489.

7 German records indicate that Kingsley was shot down by a Rumpler flown by Vizefeldwebel Albert Jünger and Jeschonnek.

8 During his brief captivity the Bedouins relieved him of his silver cigarette case; by amazing coincidence it was later found in a bazaar in Damascus by Col AE Borton, OC 5 Wing RFC, who returned it to Kingsley after the war.

9 Allan Jones later became Chairman of De Havilland, Australia.

10 Sir Lawrence Wackett was later the Founder, Manager and Director of Commonwealth Aircraft Corporation Ltd and died in 1982.

11 Capt James Batting later won a DFC with 114 Squadron in India.

12 Squadron Leader Ian Cullen MBE AFC transferred to the reserve in 1938.

13 Siddons and Cullen were in BE2c 4442.

14 in Martinsyde A7476.

15 three BE2es, 6775 flown by Capt Clear, 7132 by Dempsey and 6774 by Lt Barlow accompanied by a Martinsyde flown by Capt Freeman.

16 Maj Arnold Clear later served with 111 Squadron and left the RAF in 1919.

17 in BE2c 4442.

18 in BE2c 4485.

19 in Martinsyde A1576.

20 in DH1a 4608.

21 Clarence Palmer, from Norfolk, was repatriated in 1918 and left the RAF the following year.

22 Although other records indicate that they may have been shot down by anti-aircraft fire.

23 George Dell-Clarke suffered from a mental breakdown after his traumatic experiences with 14 Squadron and was unfit for the rest of 1917. However he joined 60 Squadron in France in July 1918 but was killed in a flying accident a few days later.

24 in Martinsyde A1577.

25 22-year old Francis Bevan of the South Wales Borderers came from Newcastle Emlyn.

26 Martinsyde A1577.

27 A graduate of Clare College Cambridge, Hugh Kirby had previously served as an observer with 30 Squadron; after 14 Squadron he went to the Wireless Telegraphy School and left the RAF in 1919.

28 Reginald Baillieu survived the war and died in 1965.

29 Ross Smith retrained as a pilot and returned to 67 Squadron. He ended the war with 3 DFCs and 2 MCs. After a distinguished post-war flying career during which various feats earned him a knighthood, an AFC and £2,500, he was killed in a flying accident in 1922.

30 BE2e 6770.

31 From London, 27-year old Cecil Gibbs had previously served as a Corporal in the City of London Yeomanry.

32 George Deacon was posted to 111 Squadron on its formation and won a MC in 1918. He retired from the RAF as a Wg Cdr in 1935.

33 Like Deacon, Robert Steele moved to 111 Squadron. He was awarded the DSO in 1918 but left the RAF in 1920.

34 Reginald Skinner was a pre-War regular army officer and he rejoined the Royal Artillery after the War, retiring as a Major in 1937. He served in the RAFVR during World War 2 as a Wg Cdr in the Balloon Branch.

35 Kenneth Sclanders MC (1893-1970) was a Flight Commander with 14 Squadron for much of 1917 and 1918; he left the RAF in 1919 and is buried in Malta.

36 The son of a Rear Admiral, Cuthbert Fellowes left the RFC in 1919 and became Land Agent to Lord Rothschild and Lord Jowitt. He married Elspeth Slessor, the sister of John Slessor.

37 Ivan Gardiner was killed when the HT Leasowe Castle was torpedoed in May 1918.

38 19-year old Malcolm Crerar came from Hamilton, Ontario.

39 Robert Jenkins MBE MC was killed in a flying accident in 1922.

40 in BE2c 4152.

41 Martinsyde A1582.

42 The Rumpler was flown by Vizefeldwebel Gustav Kautzmann and Leutnant Stiggell.

43 BE2e 6824.

44 Robert Thomas had served in the Boer War and was one of three brothers serving in France under their father Brig-Gen Sir Owen Thomas. Unfortunately none of the three brothers survived the War. Thomas had served with 34 and 12 Squadrons and had been awarded the Croix de Guerre.

45 The Reverend John Howells, aged 30, originally from Tenby had been a Wesleyan Minister in Manchester before the War. Commissioned into the Lancashire Fusiliers he had served at Gallipoli.

46 BE2e A1803.

47 A native of Edinburgh, Neil Riddell was posted to 111 Squadron in August 1917.

48 21-year old John Muller was killed in action while flying with 113 Squadron in October 1917.

49 Arthur Boddam-Whetham DSO was killed in an aircraft accident at Ramleh, Palestine in August 1919.

50 Capt Clear in DH2 A2628 and 2Lt Steele in DH2 A2623.

51 Bristol Monoplane A5141.

52 Kingsley in Vickers Scout A5236, Crerar in Vickers A5231 and Fellowes in Bristol Monoplane A5141.

53 Crerar in A5232 and Kingsley in A5236.

54 Vickers Scout A5231.

55 Reginald Morton trained as a pilot and rejoined 14 Squadron in the closing days of the War. He left the Service in 1921.

56 in BE2e A1811.

57 This was Vizefeldwebel Kautzmann's observer, Leutnant von Oettinger.

58 in BE2c 4152.

59 From a wealthy background, Frederic Bates (1884-1957) was educated at Winchester and Trinity College Cambridge. After serving with distinction with 14 Squadron, Bates went on to command 47 Squadron. After the War he joined the Board of Cunard and various family companies.

60 in BE2e A1839.

61 in Vickers Scout A5231.

62 Bristol Monoplane A5139.

63 James Mitchell transferred to the Equipment Branch in 1918, eventually retiring as a Gp Capt in 1951.

64 After serving with 14 Squadron Frank Williams was sent to 57 TS in Egypt but tragically died as a result of serious burns by a fire in his living quarters.

65 Walter Showell (1893-1949) was a "superb craftsman" in both metal and wood; after the War he became the Handicraft Master at George Dixon Grammar School in Birmingham and was author of the book "Woodwork – a Textbook for Handicraft Students".

66 in BE2c 4483.

67 in BE2c 4478.

68 Thomas Henderson renewed his acquaintanceship with TE Lawrence when he flew the latter from Paris to Arabia in 1919.

69 BE2c 4488.

70 Capt Bevan in 5421 and Lt Henderson in 4488.

71 Squadron Leader Harold James OBE (1895-1969) retired in 1931 and settled in Cairo. During the Six Day War of 1967 War the Egyptian authorities arrested him as a spy. He was released to return to UK but died during a holiday to Malta two years later, and is buried there.

72 Hugh Fordham was a Major at the Air Ministry in 1918; he left the RAF the following year.

73 Maj Ross in 4478 Capt Bevan in 5421 and Lt Henderson in 4488.

74 in BE2c 4483.

75 Federick Stent went on the command "X" Flight, the independent Flight working with Lawrence, and then 111 Squadron. He retired from the RAF as a Wg Cdr in 1936 and was killed in a flying accident two years later while practising for the King's Cup Air Race.

76 BE2c 4473.

77 Capt Stent with Air Mech 1st Class Pound in 4478 and 2Lt Siddons with Lt J A B Lane in 5421.

78 James Lane of the 18th Hussars left the Army in 1919 to run a riding school in Kent. He served with the RASC during World War 2.

79 BE2c 4483.

80 Capt Stent with Air Mech 1st Class Shaw in 4488 and 2Lt Battingwith Sgt Courtnadge in 4478.

81 BE2c 4529.

82 in BE2cs 4488 and 5421.

83 Lt Henderson in 4488, Lts Siddons in 5421 and Fenwick in 4478.

84 William Fenwick joined the Lincolnshire Regiment from Marlborough school in 1913. He remained in the RAF after the War and died in Iraq in 1928 while serving with 5 Armoured Car Company.

85 in BE2c 5421.

86 ACM Sir Charles Medhurst KCB OBE MC (1896-1954) retired from the RAF in 1950. Prior to joining 14 Squadron he had served in France with 13 and 60 Squadrons. During World War 2 Medhurst served in a number of senior appointments including Vice Chief of the Air Staff and AOC-in-C Middle East Command. His final post was as Chief of the British Joint Service Mission to Washington.

87 in BE2e 6770.

88 in BE12s A566 and A6323.

89 Joseph Maingot served with 14 Squadron until March 1918 and survived the war.

90 in BE2e 2772.

91 30-year old Thomas Stewart left 14 Squadron for 222 Squadron at Malta in July 1917.

92 in BE2e A1839.

93 A South African, Swithin Hodges had already received a MC for his work as a Flight Commander with 53 Squadron flying RE8s in France. Hodges took command of 17 Squadron in April 1918.

94 Henry Hanmer had previously served with 14 Squadron in 1916 as an observer. Described in the citation for the DFC he won while serving with 142 Squadron as "a brilliant and very gallant airman" Hanmer retired from the RAF as a Gp Capt in 1941. He later married the daughter of the Earl of Enniskillen.

95 in BE2e 3066.

96 Arthur Hopkins had been a Methodist minister before the War; after hostilities he returned to the clergy but died of cancer in 1924.

97 Clarence Graham was Mentioned in Dispatches in 1918 and remained in the RAF after the War, however in 1923 he failed a pilot training course on Bristol Fighters due to poor eyesight and he eventually left the service in 1930.

98 in BE2e A1811.

99 Born in Withington near Crewe, Robert Brewis left the RAF in 1919 but served in the Administration & Special Duties Branch of the RAFVR during World War 2.

100 Before the War Frederick Wood had been a broker in London. He left the RAF in 1919.

101 in BE2e A1839.

102 Percy Wells won the DCM in Mespotamia. He joined 31 Squadron in 1919 and left the RAF in 1920.

103 From Jamaica, 19-year old Allison Bartlett left the RAF in 1919.

104 Eric Sawtell, from Melksham, left the RAF in 1921.

105 Donald Cumming joined 31 Squadron the following month where he won a DFC: after the War returned to the Indian Army.

106 William Beer had just been commissioned and completed his pilot training having previously served as a Flt Sgt mechanic with the Squadron. He had been mentioned in Dispatches for his work a year earlier.

107 Arthur Kaye (1891-1969) resigned his commission due to ill health in 1920 and joined the family wine merchant business in Liverpool.

108 Charles Hallett, a farmer from Somerset, left the RAF in 1919.

109 Aged 26, Alan Roxburgh hailed from Jamaica.

110 in BE2e A1365.

111 in BE2e 3092.

112 RE8 A3799.

113 in BE2e A3093.

114 BE2e A1802.

115 Cecil Manson had joined the Royal West Surrey Regiment directly from the Cambridge University Officer Training Corps in 1914. He left the RAF in 1919 but served in the Administration & Special Duties Branch of the RAFVR from 1940 to 1954, serving under Sir Charles Medhurst and Stephen Pettit in Air Intelligence during World War 2. He retired to New Zealand.

116 Pryce Taylor, from Essex, trained as a pilot during 1918 but he retired from the RAF in 1921.

117 in BE2e A3093.

118 Originally from Antigua, Arthur Essex (1899-1973) later flew with 111 Squadron and emigrated to the USA after the War. He is buried in Camano Is, Washington.

119 2Lts Essex in A8664, E Bell in A7132 and Lt Hallett in A1323. Edward Bell was admitted to hospital with influenza in December 1918; he was transferred to trhe Unemployed list in 1919.

120 Donald Finlayson from Inverness had been a bank clerk with the Standard Chartered Bank before the War; he transferred to the Technical Branch in 1919.

121 Arthur Thompson returned to the Northamptonshire Regiment after the War eventually retiring in 1938.

122 Although Bates was badly injured he survived to fly again and commanded 47 Squadron in Salonika.

123 Douglas Aitcheson returned to UK to recuperate but died in April 1918 at the age of 21 due to septicaemia resulting from his injuries.

Chapter 3

1918
Beyond Jerusalem

Operations in Judea

The appalling weather of December 1917 continued into the beginning of 1918. Heavy rain and low cloud over the Judean Hills limited flying operations throughout January and February, frequently making flying impossible. When flying was possible 14 Squadron typically mounted two tactical reconnaissance sorties and a similar number of artillery co-operation sorties each day. Reconnaissance aircraft were always armed with bombs which they used to attack targets of opportunity. On one such attack[1] on 3 January, Capt Sclanders and Lt E C Booker[2] achieved a direct hit on a dugout on the Jericho Road. On the same day Capt Hanmer, Lts E S Sawtell and D Colyer[3] from the Squadron joined another three from 113 Squadron for a raid on the aerodrome at El Fule, each dropping six twenty-pound bombs from 5,000 feet. This was Hanmer's and Lt J L Benvenisti's[4] first operational flight in the new RE8, and all did not go smoothly for them. Firstly they were delayed when it took longer than usual to haul the heavy RE8 up the hill at Junction Station and secondly the engine refused to start at first. Eventually they set off some distance behind the rest of the formation, which they eventually caught up as the latter was returning from the target. "There were still one or two of our machines hovering about in the direction of Arfuleh – another ten miles on – so [we] pushed on towards them and getting over the junction let the bombs go. To my intense annoyance I saw no explosions and immediately after had a very good idea of what had happened – the safety pin had in all probability not been taken out. There was nothing to be done then but to make for home. I came up with another RE8 on the way and together we proceeded." At this stage Hanmer suggested that Benvenisti should test his gun, which he did, only to have it jam. "Thinking him to be a good gunner," recorded Hanmer, "I did not worry at first but when the gun did not start up again after several minutes delay I looked round and there was my perfectly good observer in a muck sweat at the bottom of his cockpit with his gun in little bits and himself quite incompetent to get it together again!" Luckily no enemy aeroplane found them. The following day another three aircraft bombed the camp at El Tayiben and transport at Silet Ed Dahr. Throughout the first few months of the year, a number of joint operations with 113 Squadron were flown against enemy camps, including a raid on Ramin by two 14 Squadron aircraft (out of a total of four) on 18 January, on Miskeh by one aeroplane (of a total of six aircraft)

Two future Air Marshals, Maj C E H Medhurst & Lt D Colyer enjoy their pipes outside a tent in early 1918. (Ray Vann-Mike O'Connor 220-19)

on 3 February and by three out of eight aircraft on the same target the following day and on Shumit Nimrin by five out of eight aircraft on 5 March.

The poor weather also affected enemy air operations and as a result there were only a small number of attacks on British aircraft during the early part of 1918. The first of these was just after midday on 18 January when an Albatros attacked Lts Beer and Graham as they returned[5] from the bombing raid on Ramin. Graham fired a drum at the Albatros but his gun then jammed with a broken extractor. Beer was able to dive and extend away from the Albatros as Graham struggled to change the bolt on his gun, and generated enough distance to turn back and engage the enemy aircraft with his front Vickers gun, at which the Albatros withdrew northwards.

Flying amongst clouds in hilly terrain brought a new challenge to pilots. When the clouds lay on the hills it was no longer possible simply to fly lower and go under the cloud as they had over the coastal plain. Now pilots had to decide whether to attempt to fly around, over or through the cloud. Sometimes it was possible to fly around

RE8 A3812 of "A" Flight 14 Squadron. Lts W J Beer and C E V Graham were attacked by an Albatros on 18 Jan 1918 as they returned in this aircraft from a bombing raid on Ramin. The aircraft was also attacked by three enemy scouts on 9 Mar while Capt H I Hanmer and Lt R A Tarleton carried out a Contact Patrol near Et Tayib. The machine finally succumbed to the effects of ground fire on 22 Mar 1918 when Hanmer and Tarleton had to forced land at Jericho after the oil tank was holed. (Ray Vann-Mike O'Connor 40-12A)

clouds, though often the result was to find oneself in a cul-de-sac valley. The ability to fly over the clouds depended on the performance of the aircraft and frequently it simply was not an option for the BE2e, though on one occasion Capt Hanmer managed to reach 9,000 feet as he climbed above the clouds in a light weight BE2e. Hanmer also tried flying through the clouds and on his first attempt he found that by flying on a constant compass course for twenty minutes he came out of the clouds almost directly over the aerodrome. However any thought that this method might be an easy solution were dashed on his next attempt when a fortuitous gap in the clouds revealed a large hill straight ahead that he would certainly have hit if he had carried on flying blind. Others were not so lucky: on 21 February 2Lts Beer and H T Thorp[6] were both killed when flew into a hillside near Jerusalem, while attempting to fly through a cloud.

With the arrival of the powerful RE8, 14 Squadron at last had an aeroplane that had adequate performance for operations over the high ground of the Judean Hills. The aircraft had begun arriving in December 1917 but it was not until March 1918 that the last of the BE2e aircraft finally left the Unit strength. With fifty percent more engine power than the BE2e, and increased performance to match, the RE8 proved much more popular in the Middle East than it did on the Western Front. Lt Colyer was "amazed on returning to England after the war to find out what a bad reputation the RE8 had." Colyer added that "although … crashes were not infrequent I never saw one of these aircraft catch fire." Hanmer recalled that "people soon got to like the RE8s. They were heavy no doubt, but with very little practice they could be 'chucked about' quite easily and comfortably … it was [also] a great treat being able to get one's height so quickly." Apart from improved performance, the new type also had much better accommodation for the crew; the observer was seated behind the pilot, which gave him a clear field of fire over the tail. The proximity of the cockpits meant that crew members could communicate with each other more easily and this layout was much better suited to artillery work where the pilot concentrated on the observation and the observer stayed alert for enemy aircraft. From 14 Squadron's perspective, the only drawback with the new type was that it took sixty labourers to haul a RE8 to the top of the launching slope at Junction Station, rather than the thirty required for a BE2e!

Re-equipment of the Corps squadrons in Palestine with the RE8 was mirrored by improvements in RFC's fighter aircraft: 1 Squadron Australian Flying Corps (AFC) was now equipped with the Bristol F2b Fighters and 111 Squadron was flying the SE5a. The spring of 1918 saw a further enlargement of the RFC in Palestine: 142 Squadron was formed in the March to support the Desert Mounted Corps and it was swiftly followed by 144 Squadron, a dedicated day bomber unit under 40 (Army) Wing control. As 142 Squadron commenced its work-up for combat operations, five of its crews were detached to 14 Squadron for training during April and May.

A light-hearted diversion occurred during January when Maj Medhurst, Capt Hanmer and Capt Thompson the Wireless Officer went to visit Capt Bates in hospital after his crash at the end of the previous year. The young men were greatly excited to see female nurses at the hospital and by good fortune they found that the nurses were leaving the hospital at the same time as they left to return by road to Junction Station. With a little encouragement from the officers, Bamford, their driver, managed to join the nurses' motor convoy. After much waving and cheering, they left the convoy as it neared Junction Station, rushed to their aeroplanes, and took off to give an impromptu air display. These antics had the desired effect: the nurses stopped their vehicles to watch and thereafter the Squadron officers frequently enjoyed the company of the nurses at social functions in Jerusalem.

The Squadron was heavily involved in XX Corps' operations to the northeast of Jerusalem on 19 to 21 February . On the first day Rummon, Arak Ibrahim and Ras Et Tawil were captured. 14 Squadron aircraft mounted six tactical reconnaissance sorties on this day and during one of these patrols, artillery fire was called in by the aircraft to disperse a force of 300 enemy troops. In addition seven successful artillery shoots were conducted and two aircraft carried out a bombing and strafing attack against enemy infantry near Ghoraniyeh. Another four tactical reconnaissance and three contact patrols were also flown. On 21 February Jericho and Talat Ed Dum were captured. The following day BE2e flown by Capt S L Pettit[7] and Lt R A Tarleton[8] was sent out on a special patrol to locate a friendly cavalry formation which had lost touch with its headquarters.

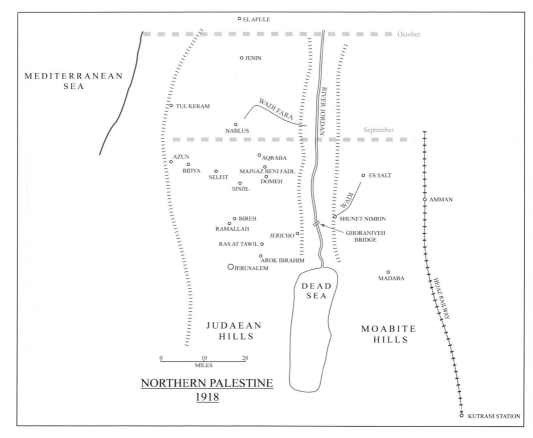

MEDITERRANEAN
SEA

EL AFULE

October

JENIN

TUL KERAM

WADI FARA

RIVER JORDAN

NABLUS

September

AZUN

AQRABA

BIDYA

MAJNAZ BENI FADL

SELFIT

DOMEH

ES SALT

SINJIL

AMMAN

BIREH

SHUNET NIMRIN

RAMALLAH

JERICHO

GHORANIYEH
BRIDGE

RAS AT TAWIL

AROK IBRAHIM

JERUSALEM

DEAD
SEA

MADABA

JUDAEAN
HILLS

MOABITE
HILLS

HEJAZ RAILWAY

0   10   20
MILES

NORTHERN PALESTINE
1918

KUTRANI STATION

One effect of the enforced idleness caused by the poor weather was that some of the pilots put their minds to the invention of alternative methods of fighting. One of the most ingenious was an attempt to interdict Turkish supply-boat traffic on the Dead Sea by means of a "hydroplane". This machine comprised the forward fuselage of a Martynside scout, mounted on floats, and armed with two Lewis guns. The machine itself, which was nicknamed *Mimi*, was made by personnel of 1 Squadron AFC, but the operational crew was to be provided by 14 Squadron in the form of Capt Dempsey and Lt Bell. At 0445 hrs on 1 March *Mimi* was launched from the northwestern corner of the Dead Sea, crewed by Dempsey with Capt P D Drury and Air Mech Doig of 1 Squadron AFC. The target was the anchorage used by Turkish supply boats at Rujm El Bahr near the mouth of the Jordan. Unfortunately as they closed to almost a kilometre of their objective, the rudder mechanism failed and Dempsey lost control of the hydroplane, which nearly capsized in the strong winds and the strong currents. It was only thanks to the efforts of Drury and Doig swimming while holding the floats that *Mimi* was kept upright, but with little directional control

"Mimi" the wingless Martinsyde hydroplane on the Dead Sea. Capt Dempsey with members of the crew in late February 1918. (AWM P01184-005)

the current swept the hydroplane and her crew away to the westerly shore of the Sea, some miles south of their start point. Here they were rescued by their ground-party, but it was apparent that *Mimi* was by now beyond saving. Instead, Dempsey came up with another plan which involved taking the floats off the hydroplane and instead using them as four-man canoes. A second attempt was made at 1900 on 2 March with the two canoes manned by Dempsey, Bell, Drury, Doig and Air Mech Davies of 1 Sqn AFC plus Cpl Jane and Ptes Masters and Stamp of 2/20th London Regiment. After seven hours of paddling against the strong current they reached the eastern shore of the Dead Sea, unable to get any further north because of the currents. Instead of destroying enemy boats, they made a brief reconnaissance of the eastern shore and then paddled back – this time going with the current and arriving back after only four hours.

During January Hanmer was on leave in Cairo and while there he bumped into Maj Gen Salmond. He took the opportunity to expound the idea that each Corps squadron would benefit from having one or two scout aircraft attached to each Flight to provide escorts for the reconnaissance aircraft, just as 14 Squadron had done previously with its de Havillands and Bristol Scouts. Salmond seemed interested in the idea and invited Hanmer to discuss the idea further with his chief of staff Col N D K MacEwen[9]. Two months later when surplus Nieuport Scouts arrived in Egypt, Hanmer found to his delight that a handful of these aircraft were indeed allocated to the Corps squadrons. Whether this was due to his intervention or not, Hanmer didn't know, but he believed that this episode was another example of the way in which Salmond "was always ready to listen to what his pilots thought and had to say about things. If he could carry out their ideas he always did."

An improvement in the weather conditions over Judea at the beginning of March was reflected in the total of 480 flying hours, including 95 tactical reconnaissance

14 Sqn aircrew circa March 1918. Back Row l-r: Lt D R Mackie [pilot], Lt G W S Holdrness [observer], Lt P M Ashton [observer], Lt C M Hallett [pilot], Capt G N Wales [pilot], Stownard [?]. Middle Row: Lt R B M Jenkins [pilot], Lt E Bell [pilot], Lt J H Maingot [observer], Lt G C Shortbridge, Lt P R Bowen [observer], Lt A H Waugh [observer] (with helmet). Front Row: 2Lt H Oldham [observer], Lt J Webster [pilot], Capt W S Reid [pilot], Lt P L Ward [observer], Lt P G Wells [pilot] (with hat), Lt E S Sawtell [pilot] (with pipe). Lying in front – G A Mitchell [pilot]. (Ray Vann-Mike O'Connor 221-26)

sorties flown during the month during the month, against totals of around 300 hours and 45 sorties in each of the two preceding months. The Jordan Valley, and especially the area around the Ghoraniyeh Bridge was reconnoitred twice every day during the first week of March, and clearer weather enabled crews to carry out photo reconnaissance tasks. On 1 March Lt J B Carr[10], in the back of 2 Lt H Oldham's[11] aircraft[12] took some excellent photographs of the area. On 9 March, the XX Corps front was pushed forwards again towards Nablus and a number of contact patrols and artillery shots were flown over the next three days in support of ground operations. Enemy aircraft were much in evidence on 9 March, though they were not particularly effective. On that morning Capt Hanmer and Lt Tarleton were on a contact patrol near Et Tayib[13] when they noticed three scout aircraft approaching them. At first Hanmer took them to be friendly Nieuports, but realised that they were decidedly unfriendly when the centre aircraft opened fire on the RE8. Hanmer immediately turned away from them, heading for the safety of British lines and also giving Tarleton a clear shot at the enemy; however as soon as Tarleton returned fire,

72

the enemy scouts retired. As they resumed their patrol, Hanmer and Tarleton saw a formation of six hostile aircraft closing on a single RE8[14]. This was flown by Lts R B M Jenkins[15] and P L Ward[16] on an artillery shoot. Although there were six enemy aircraft, only one, a single seat scout engaged the RE8, diving onto the front quarter. Ward fired a short burst of ten rounds at the scout and this was apparently enough to dissuade him from attacking further: the scout continued its dive under the RE8 to disengage and head back to Turkish lines.

This lack of aggression by German aircraft even when they enjoyed every advantage of numbers, position and performance seemed remarkable but was not isolated. On 20 March an RE8[17] flown by Lts D Alliban (of 113 Squadron) and P R Bowen MC[18] was attacked by two Albatros single-seaters and an AEG two-seater from up-sun, as they carried out a reconnaissance of the Ghoraniyeh bridge. The Albatroses attacked with a speed advantage from the stern one after the other and Alliban fired at them with the front gun as they overtook him; meanwhile the AEG flew alongside so that its observer could engage the RE8. As the AEG closed to 300 yards, Bowen opened fire, at which all three enemy aircraft withdrew eastwards leaving the RE8 to continue its patrol. Two days later Bowen was attacked again[19], this time while flying with Lt Cotton. On this occasion two enemy scouts engaged from below, but sheered off towards Amman when Bowen fired at them.

Operations East of the Jordan

The question of communication with ground units, which had concerned the Squadron almost since its arrival in Egypt was exacerbated by the hilly terrain of eastern Palestine. In the open terrain of Sinai or the coastal plain of Palestine aircraft could simply land alongside army units to deliver information and be given tasking, but in Judea this was often not possible. Moreover, the high hills intersected by deep valleys meant that Corps HQ, with no line of sight with its front line units, relied heavily on contact patrols to keep them updated and to deliver messages to dispersed units. Thanks to the Squadron's Wireless Officers Lt F H R Law[20] and 2Lt K Fraser, the problem of communication between Squadron HQ and Corps HQ was solved by establishing a wireless link between Junction Station and HQ XX Corps: this link in turn enabled the exchange of strategic information between formations. However, the more fast-moving tactical information gleaned during reconnaissance flights needed a more flexible system of transfer. Attempts had been made previously in 1916 (by Maj Bannatyne) and 1917 (by Capt Stent) to pick up messages from the ground using a hook attached to the wireless aerial. Although these attempts had been partially successful, the technique was very hit-and-miss and had not subsequently been adopted. However in early 1917 Capt H C Brocklehurst[21], the RFC Liaison Officer with the cavalry, and Capt Hanmer turned their attention to developing a practical method of picking up messages by aircraft. Their solution was to fit the aircraft with a weighted cable made from a length of aerial wire with a number of hooks on it, much like a mackerel line. The cable could be wound in or out by the observer to adjust its length. On the ground, the message bag was hung on a loop of cord slung between two poles, orientated across the wind, about twenty-five yards apart. The technique was for the pilot to fly into wind as low as he could between the poles and for the observer to adjust the length of the cable so that the streamers on the weighted end trailed just above the ground; the cord was caught by one of the hooks and because it was a continuous loop it remained caught on the hook no matter which part of it had first contacted the hook. Then cable, cord and message bag could be hauled aboard the aircraft. With a little practice this manoeuvre could be easily mastered by all pilots and it provided a consistent method of picking up messages. The technique would be put to good use during operations east of the Jordan in the second half of March.

With the front lines static once more, Allenby decided to grasp the offensive again by mounting a raid on Amman. His objective was to cut the Hejaz railway by destroying the bridges Amman, thereby isolating the Turkish garrison at Ma'an and opening the possibility of linking with the Arab Sherrifan forces. The troops for the raid were supplied by XX Corps' 60 Division and the ANZAC Mounted Division, all under the command of Maj Gen F S M Shea and collectively named "Shea's Force." The plan was for 60 Division's infantry to cross the Jordan at and advance along the Wadi Nimrin to secure Es Salt; the ANZAC cavalry would then dash to Amman taking the RE demolition teams with them. The success of the operation would depend on speed: the demolition work would need to be completed before the Turks could reinforce Amman.

Because of the distances involved from Junction Station, "A" Flight was detached to an advanced landing ground at Jericho to support the ground operation. Although the makeshift aerodrome was in more convenient proximity to the operational area, it was far from ideal. The landing ground itself was crossed by a number of small ravines, which were to cause a number of ground accidents, and strong air currents within the steeply-sided Jordan Valley, nearly a thousand feet below sea level, made flying conditions difficult. Neither of these factors was helped by the return of heavy rain, which also caused serious problems for Shea's Force. Weather delayed the crossing of the Jordan, which had risen nine feet overnight, and by the time the main force had crossed the river on the evening of 23 March the whole operation was running three days late.

"A" Flight had started preparation work for the raid on 20 March: three enemy gun positions were attacked by aircraft and on the following day four successful shoots were carried out against enemy batteries. In addition, a total of 900 machine gun rounds were fired at various moving targets in the tactical area. Then, on 22 March, Lts A C Reed[22] and W B Cochran[23] made a final reconnaissance[24] of the enemy positions at Es Salt, Ghoraniyeh and Madeba.

Sheas's Force slogged through the rain, capturing Shunet Nimrin on 24 March and two aircraft[25], flown by Lt D R Mackie[26] with Lt Graham and Lt Reed with Lt Cochran, supported the action by dropping fifteen bombs and firing 900 rounds at enemy troops and transport. Es Salt itself was captured the next day. By 26 March the foremost units of the cavalry had reached Amman, but a complex tactical situation

Lt A Dix Lewis & 2Lt C Sweetman in a RE8 bound for Es Salt. Alan Dix-Lewis returned to the Middlesex Regiment in 1922, retiring in 1930; after returning to the army in 1939 he retired for a second time as a Major in 1944. Charles Sweetman, a telephone engineer in Nottingham before the War, had been an Air Mechanic; he was commissioned in 1918 and left the RAF in 1920. (Ray Vann-Mike O'Connor 229-209)

was developing and the ANZAC Divisional Headquarters was separated from its own units by ten miles and from Shea's Headquarters by another twenty miles, and none were in direct touch with each other. The situation lent itself to using the new message-lifting skills. Capt Hanmer dropped a message giving his report and asked that HQ ANZAC Division write their tactical appreciation for him to pick up later for delivery to Shea's Headquarters. Capt Brocklehurst persuaded another officer to help him hold up the loop of cord between them and Hanmer picked it up at the first attempt. At a stroke communication had been re-established between the scattered components of Shea's Force. However, Brocklehurst decided that holding up the loop by hand was rather too hairy and he would revert to using poles in future! The following day, the system was further refined when Hanmer with Lt Carr flew past[27] the ANZAC Headquarters en route for the morning reconnaissance. Here they picked up detailed written instructions of the Headquarters' requirements for reconnaissance of the roads to the north and south of Amman. This was probably the first time that an aircraft had effectively been tasked while airborne. On their return from the sortie, Hanmer and Carr dropped their reconnaissance report to the cavalry Headquarters and picked up their report to Shea, once again linking the Force Commander with his dispersed units.

The number of tactical reconnaissance sorties from Jericho was increased to five or six per day and reconnaissance aircraft dropped bombs on enemy troops and on Amman station. On 27 March three 14 Squadron aircraft, accompanied by four more from 113 Squadron carried out a bombing attack on Amman station, scoring a direct hit on a train. The next day another seventeen bombs were dropped on Amman station by reconnaissance aircraft. Over the next three days the ground forces withdrew from Amman to the Jordan after an operation which had been only partially successful. Reconnaissance aircraft provided cover for the forces throughout this phase, while bombing attacks kept up the pressure on Turkish forces east of the Jordan. Amman station was bombed by Capt Pettit and Lt Colyer on 3 April, by four aircraft the next day and by another pair the day after that. "A" Flight finally withdrew from Jericho on 4 April.

During the middle of the April the whole Squadron reverted to routine reconnaissance and artillery patrols. The priority for the latter was counter-battery work and eight batteries were engaged in the three days from 11 April. Further counter-battery work was carried out on 28 April during which four batteries were engaged. Meanwhile, the Squadron's reconnaissance missions were tasked to monitor the movements of enemy forces between Es Salt and the Shunet Nimrin area, in preparation for a second raid across the Jordan. This second raid, originally planned for later in May was brought forward after a delegation from the Beni Sakhr tribe indicated that they might be prepared to join the fight against the Turkish forces amongst the Moabite Hills, if the British Army attacked first. Once again a joint force comprising the infantry of 60 Division, and the ANZAC Mounted Division, this time under command of Maj Gen E W C Chaytor prepared to cross the River Jordan.

The advanced landing ground at Jericho used by "A" Flight during the first Amman raid had been hard on aircraft and crews, and with temperatures reaching the high nineties (in Farenheit) in Judea in the late spring Jericho would no longer be suitable for sustained flying operations. Instead the Flight deployed to Jerusalem on 28 April. The offensive towards Shunet Nimrin and Es Salt commenced on the last day of the month, with "A" Flight contact patrols supporting the advance throughout the day. The ground operations continued for the next four days, during which time 14 Squadron aircraft flew as many as fifteen tactical reconnaissance patrols a day. A number of bombing attacks were also made on enemy troops near Ain Es Sir.

The weather for the second raid was much better than it had been a month previously, but progress on the ground was hampered this time by strong resistance by the much reinforced Turks. With casualties much higher than expected among Chaytor's soldiers, first aid supplies began running out at the tactical Casualty Clearing Station at Es Salt. On the evening of 3 May aircraft were dispatched to drop medical supplies to the troops at Es Salt. This simple-sounding mission was not without its problems, for Es Salt lies in a bowl in the Moabite Hills, and even the RE8 lacked sufficient performance in the heat of the early summer to climb out of the bowl. One of the pilots involved was Capt Hanmer who found that after making his drop his only means of escape was to fly down the road towards Shunet Nimrin and into the Jordan Valley.

During a contact patrol on 3 May Lt R C van der Ben, the observer[28], was severely wounded in the leg by ground fire. He returned fire with his machine gun and then instructed his pilot to carry on with the patrol while he completed the reconnaissance. Van der Ben, who was awarded a MC for his actions, was one the crews detached from the newly-forming 142 Squadron. On the same day two other RE8s were badly damaged by ground fire, resulting in two forced landings at Jericho: the engine in Capt H A Courtenay's[29] and 2Lt T E Gohl's[30] aircraft[31] was shot through, as was the petrol tank in Capt W Elliott's[32] and Lt Cochran's machine[33].

By 5 May Chaytor's Force had withdrawn once again to the western bank of the Jordan, but "A" Flight remained at Jerusalem for another week. During this time a number of joint bombing attacks were carried out with 113 Squadron aircraft. Of the three aircraft which bombed Amman station on 7 May, Capt G N Wales[34] scored two direct hits on a train and Lt J E Carpenter[35] managed to start a fire in the buildings. Two days later another three attacked the aerodrome at Jenin.

Aerial Combats

During a routine artillery shoot near Sinjil on 29 March an enemy LVG aircraft made a single pass attack on an RE8[36] flown by Lts L Clark of 113 Squadron and G W Holderness[37] of 14 Squadron. The LVG sheered off after Holderness fired eighty rounds at it, and the RE8 was then able to continue the shoot. Five days later another RE8[38], flown by Lts Wells and P M Ashton[39], was engaged by two Albatros scouts during a tactical reconnaissance near Amman, but no damage was done to the aircraft. A more involved engagement occurred on the afternoon of 8 April during which two of the Squadron's RE8s[40], flown by Lt Mackie with Lt Carr and Lt G J Turner[41] with Lt Ward, were involved with a formation of up to seven enemy aircraft as they carried out artillery co-operation duties. Mackie's aeroplane was at 7000 feet over Bir Ez Zeit when the crew noticed a formation of aircraft being engaged by anti-aircraft fire. They closed to investigate and saw three single-seat Albatros Scouts and two two-seater AEG aircraft heading back towards the enemy lines. Mackie turned to follow them whereupon the scouts detached and attacked the RE8 from up-sun. For the next ten minutes the scouts dived on the RE8 as Mackie flew in a wide circle, trying to make it difficult for the scouts to track him while presenting Carr with a with a chance of shooting back at them. The scouts eventually disengaged, leaving the badly-damaged RE8 to return to base. About ten minutes later it was Turner and Ward's turn as they saw the formation, which had by now been augmented by another two AEGs, heading northwest about 1000 feet above them. Turner pulled the nose up as he passed under the enemy aircraft and fired at them before turning to follow them. Once again a pair of Albatros detached for a single pass, but this time the single-seaters' attack was accompanied by heavy fire from the two-seaters and Turner was forced to disengage.

Unfortunately, Turner and Ward were less lucky two days later when they suffered an engine failure soon after take-off. The aircraft[42] spun into the ground, killing Turner and seriously injuring Ward. Even without the attentions of enemy aircraft or artillery, military flying in 1918 was still a dangerous business. Later in the month four more officers were injured in flying accidents in the space of just two days: Lt H S Newman[43] and 2Lt J F Thompson spun in on 28 April and 2Lts J E Bennett[44] and W E Hall[45] crashed the following day. Another aircraft accident on 7 May resulted in injuries to Lt Bell as he returned from the raid on Amman.

However, on the same day that Turner's luck had run out, Fortune smiled on Lts Hallet and Carr during an engagement with an Albatros near Selfit. The Albatros was escorting an AEG reconnaissance aircraft, but left its charge to carry out a number of very aggressive attacks on Hallett and Carr's RE8[46]. On one pass the Albatros closed to within twenty feet and Hallett feared a collision was inevitable. Perhaps this near-miss frightened the German pilot, too, because he then disengaged, but after the action Carr found three bullet holes in his coat. Lts R B M Jenkins and R M Campbell[47] were also lucky three hours later when three Albatros came across their artillery patrol. Only one of the enemy scouts engaged them, but that single pass was enough to hole the RE8's[48] oil tank and they had to return to Junction Station.

From the middle of April onwards, contact with enemy aircraft became a rare event. The deployment to the theatre of high performance SE5as of 111 Squadron, 1 Squadron Australian Flying Corps' Bristol Fighters and the Nieuports flown by all the "Corps" Squadrons gave the RAF the tools with which to achieve air superiority.

One of the last engagements by 14 Squadron reconnaissance aircraft was on 1 May when four Albatros attacked an RE8[49] over Domeh. The Germans appeared from out of the sun and split into pairs, attacking from front and rear simultaneously. As the pilot 2Lt H J Crompton (of 113 Squadron) manoeuvred the RE8, Lt G J Williams[50] fired at an Albatros which had closed to within a hundred yards. The Albatros immediately reared up and spun away, but unfortunately it disappeared behind a hill before Williams could verify that it had crashed. At this the others broke away leaving Williams fairly certain that he had scored a kill.

Back to the Routine of Trench Warfare
"A" Flight finally returned to Junction Station from Jerusalem on 14 May by which time the Squadron's activities had once more resumed the routine of tactical reconnaissance, artillery shoots and photography. As temperatures rose once more with the coming of summer, flying became restricted to the early morning and late evening. Undoubtedly the mainstay of 14 Squadron's work during the summer was the unglamorous but nevertheless vital work of photographic reconnaissance and the Unit consistently produced the highest number of photographic negatives of any of the squadrons in theatre.

Throughout the summer Allenby had been planning his next move. It became clear that his main attack would have to come on the western flank, a mirror image of his tactic at Gaza. However in order to achieve surprise, the Turks were encouraged to believe that the attack would once again be delivered in the east. Large dummy camps filled with canvass horses were set up and mules towed sleighs to generate

RE8 over the Jerusalem to Bireh Road. (Ray Vann-Mike O'Connor 215/27)

enough dust clouds to give the impression of forces massing on the eastern flank. Meanwhile the real flow of troops, carried out at night and in strict silence, was in the opposite direction. The role of the RAF in this deception was firstly to deny the enemy the ability to conduct aerial reconnaissance over the British lines and secondly to carry out offensive raids which would keep the Turks thinking that the main attack would come on the eastern flank. The contribution of 14 Squadron was to carry out regular bombing attacks against targets in and around Amman, in conjunction with 113 Squadron. Four aircraft (plus two from 113) bombed the Station and the aerodrome on 31 May, while Lts R J W Palmer[51] and Hallet (plus three from 113) bombed the Station and the bridge on 3 June and five aircraft (Lts Palmer, J G Argles[52], Mackie, Bell and J Webster MC accompanied by a further six from 113) repeated the exercise the next day.

With the arrival of 142 Squadron larger attacks were possible and a force of thirteen RE8s (including four from 14 Squadron) raided Amman on 11 June. This effort was continued at approximately weekly intervals over the next three months. The raid against Amman on 13 July was successful in scattering a large force of enemy cavalry. The 14 Squadron pilots, Capts N A Bolton[53] and Wales and Lts Carpenter and J E Atkinson[54] reported that they had attacked cavalry who were deployed in groups of about 250 on horses and camels. Each aircraft dropped eight bombs on the enemy troops from about 800 feet and between them the aircraft fired about 2,800 machine gun rounds while chasing and scattering the cavalry.

Another regular target was Kutrani Station which was bombed by twenty RE8s from the three Squadrons on 16 June. During this raid the six aircraft from 14 Squadron achieved direct hits on trains, track and trench positions. The Squadron also provided six aircraft against the same target on 5 and 15 June and five aircraft (as part of a force of twelve RE8s) on 15 August, during which raid they scored two direct hits on trains and anther direct hit with a 112-pounder on the rail tracks.

Artillery work also continued. By mid-1918 both aircrews and artillerymen were well practised in gunnery with aerial observation. Much of the work of the aerial observer was in locating enemy batteries and perhaps the most rewarding of such patrols for aircrew was when they managed to locate and neutralise anti-aircraft guns. On 20 June an aircraft spotted an anti-aircraft gun and engaged it with a 60-pounder battery which silenced it with a direct hit, and another anti aircraft battery was similarly silenced two weeks later. The routine was punctuated by the occasional losses. 2Lt L E T Burley[55] was wounded in action when his RE8[56], flown by Lt Bell, came under machine gun fire on 5 July and on 29 July Capt Pettit and Lt Williams were shot down[57] while attacking an anti-aircraft battery. They were both later reported to be Prisoners of War.

By the beginning of June all the 142 Squadron crews had returned to their unit, and during this month, too, the aerodrome at Junction Station was renamed "Surar Junction." Surar Junction was also home to 144 Squadron, a 40 Wing unit equipped with DH9 aircraft, while the other two 5 Wing squadrons (113 and 142) were at Sarona and the remaining three 40 Wing squadrons (1 AFC, 111 and 145) at Ramleh. By now 14 Squadron also had its complement of Nieuport scouts which were based at the advanced landing ground at Jerusalem. These aircraft were use to fly standing "Hostile Aircraft Patrols" but the pilots were expected to be fully operational as tactical reconnaissance pilots, too. However the RE8 continued to be the mainstay of the reconnaissance work. The aircraft were always loaded with bombs and crews were encouraged to attack targets of opportunity. One such attack was on 9 July when a reconnaissance aircraft crewed by Lt G A Mitchell[58] and A H Waugh[59] attacked a body of one hundred enemy infantry and their camels.

In raids which are reminiscent of the attacks by Yates and Hill on the water supplies at Bir Hasana in early 1916, two attempts were made to neutralise the water cistern at Khan Lubban. A pair of aircraft was tasked against the target on 7 August. Lt Mitchell and Capt Bolton both dropped a 112-pounder bomb and several 20-pounders, but no hits were obtained. Two days later Mitchell tried again, this time accompanied by Lt Bell. This time Mitchell's 112-pounder hit the earthworks and Bell's landed in the garden, but despite these close misses, no real damage was done.

In mid-August XX Corps' 10 Division carried out a series of trench raids, aimed at intimidating the Turks and also capturing prisoners to obtain intelligence. 14 Squadron aircraft were closely involved in the preparatory work for the raids by carrying out special reconnaissance of the positions to be attacked and constructing a photo-mosaic of each target area. In addition the Squadron's Nieuports were tasked to keep enemy aircraft from observing the build-up of forces prior to the raids. The raids which were carried out on 13 and 14 August were a great success and resulted in the capture of seventeen Turkish officers and two hundred and thirty Other Ranks. Later in the month three aircraft bombed the Turkish 53 Division's field bakery and main store at Aqraba.

The Battle of Mergiddo

Preparations for the offensive continued through September with routine reconnaissance and artillery co-operation patrols. On one such flight over Yetma on 15 September, Capt Bolton and 2Lt R C Revelle[60] came under heavy anti aircraft fire; one shot was close enough to damage the aircraft[61] and kill Revelle.

The offensive opened at 0430 hrs on 19 September with a brief barrage and the advance of XXI Corps' cavalry. At dawn, the RAF attacked a number of Turkish Headquarters units. Five aircraft from 14 Squadron were tasked against three Turkish Corps and Divisional headquarters: Lt Atkinson attacked the headquarters at Jalud at 0530 hrs, Lt B R Harris[62] bombed Sheikh Abu Zarad at 0535 hrs, and Capt Bolton and Lt Carpenter attacked Mejdel Beni Fadl at 0545 hrs. During these raids there were two direct hits on tents from the three 112-pounder and twenty-three 24-pounder bombs which they dropped. They also fired over two thousand machine gun rounds into these targets. Capt Sclanders was also airborne at daybreak and he engaged an anti-aircraft battery and motor transport on the Domeh Road.

As the day progressed, elements of the Turkish 7th and 8th Armies attempted to withdraw eastwards and they came under sustained air attack from all three Corps squadrons. Six of 14 Squadron's aircraft attacked transport and troops on the roads between Azun and Bidya from low level with bombs and machine gun fire and six more, including two Nieuport Scouts, attacked troops and transport near Tul Keram from very low level, dropping a hundred Mills grenades on densely packed targets. Two more raids by five aircraft and four aircraft also targeted the same concentrations, wreaking carnage. In his biography of Allenby, Sir Archibald Wavell describes this action as "deadlier if less spectacular" than the massacre that was to come two days later in the Wadi Fara. On 20 September 14 Squadron's focus of operations moved ten miles southeast to the area north of Aqraba with raids by two aircraft, seven aircraft and six aircraft against troops and transport withdrawing from Aqraba towards Nablus. Nine reconnaissance missions were flown including four contact patrols, and aircraft were also involved in artillery co-operation duties. However the problem for artillery aircraft was that the targets were moving backwards from the front so fast that they were often out of range of friendly guns. One artillery aircraft located an enemy battery but with no friendlies within range, the aircraft engaged the battery itself with machine gun fire.

That night the Turkish 7th Army withdrew from Nablus and attempted to retreat eastwards to the Jordan Valley. Their route took them into the head of the Wadi Fara, and it was here, in a narrow track bounded on one side by a steep hillside and on the other by a precipice, that they were located by a reconnaissance aircraft the following morning. Aircraft from all RAF squadrons were sent to the area, arriving in continuous relays to bomb and strafe the densely packed troops and their equipment. When Lt Colyer landed at Jerusalem he was ordered to refuel and re-arm immediately and set off for the Wadi Fara: "When the order for bombing was received I had just landed... Fearing that the target might be too fleeting a nature to allow delay, we did not wait to have bombs placed on the bomb racks, but my observer took them with him in the back seat and when we arrived over the target flung them overboard onto the mass of troops below... When I arrived over the Wadi Fara with the one other aircraft which accompanied me from Jerusalem I found a heterogenous collection of aircraft – SE5s, RE8s, Brisfits, Armstrong-Whitworths all circling and swooping over the unfortunate Turks who were strung out in a column... along a narrow road for miles. Each formation chose its own height to bomb and then dived down to use its machine guns regardless of the fact that there were other aircraft doing the same thing overhead. In this way our action was much hampered and the multitude of aeroplanes constituted a definite danger to each other. On several occasions on looking up I saw a formation or single aircraft above

Lt John Webster and Sgt Ethelbert Purling were killed in action in RE8 B6561 over the Wadi Farar on 21 September 1918, possibly as a result of being hit by bombs dropped by other aircraft attacking the retreating Turkish Army. The aircraft is painted in an experimental silver colour. (Ray Vann-Mike O'Connor 40-14A)

me about to drop its bombs oblivious of the fact that my aircraft was in the way."

During the course of the day, 14 Squadron dispatched three formations of six aircraft to the Wadi Fara, each formation dropping about forty bombs and firing three thousand machine gun rounds into the column. By the end of the day the Turkish 7th Army ceased to exist after a chilling demonstration of the effectiveness of air power. Colyer "...went down to the valley in a car two days later and I have never seen so terrible a sight. Dead men and horses were lying everywhere, some caught on rocks halfway down the gully some run over and crushed to death by the guns in their headlong rush drawn by maddened teams... one almost felt sick at the thought that one had been... responsible for such carnage." However, the fight was not entirely one-sided: a 14 Squadron RE8 was brought down during the attack, killing the pilot Lt J Webster[63] and his observer Sgt Mech E J Purling[64]. They may have been the victims of Turkish rifle fire, though Colyer thought it more likely that they were inadvertently bombed by another aeroplane.

With Turkish resistance west of the Jordan smashed, 14 Squadron now turned its attention once again to the Jordan Valley and the Turkish 4th Army in the hills of Moab beyond. Two aircraft attacked troops and transport in the Valley directly to the east of Nablus and three others attacked four suspected enemy batteries near Shunet Nimrin. These latter aircraft did not claim any hits but they did succeed in making the batteries cease fire. On 23 September three waves each of five aircraft joined sixteen from 113 Squadron in attacking troops and transport on the Es Salt road as the Turkish 4th Army fled northwards.

Apart from the "formal" offensive action of bombing raids, 14 Squadron RE8 aircraft also dropped over two hundred bombs on targets of opportunity as they had carried out reconnaissance and artillery co-operation missions during the five days of battle. The Unit's Nieuport scouts had also been very active operating as pairs against enemy artillery batteries and reinforcements. These aircraft proved most effective when they found artillery units in vulnerable phases of limbering up to move.

The last photograph of 14 Squadron before the unit's disbandment at Tangmere in February 1919. Maj C E H Medhurst OBE MC is on the far right and Capt D R Mackie MC is third from right. (J Divall)

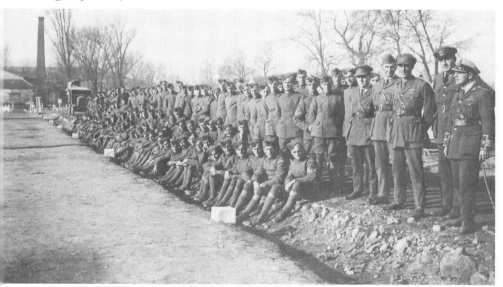

By 24 September the front line had been pushed northwards beyond the Plain of Esdraelon. 142 Squadron had established itself at a forward landing ground on the Turkish aerodrome at El Afule and 14 Squadron started sending aircraft forward to operate from El Afule from 27 September. This aerodrome had only a few days before been some forty miles behind the enemy front lines – now it was well behind the British lines. This distance between airfield and both its supply base and its tasking headquarters caused something of a logistical nightmare. One of the main tasks of the 14 Squadron aircraft was to ferry fuel and oil from Surar Junction up to El Afule in support of 142 Squadron's reconnaissance of Damascus. A further task was to act as a communications relay between HQ 5 Wing and the advanced landing ground. However, the rapid advance and move to El Afule had taken its toll of 142 Squadron's Armstrong Whitworth FK8 aircraft, whose undercarriage was not well-suited to operating from rough ground, so 14 Squadron was transferred to assist with supporting the Desert Mounted Corps. For the first three days of October this task was mainly one of flying contact patrols to locate British cavalry units who were hot on the heels of the retreating Turks. On 7 October one aircraft located HQ 5 Cavalry Division and another HQ 4 Cavalry Division, enabling communication to be re-established with these units. The following day "C" Flight 142 Squadron, which still operated the RE8, arrived to take over the task and 14 Squadron returned to Surar Junction.

With the campaign in Palestine rapidly reaching its conclusion, there was no further tasking for 14 Squadron and flying dwindled. On 15 October it was decided that two squadrons should be sent to Salonika where forces were being gathered for an offensive northwards into Austria-Hungary. Nine days later, exactly a week before the Turkish Armistice marked the end of the Palestine Campaign, 14 and 144 Squadrons were ordered to Kantara to embark for Salonika. For most of the Squadron the move to Kantara was relatively straightforward: the aircrew who simply flew the aircraft along the coastal route to Egypt, and the groundcrew loaded Squadron's heavy equipment onto the railhead at Junction Station arriving in Kantara the next day. However things were much tougher for the unlucky few who were with the stores and equipment which had been moved as far north as Haifa in the expectation of further advances: now it all had to come back southwards.

At Kantara, the aircraft were dismantled and crated ready for shipping; unfortunately the aircraft crates would not fit through the hatchways on the ship and a new vessel had to be found. Meanwhile, 14 and 144 Squadrons' personnel and their equipment, embarked on the SS *Maryland*, arriving at Mikra Bay on 6 November. Here confusion reigned about what to do with them until their aircraft arrived. In fact it was 11 November before a suitable ship was located at Port Said for the aircraft and by then all of the plans had been overtaken by the Armistice. The aircraft were not dispatched and on 9 December after a short sojourn in Mikra, 14 Squadron's personnel were packed aboard a train heading for home. Now only at cadre strength, the Unit arrived at Tangmere on 1 January 1919 where it was disbanded on 4 February.

Notes

1 in BE2c 4437.

2 Ernest Booker had been a salesman in Australia before the War. He was demobilised in 1921 and returned to his native Canada.

3 Air Marshal Douglas Colyer (1893-1978) was Air Attache in Paris, Madrid and Lisbon during the 1930s and was ACAS (Policy) for the latter half of WW2. After retirement from the RAF in 1946 he served as Civil Air Representative for Europe until final retirement in 1960.

4 A French and German linguist, Jacques Benvenisti had studied at Christchurch College, Oxford and the University of London before the War. His translation of the life of St Francis of Assisi was published in German in 1927.

5 in RE8 A3812.

6 Henry Thorp had originally enlisted as a Private in the London Regiment before being commissioned into the RFC.

7 Stephen Pettit was Mentioned in Dispatches for his service while in captivity as a Prisoner of War. He left the RAF in 1920 but served again in Air Intelligence as a member of the RAFVR during WW2, retiring as a Sqn Ldr in 1954.

8 Originally from Dundee, Robert Tarleton joined the Jodhpur Railway as an engineer after the War and rose to become the Superintendent. He was killed in a light aircraft crash near Jodhpur in 1936.

9 AVM Sir Norman MacEwen CMG DSO (1881-1953) retired from the RAF in 1935 and was Chairman of the charity SSAFA from 1936-49.

10 James Carr left the RAF in 1919 but served with the RAFVR during World War 2.

11 Harold Oldham won a DFC for his Contact Patrol work in September 1918; he left the Service in 1919.

12 RE8 B6472.

13 in RE8 A3812.

14 RE8 A4432.

15 Born in 1895 and educated at Haileybury College, Richard Jenkins left the RAF in 1919 for a career in civil engineering; he served in the Royal Engineers during World War 2.

16 Pascoe Ward was injured in an accident in April 1918 but soon returned to flying duties. After the War he returned to Devon and transferred to the TA battalion of the Devonshire Regiment. He served with the Regiment during World War 2 as a Maj and earned the MBE for his service.

17 RE8 A3811.

18 From Abergwili near Carmarthen Parcell Bowen earned a MC while serving with the Machine Gun Corps in Palestine in 1917. He won his first DFC when with Lt Robert Fawcett he carried out a difficult reconnaissance sortie on 22 Sept 1918 and a bar to the DFC in Russia the following year. On that occasion he and his pilot were wounded by ground fire and the pilot passed out; leaning over the pilot, Bowen flew the aircraft 100 miles back to base. Subsequently Bowen was involved in secret undercover operations in Ireland, where he was murdered by Irish Nationalists in 1921.

19 in RE8 B5863.

20 Francis Law later served in the Equipment Branch of the RAFVR from 1939 to 1954.

21 Lt Col Henry Brocklehurst FRGS FZS (1888-1942) 10th Hussars was killed in action in Burma. An accomplished big game hunter, he served between the wars as Game Warden to the Sudan Government and wrote the book "Game Animals of the Sudan".

22 Ambrose Reed had served as a Corporal in the New Zealand Mounted Rifles before being commissioned into the RFC in 1917; he left the Service in 1919.

23 William Cochran left the RAF in 1919.

24 in RE8 B5861.

25 Lts Mackie and Graham in A3805 and Lts Reed and Cochran in B5861.

26 Born in St Vincent in the West Indies in 1887, Douglas Mackie was the RFC's first "coloured" pilot. He left the RAF in 1919 to resume his career as a civil engineer, spending much of his working life in west Africa.

27 in RE8 A3805.

28 in RE8 B5057.

29 A pre-War Regular, Hugh Courtenay DFC returned to the RASC, eventually retiring as a Col in 1943.

30 Thomas Gohl, from Capetown, was posted to 142 Squadron a fortnight later.

31 RE8 B5056.

32 ACM Sir William Elliott (1896-1971) later served 142 Sqn in Palestine and 47 Sqn in Russia during WW1; he rejoined 14 Squadron in 1921. Elliot was AOC-in-C Fighter Command 1947-49 and later chaired the British Joint Services Mission to Washington.

33 RE8 B5057.

34 From Glamorgan, Geoffrey Wales (1896-1971) served with the Welch Regiment before joining the RFC. He resigned his commission in 1920 and eventually settled near Chatsworth.

35 John Carpenter, who was mentioned in Dispatches in 1918, left the RAF in 1919.

36 RE8 A3693.

37 George Holderness DFC retired from the RAF in 1919 but served with the Administration & Special Duties Branch of the RAFR in World War 2.

38 RE8 B6473.

39 Percival Ashton had been a member of Manchester University OTC at the outbreak of War.

40 Lts Mackie and Carr in B5657 and Lts Turner and Ward in B5007.

41 A Canadian, George Turner (1891-1918) had previously served as an infantryman in the Canadian Scottish Regiment.

42 RE8 B5007.

43 Originally commissioned into the Welsh Regiment, Henry Newman left the RAF in 1921 but rejoined again in 1940, serving in various branches until 1954.

44 John Bennett joined the Fife and Forfar Yeomanry from the Inns of Court OTC in 1915; he relinquished his commission in 1921.

45 William Hall had previously been a Private in the Army Service Corps.

46 RE8 B5057.

47 Robert Campbell, from Edinburgh, left the RAF in 1919; he rejoined the RAFVR Technical Branch in 1941 but died in 1943.

48 RE8 A4432.

49 RE8 B5857.

50 Shot down in July 1918, George Williams was repatriated in Oct 1918 and rejoined the Herefordshire Regiment.

51 Robert Palmer served in the Administrative & Special Duties Branch of the RAF Reserve during World War 2.

52 John Argles served as a pilot with the RAF in the early 1920s and transferred to the RAF Reserve in 1925. He was active in the Administration & Special Duties Branch of the RAFVR ending World War 2 as a Gp Capt and having been awarded a CBE.

53 Norman Bolton had previously served with 6 and 21 Squadrons on the Western Front, where he had been awarded the Order of Leopold and the Croix de Guerre. He left the RAF in 1919.

54 John Atkinson left the RAF in 1919 and moved to Schenectady, Nw York.

55 On recovery from his wounds, Leonard Burley joined 142 Squadron.

56 RE8 B6560.

57 in RE8 B6609.

58 A pre-War farmer in Australia, George Mitchell returned to Australia at the end of 1918.

59 Albert Waugh, who served with the RAF occupation forces in the Rhineland immediately after the War had been a "practitioner in dentistry' in Wolverhampton before the War.

60 Roy Revelle had been a law student at Clements Inn, London.

61 RE8 B7710.

62 Bertrand Harris had originally enlisted as a driver in the Honourable Artillery Company in 1914; he was appointed to a permanent commission in the RAF in 1919, but he died of pneumonia, aged 27, in 1922.

63 John Webster, the only son of Dr J A Webster was a native of Tasmania, had won the MC while serving with the West Yorkshire Regiment prior to transferring to the RFC.

64 Originally from Norfolk, 22 year old Ethelbert Purling had served with the 2/4 Norfolk Regiment in the Dardanelles before transferring to the RFC.

Chapter 4

1920–29
Inter War Years 1

A New Beginning

As the newly-formed RAF shrank in the aftermath of the First World War, a number of squadrons found themselves left behind in obscure corners of the Empire. Amongst these, 111 Squadron commanded by Sqn Ldr C E H Medhurst OBE MC was based at the old Turkish aerodrome at Ramleh in Palestine. Medhurst, who had commanded 14 Squadron through Allenby's campaign of 1917 and 1918 now led a unit equipped with twelve Bristol F2b Fighters, which had been inherited from 1 Squadron Australian Flying Corps at the end of the War. The Squadron shared its home with 2 Armoured Car Company RAF, the two units being the RAF's contribution towards the military support for the British administration of Palestine. The remainder of that support was given by three Battalions of British infantry and one of Indian cavalry.

Palestine, about the same size as Wales, had a population of about three-quarters of a million people of which about ninety percent were Arabs. However Zionist immigration, which had begun in the previous century, had already engendered a wakening sense of nationhood within the resident Jewish community. Additionally, the Balfour Declaration of 1917, which approved in principle the establishment of a Jewish homeland, had opened the way for further massive immigration of Jews fleeing from persecution in central Eastern Europe. Perhaps not surprisingly this large influx of foreigners to the region caused great unrest amongst the indigenous Arabs, who regarded the entire Levant, including Palestine, as being the Arab homeland. Thus the competing interests of the majority Arab population and the minority Jewish community presented the military administration with a major task in maintaining law and order in Palestine.

With hostilities over in Europe, Sir Hugh Trenchard started to lay plans for a peacetime RAF. He envisaged a Service comprising thirty-two squadrons, the majority of which would be based in the Empire. These overseas-based squadrons would be used to police the wilder parts of the Empire (such as Iraq, North-west India and Palestine) where the speed and reach of aircraft would enable a few small flying units to replace larger (and more expensive) army garrisons. This new strategy of Air Control would ensure the peacetime survival of the RAF. In December 1919 it was decided that the squadrons of the peacetime RAF would bear the Squadron Numbers of units which had distinguished themselves during the War. Among these thirty-two

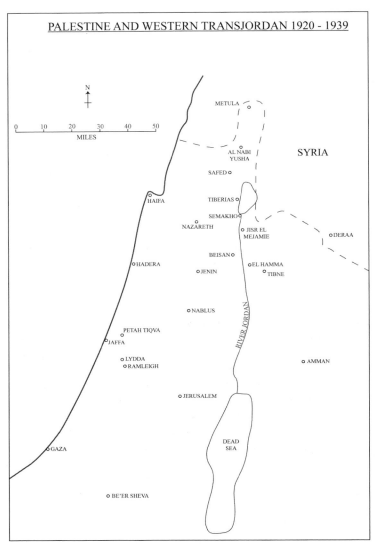

PALESTINE AND WESTERN TRANSJORDAN 1920 - 1939

numbers was that of 14 Squadron, thus establishing the Squadron as one of the most senior units in the RAF. The decision was taken to renumber 111 Squadron at Ramleh to become 14 Squadron from 1 February 1920: it was an entirely appropriate choice since 111 Squadron itself had originally been formed from 14 Squadron's "A" Flight in 1917 and Medhurst also provided a direct personal link to the wartime 14 Squadron.

The "new" 14 Squadron, by now under command of Sqn Ldr W L Welsh[1] DSC AFC, saw its first action on 23 April 1920 when it was called to assist in operations against a dissident Arabs in the north of the country. Arab emotions were running high after anti-Jewish rioting in Jerusalem earlier in the month and an armed Arab band was reported to have attacked a goods train between Semakh, on the south coast of the Sea of Galilee, and Jisr El Mejamie, about ten miles further south. One aircraft carried out a reconnaissance of the area and reported much activity in the Jordan Valley about eight miles north of Beisan and that the railway and telegraph lines had been cut. The Signals Officer who set out from Beisan to repair the telegraph was chased away by 300 Arabs and a troop of Central Indian Horse which set out to investigate from Semakh was engaged a band of armed insurgents. Although there were only about thirty insurgents, they fought fiercely and two more cavalry troops had to be called in as reinforcements at dusk fell. Early next morning some two thousand well-armed Arabs attacked the garrison at Semakh. The initial charge was repulsed, but the Indian cavalry commander decided to fall back to the railway station and the camp. A 14 Squadron aircraft arrived on the scene at 0830 hrs and attacked the enemy with machine gun fire but the pilot was wounded by ground fire and had to land near the cavalry camp. A second aircraft arrived an hour later and landed near the cavalry camp to get instructions. Once fully briefed on the situation, the pilot took off again and engaged the attackers with bombs and machine gun fire, inflicting serious casualties. Three other aircraft arrived at intervals thereafter and between them they managed to disperse the assailants. In the Army view the RAF's support had been invaluable and was largely responsible for the withdrawal of the enemy. However Arab resentment continued to simmer and two weeks later an aircraft was forced down to the east of the Sea of Galilee. Although the Arabs burnt the aircraft, they sent the crew back to Semakh unharmed

The remainder of the year's task was mainly routine operational support of the army and police forces. Aerial photographic surveys were also carried out throughout Palestine and so was routine flying practice. In addition crews kept up to speed with weapons training, including practice bombing with 9-pound bombs and air-to-ground firing with machine guns against floating targets set up in the sea off Jaffa. Bombing was also practised using an apparatus known as the Batchelor Mirror. This was a large mirror on the ground at the target location, on which the image of the aircraft was tracked by an observer; the aircraft fired a Verey light to signal a simulated bomb drop and the position of the aeroplane's image on the mirror in relation to various graticules engraved into the mirror indicated where the bomb would have landed in relation to the target. A busy sporting calendar on the Station and also throughout Palestine also ensured that no-one was idle!

Accidents and forced landings were very much part of flying relatively primitive aircraft in an unforgiving environment. In most cases the aircrew were able to walk away from accidents unhurt, but there were also fatalities from time to time. Fg Off N Fitzgerald-Eager[2] and his gunner AC1 P W J Thackery[3] lost their lives in an example of how the Sinai Desert was every bit as unforgiving after the War as it had been during the campaign of 1916. They were flying[4] from Ramleh to Ismailia on 14 June 1920, but flew off course and became lost. They forced landed in Sinai

Fg Off C H Flinn, the saviour of Hadera, seen here while serving with Z Force in Somaliland in 1920; the aircraft is a DH9. (IWM HU35683)

Desert about thirty miles west of Nekhl. Both men died from exposure in the desert, and Thackery's body was not located until three months later. In April the following year Fg Off P J Cox[5] was killed and Fg Off C Pilkington[6] AFC was seriously injured when their aircraft[7] suffered an engine failure at Ramleh. Unfortunately Cox stalled the machine while manoeuvring to make a forced landing and the aircraft crashed.

The Squadron's next major operational involvement was in the disturbances of May 1921. Since the end of Ottoman rule, tensions between Palestinian Arabs and Jewish settlers had been building and they reached flashpoint on 1 May when a May Day procession by Jewish communists in Jaffa degenerated into a street brawl. When the Palestine Police intervened, the communists sought refuge from them in the Moslem quarter, to the violent indignation of the Arabs; murder and mayhem soon followed and continued for the next few days. Martial Law was proclaimed on 3 May, but by then the disturbance had spread to other districts. A well-armed band of some four hundred Arabs led by Sheikh Abu Kishek took the opportunity of the chaos to settle old scores and they attacked the Jewish settlement of Petah Tiqva[8] on the morning of 5 May. While two squadrons of the 8th Indian Cavalry came to the rescue, a 14 Squadron Bristol Fighter flown by Fg Off C H Flinn[9] was sent to disperse the attackers by flying low over them. Flinn found a large Arab raiding party to the south of the village and dropped four bombs in front of them, causing them to withdraw towards Yahudiya; he then dropped a note to the cavalry squadron commander, Lt T B Vickers[10], helping the latter to locate the attackers and disperse them at the charge.

The next day, Flinn was again in action, this time at Hadera. Here Arabs from the nearby village of Tulkarem were preparing to attack the Jewish settlement. Unfortunately the armoured car which had been sent to intervene was stuck in soft sand a few miles away and only a tiny force of ten policemen stood between five hundred frenzied Arabs and the Jewish colonists. At 1020 hrs, Flinn took off from Ramleh to reconnoitre the area. He had instructions that he was not to take offensive action unless it was absolutely necessary, but it was obvious when he arrived over Hadera thirty minutes later that he was the last line of defence for the Jews. He was able to prevent the Arabs from attacking for a while by dropping bombs and firing his machine gun in front of them, but inevitably his fuel ran low and he had to make a dash for Jenin to refuel. Once there, Flinn telephoned Ramleh and asked for another aeroplane to be sent, before he took off again. Meanwhile the Arabs had taken advantage of Flinn's absence to start their attack and when he returned to Hadera at 1235 hrs he found that they had infiltrated the southeast quarter of the settlement and were in the process of looting and burning the buildings. Flinn's return caused panic amongst the attackers who began to flee; he dropped four more bombs amongst them and harried them with machine gun fire. At this point another Bristol Fighter, flown by Flt Lt E J D Routh[11] arrived on the scene and the two aircraft, together with the armoured car which had freed itself from the sand, were able to ensure that the attackers were completely routed by 1400 hrs.

Low flying aircraft were used to support the police in dispersing large crowds outside Jaffa, and they proved to be most effective when a bomb was accidentally released during the demonstration. Bombing a crowd went against all the principles of "Air Control" but it nevertheless worked in this case and the rioting stopped almost instantly! The threat of air attack was also sufficient to gain the surrender of Sheikh Abu Kishek who had set up positions north of Jaffa with seven hundred armed followers: despite his apparent strength he gave up before any further military action was necessary.

The official report into the disturbances recorded that "...the lives of the colonists [at Hadera] were saved by the arrival of an aeroplane." Nor was the effectiveness of aircraft lost on the Jewish settlers and according to Israeli sources[12] it was the actions of 14 Squadron aircraft at Hadera, Petah Tiqva, and at Semakh the previous year, that sowed in the minds of the Yishuv leadership the seed of "defence aviation", the beginnings of which would eventually become the Israeli Air Force.

Transjordan

One of the results on the Cairo Conference on the future of the Middle East in March 1921 was the establishment of the Emirate of Transjordan with HRH Emir Abdullah as the Head of State. The conference provided an opportunity for 14 Squadron to renew its acquaintanceship with Col T E Lawrence: the Unit provided four aircraft to fly Lawrence to Amman to see Abdullah on 10 and 11 April. Sqn Ldr Welsh himself flew Lawrence to Amman[13] on 17 April for Abdullah's inauguration ceremony, and transported him around the new Emirate over the following ten days.

Emir Abdullah's new country to the East of the River Jordan was about twice the size of Palestine and comprised mainly of desert – or more properly steppe – on a mountainous plateau some 1,500 to 4,500 feet above sea level. This plateau was intersected by steep ravines running east-to-west and was bounded in the west by the rift valley of the River Jordan, the Dead Sea and the Wadi Araba, and to the east it merged into the deserts of Syria, Arabia and Iraq. Strategically, the British saw that control of a swathe of land which linked the Palestinian ports to the oilfields in Mesopotamia would guarantee the security both of the oil pipeline that ran across the desert and of the air route to the eastern Empire that ran above it. They also saw Transjordan as a buffer between Palestine and desert raiding parties. The country

T E Lawrence ("Lawrene of Arabia") sitting in the rear cockpit of 14 Squadron Bristol fighter H1526 at Amman on 17 April 1921. Lawrence had flown to Amman to attend the formal inauguration of Abdullah as Emir of Transjordan. The Squadron Commander, Sqn Ldr W L Welsh is in the front cockpit. Note the Squadron badge painted on the side of the aircraft. (US Library of Congress Matson Photograph Collection LC-DIG-matpc-02318)

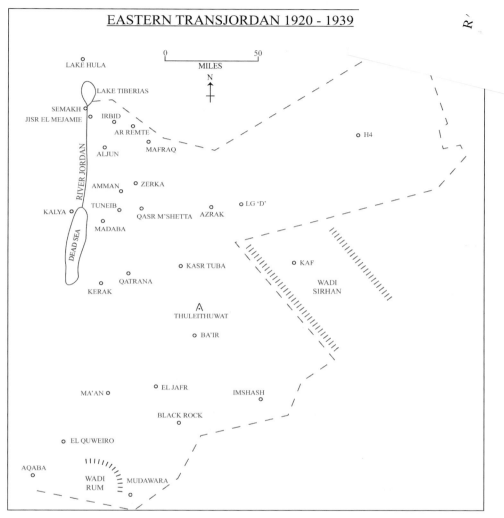

EASTERN TRANSJORDAN 1920 - 1939

itself was inhabited by a largely nomadic population. These Arabs, chiefly Bedouin from the Howeitat and Beni Sakhr tribes, were armed, fighting men who moved their flocks and camels from grazing ground to grazing ground. They regarded inter-tribal raiding as a legitimate form of amusement and method of obtaining wealth. Their neighbours in Arabia were similarly minded and did not regard the international boundary as having any particular significance. Thus the enforcement of law within Transjordan and the maintenance of the country's security would provide a challenge to those charged with these responsibilities.

Although both responsibilities fell to the locally-recruited (but British-led) Arab Legion, they were underwritten by the RAF by means of Air Control. To achieve this,

F assets would need to be based in-country: a flying station was established at the .ormer Turkish aerodrome at Amman. One section of armoured cars from 2 Armoured Car Company was moved to Amman permanently and provision was made for aircraft to be detached there from Ramleh whenever they were required.

The first opportunity for the Squadron to participate in the affairs of Transjordan came at the end of April 1921. Matters had come to a head in a dispute over cattle between tribes in Madeba. The Emir's representatives who had been dispatched to resolve the argument were killed and the Emir requested military support to reassert his authority. Unfortunately all the available ground forces were heavily involved in attempting to quell the Jaffa rioting, leaving aircraft as the only option. 14 Squadron's aircraft were duly dispatched to Madeba and provided the necessary show of force which had the desired effect. In September aircraft were again sent to Amman to help deal with disturbances there, and as a result, a new 14 Squadron "C" Flight was formed at Amman with four DH9A aircraft to operate semi-autonomously from the new station. This was the beginning of a close association with the country that would last until the outbreak of the Second World War.

Trouble was anticipated in Palestine on the anniversary of the Balfour Declaration in November, and aircraft carried bombs when on patrol. However, nothing unusual was seen and all remained peaceful. On 8 November Sgt Maj Haug and Cpl Lucas set off from Ramleh for Amman[14], but somehow managed to overshoot their intended destination by a hundred miles. Search parties were organised and twenty-nine search flights were made before the crew was located and rescued on 12 November. The aircraft was eventually recovered on 18 November and flown back to Amman. Fg Off W G Meggitt[15] MC and Fg Off D L Blackford[16] took photographs of Kafrini district during the month and the Squadron's aircraft also co-operated with police and army during an operation to confiscate cattle in lieu of unpaid fines that had been levied as a result of the Disturbances in May.

During June 1921 a Flight from 30 Squadron supporting a ground survey party led by Maj Holt of the Royal Engineers established a route from Baghdad westwards to Ramadi. Although 14 Squadron was not directly involved with this pioneering work, later in the month Sqn Ldr Welsh led a ground convoy which set out eastwards from Amman with spare parts for the 30 Squadron aircraft. On 9 July a 14 Squadron Bristol Fighter accompanied a DH9A of 30 Squadron to Azraq when the latter became lost and landed at Ramleh.

Sqn Ldr Welsh handed command of the Squadron to Sqn Ldr J S T Bradley[17] OBE at the beginning of December 1921. Bradley was remarkable in that his Command was his first flying tour after qualifying as a pilot. After wartime service in the Machine Gun Corps he had joined the RAF as a staff officer on the basis of his expertise in machine guns and had only learnt to fly in 1921. Perhaps his chief claim to fame, though, was that he had organised the first of the RAF Pageants at Hendon in 1920 and in 1921 – a feat which illustrated his organisational flair.

The start of Bradley's tour of command coincided with the next major problem in Transjordan, an inter-communal dispute at Kerak. Two factions there were so

A Bristol Fighter picking up a message in 1922/23. The message was put into a bag which was suspended on a rope between the two poles; the rope was then grappled using a hook suspended from the rear cockpit of the aircraft. This system, which was first used by 14 Squadron in 1917 provided an effective means of communication between ground forces and aircraft in the days before radio. (RAFM AC72-19-4-7-1)

involved in fighting each other that they no longer bothered to pay their taxes to the Emir. The Emir was not pleased and it was decided that a show of force was needed to point out to the parties the errors of their ways. Five Bristol Fighters were dispatched from Ramleh at 0800 hrs on 15 January 1922, but one aircraft had to turn back because of engine trouble. An hour later, the remaining four arrived in formation over Kerak at precisely the same moment as the Arab Legion entered the town. The aircraft then split up, with two of them taking photographs of the area while the other pair put on an energetic flying display, zooming and diving low over the crowd firing Verey lights as they went. The inhabitants were utterly terrified by the aircraft and the Arab Legion had little difficulty in dispersing the crowd and bringing an end to the affair.

The Squadron made several reconnaissance flights over the festival of Nebi Saleh during April, in order to keep an eye on events and ensure that there was no trouble. Far from causing any resentment by this action, the Squadron was rewarded two days later by a visit from a Sheikh who wished to pass on the appreciation of all the local Sheiks for the way in which the Squadron had honoured them by escorting the procession!

In early 1922 the Air Ministry formally took responsibility for the military control of Palestine and Transjordan. In practice this new arrangement merely formalised the status quo as far as 14 Squadron was concerned, but it did mark the beginning of a reduction in the number of British troops in theatre and therefore a shift in the burden of responsibility towards the Squadron. 1922 also marked the formalisation of British involvement with Palestine and Transjordan by the League of Nations Mandate. This document signalled the transformation of British interest in the region from being a that of a post-war occupying power, to one with the responsibility for overseeing the government both countries until such time as they could become viable independent states.

During the summer of 1922 problems were building in the Ajlun district where the villagers in Tibne Rahaba and Zubya refused to pay taxes to the Emir. Flt Lt Routh, Fg Off S D Cully[18] DSO and Plt Off C D Pyne[19] were detached to Ar Remte on 13 June to carry out demonstration flights and leaflet dropping over Tibne and the surrounding villages, as a means of persuading the villagers to change their mind. However this measure apparently had little effect, because the following month the Squadron was tasked to support the Arab Legion in bringing the district under submission of the Emir. For this operation, a special bombing Flight of Bristol Fighters, supplemented by two Amman-based DH9As, operated from Amman with a forward landing ground at Mafraq. Intensive bombing was carried out on 5 and 7 July, during which 147 20-pound bombs were dropped and 2,800 rounds of Lewis gun ammunition were expended. This action softened the resistance in the area sufficiently for the Arab Legion to move into the district two days later and bring the Sheikh to order.

While the Authorities in Amman were dealing with the problems in the north of the country, they also received intelligence that the Wahabi followers in Riyadh intended to attack the south of the country. An aerial reconnaissance of Kaf, in the Wadi Sirhan about ninety miles southeast of Amman, on 17 June found nothing. Two days later, though, a small Wahabi raiding party did attack Kaf and as a precaution against further threats from this direction, a Flight of aircraft was dispatched to reinforce Amman. However one aircraft was written off in a crash on 29 July and as a result of further unserviceabilities only one serviceable DH9A remained at Amman by mid-August. The Squadron was therefore poorly placed when a major raid by a thousand Wahabis streamed across the border in the early hours of 15 August. Having killed thirty-five villagers at Taneib and Umm El Awad, the raiders were engaged by Beni Sakhr warriors about ten miles south of Amman. At this stage RAF Amman was still unaware that the raid was taking place, but fortuitously the single serviceable DH9A happened to overfly the battle during a routine flight to re-supply Ziza. Although the pilot remained completely ignorant of the struggle going on beneath him, both sides on the ground were convinced that the aircraft heralded the imminent arrival of a section of armoured cars and more aircraft. Fearing the overwhelming firepower of aircraft and armoured cars, the Wahabi fell back, while the Beni Sakhr, emboldened by the same prospect, followed in hot pursuit. Thus, completely by

Personnel from 14 Squadron and 2 Armoured Car Company circa 1924. The flying squadron and armoured car company worked closely together. Note the Squadron badge painted on the radiator grille of the Bristol Fighter. (Jack Mark via Cliff Mark)

accident, 14 Squadron managed to curtail the insurgency. A reconnaissance by the same aircraft a little later in the morning revealed a large body of camel- and horsemen near Yadudi, but it was impossible to tell whether they were friend or foe. Bristol Fighters were sent to Amman and were ready for operations the next day, but despite a large number of sorties flown to try and locate them, the Wahabi had escaped unhindered back into the Arabian desert. As a result of this episode a Long Range Bombing Flight was set up with two aircraft modified with the fitment of an extra 18 gallon fuel tank. The aircraft deployed to Amman on 4 September in anticipation of further Akhwan raids, but when none took place the aircraft returned to Ramleh three days later.

On the last day of the month Fg Off W Elliott[20] DFC* and Mr R V Vernon[21] of the Colonial Office were seriously injured when the engine[22] failed during take off at Jerusalem.

Operations against dissident tribes virtually ceased over the winter months, leaving Squadron personnel to concentrate on matter such as sport. The Squadron's football team played eleven or twelve matches a month, remaining unbeaten during the season and winning the Palestine Association Football challenge Cup in the April of 1923. Another diversion from more serious operations was the project, led by Flt Lt R S Sorley[23] DSC DFC, to take aerial photographs of the archaeological sites in Palestine for the Palestine Government.

The Air Pageant of 1923

Inspired by his success at organising the Hendon Air Pageant, Bradley decided to organise a similar event in Palestine in 1923. During the afternoon of Tuesday 15 May 14 Squadron hosted "Annual Aerial Manoeuvres," which was probably the largest social occasion of that year in Palestine. Special train and bus services were even laid on from Jerusalem, Jaffa and the surrounding areas to help bring in the crowds. Over seven thousand people attended the event including the High Commissioner, the Air Officer Commanding and various other dignitaries and their ladies. The crowds themselves were in for an impressive and exciting spectacle which started with a relay race between three teams. Each team consisted of an Avro 504, a Bristol Fighter, and a DH9A. The race started with the three Avros racing away towards El Kubab, some four miles away, each aeroplane trailing a coloured streamer to identify the pilot. On their return to Ramleh each Avro landed close to his team's Bristol Fighter where an observer waited to be handed a tally disc by the Avro pilot, before sprinting across to the Bristol and clambering aboard. The Bristols then set off over the same course and finally the whole procedure was repeated with the teams' DH9As. The race was closely fought but at the end, by the narrowest of margins, victory went to Flt Lt T E Salt[24] (Avro), Fg Off Culley (Bristol Fighter) and Fg Off I M Morris[25] (DH9A).

There followed a mock aerial combat between Fg Off R R H Bruce[26] and Fg Off J Marsden[27] in Bristol Fighters. Both pilots thrilled the crowd with a variety of aerobatics in fine style, and the onlookers were particularly impressed when one aircraft completed a half loop and then remained inverted for over a minute! After stunting around for a while, the two aircraft then closed for a fierce machine-gun duel; eventually one was "shot down" by the other and glided in to land.

Then it was back to racing, this time amongst 14 Squadron Bristol Fighters who were competing for a Challenge Cup presented by the High Commissioner. The aircraft took off at one minute intervals, and the stream of aircraft set off around a twenty seven mile triangular course. After quarter of an hour the excitement mounted as a swarm of Bristol Fighters charged back to the airfield at full pelt. The fastest lap was by Fg Off C J Collingwood[28] in nineteen minutes forty seconds, but he was subsequently disqualified and the Cup went instead by Flt Lt R Harrison[29] DFC with a time just seven seconds slower. Fg Off Marsden came second and Flt Lt Sorley third.

The Finals of a "Spot Landing" contest for Bristol Fighters and DH9As followed. This was for a Challenge Cup presented by Major-General Sir Hugh Tudor, KCB, CMG and the eliminating rounds had been flown on previous days. The pilots climbed to 2,000 feet over the airfield, then switched off their engine to glide down to land as close as possible to a fifteen foot circle on the aerodrome. Each pilot had two attempts and Plt Off C L Falconer[30] got closest, landing within ten feet of the circle.

Then came an interesting demonstration of picking up messages without landing – essentially using the same system that had been pioneered in 1918 by 14 Squadron's

Capt H I Hanmer with his RE8s in the Judean Hills. Just as in Hamner's day, the message was put into a small bag which was attached to a coloured streamer and slung between two poles. The crowd watched closely as Fg Off Collingwood manoeuvred his aircraft and they were suitably thrilled when he caught the streamer with the grapnel hanging beneath him. Having picked up the message he then flew a circuit and dropped the bag back near the poles, where it was picked up by a waiting attendant. The greatest excitement and entertainment yet of the day came with a balloon hunt. Each pilot took his turn to take off and climb over the airfield. When he was in position he fired a Verey light as a signal for three large helium balloons to be released simultaneously from different parts of the airfield. The pilot then had to charge down and destroy all three balloons with the propeller or other parts of the aircraft, as quickly as possible. This proved rather easier said than done, and the crowd was kept happily amused by balloons which eluded their attackers' best efforts. However Flt Lt G Martyn managed to pop all three of his balloons in a very creditable one minute and one second, thereby wining the Trophy.

One of the stars of the 1920 Hendon Pageant was Flt Lt J Noakes[31], who created somewhat of a sensation at that event with his demonstration of crazy flying in an Avro 504. Bradley had persuaded him to give a repeat performance at Ramleh and he gave what "Flight" magazine described afterwards as an "extraordinary display of aerial antics" which thrilled the spectators. Noakes' display was followed by the Palestine Aerial Derby, a handicap race open to all types of aircraft who wished to compete for a Challenge Cup, presented by Wg Cdr T O'B Hubbard[32] MC AFC. The competitors started in their handicap order and flew one lap of the course which the Bristol Fighters had followed in their race. Thirteen machines lined-up for this event and set off in close succession – an impressive spectacle. After quite a long interval the leaders came into view in the distance and there was great speculation in the crowd as to whether the bookie's favourite, a Vickers Vimy, piloted by Flt Lt G Martyn[33] was in the lead. They were not disappointed: Martyn's Vimy was indeed leading the field and went on to complete the course in a winning time of around 25 minutes.

The most spectacular event though, surpassing even the balloon hunt, came as the Grand Finale. An "enemy factory" had been set up in the middle of the airfield and a formation of three Bristol Fighters swooped down over it. The factory opened up on the aircraft with machine-guns, and the aircraft responded with bombs which created pleasingly huge amounts of noise. After this first round, the aircraft circled the factory briefly before flying off, only to return almost immediately for another dive bombing attack. This time a well-aimed salvo of bombs completely demolished the building. The huge blaze in the middle of the airfield, accompanied by the explosions of the enemy magazines, and the victorious formation circling overhead was a magnificent spectacle in the late afternoon. And just as everyone thought that the proceedings were at an end, a final *Bang*, accompanied by a Very rocket, added the crowd-pleasing finishing touch to all the excitement. After prize-giving by His Excellency the High Commissioner, the proceedings were brought to a close by the band of the 31st Lancers playing "God Save the King."

The Grand Finale at the Palestine Air Pageant, 15 May 1923. A Bristol Fighter flies over the dummy "factory" which has been bombed. (RAFM AC 72/19/4/2d)

Two months later it was back to operational flying with two Bristol Fighters co-operating with the Gendarmerie in an attempt to capture of a gang of bandits who were raiding the Nazareth to Tiberias road. Despite searching the area between Be'er Sheva, Hebron, Gaza and Ramleh nothing was found, but the exercise of operating with the Gendarmerie provided some valuable lessons. In September a Flight of aircraft was once again dispatched to Amman in readiness for Adwan raiding – but once again they were not required.

The Squadron's operational focus remained in Tansjordan during the autumn with a dispute between the Emir and the Sultan Adwhan. An attempt to try and find a peaceful solution to the differences between them through a conference on 3 September failed and the Government decided to resort to military force. The Sultan's reaction on being given an ultimatum to surrender to the Emir by 17 September was to make a pre-emptive strike himself. After sending a message on 15 September that he would not take responsibility for what happened to any British forces sent against him, he moved to capture a number of Arab Legion posts, set up roadblocks along the Amman to Jerusalem road and cut down telephone and telegraph lines. Military action which had been planned for 17 September was brought forward by twenty four hours and at 0505 hrs on the morning of 16 September two DH9A aircraft, E877 flown by Flt Lt W S Magrath[34] and Fg Off Morris and E8713 flown by Fg Off J R Bell DFC with Mr Philby[35], were dispatched to Suweilah to reconnoitre the area. A thick mist prevented them from seeing anything on the ground so Bell returned to Amman; however Magrath remained in the area and when the mist started to lift an hour later, he and Morris saw a large number of horsemen advancing along the road towards Amman. They dropped a message at the Emir's camp and then directed two armoured cars towards the horsemen. The same two aircraft were airborne again at

0840 to monitor the situation and keep the Emir updated. In the early afternoon the aircraft attempted to take more direct action: Bell and Sgt Hughes took off[36] to bomb enemy forces reported in the Wadi Sir. However when they reached the area, they found that the target had disappeared and they returned to Amman without dropping. A little later three aircraft[37], led by Flt Lt S H Wallage[38] MC and Mr A L Kirkbride[39] of the British Residency staff, each loaded with machine guns and eight Cooper bombs, launched to search for enemy targets, but once again none were found and the aircraft returned to Amman after an hour's flying.

Another armed reconnaissance the following morning by Fg Off Morris and Gp Capt N D K McEwen CMG DSO (OC RAF Transjordania) in E877 and Flt Lt Magrath and AC2 Walpole in E941 also failed to find targets, but did manage to locate the friendly forces. Over the next two days 14 Squadron's DH9As continued with reconnaissance flights to track down the small bands of dissidents and then direct armoured cars towards them by dropping messages. By 20 September the revolt was over and the Sultan had fled to Syria.

On 21 September 1923, Bradley, now promoted to Wing Commander, handed command of 14 Squadron to Sqn Ldr W H Dolphin[40]. However, Dolphin's tour of command was short-lived and he handed the Squadron to Sqn Ldr A N Gallehawk[41] AFC on 6 June the following year.

By 1924 the Squadron had well and truly settled down into its peacetime routine of co-operation exercises and operations with the Palestinian Gendarmerie in Palestine, with the Arab Legion in Transjordan, with 2 Armoured Car Company and with the 9th Queen's Royal Lancers. The photographic surveys continued (for example one of Jaffa was completed in July and of Gaza in October) including further work for the archeological survey. For the 1924 "season" this was led by Fg Off Marsden supported by Fg Offs Collingwood and H N Thornton[42], and Sgt Maj E K Haug[43]. There was also an extensive programme of air-to-ground weaponry practice. In echoes of the previous year's pageant, five aircraft took part in the Aerial Exercises in Cairo in March, winning the "Balloon Hunt" and taking second place in the Message Lifting competition. The Squadron was frequently called on to transport military and civilian dignitaries around Palestine and Transjordan, and was also responsible for delivering and collecting air mails within both territories. New landing grounds were established at Kolundia (six miles north of Jerusalem) and Beisan. There were ceremonial occasions too, such as a flypast by nine aircraft for the benefit of the Mediterranean Fleet's 4th Battle Squadron who visited Jaffa in June. Three months later, three aircraft provided an aerial escort for Lord Thomson, the Secretary of State for Air, when he visited Amman while en route for Baghdad, and in November three Bristol Fighters patrolled above the Governor of Syria, General Weygand, as he travelled by train from Mulebbir to Lydda. All this activity amounted to a monthly flying task of around 250 hours.

Unfortunately this flying was not entirely accident-free. There were three forced landings in June 1924, a fairly typical monthly total, and on 27 June Flt Lt R C Creamer[44] DFC and LAC F C Perren[45] were killed when DH9A H151 spun in at

Landing Ground "D". Perhaps not surprisingly, all the pilots were required to practise forced landings a few months later.

When Squadron personnel were not involved in flying or servicing the aircraft there were plenty of social events to keep them occupied. The Squadron cricket XI played 4 matches in July and in the same month there was an airmen's dance and a whist drive in the Sergeants' Mess. Living conditions were fairly primitive, but people found ingenious ways to make themselves comfortable. "At both Ramleh and Amman," recalled Flt Lt Sorley, "we lived in BE cases [the crates in which the First World War BE2c aircraft had been packed for delivery] and some made them into most comfortable suites, dimly lit with Persian carpets and brass and copper pieces bought from the bazaars. It was pleasant to entertain each other as guests for drinks before dinner. The Mess too was more civilised and with Latroune wine from the monastery on the road to Jerusalem at a mere tenpence a bottle, the food was washed down stylishly if not always suitably." In 1924 a more permanent structure was completed, "after which we wore Mess Kit every night to accompany the Latroune wine at dinner and the general standard of entertaining was raised. Receptions and garden parties at which ladies wore flowing skirts and long white gloves made us all sit up and take notice and was a welcome change from roughing it!"

The station's swimming pool also featured prominently in social and sporting life during the summer at Ramleh. In the autumn, cricket season drew to a close with a match between the "Officers and NCOs" versus the Airmen" – a match which was won by the Airmen. The end of the cricket season marked the start of the football and hockey seasons, with Squadron teams playing in competitions and leagues throughout the Palestine Command.

The Akhwan Raid of 1924

However, it seemed that some sort of trouble was always lurking round the corner. During July 1924 large numbers of Wahabi were reported to be assembling near Kaf, just over the border in the Arabian Desert. It transpired that a force of Akhwan, or "brethren," as the members of this zealously puritanical sect amongst the Wahabis styled themselves, had started out from Al Qasim, which lies about halfway between Riyadh and Ha'il and marched up the Wadi Sirhan towards Transjordan. This force of nearly 5,000 disciplined and well-armed men on camels, plus another 200 horsemen, followed about twenty war banners. They left Qa'al Umari at sunrise on Wednesday 12 August, marching for Qasr Al Mshatta. The small Arab Legion post at Kaf were fully aware of the threat but were isolated and unable to communicate with their Headquarters. Unfortunately a small detachment of Arab Legion taking supplies to the Kaf garrison was surprised by the Wahabi, who killed them all. A hard day and night march brought the Wahabi to Qasr Al Mshatta an hour and a half before sunrise the following day. After morning prayers they split into three columns to continue their advance. The columns fanned out from Mshatta towards Kastal, Umm el Amad and Tuneib, crossing the Hedjaz railway line just before dawn and cutting down the telephone lines. They also set fire to several small villages as they passed through them.

Fortunately a RAF lorry carrying petrol en-route for Ziza was stopped by frightened locals at Quseir, who informed the airmen of the Wahabi presence to the south. In turn this news was relayed to Amman and it was decided to launch an aeroplane to corroborate the report. At 0655 hrs on 13 August a DH9A flown by Flt Lt Wallace was scrambled to reconnoitre the area around Tuneib; fifteen minutes later it was back with confirmation that a major attack on Transjordan was in progress. In the meantime, three armoured cars had been dispatched towards Yadouda to block the Wahabi line of advance towards Amman.

At 0905 hrs a formation of three DH9As led Sqn Ldr J H D'Albiac[46], from the Air Staff at Amman, took off from Amman. On his wing were Flt Lt Wallace and Fg Off Morris, and all three aircraft were armed with bombs and fully loaded machine guns. They were overhead the insurgents seven minutes later, but in order to comply with the Rules of Engagement they had to positively identify that the Wahabis before they could open fire. This identification was swiftly provided by Mr Kirkbride of the British Residency staff, who was carried in D'Albiac's aircraft, and at 0915 hrs the aircraft attacked the insurgents with bombs and machine gun fire. Although dropping bombs on a widely dispersed force caused only a few casualties, this action successfully halted the northerly advance of the Wahabi, who then turned southwards. It also had the unforeseen benefit of causing the Wahabis to rally together around their banners – thereby making themselves a more densely packed target for the armoured cars. After dropping his bombs, D'Albiac flew back towards Yadouda where he located the armoured cars and dropped a message instructing them to advance and engage the enemy. The armoured cars joined the battle at Tuneib at 0930 hrs and spent the next two hours in a running fight towards a point about twelve miles east of Ziza. The Wahabi force now covered an area of approximately two kilometres by two kilometres, with the armoured cars engaging their flank from a range of some six hundred yards. However by late morning the armoured cars were running short of ammunition. At 1050 hrs the three DH9As, now rearmed, took off once more and relieved the armoured cars at 1130 hrs. Twenty minutes later D'Albiac landed next to the armoured cars and instructed them to fall back to Ziza. Meanwhile two Bristol Fighters flown by Sqn Ldr P B Hunter[47] and Fg Off Collingwood had been dispatched from Ramleh. They took off again almost immediately, carrying Gp Capt MacEwen and Lt Col F G Peake[48] OBE (commanding the Arab Legion) who wanted to see the operational area for themselves. They found that the second attack by the DH9A formation had routed the insurgents, who started a headlong retreat back into the desert, so both Bristol Fighters landed near Ziza where Gp Capt MacEwan instructed the armoured cars to return to Amman.

However, it was decided that a further attack should be made to ensure that the Wahabis did not regroup. At 1430 hrs Flt Lt Wallace took off for his third sortie of the day in his DH9A, leading the four Bristol Fighters, flown by Fg Offs C Bousfield[49] and Falconer and Sgts O C Tostevin[50] and Sgt L Rogers, which had arrived from Ramleh just before midday. They were to carry out an armed reconnaissance to the east of Ziza. An hour later they located the Wahabis forty miles east of Ziza and

DH9As from 14 Squadron and Rolls Royce armoured cars of 2 ACC display the captured Wahabi battle standards which were presented to them by a grateful Emir Abdullah after the attempted invasion by some 5,000 Akhwan warriors on 13 August 1924 was stopped by the joint actions of both units. (RAFM X0028071-9)

manoeuvred to attack. Although by this stage the Wahabi force had become a rabble, they still fought back courageously with surprisingly accurate rifle fire. All of the aircraft were hit by small arms fire, as were Fg Off Falconer and LAC Ross. In Falconer's case he actually saw his assailant aiming a rifle at him – "I remember seeing two men up on a camel, and one hanging on by the tail. And one of them was a jolly good shot because he had a crack at me and the bullet broke one of the hinges on the elevator, went straight on through my arm, through the cockpit and out through the engine cowling. My air-gunner produced a very oily handkerchief, which I think he'd been cleaning plugs with and asked whether he could tie my wound up with that. I said 'no'. We got back safely without crashing but I was bleeding hard."

That evening a peculiar eclipse of the moon may have helped to persuade the Wahabis that their cause was lost. At any rate, the two DH9As which were launched the following afternoon to reconnoitre the Wadi Sirhan and the watering places at Azraq, Amria and Hazim could find no trace of the insurgents. The Wahabis had lost over 500 of their number killed, while 150 Transjordanian civilians had also lost their lives in this major threat to Emir Abdullah's new State. In appreciation of his gratitude to 14 Squadron and to 2 Armoured Car Company, the Emir presented each unit with one of the war banners which had been captured from the Wahabis.

One of the responsibilities of the Squadron was of Search and Rescue, and it was called in from time to time to locate aircraft from other units which had become overdue in Palestine and Transjordan. In October four Bristol Fighters were sent to find two DH9As from 47 Squadron. The search was successful: the aircraft had forced

landed and one of them had overturned, and 14 Squadron was able to rescue both aircraft and crews. Sadly another Bristol Fighter crash at Heliopolis (Cairo) on 2 October 1924 was fatal. The ballast, which had to be carried in the aircraft when it was flown solo, had not been properly restrained: it shifted and the resulting imbalance caused the aircraft to spin in from 300 feet, killing Fg Off Bousfield.

Christmas 1924 was celebrated with a fancy dress soccer match between Officers and Airmen which, interestingly, was won by an "unconverted try"! The traditional Airmen's Christmas Dinner followed with the officers waiting on the airmen, who voiced their approval at the end of the meal with a raucous rendition of "For he's a Jolly Good Fellow." In the evening it was the turn of the Warrant Officers and Sergeants to host the married families in their Mess, complete with a Christmas tree for the children. This dinner was followed by a dance and the festivities continued the next day in the Officers' Mess when all families were invited to a Boxing Day children's party. On 27 December the whole Squadron gave a fancy dress party for all the other units in the area – a party that went on until 0200 the next morning. The Festive Season eventually drew to a close with the Officers' New Year's Eve Dinner Dance which was held in their Mess. Despite the party-going the Squadron still flew when required to do so and on 27 December two Bristol Fighters were dispatched to collect the mails from three Vernon aircraft which had forced landed near Ziza on Christmas Day because of bad weather. The only cloud over the period was when Fg Off F C T Rowe[51] and LAC G Harding from the Amman-based "C" Flight undershot while landing DH9A H85 at Ramleh and hit the railway line; the aircraft was written off, but happily the crew escaped with minor injuries.

1925

Operations started again in January 1925 with four Bristol Fighters[52] of "B" Flight led by Fg Off Marsden detached to Beersheba to support a reconnaissance of the

Wadi Araba for the latter half of the month. This mission, by a mixed force of the Palestine Gendarmerie and the Arab Legion, was intended to consolidate knowledge of the area and to arrest certain trouble-makers who had already been identified. It was also a demonstration of capability both to the local Arab population, but also to the Gendarmerie and Legion themselves. Building on the experience of an exercise with three squadrons of the Gendarmerie the previous March in which it had been found that with a passenger on board a Bristol Fighter could also carry sixteen gallons of water or 165 pounds of stores, the Flight was used to re-supply the ground forces. Over the two weeks the Flight delivered 500 pounds of food, 2,800 pounds of fodder and 60 gallons of water, which was either dumped at a landing ground at Ain El Hosp, about twenty miles south of the Dead Sea or dropped directly to the troops by parachute. The aircraft were also used for reconnaissance ahead of the ground forces and for dropping messages, thereby making the command and control of the expedition far more effective. During this expedition a wireless set mounted on two camels was used for the first time, and the success of this trial opened the possibility of using wireless communication between aircraft and ground troops for future operations.

Two months later, reconnaissance patrols were mounted by Bristol Fighters within Palestine and DH9As over Transjordan to search for raiders at the start of the "raiding season", but none were seen. Unfortunately Fg Off Bruce, who had played a starring role in the 1923 Air Pageant was killed at Ramleh on 17 January in a flying accident[53] which also injured LAC A Sutton[54].

The Secretary of State for the Colonies visited Palestine in April, and his entourage, travelling in four Vernon transport aircraft were escorted by nine 14 Squadron Bristol Fighters while they were in the country. The Secretary of State visited the Squadron on 17 April and had lunch with unit personnel which was followed by a co-operation demonstration with the Palestine Gendarmerie at Kolundia. Five Bristol Fighters were involved in this demonstration; Amman's DH9As were not involved in the Secretary of State's visit, but they were instead kept busy practising high angle dive attacks using 20 -pound bombs.

Operations with the Palestine Gendarmerie in May resulted in the capture of some Arab insurgents in the Beersheba and Dead Sea area. In the same month the Squadron carried out night flying practice at Ramleh for the first time. Pilots found that on moonlit nights it was possible to land successfully using only ground flares, but without moonlight pilots needed the additional light of wingtip-mounted flares and even then only the north part of the aerodrome was useable. By the end of June all pilots had become qualified at night, but two accidents during the qualification process had resulted in badly damaged aircraft. Although these aircraft would be rebuilt by the Squadron, it was decided to stop night flying before more aircraft were put out of service. The Squadron was now limited only to its established strength of eight Bristol Fighters without the extra in-use reserves which usually helped to increase the number of aircraft available to fly.

On 27 June 1925 Ma'an was annexed into the Emirate of Transjordan. Four

DH9As departed Amman for Ma'an in the early hours of 29 June to support the ground forces, but the event passed peacefully and there was no need for the aircraft to be used. In fact the whole Palestine area was very calm during middle of the year, and although flying practice continued, Squadron personnel were more concerned with the cricket season than with operational matters during the summer. The Squadron XI played seven matches during May alone (but only won three of these) and an inter-Flight competition started in July.

However the Jebel Druze rising in Syria began to have consequences in Palestine and Transjordan from August. The Squadron started to mount patrols along the Palestinian border to stop Transjordanian tribes from crossing into Syria to support the Druze. The "Frontier Recco" was normally flown by a formation of two or three aircraft and started with an hour and a quarter's transit from Ramleh to Mafraq to refuel. From Mafraq the route followed Syrian frontier westwards to Ar Ramtha about half an hour away for another landing stop. After a short break the aircraft continued for another half an hour along the border to Semakh on the southern shore of the Sea of Galilee. At this stage the patrol was complete and after refuelling again, it was another hour and a quarter back to Ramleh. By November the situation had deteriorated further and on 12 November a section of armoured cars was despatched to Semakh; the next day two aircraft were also sent there for reconnaissance duties. In one of these aircraft[55], flown by Fg Off D Macfadyen[56], Major C A Shute[57] CBE, the Second in Command of the TJFF was able to get a good view of the operational area. "B" Flight was also engaged in operational duties around Metula at the most northerly point of Palestine. By now the flow of people had been reversed and a large number of refugees were fleeing Syria for the safety of Transjordan and the refugee camp at Azrak.

The Move to Amman
During November "A" Flight re-equipped with DH9A, and then moved to join "C" Flight at Amman in February 1926. This move meant that two Flights of DH9A were now based at Amman along with one section of 2 Armoured Car Company, while a single Flight of Bristol Fighters ("B" Flight commanded by Flt Lt G E Gibbs MC[58]), and the remaining two sections from 2 Armoured Car company remained at Ramleh. In a move to simplify this complicated state of affairs, a local decision was taken to rename the units on 22 March. Thus the DH9A and armoured car force at Amman became 14 Squadron and the Bristol Fighters and armoured cars at Ramleh became 2 Armoured Car Company. This local arrangement was not reflected in any official documents outside the Command area, but it did *de facto* lead to a change of command of 14 Squadron to Sqn Ldr J Everidge[59] MC who had been in command of 2 Armourd Car Company. Meanwhile Gallehawk became CO of the Armoured Car Company. In another development during the year, a separate armed force, under British control, was established to ensure the security of Transjordan's borders. The Transjordanian Frontier Force (TJFF) took responsibility for security from the Arab Legion, who now became more of an internal police force.

"B" Flight, 14 Squadron at Ramleh 1925. Note the Squadron badge painted on the radiator grille. This photograph includes two future Air Marshals: Gerald Gibbs (4th from the left) went on to be the last RAF officer to command the Indian Air Force in 1951 and Douglas Macfadyen (2nd from left) became AOC-in-C Home Command in 1956. (Ian Macfadyen)

On 17 April Sqn Ldr H A Tweedie[60] OBE AFC and Flt Lt Wallage were both killed when they crashed at Amman during a dual instructional sortie[61]. Another aircraft had crashed earlier in the month, though thankfully without injury to the crew, when it landed in soft ground while bringing aid to a downed Spanish Breguet. The Spaniard, flown by Capt R M Estevez and Mechanic Calvo, was one of three aircraft which had passed Amman on 11 April en route to Manilla via Baghdad; they were reported missing the following day triggering an intensive search and rescue operation. Flt Lt H E P Wigglesworth[62] DSC commanding "A" Flight commanded the operation, setting up his control point at Landing Ground "D" with Cpl G W Grayson[63] as the radio operator. For the next five days, Fg Offs J S L Adams[64], L W Mercer[65], Falconer, E C Ridlington[66] and Plt Off A C Evans-Evans[67] with Sgt F Keith, Cpl J Gamble, LACs J R Burley, H E Hazell, J E Field, F Burchett and AC1 G R Brown combed the area around Landing Ground "E". Their task was not made any easier by the fact that rather than staying with their wrecked aircraft, the Spaniards had walked into the desert and become separated. Estevez was found on 16 April and Calvo the following day.

In the spring of 1926 the operational situation on the Syrian border had escalated further and the Squadron now mounted daily patrols. In an indication of how tense things had become, the three DH9As making the border reconnaissance on 1 May were fired upon as they approached Burqa by tribesmen who mistook them for

French aircraft. One of the aircraft was damaged, but there were no casualties on this occasion.

The Bristol Fighters at Ramleh began to be replaced with DH9As from the middle of the year and Sqn Ldr Gallehawk used two of these new aircraft to carry to support his extended ground reconnaissance of Southern Palestine during the last two weeks of May. Gallehawk's armoured cars were re-supplied by the aircraft, which were also able to scout ahead of the convoy, just as they had done during the Legion/Gendarmerie operation from Beersheba the previous year. Gallehawk established a landing strip at Aqaba, thereby extending the reach of aircraft in that region, and two DH9As were able to land there successfully on 27 May. Another pioneering development involved experimentation with wireless sets carried in aircraft during June and July. In the first, Gp Capt L W B Rees VC OBE MC DFC, commanding Air Forces Palestine, accompanied by Fg Off Adams took two DH9As from Amman to Baghdad and Mosul and was able to keep in radio contact with Amman throughout the eight days they were away. In the second, ten flights were made carrying air-to-air wireless with some success.

But trouble was brewing in the centre of the country, in the area of Ma'an and El Jafr. A reconnaissance sortie on 17 June from Amman reported a body of the Howeitat encamped to the west of the Arab Legion fort at El Jafr. Nine aircraft, three from Ramleh and six from Amman took part in a demonstration over the Howeitat on 8 July. The demonstration had the desired effect and the Howeitat dispersed.

Back up to the north, a disturbance was reported at Irbid and three DH9As were dispatched from Amman on 20 August to carry out a reconnaissance in co-ordination with a half section of armoured cars. Once again it was decided that a demonstration of force was necessary to dissuade any further disturbances and five DH9As were duly sent there. Despite this busy operational programme, the Squadron cricket XI managed to beat the Jerusalem Cricket Club during the month by 36 runs!

By the end of the year it was clear that the experiment of having mixed units of aeroplanes and armoured cars was not practical and in December the units reverted to the previous status quo. The flying unit once again became 14 Squadron comprising three Flights, each of four DH9As; "A" and "C" Flights were based at Amman and "B" Flight was based at Ramleh; Sqn Ldr Gallehawk resumed command of the Squadron. Meanwhile the armoured cars returned to the aegis of 2 Armoured Car Company. A further reason for celebration at the end of 1926 was the presentation to Flt Sgt Smith of the Long Service and Good Conduct Medal.

Apart from the brief flirtation with night flying in May 1925, when flying had been limited to ten-minute circuits of the airfield, the Squadron's activities were limited to daytime flying. However, Flt Lt Wigglesworth started to develop an operational capability at night. In December 1926 he and Fg Off Falconer flew from Ramleh to Amman at night, arriving at approximately 2230; this was quite an achievement in single-engined aircraft over hostile terrain. The following month, Wigglesworth conducted two night demonstrations, one over the Druze camp at Azraq on 16 January (with Plt Off E H Collinson[68] MC in the rear cockpit[69]) and one

DH9A JR7022 which served with 14 Squadron from February to July 1926. (RAFM x0028071-1)

over Bair and Ma'an three nights later (in the same aeroplane with LAC Dyer). On both occasions he advertised his presence by dropping parachute flares, demonstrating to the locals that the RAF had the capability to turn night into day.

It was no coincidence that Wigglesworth had chosen Azraq for his first demonstration: it was becoming apparent the Druze leaders had broken their word that the refugee camp would not be used as a sanctuary from which armed men would carry out their war against the French forces in Syria. In April matters came to a head and a force comprising three sections of armoured cars under the command of Gp Capt Rees entered Azraq on 17 April. It took three months to clear Azraq completely, but by July all the Druze had returned to Syria. 14 Squadron aircraft were used throughout the operation to scout ahead of the armoured cars and to maintain communications between sections and with the Headquarters.

Another pioneering night flight took place on 15 June when Wigglesworth and LAC Matthews led[70] a pair aircraft for a night formation flight to Baghdad. Each aircraft had a thirty-two Watt headlight fitted to the rear gun mounting to allow the crews to stay together in the darkness. They left Amman at 1715 hrs GMT flying at 3,000 feet routing along the oil pipeline past Landing Grounds "D" "H" "M" and "R" where they landed to refuel at 2005 hrs. Here they also needed to effect repairs to leaking cylinders before taking off again at 2210 hrs and landing at Hinaidi four hours later. Throughout the flight the aircraft were also able to keep in wireless contact with base.

Routine Patrols

With the operational pressure off the north of the country the routine patrols of Transjordan reverted to bi-weekly flights by formations of three aircraft. The route of these patrols was either a "Northern Recco" along the Syrian border and the head of the Wadi Sirhan or a "Southern Recco" over the wilderness of south-east Transjordan returning via Ma'an. The northerly route, which served the dual purposes of dissuading Transjordanian tribes from raiding into Syria and Arabian tribes from raiding Transjordan, initially followed the railway line from Amman to Zerqa before striking across the Mafraq plain to the Syrian border at Ar Ramtha. Here the route turned eastwards to follow the Syrian border past the ruins of Umm Al Jemal; at this point the border itself became indistinct, and it was much easier to drift south to follow the clear line of demarcation between the black basalt of the Druze foothills and the lighter sands of the Transjordanian desert. This route led after about forty miles to the beautiful desert oasis at Azraq. Here crews could land and take a short break before returning to Amman.

The Southern route was a much longer patrol and crews regarded it is a tedious chore. It involved leaving Amman at first light to take advantage of the clear smooth air and flying about sixty miles south-eastwards to the desert fort at Qasr Tuba. Although Qasr Tuba could be tricky to find, the next landmark, the "three sisters" – the gleaming white chalk of the triple peaks of the Jebel Thuleithuwat – was clearly visible some twenty miles to the south, rising up from the gravel plain which extended south from Qasr Tuba. Ten miles beyond Thuleithuwat was the Arab Legion post Ba'ir, a favourite Howeitat camping ground. From Ba'ir the route then turned eastwards towards to Arabian border to another Arab Legion post at Imshash on the Arabian border on the Wadi Khedrij. A large natural landing ground next to the wells at Imshash lent itself to a convenient break after almost two hours' flying, and the aircraft often landed here so that the crews could enjoy a breakfast of sausage and beans – washed down on some occasions with an illicit bottle of beer! After taking off again, the aircraft followed the patrol line southwards to Hausa and then almost due westwards to Ma'an. Here the aircraft landed on the plateau some 4,000 feet above sea level. In the summer the aircraft did not have sufficient performance to take off again in the heat of the afternoon sun, and the crews normally took the opportunity to take a siesta until the temperatures had dropped to a more comfortable level. In the cool of the evening, the aircraft would take-off for the return leg to Amman.

Despite the relatively small community at Amman, squadron members enjoyed a lively social life in Amman in the 1920s and '30s. The majority of servicemen at Amman were single young men on a tour of duty which usually comprised three years in Iraq followed by two more in Transjordan. Some of the older officers and the senior NCOs were married men accompanied by their families and the few European families who lived in Amman were also completely integrated into the RAF's social arrangements. On the Station airmen, sergeants and officers had their own messes which served as the centres of their social lives. It was here that various functions such as dinners and dances were held. Mess life was a formal affair and, for example, officers were expected to dress in formal dinner dress for their evening meal during the week or at weekend Dining-In Nights. While the membership of each mess tended to socialise within its own social confines, Amman's uniquely isolated position meant

A DH9A, possibly JR7024, in flight over the desert near Aqaba on 18 March 1927. (RAFM x0028071-6)

that traditionally conservative social mores of the time could be relaxed and there were numerous opportunities for officers, NCOs and airmen to socialise together.

Sport also provided a vehicle for social intercourse and it played a major part in servicemen's lives at both squadron and station level. Participation in the various sports activities was actively encouraged, with time made available during the working week for sports activities. Inter-Unit competitions covered the whole of the Middle East area giving servicemen the opportunity to compete at a high level. Amongst 14 Squadron's sporting successes were the winning of the Palestine Challenge Cup for Football by beating 2 Armoured Car Company by two goals to one in July 1927 and some fine tennis in the Middle East Command Championships in November 1928. 14 Squadron's LAC Davidson lost to Sgt Atkins of 4FTS in the finals of the Open Singles, but LAC Ward beat LAC LeMaistre of 2 Armoured Car Company in the Handicap Singles.

There was also the opportunity to travel in the local area and enjoy the experience of living in the midst of Arabic culture. For the more hardy, expeditions could be made to explore the numerous archaeological sites in Transjordan, or to shoot duck in the lakes of Azraq. Jerusalem was also relatively nearby and there was frequently service transport provided for those who wished to travel there, making it a favourite for off-duty visits. For the aircrew the fleshpots of Cairo were also a particular draw. Major servicing of aircraft took place at Aboukir, so there were frequent opportunities to ferry aircraft to Egypt for servicing and bring replacement aircraft back to Amman. Such trips inevitably meant a night or two –

and sometimes more – in Alexandria or Cairo, and there was no shortage of volunteers for these duties!

By the August 1927 all three of the Squadron's Flights were based at Amman and on 26 September Sqn Ldr E G Hopcraft[71] DSC assumed command of 14 Squadron. The following February intelligence reports suggested that another major raid was being planned by the Wahabi, so the Squadron stepped up patrols of possible incursion routes and of wells in the area. Three patrols covering the northern, southern and eastern areas were flown each day. After a forecast of bad weather which threatened to close the airfield at Amman, "C" Flight, under the leadership of Flt Lt H G Crowe[72] MC, was dispatched to Ramleh on 19 February so that it could continue to operate. The gales and snow duly came and Amman was closed, but "C" Flight was able to patrol the desert as planned. On the third day of the detachment Crowe recalled that the officers "were all in the ground floor ante-room of Ramleh Mess having a pre-lunch aperitif with the windows open and the sun beating down on the lovely gardens when, with no warning sound, the pictures came off the walls and the whole place shook. Not a word was spoken but in a few seconds we had all gone through the windows to end up in the gardens with our drinks still in our hands, looking at a great column of dust from Ramleh village where the earthquake had wrecked native houses killing a large number of people. Buildings at the aerodrome were not really damaged, but aircraft in the hangars had moved damaging wing tips."

But there was more drama to come: further intelligence indicated that the Wahabi threat had moved further south and "C" Flight moved to Ma'an for further patrol

Flt Lt Henry Crowe had to resort to slashing the wings of their DH9As to stop them from flying away during the fierce gale at Ma'an on 27 Feb 1928. The wind was still blowing at 45 mph when this photograph was taken. (FAAM JMBGSL03238)

work on 26 February. That evening the aircraft were secured outside (for there were no hangars at the landing ground there) with screw pickets and ropes in the usual way. The crews "went to the hotel about a mile away for a meal, leaving an Arab Legion guard and two airmen with the aeroplanes. We had hardly finished the meal," recorded Crowe, "when the wind started to roar. It seemed to get worse so we got ready to go out to the aircraft when a tender skidded to a halt with a very frightened corporal reporting that 'the kites were moving.' The wind was worse on the exposed landing strip and we could hardly walk against it. But not only the wind was sent to try us; clouds of dust and hail added to our troubles. The wings lifted in the gale tearing the screw pickets out of the ground until they came to a small hill where a few remained with their tail skids broken in 'rigging position.' Well, we had no means of preventing them being blown further away. It was impossible and to dangerous to human life to start engines even if there had been any shelter to go to, so we slit the fabric on the lower wings to try to reduce their lift factor and then hoped for the best!" All four aircraft were severely damaged and had to be dismantled. They were returned by rail to Amman, where they were fitted with new wings, and they were flyable again some ten days later. Happily the Wahabi raid never materialised.

Lloyd Reliability Trials
In late 1927 the High Commissioner for Egypt and the Sudan, His Excellency Lord Lloyd of Dolobran, instituted a competition to test the reliability and efficiency of all the RAF squadrons in the Middle East Command. The Squadron's first trial, for the 1927 competition was conducted between 23 and 26 April 1928. It involved all twelve of the unit's aircraft and proved to be an eventful few days. The Squadron set off from Amman at 0800 hrs, reaching Abu Seir for breakfast. Here crews refuelled their aircraft using four-gallon tins of petrol, under the watchful eye of judges who timed the operation. When it came to leave Abu Seir things started to go wrong and two aircraft suffered from jammed throttles, delaying take-off by the Squadron until 1130 hrs. All twelve aircraft then set off towards Kantara, but one of them started to lag behind with a rough running engine and eventually the pilot had to land on a salt pan near Madden Station to try to effect repairs. The rest of the formation landed alongside, but discovered too late that the surface was quite soft. In the event the rough running engine could not be repaired without the expertise of groundcrew. Furthermore, by landing between Abu Seir and Kantara the Squadron had disqualified itself from the competition. With fuel now running too low to continue to Kantara, the formation leader decided to divert instead to Ramleh in the hope of reaching the aerodrome in daylight. On take-off one aircraft burst a tyre and tipped onto its nose, causing further delay while it was repaired. Luckily this aircraft was successfully repaired relatively quickly, but even so the eleven aircraft reached Ramleh after nightfall. Miraculously all eleven aircraft landed safely without the aid of either ground lights or wing flares and without hitting each other in the darkness. Not surprisingly the crews were far too tired and demoralised to refuel their aircraft again that night.

The next day the remaining ten aircraft routed via Heliopolis to reach Aboukir at 1600, but by this time, two of the aircraft's engines needed extensive work on them. The rules of the competition stipulated that any such work must be carried out by the aircraft's crews themselves and the unlucky two crews spent a busy night changing cylinders and soldering leaks. However they completed their task in time for all ten aircraft to take off from Aboukir at 0600 hrs heading for Cairo and thence back to Aboukir. This flight was uneventful and the relieved crews were able to enjoy a much-needed refreshing dip in the sea when they got back to Aboukir. Then things started going wrong again on the last day. All ten aircraft took off at 0700 hrs for Heliopolis, but one had to forced land near Katbara, and although nine aircraft reached Heliopolis, two more had to be left there because of cylinder and water leaks. This left the four aircraft of "C" Flight and three from "A" Flight to continue to Amman. Unfortunately one more aircraft dropped out en route, so only half of the aircraft which had originally left Amman returned there four days later.

"On the Lloyd Cup" 1928 – Sqn Ldr E G Hopcraft and others enjoying a break between flights during the Lloyd Reliability Trials held on 16-19 November 1928. 14 Squadron was victorious in the competition after all its aircraft completed the 1,600 mile course flown over the four days. The aircraft in the background, J7825, had the dubious distinction of being Amman's last DH9A before it crashed into a building in March 1930! (RAFM AC 86/57/2)

While the Squadron's performance was pretty disastrous, it provided some very valuable lessons. Over the next few months Hopcraft corrected the Squadron's failings in preparation for the next competition. This preparation paid off when the Competition was run again eight months later. At daybreak on 16 November, the Squadron's aircraft set of for Hinaidi (Baghdad), with all of them returning to Amman the next day before setting off for Abu Seir via Ramleh on 18 November. All of the aircraft arrived back at Amman four days after they had left it having flown some 1,600 miles: none had dropped out at any stage of the route and 14 Squadron thereby won the Lloyd Reliability Cup for 1928.

The Squadron would have to wait until the following year before they could receive the Lloyd Cup, but prizes were given at the Squadron's Sports Day on 21 April. The Squadron was graced by HRH Emir Abdullah, who presented the prizes in a day that was slightly marred by the appearance of a swarm of locusts! In fact the Emir was a regular visitor to the Squadron, and he frequently reciprocated the hospitality by entertaining the officers to Turkish coffee in his Palace. Sometimes he also invited them to dine with him; one such occasion was a feast held under a full moon in the amphitheatre in Amman, with many of the Sheikhs who had fought with Lawrence in attendance. "We were seated cross legged," recalled Flt Lt Crowe, "on rich Persian carpets laid on the earth… when we heard a hubbub. We looked around to see eight Nubian Slaves stripped to the waist carrying a huge wooden dish bearing a baby camel (which had been cooking all day) resting on a bed of rice and in a great pool of very hot gravy which splashed over the rim onto the naked shoulders of the slaves making them howl. They put the great dish down in front of the Emir, then drawing their daggers they plunged the knives into the camel's hump and cut the meat into smoking strips." The evening provided an unforgettable experience for those who were there.

The year 1928 was remarkable in that it was the first year since the Squadron's inception that no gun was fired or bombs dropped in anger. Unfortunately, however, it was a year in which fatal aircraft accidents claimed the lives of six Squadron members: Flt Lt G McCormack[73] and LAC J Kimberly[74] were killed on 28 March, Plt Off J H L Maund[75] and AC1 J J H Middleton[76] on 26 June and Sgt V R Saunders[77] and LAC F W Fletcher[78] on 31 August.

At the end of December 1928 the Squadron co-operated with the TJFF and 2 Armoured Car Company in an operation to collect a fine of camels from Fehad Ibn Zebn at his encampment near Kaf. Apart from the support of aircraft, the co-operation included the provision of a number of the Squadron's Morris 6-wheeler vehicles as troop transports. The aircraft operated on 29 December, with one DH9A staying overnight with the column. The following morning this aircraft was used to evacuate Sqn Ldr L F Forbes (OC 2 Armoured Car Company) to hospital at Ramleh after he injured his arm.

The weather broke in the New Year, bringing frequent storms with winds reaching fifty miles per hour, and snap frosts on the windless days. As a result, Amman was closed on a number of occasions, including during late February when the Squadron was stuck at Heliopolis for ten day unable to return. The aircraft had been dispatched there on 2 February for an Air display and demonstration of Aerial Drill.

After a year free of operations in 1928, the Squadron was back in action in March 1929 when it was called to intervene during raiding by the Sharafat and Uziemat tribes against the Beni Sakhr tribe. At 0630 hrs on 13 March a wireless-equipped aircraft was dispatched to Mafraq to reconnoitre Arab insurgents from the Jebel Druse raiding into Transjordan. Once again the squadron provided a number of six-wheeler Morris trucks to transport the sixty men of the TJFF, who were supported by three Rolls-Royce armoured cars from 1 Section, 2 Armoured Car Company. Receiving direction from the aircraft, the ground party intercepted the raiders at Umm el Jemal and after a short battle, supported by aircraft, the insurgents withdrew in disorder leaving twenty dead. During the action, the aircraft had fired 390 rounds and dropped eleven 20-pound bombs and had killed four of the raiders. The remainder of the Squadron was called in to finish off the insurgents and eight aircraft were airborne within fifty-five minutes of the call, but by the time they arrived on the scene, only a few stragglers remained.

The other highlight of the month was the sight of the *Graf Zeppelin* which passed over Ramleh at 1830 hrs on 27 March on one of her round-the-world tours. Routine co-operation exercises continued through April, with 2 Armoured Car Company (two aircraft from "B" Flight) at the beginning of the month, followed by three days with the TJFF. On 11 May one Flight was sent to Cairo so that the High Commissioner could present the Squadron with four trophies: the Lloyd Reliability Cup for the previous year, the Command Cup (for musketry and pistol shooing), the HQ Staff Middle East Cup (for bombing) and the Proficiency Cup (for all round proficiency). The Lloyd Reliability Trial for 1928 ran over the three days from 18 May and resulted in one aircraft being damaged in a night landing at Ziza.

The Palestinian Uprising of 1929
Throughout the 1920's there was an increasing perception among the Palestinian Arabs that their country was being exploited at their expense, and with the assistance of the Government, for the benefit of Jewish settlers. The fuse for trouble was lit when Jews erected a screen at the Wailing Wall as part of their Yom Kippur worship in September 1928. This was seen by Arabs as a violation of the long-established principle, agreed under Ottoman rule, that nothing should be built on or around the Wall. Although the British authorities, who agreed to maintain the status quo for religious observance, did remove the illegal structure, Palestinian resentment at Jewish attitudes simmered throughout the summer of 1929. Then on 15 August, the Jewish holy day of Tisha B'Av commemorating the destruction of the Temple, a Jewish protest at the Wall was enough to provoke Palestinian fury in Jerusalem the following day. On 17 August, a Jewish youth was stabbed to death and the situation worsened several days later when his funeral degenerated into further rioting. The violence escalated in Jerusalem on 23 August and rapidly spread across the country with an orgy of murder, looting, pillaging and burning as Arabs vented their pent-up

frustration against Jewish settlements. The timing could not have been worse for the authorities: the High Commissioner and the Chief of Police were both away, and in any case the army garrison had been reduced so much over the years that by now it was overwhelmed by the situation. The RAF acted swiftly to try to control the situation. When news of rioting was received at Amman on 23 August, "A" Flight, 14 Squadron was immediately dispatched carry out a reconnaissance of Jerusalem and then to land at Ramleh and await further tasking. However, it was immediately clear that aircraft had only limited capability against urban unrest that more troops would be needed on the ground to restore the order of law. So on the same day, after only one hour's notice, an armed party of four NCOs and 28 airmen under Flt Lt R A A Cole[79] was dispatched from Amman to Jerusalem and thence to Jaffa to provide aid to the civil power. A second detachment, twenty-five strong, under Flt Lt J E Truss[80] MC followed the next day.

Meanwhile reinforcements from all three services were called in from around the region, arriving over the next few days: a battalion of the South Wales Borderers was flown in from Cairo on 24 August, with the rest of the regiment and the Green Howards following by train a day later, HMS *Suffolk* arrived at Haifa on 26 August and HMS *Barham* at Jaffa on the following day, providing between them over seven hundred men for duty on land. HMS *Courageous* brought a battalion of the South Staffordshire regiment from Malta as well as its own Flycatcher aircraft on 27 August. The RAF also reinforced Palestine with Fairey IIIFs from 208 Squadron, DH9As and Bristol Fighters from 45 Squadron (both normally based in Egypt) and armoured cars from Iraq.

However, until all of these assets were in place, the burden of aiding the civil power fell to 14 Squadron. The ground parties remained deployed until 27 August and the pace of operational flying also took its toll on the Squadron's aircraft. The Unit had been operating with only eleven DH9As against an establishment of twelve aircraft and unserviceability reduced number of available aircraft still further. Six airscrews split within two days and by 26 September there were only eight aircraft serviceable. Extra DH9A aircraft were sent from 4 Flying Training School at Cairo to bring the Squadron up to full strength and by 31 August the Squadron had twelve aircraft available to fly each day.

"A" Flight's four aircraft at Amman[81] carried out a reconnaissance of the area from Nablus to Jerusalem, Gaza, Jaffa, Tel Aviv on 24 August. They reported some fighting in Tel Aviv, but were unable to intervene. Another patrol of the same area by three aircraft reported no trouble, and all was quiet when aircraft from Amman flew over Nablus in the morning and Safed in the afternoon. The following day the Ramleh detachment reported a large mob assembling at the clock tower in Jaffa; on this day a number of Arabs were murdered in Jaffa by Jews after several Jews had fallen victim to the rioters. Meanwhile Amman-based aircraft discovered large numbers of Arabs in cars driving towards Beisan from the direction of the Dead Sea, perhaps indicating more widespread incursion by Arabs from neighbouring districts. The operational pattern was set for daily dawn patrols from Ramleh to reconnoitre the hotspots around

Palestine and from Amman to check the border crossing points along the Jordan Valley.

Until 26 August, the role of the aircraft had been to co-operate with ground forces, but on that day aircraft intervened directly to break up hostile crowds. The day started with dawn patrols from both Amman and Ramleh finding that all was quiet. However, later in the morning, the four aircraft from Ramleh came across a looting party of fifty Arabs confronting the police at Haifa. The aircraft opened fire at 1050 hrs, killing two of the gang and dispersing the rest. Two aircraft which had been launched from Amman to assist at Haifa found nothing when they arrived there at 1140 hrs. The Ramleh Flight dispersed another crowd which was gathering on a hill near Maghar in the afternoon.

The following day the dawn patrol from Amman again confirmed that the Jordan Valley was quiet, and made contact with TJFF detachment at Beisan who were securing the border. A further sortie from Amman by a pair of aircraft in the afternoon covered the northerly area around Semakh, Safed Haifa and Nazereth. However, the patrol from Ramleh came across trouble near to Junction Station. At 1045 hrs[82] Flt Lt C S Riccard[83] found Arabs looting and burning a Jewish settlement at Artuf, but he was unable to intervene because his gun jammed. The next morning, on the dawn patrol, Flt Lt J H Hutchinson[84] and Sgt J I Richardson located Arab looters escaping from Beit Sahur, so they opened fire, killing three of them. Two aircraft were also launched from Amman at 0730 hrs to investigate reports of incursions of Bedouin from Transjordan into Palestine, but nothing was found.

The four aircraft at Ramleh spent the morning of 29 August co-operating with the army and an armoured car company who were clearing Beit Sahur near Jerusalem, from which Arab gangs had burnt and looted the nearby Jewish settlement at Talpioth. However while attention was turned to Beit Sahur, a massacre was carried out at Safed, in which some twenty Jews were killed and about eighty more were wounded. The aftermath of this massacre was still in evidence when two aircraft[85] arrived over Safed early the next morning. Many houses were still ablaze and the looting was continuing. The aircraft opened fire on the looters, killing two and dispersing the remainder. The same two aircraft returned to Safed in the afternoon to continue the search for armed gangs and found by then that things had quietened down and the police were back in control.

By now the RAF presence in Palestine had been considerably reinforced and on Friday 30 August a show of force was planned over the Mosque of Omar in Jerusalem, where a large crowd gathered daily for midday prayers. Eight DH9As from 14 Squadron were accompanied by four Fairey IIIF from 208 Squadron, a Bristol Fighter from 45 Squadron and three Fairey Flycatchers from the Fleet Air Arm; these sixteen aircraft arrived over Jerusalem at low level to dramatic effect just as the crowd emerged from the Mosque. Another demonstration flight by three DH9As[86] accompanied by six Fairey Flycatchers and another six DH9As from 45 Squadron was mounted for the benefit of the residents of Semakh, Tiberius, Safed and Metula two days later.

By the beginning of September the British authorities were beginning to regain control within Palestine, although it would still be another fortnight before the disturbances had completely died down. Despite being neither soldiers nor policemen, the RAF personnel who had deployed in the first few days of the uprising had acquitted themselves well; one airman who particularly shone in this unglamorous task was Sgt J S Durham who was recommended for a MBE for his efforts. With all of its aircraft back at Amman, 14 Squadron's responsibility was to ensure that insurgents from Transjordan and Syria did not rekindle the violence. The "Northern Recco" took on particular importance was flown daily. The patrol on 1 September located a hundred tents at Mafraq and three hundred loaded camels heading south from Ar Ramtha; a further fifty tents of the Beni Sakhr were reported at Samra. These sightings were confirmed by the next day's reconnaissance, and two aircraft[87] were dispatched later in the day to Semakh. Here they stayed overnight and co-operated with the Green Howards in rounding up some one hundred Arabs in the Al-Nabi Yusha district. The following day the first long "Southern Recco" for some days was flown by[88] Flt Lt C B Greet[89] with Sgt Lawrence and Fg Off A P Wayte[90]; there was nothing of interest to report, although Waite forced landed on his return.

In the afternoon of 6 September a pair of aircraft[91] was sent to Semakh to investigate a concentration of Arabs at El Hamma. The same two aircraft deployed to Semakh at 0540 hrs on 9 September to co-operate with Maj Smith of the TJFF. They remained there for most of the day, returning to Amman at 1555 hrs. On this day also, Gp Capt Playfair and Flt Lt Riccard flew to Deraa to visit the French Air Service in Syria to discuss policing of the Syrian border.

Operations wound down over the rest of September and normality returned as autumn passed. With November came the next round of the Lloyd Reliability Trial. This time the routeing was from Amman to Rutbah and Baghdad, thence returning via Rutbah to Abu Seir, Heliopolis (for night flying), Ramleh and then back to Amman. The flying took place over four days starting on 10 November, when the Squadron's complement of twelve aircraft left Amman. All went well until the last leg when one aircraft was damaged on landing at Ramleh. The rest of the Flight had to stay with the aircraft and the loss of score was enough to give the lead to 216 Squadron, who won the Trophy. Although there was some disappointment in the result of the competition, it soon evaporated with the news, announced later in the month, that 14 Squadron had been selected for the annual Cairo-to-the-Cape Flight in 1930. Undoubtedly this honour had in part been awarded in recognition of the Squadron's excellent performance during the Reliability Trials of the previous years. However Middle East Command recognised that the obsolescent DH9As were unsuitable for the journey and instead 14 Squadron would be issued with four Fairey IIIF aircraft with which to make the flight.

With the decade closing on a high note, Sqn Ldr Hopcraft handed command of 14 Squadron on 3 December 1929 to Sqn Ldr F O Soden[92] DFC. Soden, a fighter ace from the First War, arrived in great style in his private Moth aircraft which he had flown from England via Malta.

Notes

1 Air Marshal Sir William Welsh (1891-1962) had commanded 17 Sqn RNAS, 217 & 214 Sqns during WW1; he was head of theRAF Delegation to Washington DC in 1943 and stayed on in the USA after he retired from the RAF.

2 Australian-born Neale Fitzgerald-Eager had served with the NZEF during the First World War

3 20-year old Percy Thackery was from Thetford, Norfolk.

4 In Bristol Fighter E2293.

5 Pierse Cox had been granted a Short Service Commission in the RAF in Dec 1919.

6 Flt Lt Christopher Pilkington transferred to the Reserve in 1926 and died in Aug 1934.

7 Bristol Fighter H1533.

8 Petah Tiqva had been the first Jewish colony to be established by the Old Yishuv in 1878.

9 Charles Flinn (1897-1978) had been Mentioned in Dispatches for his part in operations with "Force Z" against the "Mad Mullah" in Somaliland earlier in 1920. Air Cdre C H Flinn CBE retired from the RAF in 1950.

10 Thomas Vickers was killed in action on the Northwest Frontier of India in Jul 1922.

11 Wg Cdr Eric Routh (b1895) had served with the KRRC in WW1 and retired from the RAF in 1946.

12 "Roots of the Israeli Air Force 1913-1948" Ambar, Eyal & Cohen as translated by Elimor Makevet.

13 in Bristol Fighter H1526.

14 in DH9A H1672.

15 William Meggitt (1894-1927) won his MC while an observer with 25 Sqn on the Western front and also served with 22 Sqn in France. He was killed in an aircraft accident near Crawley.

16 Air Cdre Douglas Blackford (1895-1953) was Air Attache to Washington in 1943.

17 Air Marshal Sir John Bradley (1888-1982) was Deputy Air Member for Supply in 1942.

18 A Canadian, Stuart Culley had achieved some fame for shooting down Zeppelin L53 after taking off from a barge towed by HMS *Redoubt* in 1918; the Camel he used in that engagement is preserved at the Imperial War Museum. He retired from the RAF as a Wg Cdr and died in 1975.

19 Originally commissioned into the KRRC in 1915, Wg Cdr Charles Pyne retired from the Admin & Special Duties Branch of the RAF in 1955.

20 Later Air Chief Marshal Sir William Elliott (1896-1971); he had previously served with 14 Sqn in Palestine in 1918.

21 Roland Vernon (1877-1942) spent much of his career as a diplomat in the Middle East.

22 of Bristol Fighter H1504.

23 Air Marshal Sir Ralph Sorley (1898-1974) served in the RNAS during WW1 and was responsible for writing the Operational Requirement for the Spitfire and Hurricane. He was AOC-inC Technical Command and joined De Havilland when he retired from the RAF.

24 Sqn Ldr Trevor Salt was killed in Oct 1931.

25 Ira Morris transferred to the Reserve in 1926.

26 Ronald Bruce, who was appointed to a Short Service Commission in 1921 was killed in a flying accident in 1925 aged 25.

27 Air Cdre John Marsden (1899-1956) commanded 5 Air School at Witbank South Africa in 1941.

28 Gp Capt Cuthbert Collingwood OBE DFC (1901-1996) retired from the RAF in in 1948.

29 AVM Richard Harrison DFC AFC (1893-1974) was AOC 3 (Bomber) Group in 1943.

30 Air Cdre Colin Falconer (1901-1994) spent much of WW2 as a staff officer at HQ Desert Air Force.

31 Gp Capt Jack Noakes AFC MM had served as a Sgt pilot with 29 Sqn in 1916; he commanded 51 Training Group in 1939.

32 Thomas Hubbard (1882-1962) won his MC while commanding 11 Sqn in 1916; his AFC was awarded for test and experimental flying later in the war. He retired from the RAF as a Wg Cdr in 1931.

33 Sqn Ldr Gilbert Martyn was killed in Oct 1936.

34 34 year old Walter Magrath was killed in a riding accident in Dec 1923 and is buried at Ramleh.

35 Sir John Philby (1885-1960) had been involved in the Arab Revolt and was Head of Secret Service in Palestine. He subsequently served as an advisor to Ibn Saud, but is best known through his son double agent Kim Philby.

36 in E877.

37 E877 (Flt Lt Wallage and Mr Kirkbride) E941 (Fg Off Morris and Sgt Hughes) and E8713 (Fg Off Bell and Flt Lt Magrath).

38 Stanley Wallage (1895-1926) won his MC while serving with 22 Sqn on the Western Front; he achieved 10 air combat victories.

39 Sir Alec Kirkbride (1897-1978) served in Transjordan until 1951, latterly as First British Minister in Amman; he was a good friend of King Abdullah.

40 Wilfred Dolphin had been a member of the RFC Technical Branch and most of his career was spent in technical appointments; he retired as a Wg Cdr in 1936.

41 Air Cdre Arthur Gallehawk (1893-1945) served with 7 Sqn RNAS in East Africa during WW1; he was SASO at HQ Flying Training Command in 1940.

42 AVM Henry "Bill" Thornton CBE (1896-1971) served in various diplomatic posts; on retirement from the RAF he joined the Board of the Blackburn and General Aircraft Ltd as Sales Director.

43 Erik Haug was killed in a flying accident at Kenley in Oct 1926.

44 26 year old Reginald Creamer had joined the RFC in 1917 and won his DFC in France in 1919.

45 Perren was aged 23.

46 Air Marshal Sir John D'Albiac (1894-1963) had served with 8 Sqn RNAS during WW1 and was AOC Iraq in 1941.

47 Wg Cdr Paul Hunter had originally joined the RFC as an Equipment Officer in 1916; he retired from the RAF in 1938.

48 Maj Gen Frederick Peake CMG CBE (1886-1970) founded the Arab Legion which he commanded until 1939.

49 Colin Bousfield had originally joined the RFC as an observer in 1917; he was posted to 14 Sqn in January 1924 and was killed in a flying accident nine months later.

50 Flt Sgt Osmond Tostevin was killed in a midair collision while flying a Siskin near Duxford in Dec 1928.

51 Frank Rowe transferred to the RAFVR Administrative & Special Duties Branch in 1939.

52 these included C802, D7815 and D8058.

53 in Bristol Fighter F4502.

54 Alex Sutton.

55 Bristol Fighter J6593.

56 Air Marshal Sir Douglas Macfadyen KCB CBE (1902-1968) was AOC-in-C Home Command before his retirement from the RAF in 1959. A staff officer with the Expeditionary Force in 1940, he had survived the sinking of the SS *Lancastria*. His son Ian also joined the RAF and became an Air Marshal.

57 Lt Col Cyril Shute CMG CBE of the Indian Army took command of the TJFF in 1928. He retired from the Army in 1933 but served as a Wg Cdr in the Admin & Special Duties Branch of the RAFVR during World War 2.

58 Air Marshal Sir Gerald Gibbs (1896-1992) won 3 MCs while serving with 17 Sqn in Macedonia in 1918. He retired in 1953 as C-in-C Indian Air Force.

59 Wg Cdr James Everidge (1881-1979) joined the RFC in 1915 and commanded 30 Sqn in Mesopotamia in 1918-19; he retired in 1929 but rejoined the RAFVR during WW2.

60 The acting Station Commander, Harley Tweedie had been a member of the British Delegation to Paris and while at the Air Ministry had worked on arms control in post-WW1 Germany. He was the son of the author and painter Mrs Alec Tweedie.

61 in DH9A J7108.

62 Air Marshal Sir Philip Wigglesworth (1896-1975) served with 3 Sqn RNAS during WW1 and after WW2 was Commander British Air Force of Occupation. After he retired from the RAF he was President of Renault UK.

63 Sgt G W Grayson was presented with the Silver Cross of Military Merit by the Spanish Consul in Jerusalem on 3 May 1928 in recognition of his services.

64 Wg Cdr John Adams retired from the RAF in 1946.

65 A Royal Artillery Officer attached to the RAF from 1922-26, Lawrence Mercer retired from the Army in 1939 but rejoined as a Brevet Major for wartime service.

66 Another Royal Artillery officer, Erwin Ridlington was attached to the RAF from 1922-26 and retired as a Colonel in 1948.

67 Gp Capt Anthony Evans-Evans DFC was Station Commander RAF Coningsby when he was killed while flying a Lancaster of 85 Sqn Pathfinder Force on operations in Feb 1945.

68 Curiously, Edward Collinson was a Maj in the East Surrey Regt RARO on attachment to the RAF.

69 of DH9A J8744.

70 in DH9A J7251.

71 Edward Hopcraft had won his DSC for action with the RNAS in late 1917; he was promoted to Gp Capt in 1938.

72 Air Cdre Harold Crowe (1897-1983) had been an observer with 20 Sqn RFC during WW1 and shot down 8 aircraft. He retrained as a pilot and commanded 23 and 74 Sqns in the mid 1930s and was AOC 223 (Composite) Group in Burma in 1944.

73 32 year old George McCormack had been commissioned into the RAF as an observer in 1918 and was presented to the King in 1922. After training as a pilot he served with 111 Sqn and joined 14 Squadron in Dec 1927.

74 Kimberly was aged 33.

75 Plt Off John Maund had been commissioned into the RAF in Jan 1927 and joined 14 Sqn in Feb1928.

76 Jack Middleton was aged 21.

77 Victor Saunders was aged 24.

78 Frederick Fletcher was aged 23.

79 Gp Capt Robert Cole OBE was Station Commander at Moreton-in-Marsh and Kinloss in WW2 and at Cottesmore in 1946.

80 Josiah Truss won his MC while an observer with 114 Sqn in India in 1919; he transferred to the Equipment Branch and retired as a Wg Cdr in 1944.

81 DH9As J7067, J7254, J8203 and J8112.

82 in DH9A J7254.

83 Gp Capt Cecil Riccard CBE retired from the RAF in 1951. Much of his flying after he left 14 Sqn was on flying boats.

84 Wg Cdr John Hutchinson was killed when his Magister aircraft collided with a balloon cable near Slough in October 1940.

85 DH9As J8101 and J7116.

86 H3570, J8141 and J8172.

87 J7254 and J8142.

88 Flt Lt Greet with Sgt Lawrence in J8187 and Fg Off Wayte in J7818.

89 Gp Capt Cyril Greet retired from the RAF in 1946. He commanded RAF Stornoway in 1941-42.

90 After completion of his Short Service Commission, Alline Wayte left the RAF in 1934 but rejoined and served during WW2 in the Admin Branch.

91 J8098 and J8112.

92 Gp Capt Frank "Mongoose" Soden (1895-1961) flew SE5as with 60 and 41 Sqns on the Western Front, scoring 27 victories in aerial combat. He commanded RAF Upper Heyford and Biggin Hill during WW2 and retired to Kenya after the war.

Chapter 5

1930–38
Inter War Years 2

New Aircraft
Fourteen Squadron entered the new decade with a new Commanding Officer and the prospect of new aeroplanes. Four brand new Fairey IIIF Mark IVM aircraft had already been collected from the Depot by the pilots of the Cairo to the Cape Flight in early December 1929. Other examples of the type had started arriving at Amman that month in dribs and drabs to replace the tired and increasingly unreliable DH9As, but it would take until March to re-equip the whole squadron. Designed as a 'General Purpose' aeroplane, the Fairey IIIF could carry three people and with improved load carrying capability and range over the DH9A, it was an ideal machine for the job of policing Transjordan. The aeroplane was similar in size to the DH9A, but its sleek lines and Napier Lion engine, half as powerful again as the Rolls-Royce Eagle fitted to the 'Ninack', gave it a significantly better performance than its predecessor.

The Cairo-Cape Flight
By the beginning of January 1930, the crews of the Cairo to the Cape Flight were thoroughly familiar with their new aircraft[1]. The four pilots selected for the Flight were Flt Lt C B Greet, Fg Off J H Hutchinson, Fg Off A P Wayte and Sgt J I Richardson: it was a noticeable act of faith by the Air Staff at Cairo that all of these pilots were post-War aircrew. They had been joined at Amman by Fg Off D W Gibbon[2] of 216 Squadron, who was to act as the Flight's navigator, and their three mechanics Flt Sgt E H McDonald[3], and Sgts N G N Davies and R W Timms. Together the crews had practised the various techniques they would use on their long distance flight, and passed a navigation test, which was flown in formation.

The Flight left Amman at the start of their journey on 6 January 1930 after a brief delay because of the weather. The continuing foul weather made for an unpleasant flight to Egypt, which included a forced landing by Flt Lt Greet at El Arish, but eventually all the aircraft arrived safely at Heliopolis. Here the team was completed with the addition of Air Cdre AG Board[4] CMG DSO, who was to act as HQ Middle East's representative at the various diplomatic receptions that would punctuate the journey. After the final preparations were made the Flight was ready to leave Heliopolis on schedule at 0700 on 11 January. From Cairo the route followed the Nile southwards via Wadi Halfa, Khartoum and Mongalla to Entebbe on the north shore

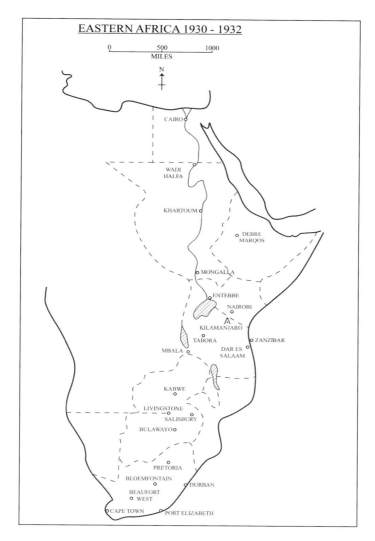

EASTERN AFRICA 1930 - 1932

of Lake Victoria. Here the Flight carried out a co-operation exercise with the 4th Battalion King's African Rifles, before continuing on to Nairobi. Another exercise, this time with 2nd Battalion King's African Rifles was undertaken at Tabora in central Tanganyika.

From there the route took the Flight to Abercorn (Mbala) on the southern tip of Lake Tanganyika, Broken Hill (Kabwe – about a hundred miles north of Lusaka) and Livingstone on the Rhodesian border, then across Rhodesia and South Africa by way of Bulawayo, Pretoria, Blomfontein, Beaufort West and Cape Town. Despite encountering some heavy rain and thunderstorms en route the Flight made good

125

progress and reached Cape Town at the beginning of February. They then started their return journey, which took them around the coast of South Africa via Port Elizabeth to Durban, then back to Pretoria. From Pretoria the Flight was accompanied for the rest of the return journey by four Westland Wapitis from the South African Air Force; amongst the South African personnel making the flight northwards was Col Pierre van Ryneveld who, as a member of 17 Squadron RFC, had fought alongside 14 Squadron in the Sinai campaign of 1916. Unfortunately at Fg Off Hutchinson fell ill with fever at Pretoria on 8 February and was admitted to hospital. His place was taken by Fg Off Gibbon and the eight aircraft set off for Bulawayo and Salisbury (Harare).

Up to this point the Fairey IIIF aircraft had performed well, although vibration from the new propellers fitted to this mark of the aircraft caused the crews to fly at a slightly reduced cruising speed. However, just short of Salisbury Fg Off Gibbon's aircraft[5] suffered a fractured oil pipe and had to forced land in four foot long grass. After repairing the fault and clearing a runway through the grass and boulders, the pilot was able to take off and continue the journey. Perhaps Fg Off Gibbon and his passenger Air Cdre Board had time to reflect on their good fortune when the Flight stopped at Broken Hill to lay a wreath at the graves of two less lucky aviators. Fg Off Y W Burnett and Sgt T L Turner from 47 Squadron had been killed when they crashed after take-off there during the Cairo-Cape Flight the previous year. From Broken Hill, the Flight retraced its steps northwards across Tanganyika towards Entebbe and then followed Nile to Cairo. On 24 February they arrived back at Heliopolis at 1300 hrs, having established a new record of 45 days to complete the journey of 13,200 miles, wiping a whole fortnight off the time taken by the 1928 Flight.

The Tribal Raids of 1930

The beginning of the new decade coincided with a resurgence in tribal raiding. It started with a large raid by Arabian tribes against the Howeitat on 2 February. A mixed force of a thousand camelmen and two hundred horsemen under the leadership of Ibn Musaad the Governor of Ha'il raided Imshash killing thirty-seven people and looting 1900 camels and 2100 sheep. Although aircraft were sent to intervene they arrived after the fighting was over and found many corpses strewn over the battlefield. One of the Howeitat sheikhs was flown to the area so that he could identify the bodies. The raiders retired back into the Wadi Sirhan and gave every indication that they were regrouping before carrying out another raid in Transjordan. A mobile column supported by six aircraft set out for Imshash on 12 February to prevent any further incursion. Patrols of the Arabian border and northern Transjordan were carried out twice daily from Amman and a Flight was detached to Ma'an to patrol the area around Imshash to Mudawara at dawn and from Mudawara to Aqaba at 1300 each day. The following month 14 Squadron aircraft supported a TJFF column during operations near Azraq to enforce a fine of camels from the Rualla tribe for their part in raiding. The column was re-supplied by air throughout the operation.

126

In the south, aircraft from the detached Flight at Ma'an supported the Armoured Car detachment which was guarding the wells at Ba'ir and another TJFF column which was making a reconnaissance of the Wadi Rhum. Two aircraft from the Ma'an detachment moved to Ba'ir itself during April after intelligence reports indicated the presence of a 400-strong raiding party close to the border. A combined force of armoured cars and TJFF troops were also deployed, but fortunately no raid materialised. However the threat of raiding continued into the early summer and a new tactic was adopted of pre-positioning a detachment of armoured cars at known watering places where raiders would have to stop either on the way into or out of the country. An aeroplane was also allotted to each of these detachments, operating from the detached location, to maintain a dawn to dusk patrol of the area and keep station over any raiding parties until the armoured car could get to them. The number of routine patrols by 14 Squadron aircraft was also increased, with two hundred reconnaissance flights in May alone.

The raiding was not confined to incursions into Transjordan: Transjordanian tribes were just as busy raiding into Arabia, as well as having inter-tribal skirmishes within the country. Aircraft also started to take more direct action to restrain raiders. On 8 May a Fairey IIIF located a raiding part of forty camels and stopped them by firing bursts ahead of them every time they moved. In this way the party was detained until armoured cars arrived on the scene to arrest the ring leaders. The following day six aircraft were again used offensively to detain a party of sixty Transjordanian camelmen returning from a raid in the Nejd. Although the raiders split into two groups, all of them were successfully arrested by armoured cars

Three weeks later three raiding parties totalling 160 raiders from the Hejaz were detected from the air near Mudawara in the extreme south and halted by TJFF columns who were guided to them by aircraft. However the Bedouin were not deterred by this setback and the same raiders tried to infiltrate into Transjordan on three more occasions the following month, but on each occasion they were successfully intercepted. As a result of these attempted raids twenty-three prisoners were taken and fifty-three camels were confiscated.

At the same time raiders were active in the north of the country, too, and 14 Squadron aircraft led TJFF columns to raiders at Hazim and Azraq. On 28 July an aeroplane was dispatched to locate a Shararat raiding party which had been reported to the north of Azraq. The pilot found the raiders at 1245 hrs and remained overhead for the next four and a half hours in an attempt to detain them until a TJFF column, which had set out from Zerqa, could reach the area. The raiders stayed put until 1715 hrs, but then tried to break out. The pilot managed to hold them back using gunfire for a further quarter of an hour, but then, short of fuel, he had to land at Azraq. By the time the TJFF reached Azraq the raiders had disappeared back into the desert, and although there were no arrests, the raid had been prevented.

The raiding tailed off during the summer but autumn brought a renewal as Transjordanian tribes moved their flocks to pastures in the east of the country. On 5 October the Howeitat made an armed incursion into the Wadi Sirhan and three days later an aircraft spotted twenty-two armed Bedouins on camels. The pilot landed alongside them and told them to return to Ba'ir; the leader admitted that he had intended raiding but had abandoned the idea after seeing the patrolling aircraft.

The standing patrols did not deter two hundred Nejd Sharawat who raided the Howeitat and Bei Alia between Imshash and Ba'ir on 26 October and made off again before aircraft could intervene. However two weeks later aircraft did stop a smaller party to the south of Black Rock (about forty miles southeast of Ma'an) at 0900 hrs en route from the Hejaz to the Howeitat grazing grounds. On this occasion the ten raiders did not stop when warning shots were fired, so using wireless the crew sought permission to fire on the group and asked for another back up aircraft. The second aircraft arrived on the scene shortly afterwards and between them the aircraft killed seven camels. This action stopped the raid and the TJFF later rounded up fifty-seven camels. On 14 November Sqn Ldr Soden observed nineteen men mounted on camels and horses assembling for a raid twenty miles west of Gharmil Khanser. He intercepted Capt J B Glubb MC[6], the Tribal Control Officer who was driving to Imshash with an Arab Legion detachment and led them towards the raiders; he then held the latter in place with a machine gun barrage until Glubb could reach them. Six days later a Nejd raiding party of eight camelmen with another fifty looted camels were caught by aircraft while they were heading for the sanctuary of the Wadi Sirhan at speed. The pilot fired warning shots and when these did not have any effect he engaged the riding camels, killing four and forcing the group to stop and take cover. With the nearest Arab Legion patrol some distance away he then used a machine gun barrage to drive the looted camels back westwards and managed to generate a distance of ten miles between the raiders and their loot before he had to return to Amman to refuel. The Arab Legion were then able to arrest the raiders and impound thirty-four camels.

Training

Despite the heavy involvement with operational flying throughout 1930, the Squadron also met its responsibilities for routine training. A number of exercises were carried out during the year with the TJFF including a major one in September when Fg Off P J H Halahan[7] worked with a number of TJFF outposts to standardise the signals used by aircraft when leading ground forces to intercept raiding parties. This was followed by an exercise at Ma'an to practise the procedures. A troop of TJFF simulated a raiding party and the aeroplane was used to direct a mechanised TJFF troop towards them. The aeroplane was successful even when the raiders complicated the scenario by splitting into two groups. The exercise was repeated by two aircraft in January 1931, and again in March with a successful outcome on both occasions.

Range work continued at Zerqa, with bombing and air-to-ground firing. Sometimes it could be a hazardous activity: one aircraft[8] forced landed at Zerqa during August 1930 after the engine failed after a bullet ricocheted off the airscrew and hit the radiator.

In October 14 Squadron was joined by a household name: Flt Lt R L R Atcherley[9] flew to Amman from the UK in his private aircraft[10]. Previously a member of the

RAF High Speed Flight, Atcherley had participated in the 1929 Schneider Trophy competition flying a Supermarine S6. Although he had been disqualified in that competition for inadvertently turning inside a pylon, he had gone on to establish world speed records for 50 and 100 kilometres. He achieved further celebrity when he won the 1929 King's Cup Air Race and, just prior to his posting to 14 Squadron, he had participated in the US National Air Races in Chicago where he had thrilled crowds with a display of "crazy flying."

Flt Lt Richard "Batchy" Atcherley was an exceptional pilot who had served with the RAF's High Speed Flight and raced in the 1929 Schneider Trophy competition. On 14 Squadron "Batchy" was well known for his mischievous sense of humour. He retired from the RAF in 1959 as an Air Marshal. (RAFM AC73-6-57)

Continuing Operations

Daily reconnaissances were continued over the tribal areas on the eastern border throughout December and by the end of 1930 one Flight was permanently detached to Ma'an to cover the operational requirements in the south of the country. However, it was clear that the strategy of using armoured cars and aircraft was not entirely successful in ensuring the integrity of Transjordan. Furthermore, the pace of operations – some 600 hours were flown in December against a more typical total of 400 – was taking its toll of aircraft. In October one Fairey IIIF[11] suffered damage to its olio legs and bottom longerons and another[12] forced landed five miles south of Snainirat (just south of the Wadi Ba'ir) with a punctured oil tank. There were three forced landings and two crashes the following month and one aircraft[13] crashed in Wadi Musa after take-off from an airstrip north of Ma'an on 4 December, fortunately with no injuries.

With no end in sight to the the problem of tribal raiding the Transjordanian authorities decided that it was time for a different approach. The day to day protection and policing of the Transjordanian tribes would be devolved to Glubb and his Desert Patrol from February 1931. Before then, however, Glubb needed to restore his prestige after an embarrassing incident: Sheikh Gereid Ibn Sweiyah had been shot in Glubb's presence on 31 December by a renegade sheikh who then fled into the Jebel Tubaik. This mountainous region in the south of the country was a "no go area" for government troops and for aircraft and was regarded as a safe haven by dissident tribes. That such someone could commit such an atrocity in front of the Tribal Control Officer (TCO) and apparently get away with it was a challenge to the TCO's credibility. Taking control of the Tubaik would demonstrate the far-reaching power of the TCO and send a strong message both to dissident tribesmen and to the tribes of Transjordan itself. Glubb's expedition, which lasted for a fortnight, left Ma'an on 6 January 1931 and entered the Tubaik. They were supported by 14 Squadron aircraft which carried out dawn to dusk reconnaissance ahead of the column. Two landing grounds were established within the Jebel area, and the show of force was further emphasised by four night cross-country flights to selected outposts. On 9 January Glubb's force confiscated 150 camels at Ferdat, the camels being loot taken from the Nejd and Hejaz. This action was sufficient to restore the TCO's prestige amongst the tribes and to demonstrate that the Tubaik was no longer a sanctuary for criminal elements. The next day the weather broke and Ma'an was hit by gale force winds gusting up to seventy miles an hour. Luckily the high winds had been forecast and the aircraft were saved from damage by lashing them to armoured cars.

Two more night flights over the Tubaik – giving a further demonstration of capability – were made by aircraft flown by Flt Lt Atcherley and Fg Off A K H Binley[14] on the night of 3 February. These aircraft landed at Ba'ir and later refuelled at Ma'an; at both airfields an experimental layout of Holt Flares on the ground provided guidance for the aircraft. Four days later Glubb requested another reconnaissance of the Tubaik and during this sortie Fg Off P K Robertson[15] forced landed 30 miles south of Hausa Wells with a fractured oil pipe. Sgt Morris who set out to rescue him was unable to find him before dark, but the following day Morris was successful in his search. In the end Morris' help was not needed as Robertson had managed to repair his aircraft, but the episode was remarkable in that both aircraft successfully used ground wireless sets to communicate with each other.

Glubb made another short expedition into the Tubaik after minor trouble in April, and on that occasion Sqn Ldr Soden caried out a dusk reconnaissance and landed at Aqaba, before returning via El Quweira and Ma'an.

Under the new arrangements the Ma'an Flight ("B" Flight was performing this duty in February) was withdrawn in February 1931 to Amman to concentrate on working in the Jordan Valley with the TJFF. Meanwhile, trouble was brewing in the north of the country. There were rumours that the Beni Sakhr and Rouwalla tribes were about to resume hostilities and Sgt Neale was dispatched to reconnoitre the area round Azraq and Hazim on 1 and 2 February. Despite landing at various locations to make enquiries he could find no evidence of anything untoward. However there was a problem with Number 2 Survey Party which was operating about twenty miles east of Azraq. The army officer commanding the party, Capt Domville, reported that the locally employed labourers were playing up and it was decided to fly a night patrol over the area as a show of force. Sqn Ldr Soden carried out the flight[16] on 3 February with LAC Davis. At dawn the next day two aircraft, flown by Flt Lt G S N Johnston and Sgt Morris were called out to locate a missing transport driver from Iraq who was due to have arrived at the Survey Party. Despite a thorough search neither the driver nor his vehicle could be found, and it was later discovered that the driver had stopped at a different location. After another call from Capt Domville on 9 February, Fg Off W D J Michie[17] carried out a dawn reconnaissance over the Survey Party which apparently finally solved the problem.

On 11 February the people of Palestine were once again were to the magnificent sight of the *Graf Zeppelin* as it flew past Jerusalem on a tour of the Middle East. That same day Fg Off L M E Jarman[18] carried out the first meteorological survey flight in the region to measure the variation of air temperatures over Transjordan. He recorded a range from +14° C at 1000 feet below sea level in the Jordan Valley to -15°C up at the top of his climb to 15,000 feet.

April 1931 was a busy month for visitors with the Chief of the Air Staff visiting the Squadron on 5 and 6 April and AVM F R Scarlett, AOC Middle East, carrying out his annual inspection on 15 April. The month was also busy for night flying with five northern reconnaissances flown at night, including landing in the Jordan Valley on two occasions. Four more night patrols were flown in May. The purpose of the night flying was to look into the feasibility of night operations and useful experience was gained. However these trials showed that it was often difficult for aircraft to maintain radio contact with Amman while flying over the Judaean Hills. Clearly such problems would have to be resolved before a proper night fighting capability, but as the desert tribes were unaware of this detail, the flights still had an important deterrent value.

In contrast to the operational tasking during the previous year and even the pace of events in the first few months of 1931, the remainder of the year was spent in a relatively leisurely routine. Co-operation exercises were carried out with the TJFF (including a firepower demonstration on 27 March) and with the army and routine border patrols continued. There was also a minor operation in the north of the country at the beginning of June when one Flight of aircraft supported a company-sized expedition to the Syrian border to halt to cross-border incursions from the north. The Squadron's aircraft were also frequently used to evacuate casualties to hospital at Ramleh or Jerusalem.

Crashes continued to be regular occurrences, too: typically there were about two accidents a month. Happily these were without any fatalities. In one incident, the Squadron crews were able to use their night flying skills to locate a downed aircraft[19]. It had been damaged during a forced landing eight miles south of the Wadi Rhum on 24 October and it was eventually located during a night reconnaissance on 26 October. The Squadron had developed a night search technique in which each searching aircraft flew along pre-arranged strip fifty miles wide firing a red Verèy light every ten minutes; when the downed crew saw a light they responded with two lights and the searcher then homed in on the ground-fired lights. Once overhead, the searcher then dropped a reconnaissance flare to enable them to identify the exact position of the downed aircraft. Another search operation, this time by day, was carried out on 7 December for an Imperial Airways airliner which had forced landed en route to Iraq. It was located at Qasr Kharana about forty miles east of Amman with all on board safe.

The East African Cruise

After the success of the 1930 Cairo to Cape Flight, 14 Squadron was selected to provide crews for an "East African Cruise" in early 1932. The crews arrived at the

Depot in Heliopolis 23 December to collect four brand new Fairey IIIF MkIVB aircraft[20]. The Flight was commanded by Wg Cdr A T Harris[21] OBE AFC from HQ Middle East and the other pilots were Flt Lt Atcherley, Fg Off Jarman and Sgt Morris. The remaining personnel were Fg Off R J Cooper[22] (a navigation specialist detached from 4 Flying Training School at Abu Seir) and five mechanics, Flt Sgt Blake, Sgts Allan, Duffy, Greave and Slee. The East African Cruise left Amman on 6 January 1932 for Egypt and departed Heliopolis for Wadi Halfa five days later, following the course of the Nile southwards over the next ten days to arrive at Jinja on 21 January. After a few days in Uganda, they moved on to Nairobi for a two-week stopover. At each stop they carried out a number of local flights and took the opportunity to "fly the flag" amongst the locals. As with the Cairo to Cape flight, there were also opportunities to exercise with locally-based troops of the King's African Rifles.

The Flight reached Mombassa on 10 February for an exercise with the Kenyan Defence Force and then continued in short hops across eastern Kenya and Tanganyika towards Dar-Es-Salaam, which it used as a hub for flights around Zanzibar and Tanganyika during the last week of February and the first week of March. Sorties included exercises with the Tanganyika Territory Police and the Zanzibar Police as well as flights over the Serengeti Plain and the Ngorongoro Crater. During the latter flights on 8 March the Governor of Tanganyika, Sir George Stewart Symes GBE GCMG DSO, flew in Atcherley's aircraft and was thrilled by the sight of such abundant wildlife. Harris also led the Flight over the summit of Mount Kilimanjaro – the first aircraft to have overflown the peak. Miraculously, after flying over hundreds of square miles of "bush" where twenty foot trees would have jeopardised a safe forced landing and hindered rescue, the only forced landing occurred on 11 March when Atcherley's aircraft[23] developed a water leak half an hour after take off from Tabora.

East Africa Cruise: The aircraft crossing the mainland at Bagamoyo en-route for Dar-Es-Salaam from Zanzibar on 2 March 1932.

By good fortune the terrain near Bukibi was suitable for an emergency landing and despite sinking into soft ground on touchdown, the aeroplane was easily repairable. Five days later, now operating from Nairobi, there was another close shave when Sgt Morris' aircraft[24] overran the landing area at Wajir narrowly missing a large tree that would almost certainly have wrecked the aircraft; in the event a few scratches and dented pride were the only damage! The presence of aircraft in northern Kenya gave an opportunity to check the border with Italian Somaliland and the Flight was given the task on 16 March to inspect and photograph the border track between the two countries. In the last week of March the East African Cruise retraced its steps northwards and returned to Heliopolis just after midday on 29 March.

Jackie the Lion

When the East African Cruise flight returned to Amman it brought with it an unexpected souvenir, in the form of a lion. Atcherley had a strong sense of mischief and while he was in Africa the prospect of returning home with a pet lion proved too much of a temptation for him. On 24 March he had flown to Juba to collect a small lion cub, recorded in his log book as "Jackie the lion with the low pressure claws." Back at Amman, Jackie became a popular member of the Officers' Mess, where he forged a close friendship with Guts the Alsatian, another member of the 14 Squadron menagerie. Inevitably even small cubs grow into big lions, and Jackie soon grew too big to keep as a domestic pet. When he began to stalk other animals, as well as the Mess servants, it was clear that something had to be done. An elegant solution to this problem was found by presenting him as a gift to the King of Egypt. There were a few tense moments during the presentation ceremony when Jackie managed to slip free from his collar and escape from his handler, but all ended well and Jackie soon settled into his new home at Cairo Zoo. Here he lived into a respectable old age.

Meanwhile the year had started quietly in Amman. Two aircraft were dispatched to Ma'an on 18 January to keep an eye on the Beni Atia tribe who were crossing from Hejaz into Transjordan, but there was no trouble. But winter weather was on the way and snow storms hit Amman at the beginning of February causing chaos for eleven Wapiti aircraft from 55 Squadron who attempted to fly from Iraq to Amman. All the aircraft left Rutbah successfully on 6 February, but only five of them arrived at Amman. Unfortunately the heavy snow prevented any search for the missing aircraft until two days later. Even then Amman was almost unusable and the 14 Squadron aircraft detached to Zerqa for the operation. Five Wapitis were found on 8 February near Imtan just across the border in Syria but it took two further days to locate the last one which had forced landed fifteen miles further north. A recovery convoy escorted by the TJFF was sent to collect this last aircraft.

Over the next three months night flying continued, including another night searching exercise, and a number of co-operation exercises were carried out with the TJFF. "B" Flight worked with the TJFF in April while "A" Flight dispatched five aircraft to Semakh for ten days under canvas with the TJFF in May. This co-operation paid dividends the following month during a joint operation to close the south-eastern border with the Hejaz. In late May Sheikh Hamed Salem ibn Refada had crossed into the Hejaz intending to raise a revolt. By the beginning of June he had a force of nearly a thousand rebels operating in the area, but this force depended on supplies from Transjordan. It was decided to sever this supply route and "Semforce" comprising three troops of the TJFF and a section of armoured cars deployed to southern Transjordan under the command of Gp Capt I V N Fowler AFC. The four aircraft of "A" Flight led by Flt Lt I G E Dale[25] were detached to Ma'an on 15 June to join the operation and flew 117 reconnaissance patrols from Ma'an over the next two weeks. The operation continued for the next two months with daily patrols by "A" Flight aircraft despite temperatures reaching 109°F. By the end of August the Flight had clocked up 1,245 hours in 1,139 sorties. It was remarkable that during this time their were no forced landings or major unserviceabilities despite the harsh conditions and high flying task; much credit for this must go to Sgt A J Briggs whose personal interest and leadership ensured that the aircraft were exceptionally well cared for. The aircraft were also used to evacuate casualties from Ba'ir, Ziza and Ma'an plus two wounded survivors of an attack on a Desert Police Patrol which was ambushed on 13 July. Although Refada's forces were defeated by Ibn Saud's army at Dhaba in July, Semforce continued to round up groups of rebels trying to re-enter Transjordan, and was also busy ensuring that Saudi troops did not attempt to cross the border. "A" Flight eventually returned to Amman on 2 September.

During July Flt Lt Atcherley[26] organised some experimental night flying at Amman. He realised that a more robust system of night airfield operation was needed before the full operational potential of night flying could be realised. In one set of

Fairey IIIF J9661 crashed while Sgt R W McCheyne was practising forced landings on 29 April 1932. 24-year old Robert McCheyne survived the crash, but he died in the RAF Hospital Sarafand two months later and is buried at Ramleh.

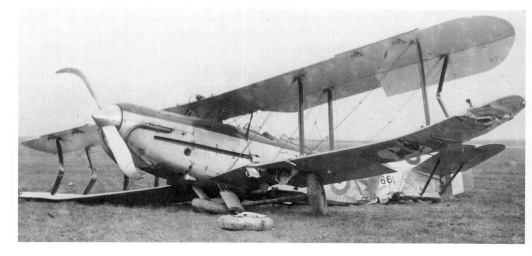

14 Squadron Fairey IIIF flying over the Wadi Rum en route from Amman to Aqaba, 1932.

trials different configurations of aircraft-mounted flares were used to illuminate the landing area. These confirmed that wing-mounted flares were more effective than tail-mounted flares. A second trial used ground flares with auto-ignition which were set out to mark the landing area and these were then fired at an agreed time by pre-set alarm clocks. This method proved to be a very effective aid to navigation and landing. Finally, an operational trial involved the "scramble" of aircraft at night after a simulated raiding party was reported. The "raiders" were 130 miles away from Amman when the alarm was raised and the aircraft located their target a mere hour and seven minutes later. On this occasion bombs and guns were also used at night.

Arrival of the Fairey Gordon
The Squadron had suffered its first fatal accident for four years on 23 May when Fg Off E V N Bramley[27] and LAC G W Moore[28] were killed in a flying accident. The aircraft was returning from the Depot when it entered a spin near Gaza and did not recover. The third occupant of the aircraft LAC L C Menet[29] escaped from the aircraft by parachute. This accident raised a question about the effectiveness of the upper wing slats on the Fairey IIIF and Flt Lt Atcherley carried out a trial at Amman on 21 June with two Fairey IIIFs[30] in which he successfully spun, rolled and looped both aircraft. Although this exercise restored full confidence in the aircraft, a new type was already on the way to re-equip the Squadron: the first Fairey Gordon arrived at Amman in July. The Gordon was based on the same airframe as the IIIF, with some minor refinements, but had a new Armstrong Siddeley Panther radial engine. The Panther took away some of the streamlined elegance of the IIIF, but it did bestow

significant improvements to the Gordon's performance, particularly on take-off at heavy weights.

Two more Gordons arrived in July 1932 and seven the following month. In a departure from normal practice where pilots simply trained themselves in flying a new type, one of the Gordons[31] was converted to dual controls for instruction. By the end of September "A" and "B" Flights had both converted to the Gordon. Both Flights practised air firing and bombing at Zerqa and the following month qualified in their weaponry classification with scores of 79.58 yards for bombing and 62.45% for firing. Another annual task was production of the "track map." Since there was no usable map of the country, each year the Squadron produced a blue print in conjunction with the TJFF and the Desert Patrol which showed the relative positions by dead reckoning of various tracks, landing grounds, Desert Patrol posts and landmarks. The track map proved to be the most practical aid to navigation in the desert.

Continuing the development of night flying skills, three Fairey IIIFs of "C" Flight set out on 14 October for the first ever night formation flight to Iraq. Flt Lt Atcherley led the flight in J9826 with his crew comprising LAC Carter and LAC Corbett. They followed the pipeline track to Rutbah, arriving there to refuel at 2035 hrs GMT. An hour later they took of again heading for Baghdad, and despite poor visibility because of blowing sand arrived successfully at Hinaidi at 0020 hrs. During the entire flight only wingtip flares had been used. The return leg was flown the following night and on this case Holt flares were lit at Rutbah to act as a beacon. Unfortunately one aeroplane had to remain at Rutbah because of a defective magneto, but the others made it back to Amman at 0035 hrs on 16 October. Once again the only lighting for all landings was provided by wing flares. The trip had demonstrated that air traffic movements by night were perfectly feasible, provided that a suitable system of beacons could be established along the route.

On 29 October 1932 Sqn Ldr L H Cockey[32] assumed command of the Squadron. As Christmas approached there were reports of a large body of Akhwan massing near the border. This represented a real threat to Transjordan and the south-eastern reconnaissance which had been routinely flown twice a week was increased to twice daily patrols from 26 December. The armoured cars were also put on alert, but the Akhwan dispersed and the New Year passed peacefully. In January a concerted work up in formation flying started in preparation for the following month's RAF Middle East Display. During the third practice sortie of the day on 3 January Plt Off G R Moorby[33] flying in a Gordon[34] found himself overtaking his leader, Flt Lt Atcherley in in a Fairey IIIF[35]. As Moorby tried to correct his position he was caught by the leader's slipstream and collided with Atcherley's tailfin. With the fin bent over at an alarming angle AC1 C Stocks[36], in the back of the IIIF, decided that it was time to leave and abandoned the aircraft; unfortunately his parachute opened too late and he was killed. Both aircraft subsequently landed safely. Twelve aircraft left Amman on 28 January for Heliopolis where practice continued for the next few days. The RAF Middle East Display took place on 3 February and 14 Squadron participated in two events with 6, 45 and 55 Squadrons. In their absence heavy rain had rendered the

14 Squadron formation 28 February 1933. Note that aircraft "L" is a Fairey IIIF whereas the others are Gordons. (Thomas Blackett)

airfield at Amman unusable, so it was not until 7 February that they could return home.

Routine flying training, including night flying, filled most of the spring of 1933. The Squadron was fully involved with the Imperial Forces exercise throughout Palestine and Transjordan at the end of March. For this exercise "A" Flight was detached to Jisr El Mejamie and "B" Flight to Ma'an, while "C" Flight was held in reserve at Amman. The aircraft co-operated with ground forces at Beisan, Semakh and Rosh Pina, including night flying on moonless nights. For these latter sorties an automatic beacon designed by Atcherley was used with great success.

The second fatal accident of the year occurred on 28 April and once again it involved someone falling from an aeroplane. Gordon K2632 flown by Plt Off W J H Ekins[37] with Fg Off J Bradley[38] and LAC R H G Willmott as his crew had just delivered the mail to Rutbah and was returning to Amman. As the aircraft approached Zerqa at 6,000 feet it hit severe turbulence. The two passengers were thrown overboard, but only Bradley was wearing a parachute. Willmott was killed, and although Bradley's parachute saved him on this occasion, he was only to live for another two months: John Bradley was killed on 12 June when one of the Squadron's Morris six-wheeler lorries overturned on the Jerusalem to Ramleh road. This accident also severely injured AC1s Mounsey and Lewis.

Arab-Jewish resentment erupted once again in the autumn when rioting broke out in October. On 28 October nine aircraft from 14 Squadron joined another nine from

6 Squadron for a demonstration flight over Tel Aviv, Tul Kerem, Haifa, Nablus and Jerusalem. Two days later a pair of Gordons was tasked with a reconnaissance of the area immediately west of the Jordan, but they nothing to report. Over the next few days further patrols were carried out along the Jordan, but again all remained quiet and it seemed that for the time being the problem had been resolved.

Ceremonial Interlude
Certainly things had quietened down enough for much of 1934 to be taken up with ceremonial flying. Once again the Middle East Display was held at Heliopolis in February with participation by ten aircraft from 14 Squadron. The Squadron also mounted nine aircraft formations for the King's Birthday Parade at Jerusalem on 4 June and to salute the Emir Abdullah on his return from London on 20 July. In March two Flight-sized expeditions were mounted: three Gordons accompanied Amman's Station Commander Gp Capt F L Robinson DSO MC DFC for a fortnight long tour of Sudan on 16 March and on the same day three more Gordons set off in the opposite direction to accompany His Excellency the High Commissioner of Palestine for a week-long trip to Baghdad.

A major photographic survey of the southern frontier of Transjordan was carried out by 14 Squadron from February to May. A Special Flight of three Gordons was formed using one aircraft from each of the Squadron's Flights. The Survey Flight left Amman on 20 February under the command of OC "A" Flight, Flt Lt F H Ronksley[39] MC. Ronksley was relieved by Flt Lt R W M Clark[40] on 19 April and the Flight eventually returned to Amman on 23 May having completed 450 hours of photographic flying.

During October each Flight was detached to Ismailia to carry out air-to-air firing against a target towed by another aircraft. This was the first time that the Squadron had practised air-to-air flying since the World War! There followed a major exercise to check the Tansjordan Defence Scheme. The exercise, carried out between 5 and 7 November involved the Squadron's aircraft, the TJFF, Arab Legion and the Armoured Car Company operating together to practise their response to an external attack on Transjordan.

Poor weather limited flying during December and although on 20 December when neither the RAF nor Imperial Airways considered it safe to fly, an airliner belonging to KLM[41] continued its journey en route to Batavia. It was reported missing on 21 December by which time the weather had improved sufficiently for ten of 14 Squadron's Gordons to launch on a search for the aircraft. Eventually the burnt out wreckage was found in the Wadi Hauran about fifteen miles southwest of Rutbah. All four crew and three passengers had been killed in the crash.

The beginning of 1935 was once again dominated by the Middle East Display, with twelve aircraft flying to Heliopolis to participate. Once again 14 Squadron joined the other bomber units in the Middle East, 45 Squadron flying Fairey IIIFs, 6 Squadron, also equipped with Gordons and 55 Squadron's Wapitis for a massed flypast. Once again the Squadron mounted nine-aircraft formations to celebrate royal occasions: formations over Haifa and Jerusalem on 6 May and over Jaffa and Tel Aviv on 7 May marked the King's Silver Jubilee, while a further one was mounted over Jerusalem on 3 June for the King's Birthday Parade.

With the operational situation now quiet in both Palestine and Transjordan there was an opportunity for crews to deploy on "training cruises" to other areas within the Middle East Command area. Exposing crew and aircraft to operating over unfamiliar territory had great training benefit; it also meant that if the Squadron was called to reinforce other units, crews would already have an idea of the lie of the land. Four aircraft left for a "training cruise" of Iraq on 22 February and over the next four days called in at Kerbala, Baghdad, Suleimania, Kirkuk, Diana and Mosul. Another cruise set off for Sudan on 22 May. This latter cruise comprised the four aircraft of "A" Flight under command of Flt Lt R A B Stone[42], and stopping off at Helwan and Wadi Halfa they reached Khartoum on 24 May. After three days in Khartoum they returned via Wadi Halfa and Heliopolis to reach Amman on 29 May.

During June Sqn Ldr Cockey was promoted and posted from the Squadron. His replacement, Sqn Ldr T C Traill DFC[43] took over command of 14 Squadron on 1 August 1935.

As part of the RAF's expansion scheme, and in the shadow of the Abyssinian Crisis, a fourth Flight, "D" Flight under Flt Lt J G Franks[44] was added to the

On 18 May 1937 Plt Off C J S Robinson managed to taxi his Fairey Gordon K2724 into a private car on the aerodrome. Fitter Harry Barnes, right, does not look impressed! Robinson wrote off this aircraft the following month while circuit flying at Beisan. (Harry Barnes)

Squadron in September. The Flight's Gordon aircraft were supplied by 6 Squadron (which itself was re-equipping with the Hawker Hardy) and the Flight started an intensive work-up to prepare themselves for operations. Over the next three months they practised dive- and high level-bombing, air firing, night flying, photography, formation flying, searching and reconnaissance skills.

Meanwhile the remainder of the Squadron was heavily involved in exercises with the TJFF in September and the Royal Navy in October. On 19 September a firepower demonstration was laid on for the officers and NCOs of the TJFF. It was decided that the best way to show the effectiveness of aerial weapons would be to bomb a target representing troops in the open. A target array was built to represent a hundred men dispersed over an area of 120 yards by 60 yards, each man modelled by three two-gallon oil tins stacked on top of each other. Thanks to this scientific approach the demonstration had also become something of an experiment and it attracted the attentions of both the Air Staff at HQ Palestine and Transjordan and HQ British Troops, both of whom sent representatives to watch the proceedings. Three Gordons took part in the demonstration, each one making three attacks. In each attack the aircraft dropped a stick of 20-pounder bombs in pairs, each stick having an interval of about 100 yards between pairs of bombs. The first pass was made in vic formation in a dive from 4,000 feet, with each aircraft releasing eight bombs from around 1,500 feet. The next two attacks were made in line astern, dropping four bombs per aircraft on each pass. After the demonstration quite a few oil tins remained standing, but when they were examined more closely it was clear that all except three had been hit and that most had been hit several times by splinters or stones.

The Squadron was called to support an exercise by the 3rd Cruiser Squadron on 2 October. Four aircraft of "C" Flight carried out an anti-submarine patrol sweeping thirty-five miles out to sea. Three days later another such patrol was carried out and on 6 October the Flight deployed with the Squadron Commander to Haifa landing ground. Here they camped for the next five days while flying further sorties in support of the naval exercise. They returned to Amman on 11 October. That evening the Squadron received an urgent call for medical assistance after a TJFF sergeant-major had been taken ill at Ma'an. He was suffering from retention of urine and was in great pain. Night flying equipment was fitted to a Gordon and just after midnight Flt Lt C V Howes[45] set off for Ma'an with the Station doctor, Fg Off J C Blair MB ChB. On Blair's advice the patient was evacuated to Amman, arriving there at 0400 hrs. Traill noted that "it is not likely that the sergeant-major had flown before and he had certainly not been up at night and we gathered that he had been relieved of his difficulty by the time Howes landed him back at Amman."

1936

"D" Flight completed their work-up on 8 January 1936. Sadly rather than remaining with 14 Squadron, they were immediately re-equipped with Vincents and sent to join 45 Squadron as part of the response to developments in Abyssinia. January was also notable for two searches for missing aircraft. In the first, the Squadron was ordered to search for an Italian aircraft that had gone missing on a flight from Benghazi to Basrah on 2 January. Fifty-nine hours of searching was carried out before the news came in that it had been located in the desert west of the Nile! At 1630 hrs on 29 January the unit was tasked with searching for a Tutor which was missing from a flight from Ramleh to Ma'an. The Palestine portion of the route was being searched by 6 Squadron and 14 Squadron was given the Transjordanian section. Two aircraft[46], flown by Fg Off M A Aylmer[47] and Sgt D J Donaldson[48] with LAC I F B Walters, took off at 1810 hrs for a dusk search of a ten mile wide strip extending from the southern tip of the Dead Sea to Ma'an. The searchlight at Ma'an was lit to serve as a beacon. The first search was fruitless, although at one stage Aylmer thought he had located the aircraft, only to find that it was the police post at Shobek answering his signals. Meanwhile reports had been received from Mudawara of an aircraft heading north along the Hejaz railway. Armed with this information the second search team, comprising Flt Lt E B Grace[49] with Cpl Williams and Fg Off G L Cruickshanks[50] with LAC Bird launched in darkness at 2200 hrs and headed directly for Ma'an. Grace started firing his Verey Lights every five minutes and soon get replies from south of Ma'an, however as he approached the source of the flares they stopped. It later transpired that the downed crew had now run out of flares. Not to be deterred, Grace dropped two reconnaissance flares and by the light of these he was able to identify and locate the Tutor. Grace and Williams then worked out a Dead Reckoning position for the Tutor which they transmitted to base, and having rejoined Cruickshanks they started to recover to Amman. The weather steadily deteriorated as the pair headed north and just beyond Ma'an they flew into cloud and became separated. Cruickshanks climbed to 9,000 feet in an attempt to climb above the cloud and Grace descended to 4,500 feet to try and get below it. In the end neither was successful and both arrived overhead Amman from different directions after nearly four-and-a-half hours' night flying including twenty minutes of instrument flying in difficult conditions. The following morning the Tutor was found by an aircraft from Ramleh within four miles of the DR position given by Grace and Williams. The whole episode was a piece of remarkable airmanship: firstly locating the downed aircraft at night and logging its position so accurately and secondly recovering to Amman in testing conditions with relatively primitive instruments and with no assistance from ground-based equipment. All the more remarkable is that Williams had already flown three-and-a half hours on the afternoon of 29 January and was up again at 0600 hrs on 30 January to fly another naval exercise sortie. Perhaps it was not too surprising that after landing from the final sortie he was admitted to hospital with suspected pneumonia!

The Palestinian Uprising Begins

From the Arab perspective the only change since their uprising of 1929 was that the rate of immigration of Jews into Palestine had accelerated. The anti-Semitic tide of fascism sweeping across central Europe had caused the numbers of Jews seeking refuge in Palestine to increase exponentially: in 1930 about 5,000 annual immigrants arrived in Palestine, but by 1935 the annual immigration figure had risen to around 60,000. In November that year Sheikh Al-Din Al-Qasam, an anti-Jewish/anti-British terrorist and something of a hero amongst the Palestinian Arabs was killed in a fire-fight with British forces near Jenin. This event precipitated a new wave of ill-feeling which erupted into sectarian violence six months later. A General Strike by Arabs throughout Palestine followed in April 1936 and the violence escalated into a terrorist campaign against both Jews and the British. With the situation deteriorating rapidly, two aircraft from "C" Flight were detached to Jisr El Mejamie on 22 April to support troops of 13th Infantry Brigade in the Jordan Area. The troubles in Palestine deepened in May and the remainder of Flt Lt Howe's "C" Flight also moved to Jisr El Mejamie. The "Jordan Air Contact Zone" covered the area immediately west of the river Jordan roughly between Beisan in the north and Jericho in the south. The rest of the country was covered by 6 and 208 Squadrons at Ramleh and 33 Squadron at Gaza. Army convoys included mobile wireless vehicles known as "Roadex" and if air support was required the Roadex would transmit a "XX" call with its callsign and co-ordinates. This would be picked up by the RAF relevant detachment which would then launch a pair of aircraft to the given co-ordinates. Aircraft flew in pairs to provide each other with cross-cover, and it was found that any more than two aircraft generated a real risk of collision. Once the aircraft reached the Roadex further communication was by pre-arranged signals by Verey light or Aldiss light. The guerrillas usually knew the country well and made effective use of any available cover, such as olive trees, to conceal themselves from the air. As a result the aircraft had to fly low (around 500 feet above the ground) in order to have any chance of detecting them, and at this altitude crews were frequently subjected to accurate small arms fire.

Fairey Gordon KR2637 of "B" Flight is readied for flying at Amman.

In the last week of April "C" Flight carried out fifty reconnaissance patrols, including a night sortie in which flares were dropped to deter crop burning. Over the next two months dawn and dusk patrols were flown on each day, which discouraged much of the arson which had been occurring just after dark. On several occasions reconnaissance flares were dropped on the position of reported illegal activity and although the aircrews could see nothing useful in the light, the army reported that the flares had a useful deterrent effect. A further frustration for crews was that they were frequently called out to investigate "heavy firing" only to discover that by the time they had arrived on the scene the small handful of snipers were already long gone. However aircraft did open fire on three occasions in July, once during daytime and twice at night. Aircraft were also used to drop pamphlets into Arab villages.

The facilities at Jisr El Mejamie were basic with only about 1,000 yards available as a runway; for night flying the aircraft simply took off and landed between the headlights of two cars. With a high intensity of operational flying ("C" Flight flew just under two hundred hours in July alone) from such a primitive landing strip it was hardly surprising that there were some accidents at Jisr El Mejamie: on 17 August Plt Off J C M Lunn[51] struck a boulder after landing[52] and the following month another Gordon[53] was wrecked after Sgt R H Payne[54] undershot the landing area at night and overturned the aircraft. Fortunately in both cases the crews were unhurt despite the aircraft being written off. After four months of operations, "C" Flight returned to Amman and was replaced at Jisr El Mejamie by "B" Flight. The pace of operations slackened somewhat after Martial Law was declared in Palestine in October and the emphasis for "B" Flight moved to supporting 13th Infantry Brigade or the TJFF while escorting convoys or in searches for weapons caches.

Despite the nature of operations, there were also lighter moments. Traill recalled that "we had to do a lot of low flying up and down the West bank and the shepherds with their many flocks of sheep and goats took advantage of this to get as close as they could when they saw us coming and use their slings at us. I do not know if David would have done any better, he must have been a very good shot, but they never allowed enough deflection and we usually saw the stone curving away behind the rudder. One day I took an egg with me and when a shepherd attacked me I pulled up and dive bombed him with it. It must have been a near miss because when I came round again flying low he was waving and laughing and perhaps a little relieved that it was only an egg. I waved back and we parted in very good humour, each with a story to tell!"

Back to Training and Ceremony
Another training cruise to Khartoum was made on 25 January 1937 by five aircraft drawn from "B" and "C" Flights. They returned on 1 February in time for the work up for the annual RAF Middle East Display. Once again there was intensive practice for the April Display. Unfortunately this practice cost an airman his life in an accident which was almost a repetition of the tragic mid-air collision of 1934. On 23 March a Gordon[55] flown by Sgt F N Heapey[56] collided with another[57] crewed by Flt Lt Aylmer

The wreckage of Fairey Gordon K2741 after a mid-air collision on 23 March 1937 with another Gordon, K2706. The pilot of K2741, Flt Lt M A Aylmer, parachuted to safety, but unfortunately his passenger AC1 Ronald Walker was killed.

and AC1 R Walker[58], slicing the tail section off the latter aircraft. Aylmer parachuted to safety, but Walker did not escape from the aircraft and was killed; Heapey managed to land safely at Amman. The remainder of the work up was successful and accident-free and the Squadron departed en masse for Heliopolis on 12 April for the rehearsals. The Display four days later went well and the Squadron returned to Amman on 17 April.

Later in the month Aylmer and Grace carried out an endurance trial with long-range fuel tanks fitted to the Gordon. Taking off at 0438 hrs on 29 April they headed south towards Aqaba then followed the border northwards over the Jebel Tubaik to Azraq and thence to H4 on the pipeline to Iraq, before returning to Amman at 1245. They had covered over eight hundred miles giving an average groundspeed of around one hundred miles per hour. On landing they still had enough fuel and oil remaining to have stayed aloft for another two hours. Another long-range sortie took place on 6 July when Sqn Ldr Traill and Flt Lt C L Gomm[59] flew non-stop from Amman to Baghdad to deliver the official translation of the Royal Commission's report on Palestine.

The Squadron Badge
Since 1918 RAF squadrons had taken to decorating their aircraft in various unofficial markings and badges. The Air Council decided that the badges were an important

part of unit identity and in 1935 they created the post of Inspector of RAF Badges formalise and approve official badges for individual units. In 14 Squadron's case the "Winged Crusader" badge which had adorned the Unit's aircraft since 1920 was put forward for approval. The origins of the badge were in the First World War and Allenby's campaign through Palestine, where servicemen saw themselves as latter-day Crusaders fighting through the Holy Land to rid it of Ottomans in the same way the original Crusaders had fought the Saracens. The shield bearing the cross of St George reflected this Crusader spirit and also referred to Lydda, near the Squadron's first post-War base at Ramleh, which was the alleged birthplace of St George. How the badge itself had been used during the First Wold War is difficult to tell, but it seems likely that Medhurst re-introduced the Squadron's wartime badge to establish the Unit's identity when the number was changed from 111 Squadron to 14 Squadron in 1920. However, none of this heritage impressed the Chester Herald who had been appointed as the Inspector of Badges. His first objection was that a shield bearing the St George cross was not permitted because it was already exclusively the badge of the City of London. The second was that the badge had no motto.

Traill fought hard to keep the shield, even quoting the example of HMS *Crusader* whose badge was a crusader's shield. But much to the disgust of the Squadron, the Chester Herald imposed his solution to the problem by replacing the shield with a circular "plate". The motto, however, was a little more difficult, but it did present the Squadron with an opportunity to get its own back on the Chester Herald. Traill felt that an Arabic motto would be fitting as the Squadron had served its entire operational life in Arabic-speaking countries; he also thought that the Emir might be the person to suggest something appropriate. He consulted with Peake Pasha who, accompanied by the Minister of Education, sought an interview with his Highness. "We were a little afraid," Traill admitted, "that the Emir might put us in an embarrassing position by suggesting something much too long, but not a bit of it: he soon saw what was wanted and told them to be quiet. After a moment's thought he came out with five words from the Koran[60], with chapter and verse, meaning 'I spread My Wings and I Keep My Promise'. We were honoured and delighted."

However, the Chester Herald was less than impressed with the idea of an Arabic motto as was Sqn Ldr V R Gibbs DSC at the Air Council, who wrote "frankly I do not like the idea of a motto in Arabic on one of King Edward's aircraft." Gibbs thought that the RAF should be even-handed to both Arab and Jew and therefore that the motto should not be in either Arabic or Hebrew. "'I Keep My Promise' sounds a good motto even in English," he suggested. This idea was taken up by the Chester Herald who tried to push Traill towards the English version. Traill was having none of this, though, and pointed out that it would be "discourteous to his Highness the Emir to refuse his offer..." adding a reminder that his Highness was also a direct descendant of the Prophet, whose words were being quoted. Meanwhile he had also written to Medhurst, now at the Air Ministry, for support and on the latter's advice approached His Excellency the High commissioner of Palestine and Transjordan. His Excellency proved a most enthusiastic supporter of the cause and with his sponsorship the matter was taken directly to the Secretary of State himself, who said that he had no objection and cordially approved the motto. In the end the Herald, now presented with a *fait accompli*, had to admit that "the Squadron's tenacity is itself deserving of getting the motto they want!"

The Badge was formally presented to the Squadron at a ceremonial parade in Amman on 12 August by AVM C T MacLean DSO MC, AOC Middle East, accompanied by Air Cdre R M Hill AFC MC, AOC Palestine and Transjordan.

A Deteriorating Situation

In November 1937 the violence started to escalate once more when Arab guerilla groups started ambushing vehicles belonging to the Palestine Potash Company as the negotiated the road between Kalya, on the north coast of the Dead Sea, and Jerusalem. As a precaution against these attacks 14 Squadron was tasked with providing air escorts for convoys of trucks over the next six months. The escorting aircraft was supposed to fly far enough away from the convoy that it could not be seen in the hope of tempting the rebels into the open so that they could be engaged. In practice, though, crews found that they had to be almost overhead the convoy at about 6,000 feet in order to pick up the SOS signal. As a result the aeroplane was fully visible to any would-be attackers and unsurprisingly the attempt to entice the rebels into open battle failed. But it was at least successful in getting the potash to Jerusalem safely. Eventually the threat waned and the escorts were discontinued in April 1938.

The deteriorating situation in Palestine mirrored a larger-scale one in Europe as Germany flexed its muscles. The RAF continued its expansion and moved closer to a war footing. In December 1937 crews practised flying in gas masks.

Fairey Gordon K2742 operating from Ma'an 1938. The aircraft was eventually transferred to New Zealand.

'C' Flight 11 Nov 1937. Many of the men in this photograph from the last days of the biplane era flew and fought in the Wellesley.

Back Row l-r: George, Bartholemew (*Wellesley air gunner*), Millar, Crofts (*Killed August 1938*), Fielding

Second Row: Maguire, Small, Gee, Norman, Gardiner, Segrave (*Killed February 1939*), Rowe, Osben, Blair

Third Row: Cpl Howard, Cpl Dowling, Sgt Chick (*Killed February 1939*), Sgt Norris (*Prisoner of War September 1940*), Sgt Sweeting (*Killed August 1938*), Sgt Broadhurst (*Killed September 1940*), Cpl D'Arcy (*Prisoner of War September 1940*).

Front Row: Flt Sgt Crouch, Fg Off Fenwick-Wilson (*retired in 1946 as a Wg Cdr having Commanded 405 & 218 Squadrons*), Flt Lt Aylmer (*Killed November 1939*), Plt Off Stapleton (*retired in 1968 as an AVM having Commanded 14 Sqn*), Sgt Houghton.

On 19 January 1938 the Squadron deployed eleven aircraft to Ma'an for a two-day exercise with the TJFF. Twenty-two camelmen from the Arab Legion with two cars were hiding somewhere in 1600 square miles of desert in the Western Tubaik representing a five-hundred strong raiding party threatening Ma'an. The "friendly forces" of Soucol were to try to locate and intercept the raiders before they could reach Ma'an. The plan was to fly relays of aircraft so that there were always three aircraft over the area keeping a continuous reconnaissance until the raiders were found. In the event the raiders were found during the second wave at 1000 hrs and the aircraft were re-rôled as a strike force. In reality the aircraft would have continued to attack the enemy throughout the day but for exercise purposes the aircraft again changed rôle to shadow the enemy force and report their progress to Soucol by wireless. On this occasion the Squadron's night flying skills were not exercised, and instead the aircraft had to re-locate the raiders, who had marched through the night, before they could reach Ma'an. They launched in darkness at 0555 hrs and an hour later had located the raiders six miles south of Ma'an, in time for the grand finale of the exercise when the raiders were met by the full force of Soucol.

This was the last major exercise of the "old ways" of policing the Middle East in biplanes. Major change was about to come: in March 1938 the introduction of the new generation of Wellesley monoplanes and the simultaneous expansion of the Squadron marked the end of the biplane era. Perhaps the last words should go to Tom Traill: "I have described life in 14 Squadron because I loved it, because it was something that will not happen again and because it was typical of service overseas between the Wars: service that did much to train the Air Force that went to war in 1939. Apart from shooting and bombing exercises it was not tactical training for modern war but it was of the highest value in developing pride in the service and a sense of fellowship involving mutual confidence and respect between all ranks."

Notes

1 The four Fairey IIIFs were J9660 (flown by Greet and Gibbon), J9657 (Hutchinson and Board), J9659 (Wayte with McDonald and Timms), and J9661 (Richardson and Davies).

2 Douglas Gibbon was killed in England in Nov 1930 while flying an Avro 504.

3 Engineering officer Gp Capt Ernest "Mac" McDonald MBE from Portsmouth was killed in action in France in November 1944 aged 44; he was posthumously awarded the CBE.

4 Andrew Board (1878-1973), who retired from the RAF in 1931 had commanded 5 Sqn RFC in 1915-16. He was no stranger to 14 Sqn, having commanded the Palestine Group in 1920.

5 Fairey IIIF J9657.

6 John Bagot Glubb (1897-1986) joined the Royal Engineers in 1915. He transferred to the Arab Legion in 1930 and rose to command the Arab Legion until 1956.

7 Patrick "Bull" Halahan (1908-1982) commanded 1 Sqn RAF during the Battle of France 1939-40.

8 Fairey IIIF S1175.

9 Richard Atcherley (1904-1970) – universally known as "Batchy" – was a pilot of exceptional ability. After a distinguished career he retired from the RAF as Air Marshal, AOC-in-C Training Command.

10 Avro Avian monoplane G-AAYW.

11 S1197.

12 J9792.

13 Fairey IIIF S1183.

14 Allan Binley was killed in Bombay flying a DH Moth in Nov 1934.

15 Paul Robertson relinquished his Short Service Commission in 1933 but rejoined the RAF in the Administrative Branch in 1942. After WW2 he transferred to the Aircraft Control Branch and eventually retired in 1959.

16 in J9670.

17 Air Cdre William Michie CB retired in 1960 as Senior Technical Staff Officer at Transport Command.

18 A New Zealander, Air Cdre Lancelot Jarman (1907-1986) retired from the RAF after a distinguished career.

19 Fairey IIIF J9801.

20 The aircraft were K1703, 1704, 1705 and 1713.

21 MRAF Sir Arthur Harris (1892-1984) achieved fame as AOC-in-C Bomber Command during WW2.

22 Gp Capt Reginald Cooper was dismissed from the service by Court Martial in 1943.

23 Fairey IIIF K1703.

24 Fairey IIIF K1705.

25 Wg Cdr Ivor Dale DFC was killed in action in Feb 1945 while commanding 21 Sqn.

26 While commanding RAF Drem in 1940 Atcherley eventually perfected his night landing system – the "Drem System" – which was subsequently adopted as standard across the RAF.

27 Educated at Brighton College, 21-year old Eric Bramley had been commissioned into the RAF in Dec 1929.

28 Gerald Moore aged 24.

29 Leslie Menet.

30 Fairey IIIFs J9642 and K1158.

31 Fairey Gordon K2635.

32 Air Cdre Leonard Cockey (1893-1978) retired from the RAF in 1945. He had joined the RNAS in 1917 and flew with 1 Naval Sqn. In 1918 he was part of the trials team aboard HMS *Argus*, the world's first "through deck" aircraft carrier.

33 George Moorby resigned his commission in 1934.

34 Gordon K2636.

35 Fairey IIIF K1158.

36 Stocks was aged 23.

37 After serving with 45 Sqn William Ekins transferred to the Royal Indian Army Service Corps in 1939 and was killed in Mar 1941.

38 John Bradley was aged 21.

39 Francis Ronksley had joined the Royal Engineers from Repton School in Sept 1914. He transferred to the RFC in 1917 and served with 80 Sqn on the western Front. Previously a Section Commander with 2 Armoured Car Company, he retired as a Flt Lt in 1934.

40 Gp Capt Ronald Clark OBE DFC retired from the RAF in 1955.

41 Douglas DC-2 PH-AJU "Uiver".

42 Gp Capt Ralph Stone retired from the RAF in 1946.

43 AVM Thomas Traill CB OBE DFC (1899-1973) achieved 8 victories while serving with 20 Sqn during WW1. He retired from the RAF in 1954, and one of his last duties was to present the Sqn Standard to 14 Sqn in that year.

44 AVM John Franks (1905-1960) retired from the RAF as President of the Ordnance Board.

45 Gp Capt Charles Howes DFC retired from the RAF in Mar 1949.

46 Sgt Donaldson was flying Gordon KR1715.

47 Sqn Ldr Michael Aylmer was killed in Nov 1939.

48 Flt Lt David Donaldson was killed over Denmark while flying a Halifax of 158 Sqn in Apr 1943.

49 Eric Grace transferred to the reserve in 1938 and served as a Sqn Ldr during WW2.

50 Originally from Durban, Wg Cdr Graham Cruickshanks was shot down and killed over Berlin while commanding 214 Squadron in Sep 1941.

51 Wg Cdr James Lunn AFC retired from the RAF in 1961.

52 in Gordon JR9829.

53 Gordon K2606.

54 Flt Lt Ronald Payne retired from the RAF in 1947.

55 Gordon K2618.

56 Fg Off Francis Heapey was killed in Nov 1941 aged 29.

57 Gordon K2706.

58 Ronald Walker aged 21.

59 From Brasil, Wg Cdr Cosmé Gomm DSO DFC was killed over France while returning from a bombing raid on Milan in Aug 1943 while commanding 467 Sqn.

60 Written phonetically, the words are "Anna assif we anna affi".

Chapter 6

1938–41
The Wellesley Years

Expansion and Re-equipment

Until early 1938 Amman was virtually untouched by the massive expansion of the RAF's home commands which had been triggered by Germany's growing militarism. In the relative backwater of Transjordan 14 Squadron continued to operate twelve biplanes just as it had done when Medhurst reformed the Unit at Ramleh nearly two decades previously. The only evidence of wider recruiting by the Service was the presence so many young officers from across the Empire. Traill recalled that "the pilots of 14 Squadron were the usual mixture: Canada, South Africa, Rhodesia and Brazil were represented (the Rhodesian was the only one to survive the war) and the combination with the home-grown was finer than either could have been alone." In early 1938, however, the full effects of the Service's expansion and rearmament programme reached Transjordan. From March that year 14 Squadron's establishment of personnel and aeroplanes increased dramatically: the three Flight structure remained, but instead of four obsolescent biplanes, each Flight would now have six modern monoplanes plus a further two "In-use Reserve" aircraft. Another three aircraft would constitute a Squadron reserve, thereby more than doubling the size of the unit to twenty-seven aircraft. All these aircraft would need to be serviced, armed and flown, and to meet these tasks the Squadron would need to expand to a total of 127 personnel.

The aircraft chosen for the re-equipment of the Middle East squadrons was the Vickers Wellesley, a single-engined monoplane with a crew of two or three. The Wellesley boasted many new features such as enclosed cockpits, a variable pitch propeller, hydraulic flaps and retractable undercarriage. The aircraft's seventy-four foot wingspan was nearly twice as big as that of the Gordon, while the Wellesley's performance also represented a doubling of speed and payload over its predecessor. Perhaps the most important features, though, (as would become apparent two years later) were its phenomenally long range and its immensely strong geodetic structure. The first two Wellesleys arrived at Amman on 19 March and re-equipment was completed just three months later.

Early in the conversion phase Traill handed command of the Squadron to Sqn Ldr A D Selway[1]. An experienced flying instructor, Selway was an ideal man to oversee the introduction of such a radically different new type to the Squadron.

The King's Birthday Flypast 9 June 1938 – the Squadron formation led by Sqn Ldr Selway turns westwards towards Amman. L2644 was written off in a landing accident on 28 October 1938.

Although the most experienced pilots converted to the Wellesley by the simple expedient of flying an old Gordon to Aboukir and swapping it for a Wellesley, Selway insisted on flying with all of the newer pilots to ensure that they were operating the Wellesley correctly. One of the first question marks over the aircraft was whether it would be able to operate on the landing grounds in the wilds of Transjordan. With its long wings the Wellesley looked much too big to be able to land on the small airstrips used by its biplane predecessors. Selway set off with Maj Glubb in a Wellesley to find out. Performing a "Cook's Tour" of the landing grounds at Ba'ir, Jaffar, Mudawara and the Wadi Rhum they found that the Wellesley coped admirably well.

The Wellesley had its first public outing in Palestine on the King's Birthday. On 9 June Selway led a nine-ship formation on a three-hour flight over seventeen different parades in Palestine. In each case the formation's arrival was timed to coincide with the breaking of the flag. The sight of such a large formation of modern camouflaged bombers must have been an inspiring sight: certainly the army commanders were most impressed with what they saw and messages of congratulations came flooding in. However the new type was not without teething troubles: problems with the undercarriage retraction system caused a number of minor accidents in the early days. In July a failure of fuel brackets in some aircraft meant that all except operational flights were suspended for a fortnight until the fault was rectified. A rather more serious problem emerged on the morning of 5 August when aircraft from "C" Flight were practising strafing attacks on the range at Zerqa. As Sgt R H

The wreckage of Wellesley L2643 in which Sgt Sweeting and AC1 Crofts were killed when the wing broke off during manoevring for air-to-ground firing at Zerqa on 5 August 1938.

Sweeting[2] pulled out from a gunnery pass the wing broke off and the aircraft[3] flew straight into the ground, killing Sweeting and his gunner AC1 W H Crofts[4]. Used to the more manoeuvrable Gordon, Sweeting had unwittingly overloaded the wing structure by pulling too hard while recovering from his dive. Subsequently the wings had to be taken off all the aircraft and new high tensile bolts fitted.

Developments in Palestine
Meanwhile the Palestine troubles continued and 14 Squadron's operational commitment meant that the new aircraft were used for operations almost immediately. Throughout July August and September of 1938 two routine night reconnaissance patrols were flown over the curfew area around Lake Hule, about fifteen miles north of the Sea of Galilee near the Syrian frontier. A number of flares were dropped during these patrols, but as with the Gordon, it proved impossible for Wellesley crews to detect any movement on the ground by the light of the flares. Nevertheless these flights seemed to be an effective deterrant against curfew breakers. As well as this routine tasking, extra operational sorties were also needed from time to time, so the Squadron kept a roster of duty crews to be called out if necessary. One evening the duty pilot was Sqn Ldr Selway, who was preparing for a dinner party when the Squadrons Operations officer phoned him for an immediate patrol. With no time to change out of his Dinner Jacket, Selway rushed to the airfield to join his navigator Sgt

Smith. "Whilst running round the Wellesley on the ground in the dark I had not seen that the sharp trailing edge of the wing was about the height of my eyes and I dealt myself a severe blow on the bridge of my nose as I hit it and I thought it had been cut a little," recalled Selway, "...we got off and dropped the flares over Lake Hule and came back about a hour and a half later. I got into my car and went down to my house to rejoin the guests to whom my wife had explained my absence. But my cut had bled considerably and the blood under the helmet and goggles had congealed, so that when I walked into the room in my Dinner Jacket with a face coverd in blood it took some time to explain to the guests what on earth I had been doing!"

Much of the Squadron's work was carried out in support of army operations designed to stop armed arab insurgents crossing from Syria or Transjordan into Palestine and vice-versa. On 20 July a combined force of TJFF and Arab Legion troops carried out a sweeping search for brigands attempting to smuggle illegal arms across the Jordan Valley. The Squadron's Wellesleys provided air cover for this operation throughout the day from 0400 hrs to 1800 hrs via a continuous relay of aircraft. The aircraft were able to keep in communication with the ground columns by means of W/T, message dropping and ground strip codes.

Although the Squadron's immediate concern was the situation in Palestine, everyone was also aware that at the same time tension was mounting in Europe. Hitler's annexation of the Austria in March 1938 and his designs on the Sudetenland brought a real expectation of war amongst RAF personnel. As the Czech Crisis came to a head in the early autumn the Squadron prepared for deployment to its war station at Ismailia. All the equipment was packed ready to move and the Squadron stood by awaiting instructions. However, the Crisis dissipated at the end of September, giving some respite, but unfortunately there was no similar improvement in the situation in Palestine.

In fact the situation in Palestine worsened during September, resulting in an increase in the Squadron's operational task. Aircrew now flew with revolvers and each aircraft also carried a rifle and ammuntion in case of forced landing in "bandit country." Many of the tasks were at night with the Squadron's aircraft providing illumination for the ground forces. During one such operation a relay of aircraft kept up an all-night patrol over Jerusalem, dropping flares at intervals to support the troops below them. On 21 September the army requested an immediate emergency night reconnaissance over the area between Kallia and Jericho. An aircraft was dispatched to the area where it dropped eight flares.

The routine patrols of the Lake Hule area continued, and armed aircraft were also called to supplement the firepower of the ground forces at night on a number of other occasions in October. On 5 and 7 October sorties were tasked against the area of Ar Rama in northern Palestine and over the two nights thirty 20-pound bombs were dropped. By now proficient at bomb dropping from the Wellesley, the crews found that if there was enough moonlight they could drop quite accurately from six hundred feet at night. Reports back from HQ 16th Infantry Brigade indicated that these actions had a significant effect on the local populace who had not appreciated that aircraft could operate so effectively at night. As a result they had since decided to adhere to the curfew. On 8 October two aircraft were sent to drop flares in a small area to the southeast of Haifa. Operating between 2100 hrs and 0100 hrs they dropped sixteen flares in co-operation with HMS *Douglas* which fired star shells from its position in Haifa harbour.

Three days later a Hardy aircraft of 6 Squadron was shot down near Hebron; two aircraft from 14 Squadron provided air cover for armoured cars who set out that night from Jerusalem to Hebron to search for the downed aircraft. The following morning four Wellesleys joined the search, but the Hardy was not found until 13 October. Meanwhile a three day operation had started on 11 October to locate an armed band which had crossed into Transjordan from Palestine. They were reported to be at Rajeb, but a reconnaisance aircraft confirmed that they were no longer there and over the next two days Squadron aircraft co-operated with the TJFF as they combed the Ajlun Forest for the insurgents Although the insurgents were not captured on this occasion, the activity of the TJFF and the aircraft was enough to persuade them to return to Palestine without causing any trouble in Transjordan. Aircraft were also in action on the night of 12 October. A flight of six aircraft, two with flares and four with bombs flew in the light of a full moon against rebel positions in woods near Rama, Kafr Imam, Mughar, Deir Hana and Sakhnin dropping thirty-two 20-pound bombs; during this engagement one of the aircraft was hit by ground fire in four places. A similar task, carried out this time by two aircraft, was flown in the same area two nights later.

From 18 October the Squadron received an additional task: one Wellesley was to carry out a dawn reconnaissance along the coast of Palestine between Jaffa and Rafah to find any ships trying to land either smuggled weapons or illegal immigrants. This task continued through the next ten months.

"Life in RAF Amman in 1938," recorded Selway, "was pretty masculine and there wasn't much to concentrate on except flying, swimming in the pool, tennis, cricket and other games. Rough shooting and riding for a few, Trips to Crusader and Saracen ruins and visits to Jerusalem on a regular rota and in addition a perfectly appallingly bad camp cinema showing unbelievably ancient – and silent – films. We dined in the Officers Mess each night in Mess Kit with proper formality and the Sergeants did likewise in their own Mess next door. There were two officially married officers for whom quarters were provided: the station commander and the squadron commander, otherwise it was an unmarried station and no wives were permitted to accompany their husbands. As the squadron boasted only one married officer – me – it didn't really matter very much. There were about a dozen British civilians living in the town from the British Resident, the British officers in the Arab Legion and the Transjordan Frontier Force at Zerqa, 15 miles away, the remainder were officials to deal with finance, the land, law, oil and so on. There were no young ladies of any description for my officers to dally with (actually there was one in Zerqa and one in Amman) and as it was very clearly understood that Europeans did not even look at, let alone dally with, Arab girls the young pilots were free to concentrate on their flying, their games and sports and in the evenings a little drinking and singing." The Station swimming pool itself had an interesting history, since permission had been denied to build one; instead an "Emergency Water Supply" was built – complete with shallow end, deep end and diving boards!

Training

While the Squadron worked hard to meet its operational flying commitments there was still much work to be done in training new pilots and. On 8 September ten new pilots arrived from 4 Flying Training School in Egypt: Acting Plt Offs J V Berggren[5], L S Bullwinkle[6], R A Green[7], C F Greenhill[8], J E Jordan[9], Gorringe-Smith[10], Sgts A G Brown[11], J A Burcher[12], R G Gilmore[13] and G E Dickson[14]. All of these inexperienced pilots would need close supervision while they converted to the Wellesley and consolidated their flying skills.

Squadron pilots also continued to explore the full capabilities of the Wellesley. In July an aircraft had been tested up to 28,000 feet (some 8,000 feet above the ceiling of a Gordon) and another was able to complete a photo-mosaic of the Jordan Valley from 20,000 feet – easily surpassing Fg Off Jarmain's meteorological climb seven years earlier in a Fairey IIIF. Not only could the Wellesley fly higher than any of the Squadron's previous types, it could also fly much further. Three aircraft from "C" Flight flew in formation around the coast of the southern Sinai Peninsular on 26 August and landed at Helwan – a distance of about a thousand miles covered in seven hours. On 21 November Sqn Ldr Selway covered a similar distance when he led three aircraft on a long-range dummy bombing raid from Amman all the way to Baghdad and back. Five aircraft then repeated the Sinai tour the following day.

While these latter flights demonstrated the long reach of the Wellesley they also revealed a shortcoming with the aircraft's fuel system. The Wellesley had six fuel tanks, three in each wing, all of which fed into the engine simultaneously. The pilot controlled them by means of a single fuel cock which selected all six tanks either "on" or "off". In theory fuel fed from all six tanks at the same rate, so each tank would have the same amount of fuel in it, but in practice pilots found that each tank emptied at a slightly different rate from the others. This made little difference on a short flight, but during a long flight there was a tendency for the fuel in one wing to be used more quickly than the other. This in turn meant that one wing became significantly heavier than the other, leaving the pilot with a large force on the control column as he tried to keep the wings level. In most aeroplanes the solution would be to balance the fuel by stopping use of fuel from the "light" wing and using only that from the "heavy" wing, but in the Wellesley this was not possible. Clearly a complete redesign of the Wellesley's fuel system would be impractical, but after a little thought Selway came up with a simple remedy to this complex-sounding snag. The Squadron's workshops produced a gadget made of cable and elastic which was attached to the cockpit floor. When the loads of the control column became uncomfortable the pilot simply had to hook the gadget onto the spectacle-shaped grip on the control column and the elastic took the strain, providing some relief for the pilot.

14 Squadron's Wellesleys Squadron lined up at Amman for a mass launch for the benefit of the cameras of British Movietone News on 30 November 1938.

14 Squadron's Wellesleys were unveiled to the wider public on 30 November when British Movietone News visited Amman. During the short clip the announcer proudly described how the Squadron was now equipped with the most modern aircraft of the same type used on various long range record-breaking flights. Despite the news reader's enthusiasm there were some on the Squadron, including Selway, who looked with envy on squadrons who were re-equipping with the Blenheim, which seemed to be a much more modern machine even than the Wellesley. With its all-metal construction, twin engines and power-operated turret the Blenheim was indeed a generation ahead of the Wellesley, but even so the Wellesley had a much longer range and could carry a heavier bomb load. The Squadron's first major encounter with a Blenheim was not an auspicious one. On 10 December the Wellesleys were involved in a massive search for a 30 Squadron Blenheim which had gone missing from Habbaniya. All other tasks were suspended during the eight day search, which spread over Saudi Arabia and Syria. Eventually the wreckage of aircraft was located sixty miles from Habbaniya; unfortunately the crew had been killed.

The traditional festivities marked Christmas 1938, in what would be 14 Squadron's last peacetime Christmas at Amman. On Christmas Day the station personnel turned out after church parade to watch – or participate in – the traditional football match between the Cripples and the Convicts. The ceremonies were presided over by Father Christmas (in the person of the Station Warrant Officer) who paraded through the Station with his retinue. Then in the early evening it was time for the Airmen's Dinner which was served to them by the

officers before the latter enjoyed their own Christmas Dinner. On Boxing Day the festivities continued with an inter-Flight chariot race. This was won by "A" Flight, whose chariot design benefitted from larger wheels than the other two Flights, and the event was followed by a paper-chase for the whole Station.

Back to Operations
The Christmas celebrations were only a brief respite from operational flying. The New Year started with communications duties conveying a number of General Officers around Transjordan and Palestine. Additionally a photo-mosaic of Bethlehem was completed from 22,500 feet. Later in the month reconnaissance flights were mounted over the Jordan Valley on the four days between 18 and 21 January and again on 24 January, looking for any suspicious movements, but none were observed. Further reconnaissance sorties in February covered the Jordan Valley and the Ajlun Forest which continued to offer sanctuary to rebel gangs. Bi-weekly sorties over the Dead Sea were started and the coastal reconnaissances which had been started the previous October were resumed. During February a 14 Squadron aircraft located a Greek merchant vessel loaded which illegal immigrants and was able to direct the Navy to the scene to prevent the immigrants from landing.

On 13 February aircraft were called in to search for a "C" Flight Wellesley[15] which had gone missing on a communications flight between Amman and Lydda. The burnt out wreckage was found on the next day three miles south of Wadi Sir. In a tragic accident, it appeared that Plt Off Bullwinkle had flown into the hills in cloud killing himself, Sgt C J Chick[16] and LAC D J Segrave[17].

Throughout 1939 the main operational task of 14 Squadron was to provide coastal reconnaissance sorties to locate ships attempting to land illegal immigrants and arms into Palestine. Usually operating in pairs, the aircraft would cover an area about a hundred miles out to sea. Any ships seen were reported to the Palestine Police who would either board the vessels themselves or direct a RN warship to do so. Most vessels were then forced to return to their point of origin, though some attempted to turn back to Palestine. On 10 February a 3,000 ton Greek vessel, the SS *Katina* was found twenty-five miles off Tel Aviv loaded with four hundred immigrants. In March it was the SS *Sandu* with 269 immigrants, and in April SS *Aghios Nicholas*, SS *Astir*, SS *Romania*, SS *Kentresta* and SS *Assimi* all attempted to land illegally in Palestine. In May *Assimi* was again found, and SS *Nikola* deposited three hundred immigrants – all subsequently captured – when she was beached on the night of 18 May. In June SS *Colorado*, *Las Perlas* and *Frossola* were found, as, once again was Assimi, and in July *Colorado* reappeared with 378 more immigrants. Finally in August *Aghios Nicholas* returned to try again, and once more it was spotted by a 14 Squadron Wellesley. While the coastal patrol was rather unglamorous it nevertheless played a vital part in the British Authorities' policy of restricting Jewish immigration – at a time when Arab support would be needed to secure British interests in the Middle East if it came to war with Germany and Italy.

On 11 March a 6 Squadron Hardy aircraft located a band of about eighty insurgents from Syria who were hiding near Zemal. A combined force of Arab Legion and TJFF troops were sent to intercept them. However, the insurgents were both well-trained and well-armed and having shot down the Hardy, badly wounding the pilot, they engaged the TJFF in a fierce firefight. The TJFF troop commander Lt F T MacAdam[18] and four legionnaires were killed and Macadam's second in command, Mulezim T Bogdanovitch[19] earned the EGM for his actions. Air support then arrived in the form of a Gladiator and a Hardy from Palestine-based squadrons and Wellesleys of 14 Squadron. Ten aircraft were used in a relay to ensure that Wellesleys remained in action continuously from midday until dusk. Using the rear gun and 20-pound bombs, the aircraft managed to pin down the insurgents as they attempted to disengage from the Arab Legion and seek refuge in the Ajlun Forest. Eventually the band managed to withdraw into a narrow re-entrant which gave them enough overhead cover to shelter them from small bombs and machine-gun fire but still gave them a clear field of fire. From this new strongpoint they kept up accurate fire and one of the Wellesleys was severely damaged by rifle bullets. It was apparent to everyone that the insurgents had chosen their position exceptionally well: all they now had to do was to remain there until nightfall and then they would be able to slip away towards Ajlun and safety. With the TJFF troops pinned down and the insurgent's position impregnable by small bombs, the only answer seemed to be to drop larger bombs on them. But authority for larger weapons had to come from the Emir himself. This the Emir graciously granted and two Wellesleys immediately set off for Zemal, armed with 250-pound bombs. After locating the enemy position, the first aircraft tipped in for its attack and the first bomb scored a direct hit on a group of thirty insurgents. Shortly afterwards, three more bombs accounted for the rest of the band. A search of the area the following day revealed 722 sticks of dynamite and 300 detonators plus 2,645 rounds of small arms ammunition: clearly

A formation of 14 Squadron Wellesleys over the Great Bitter Lake near Kabrit in 1939. The aircraft wear the unit identification letters "BF" and have been given a temporary desert camouflage by spraying a sandy-coloured distemper over the dark green of the standard camouflage. The roundels have also been "toned down" by removal of the yellow and white colours. (Mark Postlethwait)

the insurgents were a formidable and well-trained band which was intent on doing much damage.

It was shortly after this incident that one of the participants, Fg Off D C Stapleton[20] was awarded the AFC for his outstanding flying during twenty-five counter-insurgency sorties.

As the year progressed the twin pressures of the operational situation in Palestine and the growing certainty of war with Germany dominated the Squadron's work. The number of coastal reconnaissance flights was stepped up throughout the summer, squeezing the remainder of the flying task. In May a shortage of engines meant that only the operational sorties could be flown. However once spares started to arrive, the Squadron was able to resume its preparations for war with formation cross-country flights and re-fuelling and rearming exercises. With air-to-air radios still unreliable, there was always a problem of communication between aircraft on long sorties, so Sqn Ldr Selway "designed a thing rather like a small golf bag containing

During night flying on 21 July 1939, L2670 Plt Off J B LeCavalier attempted to land at Be'er Shiva to assisit Plt Off MacKenzie who had forced landed there after an engine failure. Unfortunately LeCavalier overran the landing area and hit a ditch. The aircraft was beyond repair and was destroyed on site. Note the temporary desert camouflage and the "BF" code letters.

four three-foot long wooden sticks with a coloured triangular pennant at each end. The pilot told the navigator what he wanted to say and he looked it up in a log book we had made and held up the necessary flags in various positions in the rear cockpit." This simple method worked very effectively.

Accidents and forced landings continued to be part of squadron life; fortunately, however, there were no more fatalities. On the night of 21 July Plt Off M MacKenzie[21] suffered an engine failure at Beersheba and the undercarriage collapsed in the subsequent heavy landing. Plt Off J B LeCavalier[22] was dispatched to rescue the hapless MacKenzie, but he hit a ditch on landing, so two Wellesleys were written off in the space of a few hours. A little later Sgt H N Norris[23] also forced landed at Beersheba when a piston blew off his Pegasus engine. A rescue team with tools, spare parts and heavy engine lifting equipment was duly dispatched by road, but when they arrived after a long and trying journey there was no sign of Norris or his aeroplane. Being an ex-engine fitter, and somewhat of an impatient man, he had managed to change the cylinder himself – despite the summer heat and dust – and then flown back to Amman, much to the annoyance of the ground party!

War

International tension had been mounting in the months since the Munich Crisis and war with Germany and Italy seemed to be inevitable. The Squadron made preparations and laid contingency plans and it was not a particular surprise when Sqn Ldr Selway's telephone rang at 0200 hrs on 24 August. It was Gp Capt C N Lowe MC DFC at HQ P&TJ ordering 14 Squadron to deploy immediately to its war station at Ismailia. After a busy morning, the advance party of two officers and forty-three airmen left Amman at 1400 hrs on four Valentia transports provided by 216 Squadron. An hour later, Selway led fourteen Wellesleys to Ismailia landing there at 1730 hrs – the first unit of 1 Bomber Wing to arrive. The Squadron's main party left Amman early the next day, travelling by road to Ramleh and then train to Kantara followed by a final road convoy, to reach Ismailia after a twenty-four hour journey. Meanwhile the two Blenheim units, 30 and 55 Squadrons, had also arrived from their peacetime base at Habbaniya. Flying started on 28 August and preparations were made for the imminent war.

However, there were doubts in some circles at HQ 1 Bomber Wing about the survivability of the Wellesley in an all-out war. Only a year after being hailed as a "modern aeroplane", the Wellesley was already looking obsolete when compared to the Blenheim. There was also a clear expectation that 14 Squadron would exchange their Wellesleys for Blenheims in the near future and, in preparation for this, six pilots from were detached to each of the Blenheim Squadrons for conversion training. Eight Wellesleys were also transferred from the Squadron to Khartoum: four to 47 Squadron on 4 September and two weeks later, four more were delivered there for 223 Squadron. Meanwhile the decision was taken to relegate the remaining Wellesleys in Egypt to the reconnaissance role.

On 3 September war was declared on Germany and all units were placed on a war footing. The impact of this event in Egypt was an anticlimax: Italy had not, after all, joined the Germans, so there was no operational flying to be done and things continued much as they had done before. Training flying continued and the Wing started a work-up involving formation practice, live bombing and night flying. This regime was to continue for the next four months. The first "proper" operational event was the deployment of 14 Squadron's "B" Flight to the advanced landing ground at Qasaba a week after the outbreak of war. Led by led by Flt Lt A T H Willis[24], Plt Off S G Soderholm[25], Sgt A F Wimsett[26] and Sgt L H Moulton[27] were to prepare for strategic photo reconnaissance sorties over Italian Libya in the event of hostilities. In the event they were never used, but the detachment at Qasaba was maintained (by each Flight in turn) until 20 October. The advanced landing ground at Qasaba was used again by the Squadron in December when a combined Coastal and Air Defence exercise was run for all forces in Egypt. A formation of nine of Squadron's Wellesleys simulated enemy aircraft attacking the facilities at Helwan and Suez on 12 December. However the writing was on the wall for the Wellesley and the Squadron was withdrawn back to Amman on 19 December.

The next four months were a frustrating wait for 14 Squadron's personnel as they

Wellesley Mark II K7770 after a landing accident at Amman on 22 April 1940 with Plt Off R Willitts at the controls. A few aircraft were modified to become Mark II aircraft, which offered improved navigation facilities including an enlarged canopy over the navigator's position and a radio direction-finding loop aerial.

languished at Amman, waiting to find out what role they would be expected to play in any hostilities. A hint was given in in early February when twenty-two pilots including Sqn Ldr Selway were detached to Abu Seir for Anti-Submarine training. On their return in March the Squadron started working up in this new role, flying coastal patrols and exercises with the submarine HMS *Osiris*. Seven more pilots were dispatched to Abu Seir on 13 April, but their course was cut slightly short when they were recalled on 2 May. The Squadron was now at 48 hours readiness to move, probably to Port Sudan.

A week later, "C" Flight under Flt Lt Stapleton AFC was ordered to deploy to Port Sudan. Here they were to take part in anti-submarine exercises in preparation for the arrival of the convoy carrying the second contingent from Australia. Stapleton's five Wellesleys arrived later in the day and a sixth aircraft arrived on 13 May. The Flight started operations the following day, providing anti-submarine cover for convoy US2.

THE RED SEA & ABYSSINIA CAMPAIGN

On 17 May the rest of the Squadron was ordered to proceed to Port Sudan to join 254 Wing, commanded by Gp Capt S D MacDonald DFC[28]. With its HQ at Erkowit, just inland from Port Sudan, 254 Wing was part of the mixed and scattered British forces facing some Italian 250,000 troops in Abyssinia. Although the Italian army constituted a major threat to British interests in Sudan and Kenya, there was a more immediate problem with the substantial naval force at Massawa which was ideally placed to interdict British shipping in the Red Sea. The Italian air force in Eritrea also represented a formidable capability: two wings of Savoia-Marchetti SM79 and SM81 bombers could easily cover the Red Sea, and the Fiat CR42 fighters based at Gura would be a potent defence. Thus 254 Wing's first tasks would be to neutralise the naval forces at Massawa (three hundred miles south along the coast) and the bomber wings at Asmara and Massawa. The forces available to carry out this task would include two other Wellesley squadrons, 47 at Khartoum and 223 at Summit. They would be augmented by a handful of Gladiators from "K" Flight, 112 Squadron which was shortly to deploy to Port Sudan.

Early on 18 May the Squadron's main party started to retrace their steps to Ismailia. This time they travelled south from here to Suez, where they embarked on HMT *Akbar* for the voyage down the Red Sea to Port Sudan. Meanwhile, the seventeen remaining Wellesleys of "A" and "B" Flights flew to Port Sudan via Ismailia, each aircraft loaded with as much equipment as could be packed into the fuselage. The remaining equipment required by the advance party was carried by the four Bombay transports which accompanied them. Using the personnel and equipment of the advance party, the Squadron was able to start preparations for operational flying; planning started, too, for a bombing raid on the Italian naval facilities at Massawa which would take place as soon Italy entered the war. During this time, "C" Flight continued with anti-submarine patrols over convoys in the Red Sea.

The *Akbar* docked at Port Sudan on 24 May and for the next week all the Squadron personnel were busy with the defences for the airfield, town and harbour and getting the Squadron ready for operations. It was also an opportunity for everyone to acclimatise themselves to the intense heat and stifling humidity of Port Sudan. Conditions there were far from comfortable: almost everyone was affected by prickly heat and working on aircraft was made difficult because any exposed metal soon became hot enough to burn flesh if it was touched. When a consignment of winter mittens mistakenly arrived a little later, they were gratefully received by the engine fitters as a way of protecting their hands from hot metal! The officers found accommodation in the Red Sea Hotel, the only hotel in the small town, while NCOs had the benefit of open-sided huts; however the airmen were left to find what shelter they could until more sheds could be built for them.

However, for all the discomfort, Sgt Wimsett recalled that "for entertainment there were visits to Port Sudan where there were Bars, Cafes, and one Cinema. The standard of Cafe food was good and one could have literally as much as one could eat for about the equivalent of 20p. There was a swimming pool at the Hotel and a Sailing Club was started with two boats, donated by local residents. In the various Messes, beer was available and there was no shortage of cigarettes."

The tension with Italy had steadily increased through early 1940 and it only became a matter of time before war was declared. On 10 June the Italian liner MV

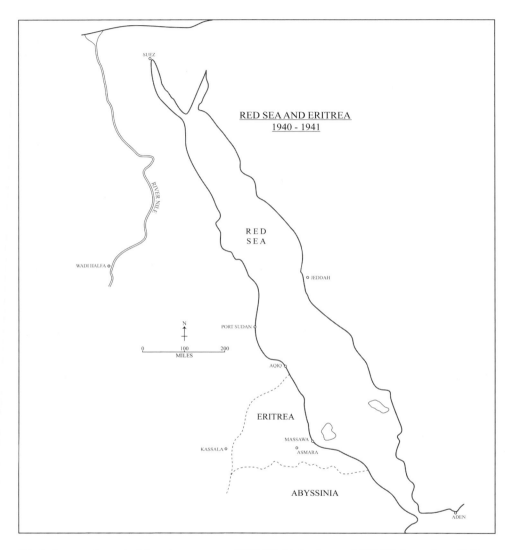

Umbria was boarded by the crews of HMS *Grimsby* and HMS *Leander* off Port Sudan, where it was forced to anchor. A little after 1700 hrs, and plainly visible to all at Port Sudan, the *Umbria* started to settle in the water: she had been scuttled by her captain who had just heard that Italy had just declared war on Great Britain. The following morning 14 Squadron's Wellesleys were bombed up ready for the pre-planned attack on Massawa. During the day 223 Squadron attacked the fighter aerodrome at Gura and 47 Squadron the airfield at Asmara. But for the moment, 14 Squadron's aircraft remained on the ground.

Massawa

Selway's planning for the attack had been meticulous: in particular he had put much thought into the timing. In order to achieve surprise he had decided to make his attack from the east shortly after sunset so that his aircraft would be invisible to the defenders against the night sky, but there would still be enough light when looking westwards for pilots to able to pick out their aiming points easily. With the blessing of "Black Mac", it was agreed that regardless of any time specified in orders, 14 Squadron's attack would take place at the first sunset after war was declared.

The main aiming point was to be the naval bulk fuel storage on the edge of Otumlo airfield, about 2 miles inland from the naval docks, which would be vulnerable to a mixture of 20-and 40-pound fragmentation bombs mixed with 4-pound incendiaries. This target would be attacked at low level by the first wave of three aircraft. The second wave following ten minutes later would drop 250-pound bombs on the airfield buildings from 2,000 feet and ten minutes after that the third wave, flying at 4,000 feet and also armed with 250-pounders, would mop up anything that was left.

At 1600 hrs Selway took off with his crew of Sgt J J W Mildren[29] and LAC A B Lund[30]. On his wing were Sgt Brown with LAC Fell and Sgt L A J Patey[31] with LAC Greaves. Climbing to ten thousand feet, Selway led his formation[32] on a southeasterly track for the two-and-a-half hour transit to Massawa. Ten minutes later the second wave[33], comprising Fg Off Soderholm, with LAC Hawson, Sgt Wimsett with LACs Hughes and Turgoose and Sgt Gilmore, with LAC F Williams, followed. They, in turn, were trailed[34] by Flt Lt A T Irvine[35] with Sgt B L Trayhurn[36], Fg Off LeCavalier and Fg Off R P B H Plunkett with Cpls D N Allfree[37] and Hughes.

Approaching Massawa, Selway descended to the dropping altitude of five hundred feet, opened the bomb doors and selected the arming switches. As darkness fell, at exactly 1830 hrs, he found the target and pressed home his attack. "I think my second container load hit the target," he reported, "for on the 'C-r-ump!' there was an immediate bright flash from under my wings, and over my shoulder I could see the glow of a petrol fire starting. The firework display by the anti-aircraft barrage of all colours was most impressive. Either Mildren or Lund had left his microphone on and all I heard as we went through all the fireworks was 'Ker-ist! Ker-ist!' in a low voice. Suddenly it was all over and we were climbing up seawards to head for home."

For Sgt Patey, who was following Selway, "there was no difficulty finding the target area, the light conditions being just sufficient to see the target. On the run in to the target the height was so low that I could see personnel standing in the entrances to the hangars. Our arrival must have caught them by surprise ... the first load of bombs was on target because fire immediately started as we broke formation in readiness for the [second] run-in. By the time we had started our second run it was quite dark and it seemed as if all hell had broken loose: tracer and 'flaming onions' together with flashes from the heavier calibre guns from the naval ships in the harbour lit the sky. Being the first experience of this sort of thing it was quite frightening to fly into to drop our remaining bombs ... and it seemed as if any aircraft going in at the height we were flying would be shot to pieces"

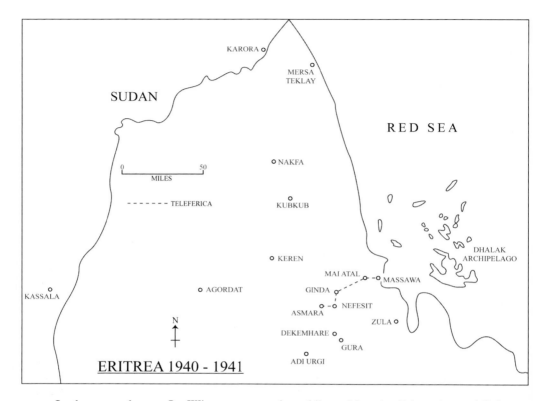

ERITREA 1940 - 1941

In the second wave Sgt Wimsett remembered "watching the flak and searchlights as our flight approached Massawa and thinking how pretty the flak looked: it was sufficiently dark to show up in red and green. On arrival the flak seemed to be going above our height, probably up to 5-6,000 feet but we also saw tracers coming up at us from small arms fire from the ground ... when we actually arrived the daylight had gone, but we could see the hangars and airfield clearly illuminated by the dump fire and several smaller fires around the airfield. Our Flight went into line astern, opened bomb doors and selected the bombs for dropping – four 250-pounders. I believe I dropped mine on a hangar on the north side of the airfield and turned south round the airfield and harbour with the air gunner enjoying himself at the back by firing at items on the ground. Coming back up the coast we did not see another aircraft until we crossed the Sudan border, when all aircraft had been briefed to switch on navigation lights. It then seemed that we were surrounded by aircraft"

The Wellesleys landed back at Port Sudan six hours after they had taken off to an enthusiastic reception from the rest of the Squadron. With well-earned beers in hand, the crews inspected the aircraft for damage – but despite the heavy barrage only three Wellesleys had been hit. However, the post-raid euphoria was muted by the loss of one aircraft: Plunkett's aircraft[38] had not returned.

But there was to be a happy ending: just after lunchtime the following day, a Wellesley touched down at Port Sudan. It was Plunkett. While returning northwards from the raid, he became unsure as to whether or not he had flown past Port Sudan and decided to land until daylight. After dropping a parachute flare, he landed on the shoreline where he and his crew slept until the morning.

That afternoon a reconnaissance sortie flown over Massawa at 20,000 feet by Fg Off LeCavalier revealed the damage to the fuel depot: nearly 8,000 tons of fuel had been destroyed by the previous night's raid. A follow-up raid by six aircraft was planned for 13 June, but it was cancelled when a thick haze of blowing sand and dust cloaked the airfield. The poor weather continued into the following day, but it did not prevent Flt Lt Stapleton from launching in the early morning for a reconnaissance of the Italian bases at Agordat, Asmara, Gura and Massawa. Nor did it, a few hours later, prevent Flt Lt Irvine and Fg Off Plunkett taking off on an unauthorised and ill-conceived raid on Massawa. Irvine had thought that the Wellesley would make an ideal single-seat dive bomber and had managed to persuade Plunkett to help him to put this hare-brained theory to the test. Taking two Wellesleys[39], they took off at 1530 hrs. The first part of the plan went well, with successful dive attacks completed. However, as they left the target area Fg Off Plunkett was shot down by an Italian fighter. Selway took a dim view of Irvine's recklessness and sent him back to Amman that evening.

Another raid was flown against Massawa on the morning of 16 June. Once again Selway led[40], with Fg Offs Soderholm, R R Helsby[41], Sgts Patey and Norris. The target was an array of corrugated metal sheds at Acico, just to the south of the port of Massawa itself, which were believed to shelter barrels of oil. Selway's formation carried out two runs over the target, dropping a mixture of 20- and 40-pound bombs, but in contrast to the first dusk attack there were no visible results.

The "Flying Fortress"

On this raid one enemy fighter was seen some distance away, and although it did not venture any closer, it triggered Selway's inventive mind into a way to improve the Wellesley's defensive armament. He had already augmented the Wellesley's single Lewis gun in the rear cockpit by adding another downward-facing Lewis gun which fired through a camera hatch in the rear fuselage floor, but he was still concerned that if the Italian fighter pilots realised how lightly defended the Wellesleys were, they would press their attacks more closely. The best way to keep the Italians at a distance, he reasoned, was to hose them with tracer bullets from as many guns as possible. The problem of how best to do this was put to the "C" Flight's Flt Sgt E T Crouch[42] with Sgts Mildren, D Farrell and B M D'Arcy[43]. Their solution was to use the small triangular windows on either side of the fuselage above the wing as gun ports. The windows were hinged at the top and could be opened inwards and upwards, leaving an opening about three feet wide by one foot deep. The Sudan Railways workshops manufactured mountings which allowed a Lewis gun on either side which could cover an arc from propeller to tailplane and could be elevated from wing level to about seventy degrees upwards. The mounting incorporated a shaped frame around the window which acted as a stop-guide to prevent gunners from accidentally shooting the aircraft structure. With this modification a formation of five Wellesleys would be able to fire twenty guns at a potential attacker! There no extra aircrew available to man the new guns, so the word went out for volunteers and the call was enthusiastically answered from the cookhouse, orderly room and administrative trades.

The war came to Port Sudan just after lunchtime on 18 June with a bombing raid by three Italian SM79s. They dropped twenty-four bombs from high level onto the northern quays in the harbour, but caused little damage. At about the same time an Italian submarine was seen on the surface about ten miles from the harbour, and made to engage one of the port tugs. However, as soon as the bombing started, the submarine dived. This episode caused great interest in "C" Flight because it showed them that their anti-submarine work over the convoys was not, as some may have thought, wasted. Three days later Fg Off MacKenzie landed from an anti-submarine patrol and reported that he had spotted a large oil slick near Barra Musa Kebir, an island approximately seventy-five miles south of Port Sudan. While investigating further, he had seen about thirty men on the island itself. It seemed likely that the men were Italians of some description, since there were no known British forces in

A close up of the locally produced gun mounting on the fuselage windows on Sqn Ldr Selway's Mk II Wellesley at Port Sudan. It was hoped that window-mounted Lewis guns firing tracer would scare off the Italian fighter pilots!

the area. The following day two tugs and a platoon of soldiers were dispatched to bring them in. MacKenzie also flew back to the island at dawn to drop a message to them to see if he could elicit any information about who they were. When MacKenzie confirmed by radio that the men were indeed Italians, Selway and Stapleton set off in the Squadron's Walrus amphibian to make their own assessment of what to do next. As the Walrus arrived at Barra Musa Kebir, they could clearly see the oil slick which MacKenzie had reported, still rising from the seabed. However the island itself was now completely – and mysteriously – deserted. Much later it transpired that the men whom MacKenzie had spotted were the crew of the Italian *Adua*-class submarine *Macallè*, which had sunk after running aground on the reef at Barra Musa Kebir six days earlier. By incredible coincidence, they had been rescued by another submarine, the *Guglielmotti*, in between MacKenzie's morning reconnaissance and the arrival of the Walrus.

The first opportunity to try out the newly up-gunned Wellesleys came on 24 June in a raid against the aerodrome buildings at Asmara. Unserviceabilities had left both 14 and 47 Squadrons short of aircraft, so it was decided that the raid should be made by a joint formation of five aircraft from each unit. Selway had already shown Sqn Ldr J G Elton[44], OC 47 Squadron, his "Flying Fortresses" as he called them, and the two men had agreed tactics to work together. Elton would lead a vic of five 47 Squadron aircraft at 15,000 feet and Selway, also leading a vic of five, would rendezvous with them over Suakin (about thirty miles south of Port Sudan). Here Selway would slot in behind and 500 feet below Elton's formation so that he was directly below the last two 47 Squadron aircraft. Selway's formation[45], comprising the three Canadians Fg Off LeCavalier, Soderholm and W D Matthew[46] plus Sgt Patey, took off at 0900 hrs and joined Elton's Flight as planned. As they approached Asmara, Elton started a steady dive to 11,000 feet (just over 4,000 feet above the airfield in the mountainous country at Asmara) for weapon release. Selway had dropped back for the attack, but he had arranged for Elton to slow down as he left the target area so that he could catch up again and re-establish the defensive formation. The raid ran like clockwork and the only Italian fighter to be seen kept well clear.

After the success of the first joint attack it was decided to try once again on 26 June. Selway led the same team and the plan was very similar to the previous raid, except that the bombs would be dropped from 1,200 feet above the aerodrome. This time the Wellesleys were greeted with heavy anti-aircraft fire as they approached Asmara and four CR42 fighters attempted to engage the 47 Squadron formation as they dived towards the target. The CR42s closed in as the ten Wellesleys started to head homewards. According to Selway "the CR42s were doing beam and stern attacks firing tracer. One of them dived underneath me and pulled up well ahead and up into a half loop and fired at me as he came back completely upside down ... he – or one of the others – was quite a good shot. There was suddenly a very strong smell of petrol and Mildren said 'Sir, there's petrol pouring into the belly of the fuselage from somewhere and it's nearly ankle deep!' and indeed the fumes were so powerful that I wondered they could put me out. I told Mildren to switch off all electrics and to stop firing the guns and that he and Lund were to prepare to bale out if I said so. I undid my straps, opened my sliding hood and the little side door and stood up and perched on the side of the cockpit and tried to keep the Wellesley straight and level with one hand. My team drew closer in formation and watched me with some concern ... fortunately there was no spark and no hot pipe and therefore no fire and after about five minutes Mildren said 'I think it's going down'. Apparently we had lost most if not all of the fuel in the starboard wing and so I had to watch out for the engine cutting. In any other aeroplane it would have meant a landing in enemy territory but not with the Wellesley with its vast reserves of fuel." Selway landed safely at Port Sudan, but not only had the Italian bullets had shot through the main fuel lines in the starboard wing, they had also torn a hole in the main tubular girder for the wing spar. Additionally there was an eight-inch hole made by a shell splinter which had just missed the control runs in the tail-box. Two other aircraft had been hit and the gunners reported that all together seven CR42s had been involved in the engagement; one of these had been driven off with smoke coming from it, while a second appeared to go down out of control. The aircrews later found out that the reason their extra guns had not had the intended "frightening effect" on the Italian fighter pilots was because they had not been loaded, as originally envisaged, with tracer rounds. In fact these were hard to come by and were not available for some time.

In the absence of anyone to enforce engineering regulations, the Squadron's engineers had a remarkably free hand in effecting repairs. Their work was closely overseen by Flt Sgt Crouch whose initiative and fine judgement was much respected. Crouch's contacts at the Sudan Railways workshops also proved invaluable when it came to making replacement steel tubes or fashioning sleeves to slip over damaged spars. In Selway's words "we had complete confidence in him and his great common sense." His locally made modifications were known a "Crouch Mods" rather than the usual term of "Air Ministry Mods."

Offensive action was curtailed for the next few days after a submarine was sighted near the Sangeneb lighthouse, which marked a reef on the approaches to Port Sudan. Anti-submarine patrols were flown on the following days and on 29 June the Italian air force revisited Port Sudan. Early that morning Wimsett was "aroused by the sound of bombs falling on the airfield. We adjourned to our slit trenches and were most amused at the sight of Flt Sgt Johns (of "B" Flt) who had slept in the nude – and was rather portly – clutching a blanket to himself like a Venus disturbed at the Bath. Overhead we saw a SM81 at about 6,000 feet, but what we did not know, was that the two Gladiators which had been detached to Port Sudan, were airborne. As we watched the Gladiators attacked the SM81, which exploded in a ball of white flame." This time "K" Flight's Gladiators were able to catch the raiders and Plt Off J Hamlyn[47] had dispatched the SM81 which Wimsett and his colleagues had witnessed.

The next day Selway led another attempt to destroy the fuel storage at Acico. With his flagship still under repair, he set off[48] accompanied by the Wing Navigation Officer Sqn Ldr C R Taylor[49]. With him were Plt Offs R J Willitts[50], T G Rhodes[51] and Sgt Wimsett, each armed with 250-pound bombs and 25-pound incendiaries; a fifth aeroplane which was also to have joined them was unserviceable. The formation arrived over their target fifteen minutes after a raid by 223 Squadron and made a diving attack from 11,000 feet down to 3,000 feet. Although all the crews were confident that they had dropped accurately it was difficult to assess the damage. On the return journey, after having bit hit several times by anti-aircraft fire over the target, Taylor reported to Selway that a strange object, like a black metal bowl, had appeared in the aircraft. On landing they were assured by Flt Sgt Johns that it was not part of some new Italian secret weapon, but merely the cover of the aircraft dynamo which had been blown off by a shell splinter!

On 3 July three Wellesleys took off for a photographic reconnaissance sortie over Zula (about thirty miles south of Massawa), Dekemhare (a similar distance south of Asmara), Gura, Asmara and Massawa. Two of the aircraft were fitted with cameras: one with vertical cameras and colour film, the other with oblique cameras with infrared film. One of the objects of the sortie was to find out if the aerodrome at Zula was being used to disperse aircraft from Asmara and Massawa to keep them safe from the RAF bombing raids. Fg Off Soderholm led the flight[52], escorted by Plt Off J A Ferguson[53] and A J Smith[54]. Just after they had made their run over Dekemhare, Soderholm turned sharply and was seen to go into some thin cloud. The other two pilots lost sight of him and continued on to Massawa before returning to Port Sudan. It was later discovered that Soderholm had been shot down by a CR42, killing him and his crew of Sgt Trayhurn and Flt Sgt J C Dawson[55].

The reconnaissance sortie had brought back enough information to plan a raid on Zula, but the weather for the next two days was too bad to fly the mission. On 5 July the weather cleared sufficiently for Flt Lt C G S Robinson[56] to lead five aircraft[57] there. The raid was unopposed and the formation dropped a mixture of 250-pounders, 40-pound anti-personnel bombs and incendiaries from 500 feet on aircraft dispersed across the airfield. Two SM79s received direct hits but it was difficult to assess how much damage had been caused to others by shrapnel. The crews also reported that the jetties at Zula were covered with stores and petrol tins and ripe for another attack. Unfortunately the weather closed in again the next day when Fg Off Helsby led a formation of five aircraft back to Zula, and they had to return soon after take-off.

Convoy Escort

At the beginning of July the convoy BN1 started its northbound passage up the Red Sea. The convoy comprising five tankers, a naval supply ship and three merchant vessels, was escorted by the cruisers HMS *Leander* and HMS *Carlisle* plus two destroyers. 14 Squadron would be responsible for seeing the convoy through the critical part of its journey past Massawa to Port Sudan. The plan was for a relay of aircraft from "C" Flight to maintain a continuous presence over the convoy. To achieve this task, sortie lengths of around six or seven hours would be needed; all this at an altitude of 1,000 feet, where the air was hot and where intense concentration was needed, would be exhausting for pilots. Stapleton therefore planned that each

Looking in a north-westerly direction at smoke amongst the hangars and airfield buildings at Asmara airfield during a low-level raid by 14 Squadron Wellesleys on 20 July 1940. During this raid Flt Lt Robinson's engine stopped completely for a few moments.

Wellesley would carry two pilots so that the workload could be shared. Although the Wellesley was a single pilot aircraft, it was possible to change pilots in flight. If the pilot's seat was unlocked it could be fully reclined so it was possible for the pilot to wriggle backwards into the fuselage, while his relief leaned over him holding the controls. Once there was enough room, the relief pilot could then climb carefully forward into the cockpit, all the while holding the controls, while his predecessor locked the seat in place behind him.

The first aircraft[58] airborne at 0300 hrs on 8 July was flown by Plt Off R A Green and Sgt Norris with Sgt Farrell acting as gunner, and an hour and a half later it was followed[59] by Plt Off MacKenzie and Rhodes with LAC W J MacConnell[60]. Three more aircraft under Sgt Burcher, Flt Lt Stapleton and Sgt Moulton continued the relay throughout the day. Over the Red Sea the flying conditions were difficult in poor visibility, but the Wellesleys were able to remain on station clearing the route ahead of the ships. At 1105 hrs Green, Norris and Farrell took off for their second sortie, eventually completing twelve-and-a-half hours flying in the day; MacKenzie, Rhodes and MacConnell also flew a second sortie, landing at Port Sudan at 1930 hrs.

Meanwhile Flt Lt Robinson led five aircraft[61] of "B" Flight on a diversionary bombing raid on the jetties at Zula, with the intention of keeping the Italians busy and hopefully stopping them from interfering with the convoy. As Robinson led his formation homeward over the Dahlak archipelago, he saw a SM81 heading south at low level, presumably returning from a search for the convoy. Putting his formation into line astern, Robinson led them in a diving attack on the enemy aircraft. "I dived after it," reported Robinson, "for it was low over the sea and gave it a long burst from my front gun. Then I overtook it and turned round it to give my chaps a chance to have a go with all their rear guns … eventually we drove it down into the sea where it crashed with a great splash." The high speed dive proved too much for Willitt's aircraft[62] and its windscreen blew in, leaving Willits with a nasty cut above his eye. With blood pouring from the wound, Willitts had to land on Aqiq island, just over the border to dress it. He was rescued by Robinson with a fresh crew later in the evening.

During the second day of its transit, the convoy was much closer to Port Sudan, so the "C" Flight crews reverted to the normal crew constitution of just one pilot. Sgt Dickson lifted off the runway at 0350 hrs to continue the escort[63]. He was followed at intervals by Sgt B T Hopkins[64], Stapleton, Sgt T W G Morren[65] and lastly MacKenzie who landed at Port Sudan at 1606 hrs on completion of the task.

Another joint raid with 47 Squadron raid on Massawa was thwarted by thick cloud over the target area on 10 July. Rather than bring their bombs back the aircraft dropped 18,000 pounds of bombs on the small Italian listening post at Mersa Tek'lay on the coast just on the Eritrean side of the border. Two days later a rather more successful raid was mounted on the airfield at Otumlo by four aircraft[66] led by Flt Lt Stapleton with another five from 47 Squadron. This time, though the Italian defences were ready for them and they were met by heavy anti-aircraft fire. There were fighters in the air, too, and one of the 47 Squadron aircraft was shot down. Four days later it was Flt Lt Robinson's turn to lead the Wing to Asmara airfield. Once again there was a stiff reception and once again 47 Squadron lost an aeroplane. Robinson revisited Asmara, at low level this time, with five aircraft[67] on 20 July. Just after he had dropped his bombs, Robinson's aircraft was hit in the engine which stopped completely. After a few heart stopping moments, the engine burst back into life. Robinson managed to get back to Aqiq before it stopped again. He was setting up to carry out a forced landing on the island when, once again, the engine started again and ran smoothly all the way to Port Sudan.

Two more raids, on 23[68] and 25[69] July were led by Flt Lt Stapleton against targets at Massawa. On the first of these the Wellesleys were attacked by a CR42 about ten minutes after they had left the target. The fighter was engaged by the rear gunners and a large flash was seen on the starboard side of its engine, after which the CR42 seemed to stall and fall away. Italian radio announced later that evening that one of their aircraft had been shot down.

Western Eritrea

At the beginning of July 1940 Italian army units had crossed into Sudan from Eritrea and seized the border town of Kassala. On the afternoon of 4 July 14 Squadron's aircraft had been put on standby to attack the Italian positions near Kassala during the initial Italian advance, but the plan was cancelled because of the poor weather. Fortunately the Italians had not pushed any further forward into Sudan, as the country was only lightly defended by ground troops. The presence of the Italians was a major threat to the rest of the country and they would have to be ejected in due course, but for the time being there was nothing that the military authorities could do but await reinforcement. In the meantime, British offensive action in Eritrea was limited to what could be achieved by the RAF Wellesley squadrons: attacks on targets at Massawa and Asmara and interdiction of the lines of communication between Asmara and Kassala. Since the beginning of July, 14 Squadron had been operating almost exclusively against Massawa and Asmara, with the exception of two reconnaissance missions mounted halfway through the month looking for military activity along the road between Karora and Keren.

At the end of the month, 254 Wing started a bombing campaign which, it was hoped, would drive the Italian colonial troops from their positions at Kassala back towards Keren. At 0730 hrs on 30 July Flt Lt Robinson led three aircraft from "B" Flight[70] to attack troops near the railway station. The formation achieved direct hits on buildings thought to contain troops, but they were badly shot up by machine guns and Robinson's air gunner, Sgt Allfree, received a serious head wound. The formation arrived back at Port Sudan at midday as Plt Off Green's second wave from "A" Flight[71] was about to set off. Green's formation did not encounter the heavy fire that had greeted "B" Flight and one pilot claimed a direct hit on an enemy machine gun post. As they left the target area they saw a formation from another squadron taking their place. The following morning Sgt Norris was tasked to carry out a photo-reconnaissance of Kassala from 800 feet[72]. By the time he arrived there, the second day's bombing had already started and a flight of Blenheims from 45 Squadron were attacking the station. Plt Off Green with Plt Off Matthew and Sgt E E Blofield[73] were also on their way to bomb the fort at Kassala[74]. The maximum bomb load for a Wellesley was 1,000 pounds and this was normally achieved by loading two 250-pound bombs into each of the bomb canisters. However a 500-pound bomb is virtually the same size as a 250-pounder and on this raid each aircraft was loaded with four 500-pound bombs in order to maximise the damage to the fort walls. Although the Wellesleys were theoretically overloaded by 1,000 pounds, the three aircraft took off easily from Port Sudan and the pilots reported no handling difficulties. There was no opposition to their attack and they successfully bombed storehouses in the fort complex.

Back to Convoy Work

Over the next three weeks, three more convoys required escorting through the Red Sea. The twelve merchantmen and six escorts of BN2 were intercepted eighty miles east of Massawa an hour after dawn on 1 August by Sgt Hopkins[75]. Over the course of the next two days, five more aircraft operated in a relay to escort the convoy during daylight hours as it sailed northwards.

Two weeks later the second southbound convoy, BS2, of two ships was escorted past Massawa by a relay of six double-crewed aircraft which kept a dawn to dusk vigil over the convoy. During their patrol[76], Plt Off LeCavalier and Sgt Norris drifted over Harmil, the northernmost island of the Dahlak archipelago. Here by chance they discovered a previously-unknown Italian airfield, which they reported on their return. They were relieved on station[77] by Sgts Patey and J R Taylor[78] who left the convoy at dusk and returned to Port Sudan at around 1900 hrs, only to find the place in darkness and an enemy air raid in full swing. The aerodrome controller signalled by Aldiss lamp that they should switch their lights off and leave the area until it was safe to return. Eventually they landed at Port Sudan after nine hours' flight.

BS2 was followed five days later by the northbound BN3, which, with fifteen merchantmen and two tankers, was the largest convoy to date. Flt Lt Stapleton and Plt Off Green took off[79] from Port Sudan at 0315 hrs to rendezvous with the convoy which had entered 14 Squadron's area of responsibility during the previous night. Once again a relay of six aircraft was mounted throughout the day to see the convoy safely northwards. Just before 1700 hrs, as dusk approached, came the event most dreaded by anyone operating a single-engined aircraft far out over the sea: an engine failure. One of the sparking plugs in blew out and Sgt Burcher found that he could not maintain altitude. With few options available to him, Burcher managed to ditch the aircraft[80] two hundred yards ahead of HMS *Kimberley*. The Wellesley floated well enough for Burcher, Dickson and Farrell to scramble out and climb into their dinghy, before they were rescued ten minutes later by the warship. Four more aircraft continued the escort the following day until the convoy sailed into safe waters.

Massawa Continued

Although 14 Squadron's primary task during August 1940 was that of convoy duty, the Squadron continued to participate in the interdiction of Italian oil reserves at Massawa. On 4 August, Flt Lt Stapleton led five Wellesleys[81] to join a Wing attack on the submarine base at Massawa. Approaching the harbour from overland, the plan was for the 47 Squadron Wellesleys to attack Sheikh Zeyad island from high level and the 14 Squadron formation to dive bomb the fuel dump at Otumlo from 3,000 feet. While the two Wellesley raids occupied the defenders and diverted their attention to the west, a flight of Blenheims from 45 Squadron would approach at low level from over the sea and bomb the submarines. All went according to plan and the Wellesleys attracted heavy anti-aircraft fire during their attack.

As they left the target area Sgt Patey heard "a terrific bang as my aircraft[82] was hit. The undercarriage lowered itself because the hydraulic system had been damaged and I immediately fell behind the other four aircraft. At the same time I felt the pain in my left arm and saw blood appear on my white flying overalls just above the elbow. The arm became numb and started to swell and I found I had difficulty using it, so it was a question of doing everything with my right hand. I found I could cope quite well so I decided to get clear of the target and and set a course for base." But things then took a turn for the worse... "about twenty miles north of Massawa two aircraft were sighted coming from astern and these turned out to be CR42 fighters. They decided to attack almost together from the astern quarters, one on each side, which made it difficult for my gunner who could only engage one aircraft at a time. As my speed was so low it was no use trying to get away from them, so I decided to prevent the fighters from making any attacks from underneath by diving down to within a few feet of the sea and staying there." Meanwhile Patey's crew of LACs Greaves and Martin, both of whom were ground crew volunteers, fought off the CR42s. While one manned the Lewis gun, the other kept him supplied with full magazines. "During their later attacks," continued Patey, "I could see splashes where bullets were entering the sea ahead of me. Things were beginning to look bad because I could see my aircraft had received quite a number of hits in the vicinity of the fuel tanks, when suddenly the fighters broke off their attacks and flew off." With just enough fuel remaining to reach base, Patey continued northwards and made a belly landing at Port Sudan before fainting from loss of blood. Luckily his wound was not, in the end, serious and he was able to return to flying duties shortly afterwards.

The Squadron also visited Massawa on 9 August (five aircraft led by Flt Lt Robinson) and 15 August (again, five aircraft this time led by Sqn Ldr Selway). Robinson also led a raid on naval facilities on Dahlak Kebir, the largest of the Dahlak islands on 22 August. At the head of five aircraft[83] he headed for Nocra, at the mouth of the large lagoon on Dahlak Kebir. Unfortunately, the weather over the southern Dahlak was poor, and unable to find the buildings he was tasked against, Robinson instead led his flight to Harmil. Here the formation dropped to 1,000 feet to strafe and bomb troops, expecting little opposition. But they were surprised when the Italians put up a spirited resistance and one burst of machine gun fire ripped into Willitts' aircraft, instantly killing his gunner Sgt A H W Matthews[84]. Another burst hit one of the other aircraft smashing its windshield, with the result that three aircraft had to divert to Aqiq for makeshift repairs before continuing home. Harmil would have to be treated with more respect in future.

Jebel Uweinat – a Secret Mission

Late on the night of 18 July Wing HQ had advised that Italian long-range aircraft were due to land at Agordat early the following morning. The Italians had been carrying out these flights for some time: transport aircraft carrying a complete – but disassembled – CR42 fighter, plus other urgent spares and supplies, were leaving Benghazi in the evening and refuelling somewhere in the desert before arriving in Eritrea in the early hours. Since these flights were carried out in darkness they were immune from interference by British fighters. The plan was to surprise them on the ground before they could return to Benghazi. At 0400 hrs, Flt Lt Stapleton took off in the lead of five aircraft[85] and headed towards Agordat. The formation achieved complete surprise and found three SM79s on the airfield. With only light ground fire, the formation split up to make individual attacks on the aircraft and airfield buildings. Two SM79s were believed to have been damaged, along with a number of airfield buildings, but the extent of the damage could not be judged because of the amount of dust caused by the bombs.

Despite its apparent success of the attack on Agordat airfield in mid-July, Italian transport aircraft continued to use the route regularly. By mid-August the staff at HQ Middle East had located the desert staging post, at Jebel Uweinat, and decided that another attempt should be made to cut the route, this time by attacking the transport aircraft on the ground as they refuelled. However, this would be no easy task: the Jebel Uweinat is a 6,000 foot-high outcrop which lies on the Libyan/Sudanese border just over four hundred miles due west of Wadi Halfa. Between the Wadi and the Jebel was a desert where, in Stapleton's words "God had taken a rest from creation. Nothing except the world's largest supply of sand and rock. No villages, water nor vegetation; trackless, barren, harsh and featureless."

Timing for an attack would be critical, since there would be a window of only about an hour while aircraft were on the ground and while there was enough daylight. Clearly, a raid on a pinpoint target after a flight over four hundred miles of featureless desert would test both the navigational skills of the crews and the long reach of the Wellesley to the full. With this in mind, Black Mac chose the crews of 14 Squadron's "C" Flight to carry out the raid: their expertise in long-range navigation, gained on the convoy patrols over the Red Sea, made them ideally suited to the task. In great secrecy, Flt Lt Stapleton led his Flight to Wadi Halfa on 24 August accompanied by Sqn Ldr Selway. For everyone involved it was a treat to escape from the unpleasant climate of Port Sudan and to enjoy the relative luxury of a hotel overlooking the second cataract of the Nile. Here they waited for the call which would tell them the Italians were on the way.

A series of codewords were intended to keep the 14 Squadron crews updated: "Cointreau" followed by a number would indicate the number of aircraft that had arrived at Tripoli from Italy. "Martini" followed by a time would inform the crews that the Italians had taken off from Tripoli and give their ETA for Jebel Uweinat. Finally, "Gin and Tonic" was the order to execute the attack. After two days of waiting and no sign of "Cointreau" or "Martini", an urgent call of "Gin and Tonic" came just after 1300 hrs. The crews rushed out to their aircraft and with Stapleton once again at the head of five aircraft[86], they headed due west. The Wellesleys were fully armed with a mix of 40-pound fragmentation bombs, incendiaries and metal spikes designed to shred tyres. In this configuration they carried only enough fuel for eight hours flight. With a flying time of almost four hours to the target area and virtually the same on the return, success would depend on the absolute accuracy of Stapleton's flying and of Sgt Dickson's navigation.

"The weather was kind," recalled Stapleton, "clear blue skies, visibility good, some ominous streams of sand scuffing the surface. In the last fifty miles the flight dropped down to low level to make an approach. At the going down of the sun, the silhouette of the conical mountain came up on cue – a jagged pile of an extinct volcano, sandblasted to a core of red and beige vertically cracked rocks. The aircraft slotted into line astern, all safety switches locked to 'off' and the airfield in the lee of the mountain appeared dead ahead in the centre of the windshield. The navigators had done their stuff." The plan was to strafe the Italian aircraft using the front gun, then come round for a second pass dropping the incendiaries and fragmentation bombs, before sowing the spikes across the landing strip and then heading for home. However it was not to be. Stapleton saw "the windsock – a somewhat tattered edition... the refuelling pumps... the landing strips, but no aircraft. All this grinding flight and there was nothing, not even a building, a shed or any transport on the place to receive explosive frustration!" A truck appeared near the airstrip and this was bombed and strafed, but with nothing else to attack, the formation dropped its bombs and wheeled eastwards. There followed a tedious four-hour flight through the darkness aiming for Wadi Halfa, another small and easily missed pinpoint amongst a vast wilderness. At 2130 hrs, the crews were rewarded – and relieved – by the sight of runway flares glimmering in the desert ahead of them. They touched down with tanks almost empty after seven-and-a-half hours flying: the engine of one aircraft stopped as it taxied in.

Later it was discovered that five SM79s had taken off from Benghazi, but were forced back after running into a sandstorm which caused three of the aircraft to crash in the desert. News of the attack at Jebel Uweinat persuaded the Italian authorities that the route had been compromised and although the "Gin and Tonic" raid had not been as destructive as had been hoped, it was nevertheless successful in closing down the resupply route.

Night Bombing

Three months of hard operational flying in the harsh environment of Port Sudan had taken its toll of Wellesleys across 254 Wing. The shortage of spare parts for a type that was no longer in production and the lack of replacement aircraft were becoming a problem. The loss of two more 14 Squadron aircraft in combat during early September did not help matters. On 1 September, a Wellesley[87] flown by Sgt Norris with Sgt D'Arcy and LAC C Lampard[88] had taken off at 0600 hrs to photograph Harmil island. After completing two runs over the island at 26,000 feet, Norris turned for a third run. "Halfway down the third leg," reported Norris, "we were attacked by three CR42s. The first burst of 20mm cannon fire hit Lampard in the leg and damaged the engine controls and hydraulics... I had no engine and nowhere to go except down. Ahead was a quite small island, rocky and uneven. I set up a classic forced landing approach, but there was a danger of overshooting into the oggin. With no flaps, we almost stalled over the shoreline and I shoved the port wing and bomb carrier into the rocky ground a quickly came to a rest. Before I could undo my straps and chute, the aircraft was surrounded by an unruly mob of Italians ... I left the aircraft and tried to reach the rear gunner's position but was prevented from doing so. D'Arcy was unable to escape until Lampard had been lifted out and carried away. His leg was almost severed and he was bleeding profusely." Lampard died from his wounds the next day.

The second Wellesley was lost to fighters ten days later during a daylight bombing raid. After dropping on a wood near Kassala which was said to contain Italian motor transport and tanks, a formation of three Wellesleys[89] started the return leg and were intercepted by two CR42s. Plt Off Ferguson's aircraft[90] was shot down in flames and although he managed to parachute to safety his crew-mates, Plt Off J Lynch[91] and Sgt T Conway[92], did not escape from the aircraft and were killed. With Wellesleys now in critically short supply, it was decided at HQ Middle East that the aircraft should be consolidated into two units, 47 and 223 Squadrons, and that 14 Squadron should be re-equipped with Blenheims.

Dwindling numbers of serviceable aircraft made it increasingly difficult to mount daylight raids by large formations. Flt Lt Stapleton led five aircraft against Nocra on 5 September and Fg Off Green led another five against Harmil the next day, but these were the last of the large formations of Wellesleys mounted by 14 Squadron. A new pattern had already been set when Green had carried out a singleton night attack on Massawa in the early hours of 29 August. Approaching Massawa from due south at 0300 hrs, Green shut off his engine and glided towards the naval repair workshops which were his target. Although there was not much moonlight, the coast stood out well and Green was able to identify the target area well enough to drop four 250-pounders and four 25-pound incendiaries onto the buildings. He achieved complete surprise and left the area without a shot being fired at him and with a large fire raging that was still clearly visible from thirty miles away on the return leg. For the next three months, offensive action by the unit's Wellesleys was limited to night attacks carried out by two or three aircraft operating as singletons. The majority of these sorties were part of a sustained campaign by 254 Wing against fuel storage facilities at Gura, with as many as sixteen aircraft from across the Wing raiding each night. Gura was attacked by 14 Squadron aircraft on six nights during September, eleven nights during October and two more nights in November; in addition night raids continued against Massawa and Asmara. The target area at Gura was not always easy to find at night, especially in the autumn weather where thick clouds and frequent thunderstorms often covered the mountains. As a result many of the raids achieved little success, but one or two did manage some spectacular results. On 20 September Sgts Moulton and W J MacConnell hit what they thought must have been an ammunition store, as a furious fire started and they saw blazing objects rolling away from the building.

One of the most successful night raids was against the airfield at Mai Edaga (just south of Gura), carried out by three aircraft on 22 September. Sgt Dickson took off[93] at 2330 hrs, followed half an hour later by Plt Off Rhodes, and a little later by Flt Sgt Patey. Unfortunately, Dickson could not locate the target, so returned home, but Rhodes was guided to the airfield by blazing sheds which had been set alight by a raider from another squadron. By the light of the flames he found a row of CR42s which he bombed with a mix of fragmentation and incendiary bombs, claiming to have destroyed two of them. He then turned his attention to some bomber aircraft which were dispersed around the perimeter of the airfield. These he strafed with his front gun. Close behind him, Patey concentrated on the airfield workshops with his 250- and 500-pound bombs.

The last offensive action by 14 Squadron Wellesleys was carried out on the night of 20 November by Sgt Dickson, with LAC Ritchie, who bombed Gura[94] and Sgt Hopkins, with Sgt Frost, who attacked Massawa.

Arrival of the Blenheim

Meanwhile, the first three Blenheims arrived at Port Sudan on 14 September 1940. Conversion started straight away, under the guidance of Flt Lt N G Birks[95] an experienced Blenheim pilot who had been posted into the unit. After studying the Pilots' Notes for the new aeroplane, pilots either watched from the navigator's seat as Birks demonstrated how to fly the Blenheim, or they flew the aeroplane under Birks' supervision, while he sat next to them. With its streamlined all-metal airframe and two Bristol Mercury engines the Blenheim was a much faster aeroplane than its predecessor and it had better visibility from the cockpit. Operationally, however, the Blenheim offered no improvement in bomb load over the Wellesley and lacked the latter's range; it also lacked the incredible strength of the Wellesley's geodetic construction. Nevertheless the Blenheim was popular amongst the aircrews and ground crews alike, though the latter noticed that the all-metal skin got much hotter than the Wellesley's fabric in the heat of the sun. With temperatures averaging around 115°F in the shade at Port Sudan, such small details took on new importance! While most of the Blenheims were standard bomber aircraft, some of those allocated to the Squadron were the "fighter version" which boasted a pack of four 20mm cannon in front of the bomb bay.

The aircraft were first used in action six days later in a daylight attack on Massawa. Flt Lt Birks led the formation[96], accompanied by Fg Off J K Buchanan DFC[97] and Flt Lt G D Hill[98], against aircraft on the airfield at Otumlo. As he dived towards his target, Birks' aircraft was hit by anti-aircraft fire and his port engine burst into flames. His wingmen saw him make a successful forced landing just north of Massawa and that evening Italian radio reported that he and his crew, Sgt J P Gillespie and Sgt J L B Cheyne[99] had been captured.

In the last week of September, the Squadron ceased operations for three weeks to concentrate on converting crews to the new aircraft type. During this time Selway handed over command of the Squadron to the newly-promoted Sqn Ldr Stapleton. Wellesley operations resumed from 8 October with night raids and anti-submarine patrols, but the Blenheims were not used again operationally until 21 October, when Sgts Hopkins and Hall carried out an anti-submarine patrol[100]. One unfortunate incident occurred during the conversion period on 26 October when a "K" Flight Gladiator mistook Sqn Ldr Stapleton's Blenheim[101] for an Italian SM79. The Gladiator opened fire wounding Stapleton in the wrist and severely damaging the Blenheim. Luckily Stapleton managed to land the aircraft at Port Sudan without loss of life. The Gladiator pilot was sent to apologise to Stapleton as he was treated in hospital, and Stapleton insisted that he drink half a pint of vinegar and tonic water by way of penitence before his apology was accepted!

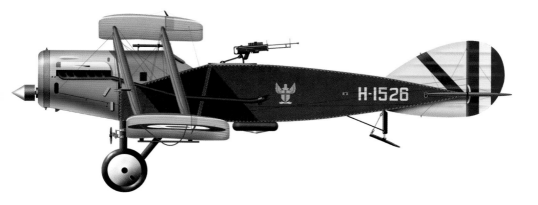

Bristol F2b Fighter H1526, Ramleh 1921.

Bristol F2b Fighter F4712, Ramleh 1924.

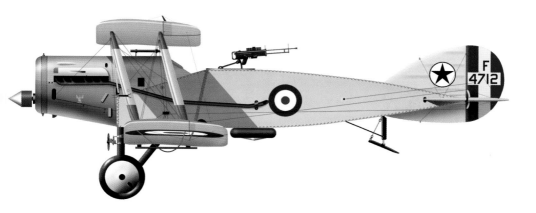

De Havilland DH9A JR7827, Amman 1927.

Fairey IIIF Mk IVM J9826, Amman 1931.

Fairey IIIF Mk IVB K1705, East Africa Cruise 1932.

Fairey Gordon Mk I K2724, Amman 1933.

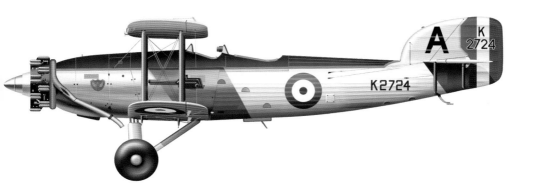

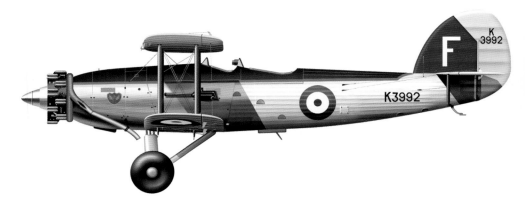

Fairey Gordon Mk II K3992, Amman 1937.

Vickers Wellesley Mk I L2697, Amman 1938.

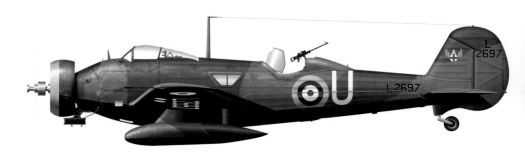

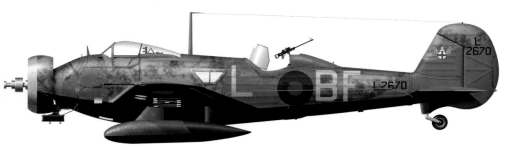

Vickers Wellesley Mk I L2670, Amman 1939.

Vickers Wellesley Mk II L2647, Port Sudan 1940.

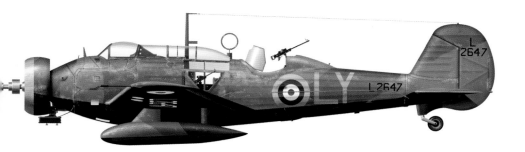

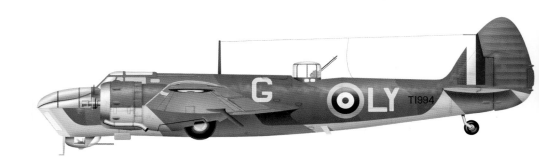

Bristol Blenheim Mk IV T1994, Port Sudan 1941.

Bristol Blenheim Mk IV Z7631, Western Desert 1942.

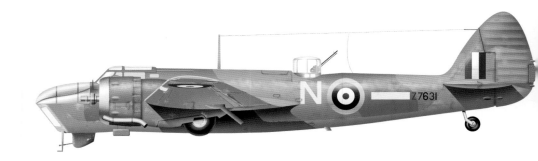

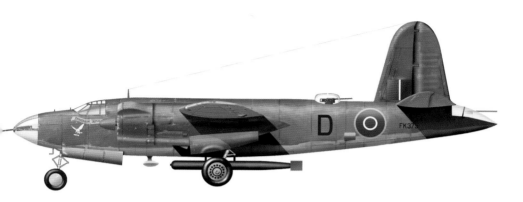

Martin Marauder Mk Ia FK375, Shallufah 1942.

Martin Marauder Mk I FK142, Protville 1943.

Martin Marauder Mk I FK145, Grottaglie 1944.

Vickers Wellington Mk XIV NB869, Chivenor 1945

Bristol Blenheim T1994 flying from Port Sudan in early 1941. The Blenheims also wore the identification letters 'LY' used by 14 Squadron's Wellesleys. (Andrew Thomas)

The start of offensive operations with the Blenheim once more was marked with another three-aircraft raid against warehouses within the naval complex at Massawa, this time led by Flt Lt Buchanan[102] on the last day of the month. The Blenheims encountered little opposition as they delivered their bombs from a shallow dive, and direct hits were scored on four large buildings. Poor weather limited flying over the next few weeks, but Massawa was visited by flights of three aircraft again on 9 and 11 November. These attacks were aimed at the quays and the destroyers berthed there.

The largest Blenheim raid yet was mounted by six aircraft on 26 November, against a storage area at Nefesit, to the east of Asmara. Sqn Ldr Stapleton led the first vic [103] followed closely by Buchanan's second vic[104]. Stapleton's plan was to fly southwards past Massawa to Dessei island in the mouth of the Gulf of Zula then turn west towards Nefesit. However as the formation reached Dessei it was intercepted by three CR42s. Following 254 Wing instructions to avoid combat, Stapleton turned eastwards to outrun the fighters. In this he was successful, but MacKenzie's aircraft had been hit in the starboard engine during the initial engagement and he was unable to stay in formation. Fearing that the engine was about to fail completely, MacKenzie turned for home. Shortly afterwards his fear was realised and the engine seized: despite jettisoning the bombs the aircraft could no longer maintain height. Faced with no alternative, MacKenzie prepared to forced land on the Eritrean coast to the north of Massawa. Meanwhile, Stapleton had realised that he could no longer reach Nefesit and he elected instead to attack the alternative target on Harat. With the remaining five Blenheims, he swung back northwards to bomb the coastal defences at Sheikh Abu. In one of the amazing coincidences of war, the formation's return leg took them over the Eritrean coast at the very point where MacKenzie was preparing to forced land. Noticing MacKenzie's aircraft beneath him Stapleton instructed the rest of the formation to circle overhead, and following the fine precedents set by 14 Squadron in the Sinai Campaign of 1916, he landed amongst the rough scrub next to

MacKenzie. After destroying their codes, MacKenzie and his crew, Sgts M E F Hitchin[105] and K C A Ball[106] DFM climbed aboard Stapleton's aircraft. The heavily-laden Blenheim eventually staggered airborne after an agonisingly long run through camel thorn and rocks. For this episode, Stapleton was awarded an immediate DFC, though the citation also noted that "courageous leadership, skill and daring are characteristic of all this officer's operations against the enemy."

At the end of November 14 Squadron was tasked to locate a fuel dump which was thought to be somewhere between Ginda and Mai Atal – a swathe of country some sixty miles long. On 29 November Fg Off LeCavalier set off to photograph the area immediately west of Ginda, while Flt Lt Buchanan and Sgt Hopkins carried out diversionary bombing raids[107] on the goods yard at Keren. A similar tactic was used on 2 December when Fg Off Green[108] carried out a photographic line search of the road and the Teleferica cable-car route between Ginda and Mai Atal[109]. While Green was carrying out his survey, Sgt Taylor bombed[110] the fort at Adi Ugri (Mendefera) and Flt Sgt Patey attacked the fuel installation at Zula in order to draw fighters away from the area of Ginda. The same area was photographed by Fg Off Rhodes two days later, but this time a diversionary raid on Adarte station, between Agordat and Keren, by Fg Off MacKenzie was not sufficient to distract the Italian fighters. Rhodes' aircraft[111] was intercepted by fighters and shot down near Ginda and the entire crew (Fg Off Rhodes, Sgt Hitchin and Sgt S C Lewis[112]) perished.

The weather both at Port Sudan and the operational area over Eritrea was very poor throughout December and for much of the month the Squadron's operational sorties comprised only the anti-submarine patrols required for convoy protection and the routine reconnaissance of the Massawa naval docks. For all operations over the Red Sea, the Squadron worked closely with the Royal Navy. One point of liaison was Cdr W H Sandford who flew on two reconnaissance sorties[113] to see sections the Eritrean coast for himself. The first sortie, with Sqn Ldr Stapleton, was flown on 30 November and the second, with Flt Sgt Patey, nine days later. It was Sandford's comment after the first of these sorties that eloquently summarised the feelings of all involved in the campaign: after a few moments in the silence following engine shutdown, Sandford was heard to utter "what a bloody country!"

Although the weather precluded large-scale daylight bombing raids, the Squadron was able to continue the pattern of small-scale night raids. On the evening of 11 December three aircraft[114] were tasked against the CITAO Motor Transport works, a new target in Asmrara. Since the target was in a heavily built-up area, 254 Wing stipulated that the aircraft were not to drop unless they had positively identified the target. Sqn Ldr Stapleton took off first with the intention of locating the target and marking it with a flare – predating Bomber Command's Pathfinder Force tactics by two years. Unfortunately his aircraft suffered a port engine failure and he had to return to base. Flt Lt Buchanan was unable to locate the target in the darkness and bombed the airfield buildings instead, but Fg Off Matthew managed to find the works after four circuits of the town and claimed "near misses".

Later night attacks met with mixed success. On 12 December Fg Off D M Illsley and LeCavalier refuelled at the 223 Squadron airfield at Wadi Gazouza before following five Wellesleys southwards. The Blenheims dropped bombs, including some with twelve-hour delayed fuses among aircraft at Gura, while the Wellesleys visited Asmara and Mai Edaga. Two nights later Sgt Hopkins attacked aircraft in the open at Zula aerodrome. He sent a wireless message reporting a successful attack and giving an ETA of 2200 hrs. A further signal half an hour before the ETA indicated that all was normal, but the aircraft[115] never returned from the mission and Sgts Hopkins, J C Hall[116] and R F Murray[117] were posted as missing. On 15 December three aircraft bombed the CITAO works in Asmara at half-hourly intervals and three more raided the airfield at Gura with some success, though Sgt Moulton was attacked by fighters before he could reach Gura. Five nights later three aircraft bombed Asmara again, claiming hits on the workshops.

The night raids on Italian airfields provoked a response from the Italian Air Force: bombers attacked Port Sudan on 15, 16 and 17 December, though little damage was done in these raids. A few days later Christmas was celebrated with as much tradition as could be managed under operational conditions: the aircrew Sergeants manned the airfield defences on Christmas Day so that the airmen could enjoy their dinner, served, of course, by the officers.

The British Offensive Opens

At the beginning of 1941, the Army in East Africa started preparations for the offensive that would drive the Italians out of Abysinnia. In the south there would be a two-pronged advance from Kenya: one Division would push into Abyssinia and two more would advance into Italian Somaliland. In the centre the "Gideon Force" of Abyssinian exiles, under the leadership of Lt-Col O C Wingate[118] DSO would move into the central highlands of the Gojjam region. In the north, the 4th and 5th Indian Divisions under the overall command of Lt-Gen W Platt CB DSO would drive eastwards into Eritrea from Kassala, with the smaller "Briggsforce" comprising 7th Indian Infantry Brigade and a Free French Brigade under Brig-Gen H R Briggs[119] moving southwards from Karora. The axes of Platt's and Briggs' lines of advance would meet at Keren, a natural stronghold which would ultimately hold the key to Asmara. However, before tactical plans for Lt-Gen Platt's offensve could be finalised, accurate maps and reconnaisance of the area between Kassala and Tesseney were needed. Flt Sgt Patey started the project on 22 December, operating from Khartoum. With Sgts Mildren and Frost completing the crew[120], he continued photographing the area until 2 January complete the mosaic. Three Blenheims also flew to Khartoum on 4 January to take part in long-range bombing raids on targets in central Abyssinia in support of Wingate's advance. They raided Bure on 5 January and Debre Marqos the next day. On 8 January one of the aircraft photographed Gallebat, before joining the other two aircraft bombing troops deployed in a wood near Tesseney.

Although the support of the army offensive would become a priority for 14 Squadron, the unit also retained its responsibility for the protection of Red Sea convoys and the interdiction of the Italian war effort at Massawa. On 5 January Flt

A 14 Squadron Blenheim carrying the unit identification letters "LY" at its dispersal at Port Sudan in early 1941. (Andrew Thomas)

Sgt Patey took off for another photographic reconnaissance[121], but this time he also had the role of distracting Italian fighters away from the Massawa area. In fact Patey was not troubled by fighters and was able to take good images of Keren. Meanwhile six Blenheims were bombing the harbour at Massawa from 4,000 feet aiming at two submarines which had been seen at the naval base. Sqn Ldr Stapleton, Fg Offs Illsley and LeCavalier made up the first vic, with Flt Lt Robinson, Fg Off MacKenzie and Sgt Gilmore the second. Unfortunately most of the bombs appeared to overshoot by about thirty yards. Sgt Gilmore revisited Massawa again the next day[122] for an armed reconniassance, which was cut short when three CR42s intercepted him. Jettisoning his bombs he was able to escape and his gunner, Sgt Smith, claimed to have damaged one of the fighters.

Massawa was also visited by three aircraft on the night of 6 and 7 January, the target being the power station on the Gherar peninsula, just opposite the naval docks. The first of these sorties[123] produced little in the way of results, but the second raid[124] obtained direct hits on the buildings. Despite an attempt to confuse the sound locators by flying at different heights, the anti-aircraft defences at Massawa were particularly accurate and all crews found that the searchlights made bomb aiming difficult. Illsley was also slightly wounded in the face by a piece of shrapnel. Flt Lt Buchanan, Fg Off Green and Sgt Gilmore attacked the CITAO works in Asmara once again on the night of 9 January. This time the night was clear and the crews reported accurate bombing. Later in the month "nuisance raids" were mounted against the searchlights at Massawa.

Stapleton and Illsley were also in action again on 9 January when they accompanied Sgt Patey for a photographic reconnaisance of the area around Kassala. The Blenheims were intercepted by a pair of CR42s on their return and although one aircraft was damaged by the fighters none of the crew were hurt. One of the fighters

184

was also badly damaged in the engagement and it was later learnt to have crashed on landing. The Kassala area was also photographed on 11 January by Sgt Moulton, and by Fg Offs Matthew and Green the following day. The latter mission was escorted by Gladiators of 1 Squadron SAAF, marking the beginnings of a shift in the balance of aerial power in the skies over Eritrea. The weather started to close again over the next few days, foiling another attempt to bomb Massawa and limiting a photo reconnaissance[125] of Karora by Sgt W L Martin[126]. A sortie was flown[127] over Karora on 15 January by Sqn Ldr Stapleton; he was accompanied in the aircraft by Brig-Gen Briggs commanding of "Briggsforce". As they photographed Karora, Aqiq and Mersa Tek'lay, Stapleton was able to give the Brigadier a good view of the ground over which he would soon be fighting. In fact this "bird's eye view" proved so valuable that Briggs sent one of his staff officers to carry out another reconnaissance on 22 January. He himself flew with Stapleton again on 27 January to inspect the Italian defences north of Massawa.

Lt-Gen Platt's advance from Kassala started on 18 January. 14 Squadron's direct support of this offensive was to provide photo-reconnaissance sorties and to interdict Italian lines of commununcation. On the morning of 24 January Flt Sgt Patey and Sgt Gilmore carried out photo-reconnaissance patrols[128] covering the areas of Agordat and Keren. Later in the morning six aircraft operated against the railway system between Agordat and Keren. Fg Off Illsley led three aircraft[129] against the railway bridge at Ad Manna. Half an hour later another three Blenheims[130] attacked the railway station at Hagaz a few miles further south. Both formations claimed "near misses" on their targets. Another photographic survey of the country between Agordat and Keren was started the next day by Fg Off Matthew[131], but he had to abandon it when a CR42 was sighted. On the same morning Flt Lt Robinson[132] was flying on a reconnaissance of the road between Karora and Elgheina when he was hit in the leg by ground fire. His observer, Plt Off A W Donald[133], pulled him from his seat and flew the Blenheim back to Port Sudan, where Robinson was sufficiently recovered to land the aircraft.

More interdiction sorties were flown on 27 January, with attacks on the Teleferica station[134] at Mai Atal and against dispersed aircraft on the aerodrome at Gura[135]. On the next day Flt Sgt Patey led three aircraft[136] against the railway station at Keren, and on 29 January Sqn Ldr Stapleton led eight Blenheims in two formations of four aircraft to bomb aircraft at Gura and Mai Edaga airfields. One of the formations was intercepted by CR42s, and although the Blenheims were hit, there were no casualties resulting from the air-to-air engagements. However, the bombing attacks did cause damage to a number of CR42s on the ground.

The photographic work also continued: Sgt Moulton with his crew, Plt Off Bosley and Sgt Taylor, spent the two days of 30 and 31 January carrying out a photo survey[137] of the ground between Agordat and Keren. Agordat itself fell to British and Indian troops on 1 February, and Moulton's up-to-date photographs were of vital importance to the Divisional comanders in planning the next phase of their offensive. Moulton was busy photographing Keren itself on 1 and also on 3 February.

185

Fg Off Illsley led four aircraft on a frustrating sortie on 1 February: they were tasked to locate and destroy aircraft on a dispersed landing strip at Arafali on the sothern tip of the Gulf of Zula. This was a flight of three hundred and sixty miles to a region of featureless swamp. Unfortunately Illsley and his team of Fg Off MacKenzie, and Sgts Gilmore and Taylor were unable to locate their target, so they flew northwards to Alghiena. Here they attacked a supposed Italian HQ where at least they had the satisfaction of seeing their bombs knock down a small hut.

Six aircraft attacked Gura once more on 3 February, scoring hits on the airfield buildings. The following day three more aircraft led by Flt Lt Buchanan set out for Gura again; at the same time another formation of three[138] led by Fg Off LeCavalier were tasked to to bomb troops and vehicles on the Keren to Asmara road. LeCavalier's formation became separated as they circled to let down through a gap in the cloud. Fg Off Mackenzie and Sgt Taylor managed to stay together, but as they approached the target area they were engaged by two Hurricanes. Despite the Blenheims firing the correct recognition signals, the fighters attacked MacKenzie's aircraft and causing severe damage. MacKenzie nursed his damaged machine back to Port Sudan, jettisoning his bombs on the way, but he could not lower the undercarriage and the aeroplane was written off on landing. Meanwhile, Taylor had managed to slip away during the mêlée and link up with LeCavalier. The two aircraft bombed enemy vehicles as planned, before they were intercepted by a CR42 which chased them northwards.

As Lt-Gen Platt's forces advanced eastwards the landing strip at Barentu, which lies about half way between Kasala and Adi Ugri, became available for use. Flt Sgt Patey and Sgt Taylor landed there on 7 February for operations tasked by the local commander. Patey returned to Port Sudan that afternoon after carrying out a photo reconnaissance of the region between Barentu and Adi Ugri, but Taylor remained at Barentu overnight, flying a number of communications sorties over the two days.

Plt Off MacKenzie's Blenheim T2115 crash landed at Port Sudan after it was severely damaged by South African Hurricanes near Gura on 4 February 1941. (W McConnell)

Over the three days of 8-10 February, 14 Squadron's efforts were concentrated against Italian road and rail transport systems in Asmara. Four aircraft led by Fg Off Green attacked the CITAO workshops on 8 February, the first daylight raid on this target. They met with heavy anti-aircraft fire and Plt Off Renniker's Blenheim[139] took a direct hit on the run into the target. The aircraft was seen to hit the ground and explode, killing all four crew[140]. The following day Flt Lt Buchanan led four aircraft against the railway station in Asmara causing considerable damage to rolling stock and on 10 February Fg Off MacKenzie led three aircraft against vehicles parked alongside the railway station.

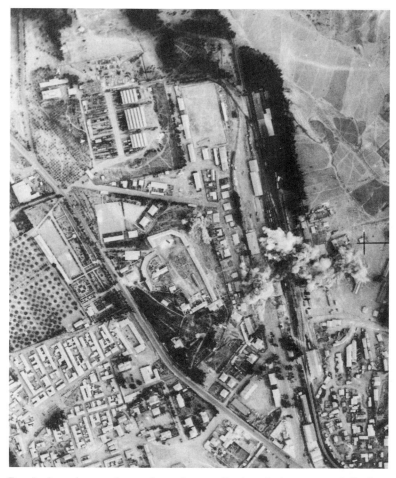

Bombs bursting on the tracks at Asmara Station during an attack by four 14 Squadron Blenheims led by Flt Lt Buchannan on 9 February 1941. This view is looking due east, along the line of the railway line.

Briggsforce Advances from Karora

While Platt's main force fought their way eastwards from Kassala, Briggsforce was advancing south from Karora down the road which ran through Alghiena Nak'fa, Kukub and thence to Keren. On the morning of 10 February Sqn Ldr Stapleton took off[141] to provide fighter protection for the troops in the area of Mersa Tak'lay, Alghiena and Karora. The weather was poor with low cloud in the area of Karora, and Stapleton was unable to locate any enemy troops. However Fg Off Le Cavalier launched later in the day in another cannon-armed aircraft[142] and strafed Italian troops on the road betwen Nak'fa and Keren. Stapleton was on fighter patrol again the next morning, and in the afternoon a pair of Blenheims[143] carried out deeper interdiction sorties towards Keren. They found a road convoy of seven lorries on the Keren to Asmara road, which they attacked with bombs and guns.

Interdiction sorties in support of Briggsforce were limited by the weather on 12 February. Fg Off Green located enemy troops[144] in the region of Kubkub, about sixty-five miles south of Alghiena, and bombed them, but neither Sgt J F Matetich[145] who arrived two hours later[146] nor Fg Off MacKenzie five hours after that, could find anything of tactical interest under the low cloud. Meanwhile, LeCavalier had mounted the fighter patrol forward of the Briggsforce front lines. The following day, Sqn Ldr Stapleton led three aircraft[147] back towards Kubkub to attack Italian defensive positions with a mixed load of 250-, 40- and 20-pound bombs. The capture of Mersa Tek'lay allowed the port there to be used for resupply and reinforcement from 15 February. Blenheims carried out anti-submarine patrols while troopships and supply vessels were unloaded over the next few days.

The bad weather on 12 February had also prevented the morning reconnaissance of Masawa harbour. By now the need to know whether any of the submarines based at Massawa and set to sea was ever more pressing, so Fg Off Illsley was dispatched[148] into grey skies that afternoon to find out what he could. The usual high altitude photographic pass was out of the question and instead Illsley opted for a risky dash over the naval docks at five hundred feet for a visual reconnaisance. This unexpected move must have taken the defences by surprise as the aircraft was not touched by ground fire. When the navy insisted on a repeat performance the next day, Buchanan used the same tactic, but by now the gunners were ready and his Blenheim[149] was hit in the wing by a burst of gunfire. From now on the monitoring of Italian naval movements was the highest priority task for the Squadron, the reconnaissance of Masawa was carried out regardless of the weather on virtually every day for the rest of the Squadron's deployment in Port Sudan.

The February weather also frustrated attempts to produce an updated photo-mosaic of Keren. Sgt Moulton carried out the first sortie on 14 February[150], but cloud in the area made flying conditions poor. On his return to Port Sudan it was found that despite dodging some particularly accurate anti-aircraft fire, none of the negatives he had taken was of any use. He tried again, with more success the next day, and managed to complete about a third of the required coverage. Fg Off Green took over the task a day later, but his camera failed, and it was not until 17 February

14 Squadron Football Team Port Sudan 1940. Even in wartime, sport played a very important part in the Squadron's life and offered everyone the chance of some relaxation and exercise. With troopships and naval vessels frequent visitos there there was much chance to play teams from other units. This team played 34, Won 26, Lost 2 and drew 6. Goals for – 168, goals against – 45. Back Row l-r: Hanson. Wood, Wilson A, Duff, Kinden, Wilson T; Front Row: Earl, Collins, Robinson, Else, Wells.

that the full photographic cover was completed by Fg Off Green and Flt Sgt Patey[151].

The captured facilities at Mersa Tek'lay also included a landing strip, which was used from 18 February onwards by 14 Squadron's Blenheims for refuelling and re-arming between operations. The Gladiators of "K" Flight also moved there on a more permanant basis. The conditions at Mersa Tek'lay were even more spartan that those at Port Sudan, but even so the ground crews there worked like Trojans in getting the aircraft turned round betwen operations. The airstrip was used to great effect on 24 February by Sgt Taylor for a reconnaisance of Nefesit[152]. His task, to confirm the location a suspected benzene storage dump and check on the weather in the target area, was completed over three sorties involving two turn-rounds at Mersa Tek'lay. On receiving details from Taylor, seven Blenheims led by Sqn Ldr Stapleton took off from Port Sudan to bomb the storage dump. The raid was not particularly successful for although a number of bombs hit the target area, some aircraft suffered hang-ups and other weapons failures.

The Battle of Keren

After their swift advance from Kassala through Agordat, Platt's Indian Divisions were

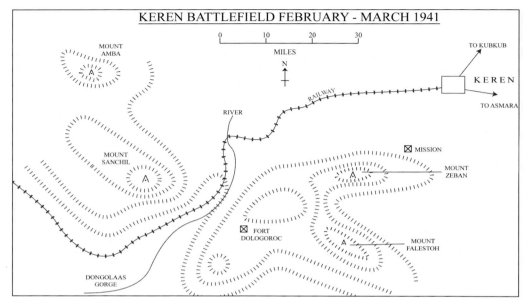

KEREN BATTLEFIELD FEBRUARY - MARCH 1941

brought to a halt in late February, at Keren. Here the way was blocked by Italian forces manning a natural barricade of steep two-thousand foot mountains guarding the Dongolaas Gorge, a narrow ravine which carried the road and railway lines into Keren from the southwest. With troops dug in on the mountains and observation posts commanding the whole of the valley beneath them, the Italian position looked impregnable. After two weeks of stalemate, the Divisional Commanders planned to carry out a decisive "big push" in mid-March. In preparation for this assault, the RAF attempted to undermine the Italian defences and interdict their lines of supply. In the last days of February, 14 Squadron were involved in large-scale operations in support of the army. On 27 February Sqn Ldr Stapleton led a formation of five aircraft against Keren itself in a raid that was co-ordinated with attacks by 47 and 223 Squadron Wellesleys. Stapleton's Blenheims carried out four bombing runs against Italian troop positions, dropping all bombs accurately in the target area. The next day six aircraft led by Flt Lt Hill attacked the railway station at Asmara and suspected transport and storage areas immediately to the west of it. On this raid the formation was escorted by Hurricanes and once again the bombs landed in the target area. Four Blenheims also set out early on 1 March to bomb troop positions again in the hills around Keren, but they arrived over the area outside the timing window for their attack. Although Fg Off LeCavalier did drop on a suspected enemy emplacement on Jebel 1792, the remaining three aircraft led by Flt Lt Buchanan[153] headed for the alternate target which was the submarine workshops at Massawa. As they left Massawa to the east they noticed a submarine on the surface just to the south of Dahlak Kebir Island. Acting on this report, Fg Off MacKenzie was dispatched at 0825 hrs on an armed reconnaissance mission[154] to find and destroy the submarine. He located the vessel close to Buchanan's reported position and dropped a stick of four 250-pound bombs on it, scoring a direct with the third bomb which caused a large oil slick to form.

Over the next fortnight 14 Squadron's efforts were concentrated against the Keren-Asmara road and rail links. On 5 March, Sgt Moulton carried an attack[155] on the railway tunnel at Arocchia, to the northwest of Asmara and then returned after refuelling and rearming at Mersa Tek'lay to attack the railway bridge just south of the tunnel. Meanwhile while Flt Lt Hill bombed a section of the Keren Asmara road. The same section of road was targetted the next day in two raids of three aircraft led by Flt Lt Buchanan and a third raid by a pair led by Fg Off Matthew. However, despite all this attention, the road appeared to be uncut. On 7 March three aircraft[156] revisited the railway tunnel on the Keren Asmara line and three days later three more attacked the road bridge. Offensive patrols were also carried out along the road between Keren, Asmara and Adi Ugri on 12, 13 and 14 March.

The main British offensive against Keren opened on 15 March. At 0340 hrs three Blenheims, led by Sqn Ldr Stapleton[157] took off from Port Sudan, followed an hour later by another three led by Flt Lt Buchanan[158]. The targets for both flights were on the battlefield of Keren itself: Stapleton led his three against the Italian stronghold of Fort Dologorodoc which guarded the mouth of the Dongolaas gorge, while Buchanan's aircraft attacked gun positions, trucks and camps on the opposite side of the gorge between Mount Amba and Mogareh. After their attacks, both formations refuelled and re-armed at Mersa Tek'lay before returning to the battlefield. On the second sortie the Blenheims worked the hills to the north of the gorge, bombing Italian artillery positions, vehicles and encampments. The following day six aircraft set out once more for Keren; this time they operated autonomously behind the Italian front lines, hunting down artilllery, vehicles and military installations. By cycling through Mersa Tek'lay twice during the day Sgt Dickson, Plt Off I Ormiston[159] and Sgt Taylor were each able to fly two sorties over the battlefield, while Flt Lt Hill, Fg Off Green and Fg Off Mackenzie managed three missions each. On the third day of the battle six aircraft[160] left Port Sudan and attacked the Fiat workshops at Asmara with four 250-pound bombs each before landing at Mersa Tek'lay. Here they were instructed to re-arm and await further orders, but they were not called for during the rest of the day.

However, this proved to be only a brief lull: on 18 March the Italians started a series of fierce counter-attacks at Keren which would last another four days. That morning, six aircraft[161] had once again arrived at Mersa Tek'lay after bombing transportation targets in Asmara; this time, however, all six were soon called to Keren to bomb Italian troop positions on Mount Zeban, a high peak which commanded the northeast end of Dongolaas gorge. The positions on Zeban were also attacked the following day by three aircraft[162], while three more[163] bombed the Mission between Keren town itself and Mount Zeban. Once again all six aircraft rotated through Mersa Tek'lay in order to fly two sorties against their targets. All the aircraft returned safely to Port Sudan that evening, despite some ferocious and accurate anti-aircraft fire, which had been absent on the previous days of the battle. Two pairs of Blenheims bombed troop concentrations on Zeban on the afternoon of 20 March, while two more attacked the same area the next morning. On 23 March two formations of three aircraft attacked Zeban, one in the morning and one in the afternoon. By now the bombing attacks were taking their toll of the Italian soldiers and their counter-attacks at Keren were foundering. The 5th Indian Division's final attack was mounted on 25 March, with support from 14 Squadron's Blenheims. The first three aircraft led by Flt Lt Buchanan left Port Sudan at 0245 hrs, followed fifteen minutes later by a pair led by Sqn Ldr Stapleton. All five aircraft were turned around twice at Mera Tek'lay during the course of the day and between them the five Blenheims dropped fifty-six 250-pound bombs on Italian troop concentrations on the road between Mogareh and the Mission. This was the first raid over the Keren battlefield where the Italian Air Force attempted to intervene: the second formation was engaged by three CR42s, fortunately without being damaged. Three more aircraft visited Keren on 26 March; although all three aircraft subsequently landed at Mersa Tek'lay, two of them were grounded there because of unserviceabilities, but Sgt H P Jeudwine[164] returned to Keren in the afternoon for a second sortie[165]. This was to be the last air attack by 14 Squadron aircraft on Keren, which fell into British hands early the next day.

Support for Wingate's Gideon Force
While the battle for Keren was fought, 14 Squadron aircraft also flew a number of sorties in the support of Wingate's advance into central Abyssinia. Early on the morning of 15 March Fg Off Matthew set off for Kassala[166] where he refuelled before flying deep into Abyssinia. By now the Gideon Force was threatening Debre Marqos (about a hundred miles northwest of Adis Ababa), although the defenders held the advantage in both numbers and tactical position; however, Wingate's forces sought to undermine the Italian will by guerilla-style attacks on small outposts. The occasional bombing raids would also sap the Italian moral. Matthew's target on 15 March was the military infrastructure in Debre Marqos and he bombed a number of buildings in the town, before returning to Kassala to refuel once more. He was supposed to return to Port Sudan that evening, but this plan was delayed by a day when he burst a tyre on landing. On reaching his home base, Matthew was sent back again almost immediately to Debre Marqos. This time he was accompanied by Sgt Matetich. The two aircraft[167] had been tasked to bomb an enemy troop concentration to the west of the town, but when they reached the area they could not locate the troops. Instead they concentrated their attention on buildings in the town itself.

Debre Marqos was visited again on 20 March by Flt Lt Buchanan, who saw much evidence of the damage caused by Matthew's and Matetich's bombs two days previously. Buchanan's target was a small bridge half a mile south of the town. As he pressed his attack, he picked up slight damage to his Blenheim[168] from rifle fire. Two days later, two aircraft were sent to attack targets north of Lake Tana. Flt Lt Hill attacked the Fort at Gondar[169] where his bombs caused a substantial fire. Unfortunately his subsequent attacks on a troop concentration two miles east of Celga and the jetty at Gorgora on the north shore of Lake Tana were less successful.

Meanwhile[170] Plt Off Ormiston had dropped on the barracks at Gondar but missed, before moving on to the airfield at Azozo a few miles further south. Here his bombs fell among hangars, but seemed to do little damage; his final run against warehouses alongside the jetty at Gorgora was also inconclusive.

The last sortie by 14 Squadron over central Abyssinia was flown on 24 March by Flt Lt Hill who attempted to strafe troop concerntrations near Debre Marqos. However he was forced back to Kassala by low cloud and had to abandon the mission.

Italian Retreat from Keren

With Italian forces in full retreat from Keren towards Asmara, 14 Squadron aircraft spent the last few days of March mopping up targets in Asmara and attacked vehicles on the Keren to Asmara road. On 27 March Fg Off Illsley strafed two convoys of about fifteen trucks, firing over a thousand machine gun rounds at these targets. However the shooting was not all one sided, and his Blenheim[171] was hit in about ten places by ground fire while Illsley himself was hit in the leg by splinters. The following day Flt Lt Buchanan and Fg Off Ormiston bombed and strafed vehicles and buildings at Ad Teclesan, about halfway between Keren and Asmara, scoring a number of hits. On this day also Sqn Ldr Stapleton led four aircraft[172] against the CITAO works at as Asmara where their mix of 250-pound bombs and incendiaries started a huge fire. Road convoys between Keren and Asmara were also attacked over the next two days by Sgt Gilmore and Sgt Dickson. Asmara itself surended on 31 March and Massawa was captured a week later, marking the end of the campaign in Eritrea.

A Last Defiant Gesture in the Red Sea

When it became obvious that the Italian resistance in Eritrea had collapsed completely, the Italian navy decided to demonstrate their fighting spirit in one glorious last gesture. Late on 31 March the six remaining destroyers of the Red Sea Flotilla, under overall command of Captain Gaspirini, set sail from Massawa. They were on a one-way mission to cause as much damage as possible to British forces in the Red Sea. Gaspirini's plan was for three of the ships to attack Port Sudan while the other three attacked Port Suez. Unfortunately, the mission started to go disastrously wrong for the Italians almost from the start when, soon after leaving Massawa, the lead ship *Leone* hit an umarked coral reef. The *Leone* was mortally damaged and after abandoning her, Gaspirini ordered the other destroyers to sink her by gunfire so that she would not alert the British to their presence. However, he was too late and the hulk was sighted early the following day by a Fleet Air Arm Swordfish, one of eighteen aircraft from HMS *Eagle* that were operating temporarily from Port Sudan. Three Blenheims[173] were immediately dispatched to attack and sink the ship, but when they arrrived overhead, the destroyer was already beneath the waves. But the British now knew that the Italian navy was on the loose. Reconnaissance of Massawa was impossible for the next few days because of low cloud and haze, but on the morning of 3 April Sgt Gilmore and Fg Off Green were able[174] to confirm that at least four destroyers had escaped into the Red Sea. By now a fleet of Blenheims, Swordfish and Wellesleys was combing the Red Sea to try and find the Italian warships. Early the next day Flt Lt Hill found an enemy destroyer near Farasan Island, off the Arabian coast, but he was unable to bomb it because of low clouds. This was the *Battisti*, which was no longer seaworthy and had left the rest of the flotilla so that it could beach itself on the Arabian coast. At about the same time a Swordfish found the remaining four destroyers some forty miles from Port Sudan. By now Gaspirini was worried about the presence of Royal Navy ships, particularly the cruiser HMS *Capetown*, and he turned away from the Sudanese coast to buy himself more time.

Meanwhile at Port Sudan, a strike force of Swordfish from 824 Squadron set off to attack the destroyers with bombs. Just after 0800 hrs Sub Lt S H Suthers[175] pulled out from an almost vertical dive over *Manin* and scored direct hits with his bombs; however despite the severe damage caused by Suther's bombs, the vessel managed to continue sailing towards the safety of the Arabian coast. Soon afterwards a second wave from 813 Squadron reached the flotilla and carried out a further attack. During this engagement Midshipman E Sergeant[176] hit the stern of *Sauro* with his bombs, causing a large explosion which capsized the destroyer almost immediately. As the Swordfish left, the two undamaged ships, *Tigre* and *Pantera*, were steaming at high speed in the direction of Jeddah, with the *Manin* limping along behind them. At 0845 hrs, Sqn Ldt Stapleton took off from Port Sudan in the lead of five Blenheims to finish off the *Manin*. The bombs exploded around the crippled warship, and Stapleton watched as "flames, thick black smoke and steam issued under pressure from every wound in the ship. Men were jumping over the side into the sea already littered with broken rafts, ammunition boxes, debris and oil. The sharks of the Red Sea had also arrived. The surrounds of the ship were stained with red and grey swatches from thrashing fish and despairing men."

For the moment, the *Tigre* and *Pantera* had managed to escape the carnage, but they were found again that afternoon by a 223 Squadron Wellesley, just off the Arabian coast. On receipt the wireless report from the Wellesley, "Black Mac" telephoned 14 Squadron and ordered three Blenheims into the air as quickly as possible: Lt Forrester, Fg Off Matthew and Plt Off Ormiston scrambled into the haze. Five Wellesleys from 223 Squadron had also been dispatched. Neither Matthew nor Ormiston were able to locate the ships because of the poor visibility, but Forrester found and attacked both of them. Joining the five Wellesleys over the destroyers, he dropped a 250-pound bomb on the *Pantera* which caused two explosions; another bomb hit the *Tigre* starting a fire. So ended the last desperate mission of the Italian Red Sea Flotilla. The episode was also a full stop at the end of the campaign for 14 Squadron: the unit left Port Sudan on 9 April. The ground party sailed up from Port Sudan on the SS *Khedive Ismail*[177] via Port Tewfik and four days later the whole unit was at Heliopolis taking charge of new Blenheims and replacement crews.

Notes

1 Air Marshal Sir Anthony Selway (1909-1984) served as C-in-C Far East Air Force in 1960 and AOC-in-C Coastal Command 1962. After retiring from the RAF he was Gentleman Usher of the Scarlet Rod.
2 23-year old Richard Sweeting.

3 Wellesley L2643.
4 Walter Crofts was 20 years old.
5 Sqn Ldr John Berggren DFC retired from the RAF in 1958.
6 22 year old Lawrence Bullwinkle was killed in a flying accident in February 1939.
7 Flt Lt Richard Green from Sutton, Surrey was killed in action in May 1941 aged 26.
8 26 year old Fg Off Charles Greenhill was killed in action flying with 274 Sqn in April 1941.
9 Sqn Ldr John Jordan survived the War.
10 Sqn Ldr J E Gorringe-Smith from Marlow, Bucks, was killed in action with 221 Sqn in May 1942.
11 28 year-old Sgt Alexander Brown from Edinburgh was killed in action with 47 Sqn in July 1941.
12 Plt Off James Burcher transferred to the Administrative & Special Duties Branch in 1943.
13 Plt Off Roy Gilmore was killed in action in May 1941.
14 Flt Lt George Dickson DFC survived the War.
15 Wellesley L2655..
16 Charles "Jimmy" Chick (1913-39) from Glamorgan was an experienced pilot who had joined. 14 Squadron in 1936. He was a passenger in the aircraft for the first leg of his journey to England for home leave. In April 1939 he was posthumously Mentioned in Dispatches for his operational flying in the previous year.
17 Desmond Segrave aged 22.
18 Francis MacAdam aged 32 was serving with the Arab Legion.
19 Theodore Bogdanovitch GC (1899-1956) had fought with the Serbian Army in WW1; he was murdered by EOKA in Cyprus while working as a security manager for the Cyprus Mining Corporation. His Empire Gallantry Medal was converted to a GC in 1947.
20 AVM Deryck Stapleton CB CBE DFC AFC retired from the RAF in 1968 having been AOC 1 Group. He subsequently worked for British Aerospace in Iran and China. His tour with 14 Squadron was remarkable in that he joined the unit as a Plt Off in 1937 and left four years later as a Wg Cdr commanding the Squadron. Stapleton was the President of the 14 Squadron Association from 2001-2009.
21 From New Zealand, Murray MacKenzie was known as "Flash" on account of his quiet manner and hesitant speech. He was missing in action in mysterious circumstances in May 1941 at the age of 27.
22 25-year old Jean "Bruno" LeCavalier from Montreal was killed in action in May 1941.
23 Flt Lt Harold Norris retired from the RAF in 1948 and joined an engineering business in Nottingham.
24 Alfred Willis (b1912) joined the Air Control Branch of the RAF after the war and retired from the Service with the rank of Wg Cdr in 1954.
25 26-year old Fg Off Samuel Soderholm, from British Columbia, was killed in action in July 1940.
26 Sqn Ldr Arthur Wimsett DFC retired from the RAF in 1968; he was shot down over Eritrea in March 1941 while flying with 47 Sqn and was taken Prisoner of War.
27 AVM Leslie Moulton CB DFC (1915-2006) retired as AOC 90 (Signals) Group. He had transferred to the Technical Branch after the War and specialised in signals and radar.
28 AVM Somerled MacDonald DFC (1899-1979) retired from the RAF in 1954. He had spent most of his flying career since 1917 in the Middle East and was known during the Red Sea campaign as "Black Mac" to distinguish him from two other MacDonalds who were denoted by their different hair colouring.
29 Flt Lt Joseph Mildren DFM retired from the RAF in 1964.
30 Flt Lt Aubrey Lund DFC later retrained as a navigator and retired from the RAF in 1949.
31 Sqn Ldr Leslie Patey DFM retired from the RAF in 1965.
32 Selway (L2647) Sgt Brown (K7725) and Sgt Patey (L2645).
33 Fg Off Soderholm (K7723) Sgt Wimsett (L2652) and Sgt Gilmore (K7723).
34 Flt Lt Irvine (L2649) Fg Off LeCavalier (K7743) and Fg Off Plunkett (L2710).
35 Educated at Eton and Balliol College Oxford, 27-year old Sqn Ldr Anthony Irvine was killed in action over Greece in April 1941 while commanding 211 Squadron.
36 Bernard Trayhurn from Dursley, Gloucestershire, was killed in action in July 1940 aged 27.
37 Nicholas Allfree, who had joined the Sqn in 1937, survived the war.
38 Wellesley L2710.
39 K7723 and K7743 respectively.
40 Selway in Wellesley L2647, Fg Offs Soderholm in K7723, Fg Off Helsby in K7725, Sgt Patey in L2645 and Sgt Norris in K7773.
41 Sqn Ldr Richard Helsby retired from the RAF in 1948.

42 Wg Cdr Edwin Crouch MBE retired from the RAF in 1947.

43 Sqn Ldr Bernard D'Arcy DFC retired from the RAF in 1966. After the war he transferred into the Air Traffic Control branch. While posted to Cyprus in 1962, D'Arcy flew with 14 Squadron once again – this time in a Hunter T7 piloted by Flt Lt D Morter.

44 AVM John Elton CB CBE DFC AFC (1905-1994) retired from the RAF in 1957.

45 Fg Off LeCavalier (L2657) Fg Off Soderholm (L2710) Fg Off Matthew (L2645) Sgt Patey (L2676).

46 Flt Lt William Matthew transferred to the RCAF in 1944.

47 Sqn Ldr Jack Hamlyn DFC retired from the RAF in 1951. During this engagement he was flying Gladiator L7619.

48 Selway (K7739) Plt Off Willitts (L2649) and Plt Off Rhodes (L2689) Sgt Wimsett (L2710).

49 Gp Capt Charles Taylor OBE retired in from the RAF 1946.

50 Sqn Ldr Richard Willitts retired from the RAF in 1959.

51 Fg Off Thomas Rhodes was killed in action in December 1940 aged 21.

52 Soderholm (L2652) Plt Off Ferguson (L2710) and Plt Off Smith (L2649).

53 James Ferguson transferred to the Administrative Branch of the RAF in 1944 and was promoted to Wg Cdr in 1958.

54 Flt Lt Andrew Smith from Sakatoon, Canada was killed in action with 274 Squadron in February 1942.

55 John Dawson aged 21 from Kent.

56 Wg Cdr Cecil Rowan-Robinson DSO DFC became secretary of the RUSI.

57 Robinson (L2649) Fg Off LeCavalier (K7767) Plt Off D M Illsley (K7725) Sgt Wimsett (K7723) and Sgt Gilmore (L2710). From Nova Scotia, Sqn Ldr David Illsley DFC was killed in action in November 1941 aged 25 while commanding 47 Squadron.

58 Wellesley L2707.

59 Wellesley K7726.

60 Flt Lt Jack McConnell (d 2007) retired from the Air Traffic Control Branch of the RAF in 1949.

61 Robinson (K7723) Plt Off Smith (L2710) Sgt Taylor (K7713) Plt Off Ferguson (K7767) Plt Off Willitts (L2649).

62 Wellesley L2649.

63 Sgt Dickson was (K7773) Sgt Hopkins (L2689) Flt Lt Stapleton (K7722) Sgt Morren (L2707) Fg Off MacKenzie (L7726).

64 Sgt Bleddyn Hopkins from Taff's Well, Glamorgan, was killed in action in December 1940.

65 From the Irish Republic, Flt Lt Thomas Morren flew Lancasters with 576 Sqn and was killed .while test flying a Bristol Brigand in July 1947

66 Stapleton (K7722) Plt Off Green (K7726) Plt Off Le Cavlier (K7723) Plt Off Illsley (L2691).

67 Robinson (K7723) Sgt Gilmore (L2649) Plt Off Le Cavalier (K7767) Plt Off Smith (K7713).

68 Stapleton (K7722) Plt Off McKenzie (K7726) Sgt Burcher (K2703) Sgt Hopkins (L2689).

69 Stapleton (K7722) Plt OFf Matthew (L2691) Sgt Patey (K7757) Sgt Morren (L2645).

70 Flt Lt Robinson (K7735) Sgts Gilmore (K7713) and Taylor (L2649).

71 Plt Offs Green (7725) Illsley (K7739) and Sgt Patey (L2645).

72 in Wellesley K7722.

73 26-year old Sgt Edwin Blofield was killed in action in February 1941 while serving with 47 Squadron.

74 Plt Off Green (K7739) Plt Off Matthew (L2645) Sgt Blofield (K7757).

75 in Wellesley L2689.

76 in Wellesley L2708.

77 in Wellesley L2703.

78 Flt Sgt John Taylor, aged 25, from Horfield near Bristol was killed in Action in May 1941.

79 in Wellesley K7722.

80 Wellesley L2703.

81 Stapleton (K7722), Plt Off Willetts (L2657), Sgt Taylor (K7767), Sgt Patey (L2645), Plt Off Illsley (L2645).

82 Wellesley L2676.

83 Flt Lt Robinson (K7723), Plt Offs Illsley (K7725), Willitts (K7767), LeCavalier (L2710) and Sgt Morren (L2645).

84 Albert Matthews from Sussex was 24 years old.

85 Flt Lt Stapleton (K7722), Plt Off Green (L2645), Sgts G M Keith (K7726), Norris (L2707) and

Moulton (L2689). Sqn Ldr George Keith DFC DFM retired from the RAF in 1950.

86 Flt Lt Stapleton (K7722), Plt Offs Mackenzie (K7726), LeCavalier (K8531), Rhodes (L2708) and Sgt Moulton (L2689).

87 Wellesley L2689.

88 Charles Lampard aged 22 was from Bristol.

89 Flt Lt Robinson (K7731), Plt Off Willitts (K7767) and Plt Off Ferguson (K7763).

90 Wellesley K7763.

91 James Lynch, aged 23, had been a Corporal Air Gunner and was commissioned only three months previously. His father had been killed in action in France in 1917.

92 Thomas Conway.

93 Sgt Dickson (L2645) Plt Off Rhodes (K7725) and Flt Sgt Patey (K7713).

94 Sgt Dickson was in K7725 and Sgt Hopkins in K7767.

95 Norman Birks transferred to the Administration & Special Duties Branch in 1941.

96 Flt Lt Birks in T2061, Fg Off Buchanan in R3899 and Flt Lt Hill in T2057.

97 A charismatic figure, Wg Cdr John Buchanan DSO DFC* (1918-1944) had won a DFC while flying Wellingtons with 37 Squadron and later commanded 14 Squadron. He was killed in action flying a Beaufighter while commanding 227 Squadron. While flying Beaufighters Buchanan shot down 10 enemy aircraft and damaged another 6, making him the highest-scoring Beaufighter strike pilot of the war.

98 Sqn Ldr George Hill (1915-2004) from Saskatchewan transferred to the RCAF in 1945, retiring in 1957.

99 Unfortunately 23 year-old James Cheyne, from Aberdeen, died five days later.

100 in Blenheim T1877.

101 Blenheim T2057.

102 Flt Lt Buchanan (R3593), Fg Offs Illsley (T1877) and Matthew (R3899).

103 Sqn Ldr Stapleton (1877), Plt Off Green (T2167) and LeCavalier (T1994).

104 Flt Lt Buchanan (R2770) Fg Off MacKenzie (R3593) and Sgt Patey (R3899).

105 Sgt Maurice Hitchin was killed in action in December 1940 aged 21.

106 Kenneth Ball DFM transferred into the Secretarial Branch of the RAF after the war and was promoted to Sqn Ldr in 1958.

107 Buchanan (T2183) Sgt Hopkins (T2167).

108 in Blenheim R2770.

109 The Eritrean Teleferica was a 45-mile long cable-car system which connected Massawa on the coast to Asmara, on the high plain some 7,600 feet above sea level.

110 in Blenheim T1897.

111 Blenheim R2770.

112 Sidney Lewis aged 23 from Aberavon, Glamorgan.

113 with Sqn Ldr Stapleton in T1877, and with Flt Sgt Patey in R3899.

114 Stapleton (T2167) Flt Lt Buchanan (T2185) Fg Off Matthew (T1857).

115 Blenheim T2167.

116 Sgt Jean Hall from Yorkshire, aged 20.

117 Sgt Robert Murray from Glasgow, aged 20.

118 Maj Gen Orde Wingate DSO** (1903-1944) achieved lasting fame as the leader of the Chindits in Burma. However in Israel he is regarded as a hero for his work with Jewish Haganah forces in Palestine between 1936-39. He was killed in a flying accident in Burma.

119 Lt Gen Sir Rawdon Briggs KCIE KBE CB DSO** (1894-1952) was later GOC-inC Burma Command.

120 in Blenheim R3899.

121 in Blenheim T1868.

122 in Blenheim T1818.

123 Flt Lt Buchanan and Sgts Martin and Moulton.

124 Flt Lt Stapleton (T1857), Flt Lt Robinson (T1818) and Fg Off Illsley (1877).

125 in Blenheim T1856.

126 26 year-old Flt Sgt William Martin was killed in action in May 1941 while flying with 55 Sqn.

127 in Blenheim T1994.

128 Flt Sgt Patey (T1994) and Sgt Gilmore (T1818).

129 Fg Off Illsley (T1877), Plt Off P E Renniker (T1822) and Sgt Taylor (T2115). Plt Off Peter Rennniker

from South Africa was killed in action in February 1941.

130 Flt Lt Buchanan (L8874) leading Fg Off MacKenzie (T1819) and Sgt Moulton (T1857).

131 in Blenheim T1857.

132 in Blenheim T1823.

133 20-year old Alexander Donald from Lanarkshire was killed in action in April 1942 while serving with XI Sqn in Singapore.

134 Fg Off LeCavalier (N3582) and Flt Sgt Patey (T1977).

135 Flt Lt Buchanan (L8874), Fg Off Green (T1822) and Sgt Gilmore (T1856).

136 Flt Sgt Patey (T1877) Sgts Moulton (L8874) and Taylor (N3582).

137 in Blenheim T1819.

138 Fg Off LeCavalier (N3582), Fg Off Mackenzie (T2115) and Sgt Taylor (T1822).

139 Blenheim T1818.

140 Fg Off Henry C P Turney, aged 22 from London, Sgt Frederick G Roy aged 20 from Norwich and Plt Off Thomas H Scorror from Rhodesia, a pilot from "K" Flight who had gone along as a passenger.

141 in Blenheim T1856.

142 Blenheim T1823.

143 Sgt Gilmore (T1823) and Sgt Dickson (T2185).

144 in Blenheim T2185.

145 Sgt Joseph Matetich, from Rhodesia, was killed in action in May 1941 at the age of 23.

146 in Blenheim T1819.

147 Sqn Ldr Stapleton (T1819), Fg Off Green (T2185), Fg Off LeCavalier (N3582).

148 in Blenheim T2185.

149 Blenheim L8874.

150 in Blenheim T1819.

151 Fg Off Green in T1822 and Flt Sgt Patey in T1994.

152 in Blenheim T1825.

153 Flt Lt Buchanan (T2185) Fg Off Illsley (T2274) Sgt Moulton (T1819).

154 in Blenheim T1822.

155 in Blenheim T2185.

156 Stapleton, Illsley, LeCavalier.

157 Sqn Ldr Stapleton (Z5767) Fg Off Illsley (T1856) Fg Off LeCavalier (T2274).

158 Flt Lt Buchanan (T1857) Sgt Moulton (T1819) Sgt Gilmore (T1822).

159 Plt Off Ian Ormiston from Rhodesia was killed in action in April 1941.

160 Sqn Ldr Stapleton (T1994) Fg Off Illsley (T1877) Fg Off LeCavalier N3582, Flt Lt Buchanan T1857, Sgt Gilmore T1822, Sgt Moulton T1819.

161 Fg Off Green T1822, Lt S R E Forrester N3582, Sgt Taylor N3557, Fg Off MacKenzie T2185, Sgt Dickson Z5767, Sgt Matetich T1857. Lt Stanley Forrester from Durban was killed in action in May 1941 aged 19.

162 Sqn Ldr Stapleton T1994, Fg Off Illsley T1877, Fg Off LeCavalier N3582.

163 Flt Lt Buchanan T1857, Sgt Gilmore T1822, Sgt Moulton T1819.

164 Sgt Harold Jeudwine from South Africa was killed in action in May 1941 aged 28.

165 in Blenheim T2274.

166 in Blenheim T1994.

167 Matthew in T2274 and Sgt Matetich in T2185.

168 Blenheim T2185.

169 Blenheim T3557.

170 in Z5676.

171 Blenheim T2065.

172 Sqn Ldr Stapleton T1994, Fg Off Illsley Z5767, Fg Off LeCavalier N3557 and Fg Off Green T1856.

173 Fg Off Illsley Z5676, Sgt Moulton T2274 and Sgt Taylor T1822...

174 Sgt Gilmore in T2274 and Fg Off Green in T1822.

175 Cdr Sydney Suthers DSC DFC (1918-2007).

176 Lt Eric Sergeant DSC★ died in Malta in January 1943.

177 This requisitioned Glasgow-built steamship was sunk by 2 Japanese submarine torpedoes in Feb 1944 with the loss of 1297 lives.

Chapter 7

1941–42
The Desert War

The Western Desert – North Africa
Back in September 1940, while 14 Squadron had been receiving its brand new Blenheims in Port Sudan, there had been significant developments nearly a thousand miles to the north. On 13 September Italian troops led by the Governor of Libya, Marshal R Graziani[1], had advanced across the eastern border of Cyrenaica into Egypt. However the invasion was more symbolic than effective and Graziani halted after only three days when he reached Sidi Barrani, sixty miles along the coast. The British response was slow in coming, but in December GOC-in-C Middle East, General Sir A P Wavell[2] CB CMG MC, launched Operation *Compass* which aimed to expel Graziani's forces from Egypt. In several phases, with unexpected success, the British pushed the Italians westwards back into Cyrenaica, continuing all the way past Benghazi to El Agheila – an advance into Libya of over three hundred miles. With the Italians now held well to the west, Wavell turned his attention northwards to Greece, which was also under attack from the Italians. Critically, many of the units which had fought so effectively during Compass were redeployed to Greece.

Unfortunately for Wavell, the situation in North Africa changed dramatically for the worse on 14 February 1941, with the arrival of Generalleutnant E J E Rommel[3] and the Afrika Korps. This development heralded the beginning of two years of desert warfare which would ebb and flow across the Western Egypt and the Libyan province of Cyrenaica. Just over a month after arriving in theatre, Rommel started what was intended to be a limited offensive, but by the end of April he had reversed the Italian losses and pushed the British back across the Egyptian border, capturing the border towns of Bardia and Sollum in the process. However, the speed of Afrika Korps' advance out-paced the deployment of the 15th Panzer Division leaving Rommel's forces overstretched and unable to take the town of Tobruk. This strategically important port was left cut off behind German lines and remained so for the next eight months. Rommel's successes also coincided with German operations in Greece which culminated in the British evacuation to Crete at the end of the month.

When 14 Squadron arrived in Egypt, Rommel was busy consolidating his positions and securing Cyrenaica. At Heliopolis, just a five-minute walk from the suburbs of Cairo, the Squadron was absorbed into the newly formed 204 Group, which would mount mobile operations in the Western Desert of Egypt. Reflecting this

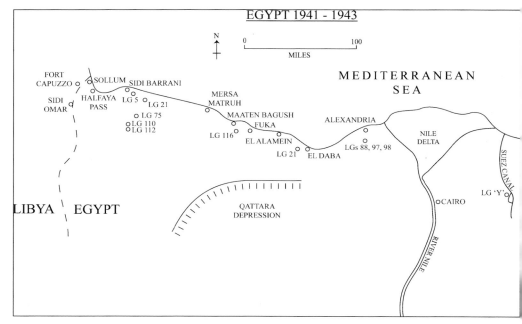

emphasis on mobility, the Squadron's structure was condensed into two fully equipped Flights which included all the logistic support to make them virtually self sufficient. Meanwhile, those personnel who had completed their overseas tour of duty were offered posting back to the UK; their places were taken by newcomers for whom the time to train would be preciously short. In this way, during the fortnight before Squadron deployed forward for operations, nearly half of its personnel (including many of the experienced technicians) had changed over.

On 15 April two aircraft were tasked to make a reconnaissance of the front lines in the Tobruk. This inaugural mission involved landing part way at Maaten Bagush where they received their instructions and where they were to land afterwards to make their report. The approach to Tobruk required adherence to a safe-lane, surrounded as it was by Axis ground troops. Fg Off G R Whittard[4], the navigator in the leading aircraft, noted the problems of navigation over this desert terrain where identifiable features could be hard to find. Although his aircraft landed safely from the sortie, Plt Off Ormiston's second Blenheim[5], which was following shortly behind did not return. This was a sobering introduction to operations in the Western Desert.

Sixteen Blenheims with twenty aircrews and their supporting personnel deployed on 1 May to Landing Ground Operational number 21 (LG 21), approximately a hundred miles west of Alexandria. LG21 was one of a vast array of tactical airstrips across the Western Desert: these landing grounds, which tended to be grouped together for mutual defence, boasted only the most rudimentary facilities to support aircraft operations. Accommodation was in tents and slit trenches, and both men and machines were at the mercy of the desert climate. Here the weather could change quickly: clear skies or coastal fogs could give way to storms and still air to violent winds which whipped up the desert sands, reducing visibility and blasting everything in their path. The conditions were a particular challenge to the groundcrew working on the aircraft. "Jobs like replacing and timing a magneto were difficult and somewhat frustrating," recalled LAC D E Francis[6]. "All our aircraft were fitted with a 'Vokes Filter' at the initial air intake to ensure that all sand was trapped before it could enter the engine. These filters contained a fabric element which was soaked in engine oil and had to be removed, cleaned in petrol and re-soaked with clean engine oil at fairly frequent intervals. This entailed removal and subsequent replacement of a large number of bolts, a really tedious task I can tell you!"

Just after 0500 hrs on 3 May ten Blenheims lifted off for three-hour familiarisation sorties up to the front line at Sollum. Nothing of interest was observed, but 14 Squadron's participation in the North African campaign had begun.

Offensive operations started two days later when four pairs of Blenheims departed in the morning to bomb enemy transport on the Tobruk-Bardia road. Small concentrations of vehicles were attacked and some hits were claimed. The defenders

Changing a Mercury engine on a Blenheim at a desert Landing Ground. Ron Page with hammer to left of engine; to right of engine: Sgt Simpson, Bill Rothwell (instrument repairer), Tony Walters (electrician). (Ron Page)

at Bardia responded with heavy and accurate anti-aircraft fire, but all aircraft returned safely. Bad weather hampered operations against the satellite aerodrome at Derna on 10 May, and Plt Off R F Johnson[7] was the only one of four aircraft[8] which took off in the early hours which reached the target. Johnson estimated between a hundred and a hundred-and-fifty enemy aircraft to be on the ground and he claimed some direct hits on them. Three aircraft on a later sortie that morning found trouble locating targets on the road east of Tobruk, and only one dropped its bombs inconclusively on eight vehicles, which were obscured by dust. By the afternoon the weather had not improved and target acquisition around Derna was difficult: although two Blenheims dropped their bombs they could not see the results. A third[9] which had taken off an hour behind the leading pair was intercepted on its way to the target. A CR42 carried out a sustained attack on the Blenheim for thirty minutes, inflicting severe damage on the aircraft and prompting the crew to jettison their bomb load in an effort to escape their attacker. With the aileron controls shot away, the barely controllable Blenheim flew back east until, in short succession, the port propellor fell off due to oil starvation and the starboard engine stopped. However, despite the severity of the damage caused by the CR42 and the subsequent crash landing to the east of Sollum, the crew were unhurt. A raid to Derna the following night resulted in another loss when Sgt G Dickson's aircraft encountered bad weather and had to divert to Aboukir where it crashed on landing in the early hours, injuring the crew.

Operation *Brevity*
The descriptively named Operation *Brevity* was conceived in the aftermath of Rommel's advance to the Egyptian border as a short counter-attack to exploit weakness in his extended front line in the area of Sollum. The operation began on 15 May with advances towards Fort Capuzzo (approximately five miles inland) and Sollum itself. Just to the south of Sollum, the Halfaya pass (known colloquially as "Hellfire Pass") which ran through the escarpment separating the coastal strip from the inland desert, was defended by Italian troops. It was against these that eight Blenheims were tasked in the early morning. The aircraft bombed infantry positions and vehicles, then carried out low-level strafing passes against the infantry, firing over two thousand rounds. By the end of the day, the pass had been captured by British troops.

Although *Brevity* had petered out within a few days, eight Blenheims were called in at short notice on 18 May to support British troops in the area between Sollum and Capuzzo. They claimed hits against moving motor vehicles, but the Squadron Commander later commented that bombing dispersed transport and personnel from 3,000 feet appeared to be largely ineffective; it was also impossible to assess accurately how much damage had been caused by such attacks. Ten days later the Halfaya pass was back in Axis hands.

21 May 1941 – A Black Day
The arrival of German forces in Africa brought not only the mechanised divisions of the Afrika Korps to the desert, but also the modern aircraft of the Luftwaffe. The

three squadrons of Fighter Wing I/JG27 had arrived at Ain El Gazala in Libya on 18 April, and were soon operating from a forward base at Gambut. Initially they were contained by Hurricanes based at Tobruk, but when these were withdrawn, the Germans began to operate closer to the Egyptian border.

Around 0400 hrs on 21 May seven Blenheims from 14 Squadron led by Sqn Ldr Stapleton departed from LG21 to attack vehicles, encampments and gun positions on the Capuzzo to Tobruk road. They had been briefed to fly in a wide formation at medium level in order to get as much coverage as much of the broad roadway as possible. Until then, 14 Squadron's experience of fighter attack had been limited to the obsolescent Italian biplanes; they were completely surprised by their first encounter with the Messerschmidt Bf109 flown by combat-experienced German pilots. Unfortunately the wide bombing formation made it impossible for the members of the formation to provide cross-cover for each other and trailing aircraft were picked off one by one by the fighters. Sqn Ldr Stapleton and Lt Forrester returned to base after successfully dropping their bombs amongst vehicles, but the remaining Blenheims[10] and their crews, most of whom were very experienced, were all lost. All five of these aircraft were shot down in approximately an eight minute period to the southwest of Fort Capuzzo by Bf109Es of 3 Staffel I/JG27[11] killing all the crew members.

The Battle for Crete

The Italians had attempted to invade Greece in late October 1940 but had been pushed back into Albania from where a subsequent attack in March 1941 also faltered. In that same month an Expeditionary Force composed mainly of British and Dominion troops from Egypt reinforced the Greeks, and the Germans also intervened to the aid of the Italians. After a short campaign, Greece fell to invading German forces and the British started a full-scale evacuation by sea on 24 April. German attention then moved to the island of Crete, which they planned to take swiftly to secure their southern flank before the imminent invasion of Russia. The attack on Crete, which began early on 20 May, was an audacious – and unexpected – airborne assault. During the morning, paratroopers dropped near the principal objective of Maleme airfield, at the western end of the island. In the afternoon targets along the northern coast were also attacked. At first, the lightly armed assault force was badly mauled, but despite suffering severe losses, the Germans managed to capture Maleme airfield the next day. This development allowed reinforcements to be flown in directly onto the island by flights of Ju52s; despite an effective sea blockade by the Royal Navy, the Germans gained the upper hand. The problem for the RAF was that Crete was well beyond the range of its fighter aircraft and was close to the operational limit for the North-African based Blenheims. Nevertheless, all available bomber squadrons were thrown against Crete.

Against this background 14 Squadron entered the battle. Things did not start well: the first sortie by five aircraft on 23 May was aborted and then sandstorms over the desert prevented operational flying from LG21 on the next day. However, the

Attacking from almost due east, Sqn Ldr Stapleton's bombs land amongst German aircraft (centre right) on the airfield at Maleme, Crete, during a bombing raid on 25 May 1941. (IWM)

morning wave of six 14 Squadron aircraft[12] on 25 May were more successful. They departed at 0400 hrs and set out for the four hundred mile flight from LG21 to Maleme, which would be a five hour round trip. The formation approached Maleme from the east, bombing from 1,800 feet and leaving more than a dozen Ju52s destroyed. Leading the second three aircraft, Flt Lt Buchanan's Blenheim was hit by anti-aircraft fire, which caused some damage to the aircraft and wounded the gunner, Sgt Ball, in the foot. Apart from this minor damage, the raid was deemed very successful. The afternoon wave, comprising a further three 14 Squadron aircraft[13], was less fortunate. This formation, led by Flt Lt Green, with Sgt H P Jeudwine and Lt Forrester took off at 1230 hrs, but all three aircraft were shot down by Bf109s of 5/JG77 which was operating with complete air superiority over Crete.

Two days later, British forces were ordered to evacuate of the island. That afternoon, a formation of three Blenheims[14] was launched to bomb enemy troops between Souda Bay and Maleme. One aircraft returned early with engine trouble, but the two others made successful attacks and headed back towards Egypt. Unfortunately, fog had formed over much of the Egyptian coast during the evening and the landing ground was completely obscured. Fg Off LeCavalier issued an SOS call 1940 hrs, but nothing further was heard, and the wreckage of his aircraft was later found thirty miles southwest of Mersa Matruh. LeCavalier's body was still in the aircraft, and that of his gunner Sgt C P A Bury[15] lay nearby, having baled out presumably at too low an altitude. Their Observer, Sgt Page, however did survive baling out and walked to safety across the desert to Mersa Matruh.

Fg Off Mackenzie's aircraft suffered a similar fate: the wireless operator Sgt McConnell made repeated attempts to obtain a radio direction finding fix but he was unsuccessful and the crew realised that they were hopelessly lost. Unsure of their position and with nowhere to land they bailed out some seventy miles south of El Dabaa, in the inhospitable Qattara Depression. Despite planning to link up at the crash site, the three men became separated and Sgts M B Fearn[16] and McConnell set out independently to walk northwards to the coast. Over the next six days a thorough search was mounted to find the aircraft and its crew. After two days of searching, a Bombay aircraft found the wreckage of the Blenheim. MacKenzie's parachute was also found about a mile away hanging on a bush, with the cords cut. Two days later the Bombay crew spotted Sgt Fearn who had managed to walk about thirty miles into a swamp. The aircraft landed to pick him up, finding him badly mosquito-bitten; he had survived by collecting water in his Mae West. That afternoon the aircraft returned and found Sgt McConnell. Too weak to stand, he was doused in water under the wing of the rescue aircraft and given some water and food. From 2-4 June either a Bombay, or a Valentia, landed each day at the crash site and a search party equipped with motorcycles, led by Lt E M Lewis[17] SAAF. However, despite combing the area for three days, MacKenzie was never found.

By the last day of May the battle for Crete was over and allied troops had either been evacuated or had surrendered. For 14 Squadron, May 1941 extracted hefty toll. The comments by AOC-in-C AVM A W Tedder[18] CB, that "... the cost [of Crete] has been heavy in relation to strength, especially in Blenheims. Blenheim dawn and dusk raids in particular have been expensive..." were particularly true of 14 Squadron which had lost over half its strength: twelve aircraft had been lost during May, with twenty-seven men dead. Sadly many of these casualties were experienced crews who had served with the unit since Palestine days. The Squadron operations diary records that at the end of the month only four operational crews and three serviceable aircraft remained.

The single major factor in the Squadron's losses had been the presence over the battlefields of the highly capable Bf109 which made medium height daylight sorties by single aeroplanes extremely hazardous. Furthermore, the piecemeal tasking of Blenheim squadrons was contributing to their vulnerability. Sqn Ldr Stapleton suggested addressing the Bf109 fighter threat by using low-level tactics and increasing the number of night sorties if singleton aircraft were used, or deploying aircraft as large formations of about six for mutual protection during daylight. He also identified the lack of a good emergency landing option if the coastal airstrips became fog-bound. Other Blenheim commanders echoed these views.

During a much needed operational lull in the first week of June, the Squadron started the business of recovering its strength. Four newly trained crews arrived, eight more aircraft added and engineers worked on the serviceability of the remainder. Sgt J T Willis[19] was one of the new pilots who arrived fresh from 70 OTU at Ismailia on 4 June. His initial impression was of a squadron still "shell-shocked" from their losses over the desert and Crete, with an unwillingness to talk much about the events.

On 7 June operations resumed with six nights of effort directed against German airstrips in Cyrenaica. During these raids the Blenheims were armed with a mixed load of twelve small 20lb bombs and also canisters containing a new experimental weapon. This was a four-pronged spike or "caltrop" and each Blenheim could typically drop 4,500 spikes in canisters. The spikes were arranged in a tetrahedron, so that when they hit the ground three prongs would act as a tripod to support the forth upward-pointing prong which would, in theory, puncture truck and aircraft tyres. It was not an original idea (the Romans had used caltrops as a defence against cavalry), and the hope was that dropping spikes would cause disruption to the movement of enemy aircraft on the airstrips. The landing grounds at Great Gambut, one 5 miles north of Capuzzo, El Adem, Bir Bu Amud, Martuba, Derna Satellite, Gazala North and South and parts of the Tobruk-Bardia road were all sewn with "spikes" and bombs. Fortunately, despite some effective searchlights and anti-aircraft fire the raids were carried out without loss to the Blenheims. However, according to a German prisoner taken near Capuzzo the raids were completely ineffective: the personnel at the target airfields were simply roused early each morning to fan out across the landing strips and pick up the caltrops. A final attack by two aircraft on the night of 16 June against Gazala South landing ground is the last recorded use of "spikes" by 14 Squadron.

Operation *Battleaxe*

After the failure of Operation *Brevity*, and the losses of Greece and Crete, Wavell came under intense pressure from Churchill to mount another offensive in the Western Desert. Thus was born Operation *Battleaxe*, which would use the same starting positions as *Brevity*, but would have the wider goal of pushing past the border area Sollum and onwards, past besieged Tobruk, to the line of Derna and Mechili. Wavell's forces for *Battleaxe* had been bolstered by the availability of more tanks and more Hurricanes which had arrived in Alexandria on 12 May after a bold dash from Gibraltar.

The battle opened on 15 June along the Libyan border, but quickly stalled: Fort Capuzzo was the only objective to be taken and stiff resistance at the Halfaya pass and Hafid Ridge (west of Fort Capuzzo) blocked the British advance. Although counter-attacks by the 15th Panzer Division on Fort Capuzzo the next day were repulsed, the German 5th Light Division was able to push past the Hafid Ridge and

Three Blenheims set off for a raid in late 1941. Note the light bomb cariers mounted under the fuselage. (Andrew Thomas)

continue south to the Libyan border at Sidi Omar. Here, on the morning of the 17 June, 5th Light Division accompanied by 15th Panzer Division crossed into Egypt, aiming to encircle the British lines.

At this point in the battle 14 Squadron directly engaged the advancing German divisions[20]. Two formations were dispatched on 17 June to attack tanks and vehicles in the Sidi Omar area. The morning wave, comprising six Blenheims[21] led by Sqn Ldr Stapleton, had only limited success, but in the afternoon Stapleton led nine aircraft[22] on a more effective sortie. Photographs from the second attack showed that at least twelve enemy tanks or vehicles had been disabled. The afternoon sortie, which was Squadron's largest Blenheim formation attack yet, was also the first operational sortie for Sgts D D Warwick[23], A Honig[24] and P N Keeley[25]. A further raid by nine aircraft the next morning was also successful: although the crews themselves could not see their results, the formation of Glenn Martins which followed them over the target reported that a number of direct hits had been scored on tanks. However, *Battleaxe* had failed and, as a political fall-out of the failure, Wavell was replaced by General C J E Auchinleck [26] GCIE CB CSI DSO OBE on 5 July.

Meanwhile farther afield, the Eastern Front opened as Germany swept into the Soviet Union on 22 June 1941, starting a campaign that was to soak up German manpower and materiel to a hitherto unseen scale.

The Squadron's final operations from LG21 on 25 and 26 June were carried out in conjunction with another Blenheim unit, 113 Sqn operating from LG15, and a South African Maryland squadron. These raids were intended to be massed attacks against the landing grounds at Gazala North and South. The mission on 25 June failed to bomb when the formation leader from 113 Squadron could not locate the target; however Flt Lt Buchanan led the same six crews from 14 Squadron the next morning to Gazala South where they dropped their weapons on dispersed aircraft. In all, twenty-five aircraft took part in the raid and although four fighters were observed taking off, no opposition was encountered.

14 Squadron Blenheim attacking mechanised troops near Sollum on 17 June 1941. (Andrew Thomas)

In contrast to May, June 1941 ended without loss to men or aircraft, and an impending move out to the Middle East brought a pause in 14 Squadron s participation in the Western Desert campaign.

The Syrian Diversion

As if the strategic disasters in Greece and western Egypt were not enough, events east of Suez had also come to the fore in the spring of 1941. Firstly, there was a military coup d'état in Iraq, where there was still significant British interest in, and control of, the oil industry and secondly, German forces were granted the use of military facilities in Vichy-French controlled Syria. These two events posed a major threat to the British interests in the Middle East.

The coup in Iraq on 1 April brought the anti-British former Prime Minister Rashid Ali, to power. British forces in Iraq were hastily reinforced during April and hostilities started on 2 May. The army steadily pushed the Iraqis back to Baghdad and the RAF also played a major role, using the obsolescent aircraft used by the Flying Training Schools at Habbaniya and Shaibah as improvised bombers. Despite support from the Axis powers provided through Vichy-occupied Syria, Rashid Ali was beaten back to Baghdad and by the end of the month he had been forced to flee into Persia. An armistice on the 31 May restored the monarch, Abdul Illah, and a pro-British government.

After securing Iraq, British, Dominion and Free French forces commenced operations against the Vichy French in Syria on 8 June. Within a fortnight advances from Palestine and Iraq led to the fall of Damascus and shortly afterwards the Vichy French capitulated just as the Australian 7th Division were poised to enter Beruit. A ceasefire on 12 July was followed by an armistice two days later.

Palestine

As these events reached a conclusion in early July, 14 Squadron packed up its affairs in LG21 and followed the order to move from the Western Desert to Petah Tiqva in Palestine. The aircraft flew directly to Petah Tiqva on 8 July, making a three-and-a-half hour flight from LG21. However, the move took substantially longer for the ground party. The forty-five strong collection of vehicles[27] needed for the squadron move had to drive to Ismalia and Kantara, then onward across the Sinai through El Arish and Gaza to reach Petah Tiqva, a journey of some 500 miles.

Unfortunately, danger in wartime was not confined to facing down the enemy; just as the move was being prepared, a fatal road accident occurred on the night of 4 July. The Squadron Equipment Officer Fg Off H Parker[28], who had been responsible for moving the ground party from Port Sudan to Heliopolis, was killed in a collision with an Egyptian ambulance as he drove back from a meeting at the forward landing ground.

The landing strip at Petah Tiqva contrasted markedly with that of the LG21: roughly hewn through a wheat field, the 1,500 yard runway was very small in comparison with the relatively open stretches of the desert landing grounds. A further complication was the power line which ran across the approach to the runway. One new pilot, Plt Off L E Leon[29] actually struck the power line during an approach, luckily escaping with part of the canopy blister next to his head being sliced off. Another pilot fresh from the UK failed to realise that in the Middle East only the outer tanks contained 100 octane fuel and these were used for take-off: in attempting to take off with the inner tanks selected, he "cut two swathes of corn" (according to Lt Lewis) with his propellors as the Blenheim staggered airborne. However at least the tented accommodation at Petah Tiqva, set amongst the trees of an orange grove, seemed far more pleasant than the open sand of the desert. There was also the novelty of having a small town nearby.

The move back from the front line gave the Squadron the opportunity to complete the task began in June of recovering to full strength. New aircrews and aircraft arrived to bring the Squadron to its establishment of twenty-one aircraft and crews and gaps among the engineering and support staff were also filled. Reflecting the number of personnel under command, about one hundred and eighty of all ranks, the Squadron Commander was promoted to Wing Commander rank and the Flight Commanders, Buchanan and Illsley promoted to the rank of Squadron Leader. With no operational tasking the Squadron enjoyed a period of training and much-needed leave throughout most of July. Ten days of leave every three months for aircrew and two weeks every four months for groundcrew became compulsory.

On 15 July, twelve aircraft were launched for a a formation demonstration over Beirut, Homs, Aleppo and Damascus and at the end of the month five aircraft set off for Nicosia. These aircraft carried out a fruitless search for a dinghy between the Cyprus and Turkish coast on 28 July.

Iran

Although the problems in Iraq and Syria had been quelled, questions remained about where Iranian allegiances lay. Iran's oil was of particular strategic importance to the British, Russians and Germans, not least because Abadan had the world s largest refining capacity. In July both the Russians and British sent ultimatums to the Iranian government insisting that the Iranians expel a number of German "technical experts" who had started working in the oil fields. When the Iranians refused to do so, the Russian and British governments resorted to military force.

14 Squadron were ordered to move to Habbaniya on 2 August for operations against Iran. A day later the ground party was on the move. From Petah Tiqva, the convoy followed the coast to Haifa and thence the line of the oil pipeline which ran across Transjordan towards Kirkuk in northern Iraq. This route led onto the high Transjordan desert to Mafraq thence the oil pumping station at H4, across into Iraq to pumping station H3, onwards via Rutbah to the airstrip at LG5 (about 115 miles west of Ramadi) and then the final stage to Habbaniya. For six days the convoy traversed desert roads which one driver, Cpl Macleod, recalled "was really a hell of a journey – the tremendous heat, the clouds of mouth-clogging sand and dust carried by the lorries. No one wanted to be behind anybody. In open desert it was devil take the hindmost. We started each day at first light to escape the fierce heat and rested from midday onwards to next first light."

With the ground party safely in Habbaniya, the aircraft set off for the three-and-a-half hour flight from Palestine on the 10 August. Lt Lewis returned to Palestine the next day and to pick up the remaining five aircraft from Lydda and lead them to Habbaniya on 12 August. An established peacetime RAF station, unlike the ad hoc desert landing grounds, Habbaniya boasted some unaccustomed luxuries. Cpl R V Ball[30] one of the Squadron cooks "...couldn t believe our luck being sent to Habb. The kitchens were all electric, the billets air cooled, like staying in a Holiday Inn, but they didn t make us very welcome. They thought we were a scruffy lot. Habb was a peace-time station complete with native servants, swimming pools, cinema etc. and real beds. We couldn't understand why the airmen there got a daily overseas allowance of ten pence to allow them to live in luxury whilst we, in the desert, got four pence. When we moved to Qaiyarah we could take the beds so we took as many boards as possible."

At Habbaniya the Squadron's flying consisted only of some formation practice. However, even so two aircraft[31] were damaged in accidents: Sqn Ldr Buchanan stalled in the finals turn and another pilot had a similar mishap, citing the sloppiness of the controls near the ground . Blame was attributed to "a certain thinness of the air near midday in this part of the east".

On 17 August the Squadron moved again, this time to Qaiyarah, near Mosul, in readiness for operations. The Advance Ground Party of thirty-eight men and eight vehicles left on that day and the balance followed five days later, arriving after an overnight stop. The aircraft made the one-and-a-half hour flight northwards on 24 August and were ready for operations over Iran the following day.

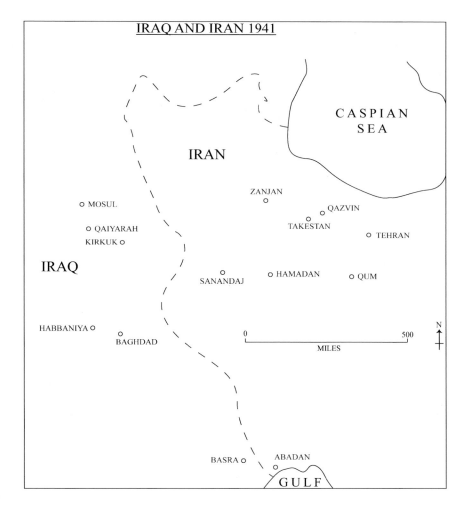

IRAQ AND IRAN 1941

CASPIAN SEA

IRAN

ZANJAN
o

o MOSUL

QAZVIN
o

TAKESTAN
o

o QAIYARAH

o TEHRAN

KIRKUK o

IRAQ

o
SANANDAJ

o HAMADAN

o QUM

HABBANIYA o

o
BAGHDAD

0   500

MILES

N

BASRA o   ABADAN
o

GULF

For 14 Sqn the comforts of Habbaniya had been swapped for a more basic existence in the northern Iraqi desert scrub at Qaiyarah: three newly-built single-roomed buildings of mud-brick served as messes and the 1,800 yard runway was a stinking construction of sand, crushed rock and sulphurous tar oil. Temperatures soared in daytime and the Blenheim s metal airframe burned the skin of those who tried to fly and maintain it. At least the presence of the Indian Divisions in Iraq and as a guard force at the airfield had the added benefit of the availability of decent curry.

The Allied intention in Iran was not to crush the nation, but rather to re-direct its political allegiance. Once the poorly-equipped Iranian armed forces had been overcome, the Allies had to set about reassuring the population of the intentions of the invading force. In contrast to the direct action in the Western Desert, the

211

Squadron's operations would be part of the psychological war and instead of bombs, tens of thousands of leaflets would be dropped over Iran s major cities, explaining that there was no quarrel with the Iranian people nor any designs upon their territory or sovereignty.

Nonetheless, the operation was still very challenging due to the extremes of temperatures and the ranges involved on what were typically five-hour sorties. The theoretical range of the Blenheim was just over 1,600 miles, but the operational modifications such as gun pods, Vokes air filters, and the roughly applied desert camouflage itself, markedly reduced that range in practice by about a third. The round trip from Qaiyarah to Tehran and back was just over 900 miles and in order to achieve this range supplementary oil tanks had to be fitted to the aircraft and the engines would have to be run on a weaker "long-range" fuel mixture. Sgt Willis explained that "the Blenheim s Mercury engines were designed to run on weak or rich mixture. The throttle box mechanism was so geared that when the throttles were thrust past zero boost the mixture controls had to be pulled back to (or leaver geared back to) rich . Under normal conditions the use of weak running hardly arose for anyone on the Squadron. My own experience was very limited in flying on weak... one occasion arose when I found that on weak the engine spluttered alarmingly... There was another minor snag for running on weak the engines ran hotter and that entailed adjusting the cylinder head gills." However, Willis also noticed some benefits in using a weak mixture at night: the exhaust plume on a weak mixture was only about nine inches long, whereas on rich it could be a very conspicuous three feet!

Coincident with the start of the land invasion, Wg Cdr Stapleton led eleven aircraft for the first leaflet-dropping mission to Tehran on 25 August. Only eight aircraft completed the round trip on which 60,000 leaflets fluttered down upon the capital. The CO had selected the British Embassy in the city centre as the aiming point and was gratified to hear some days later that some leaflets had fallen into its garden amongst the others that had scattered over the city. No opposition was encountered but although two of the three aircraft which had turned back due to engine trouble landed safely, Sqn Ldr Illsley s[32] crash landed, without injury to the crew.

A second mission on the following day involved six aircraft and 40,000 leaflets for Qazvin, about ninety miles northwest of Tehran. Again there was no opposition, but once again a Blenheim was damaged: leaflets dropped from Sqn Ldr Buchanan s aircraft failed to tear open and the intact bundle struck the port wing leading edge of Lt Lewis aircraft. The Squadron Operations Diary records slight damage though in the words of Lt Lewis himself, it bent the aileron control rod and he "had a hell of a time keeping straight and level."

On 27 August, Wg Cdr Stapleton led five aircraft over the towns of Qum and Hamadan, each city receiving 41,000 leaflets. The fourth day saw the end of Iranian resistance and Sqn Ldr Illsley led six aircraft over Sanandaj, Takistan and Zenjan with 118,000 leaflets. In contrast with the calm response noted among the population to the presence of the bombers on the previous day, the people of Sanandaj were seen to panic at the overflight.

Although the Squadron's operational task over Iran was now complete, the unit lingered at Qaiyarah for another month. September was spent with a series of formation flying practices, night flying and co-operation exercises with the Indian Divisions. All this was especially useful considering the number of new crews that had arrived just before the move into Iraq. With their experience of Eritrea and the Western Desert, Stapleton was considered keen on formation skills and Buchanan obsessive. Sgt Willis called Buchanan the "perfect gent" in the air: "he knew that Blenheims would always be struggling to take station after take-off – one had about twenty knots in hand to catch leading aircraft. He would stooge around on very wide circuits at low speed to encourage early link-ups. On course he was steadiness itself." On 9 September the Squadron was able to use its newly-honed formation skills as part of a large formation show of force around northern Iraq. Twelve aircraft each from 11, 14 and 45 Squadrons flew on a four-and-a-half-hour tour taking in Mosul to the north, Kirkuk to the south east, Baquba just north east of Baghdad, then Baghdad itself and finally Habbaniya.

Return to the Western Desert
On 4 October 1941 orders were received to return to the Western Desert and the convoy was ready to leave four days later for the two day drive to Habbaniya. The aircraft flew south to Habbaniya on the same day meeting and the whole Squadron was reunited for the formal handover of command from Wg Cdr Stapleton to the newly promoted Wg Cdr Buchanan on 10 October.

Both the outgoing and incoming Squadron commanders were highly regarded by 14 Squadron personnel. Fg Off Whittard wrote that "although both were regarded as excellent squadron commanders, they were very different characters in many ways. Deryck [Stapleton] was of a more serious nature and possessed exceptional administrative qualities, highly capable in all fields, but less spectacular than Buck [Buchanan]. He adhered to the text book more than Buck and although on the surface appearing less adventurous, displayed all the necessary daring and courage."

Stapleton described his successor as an "outstanding pilot, madly brave, strangely dilettante" and Plt Off K P Wilson[33] recalled that Wg Cdr Buchanan's "personal appearance was that of a dandy – always immaculate in shorts and shirt, with a fair moustache which he constantly curled with his fingers." But under that dandified appearance he was "a pilot's pilot if ever there was one. He was utterly fearless and flew with tremendous natural skill ... his love of operations was such that he flew on every possible occasion and in 14 Squadron kept two crews who alternated trips. Formation flying with Buck was a hair-raising experience until it was mastered. It was generally acknowledged that 14 Sqn flew closer than any other Blenheim squadron. Buck would be constantly urging each aircraft to get closer and closer in – we were often closer than half a span – and after a two-hour operation the hand on the control column would often be badly blistered."

The ground party set off west again on 12 October, staging their journey across the desert as they had done on their eastward journey in August. First they stopped

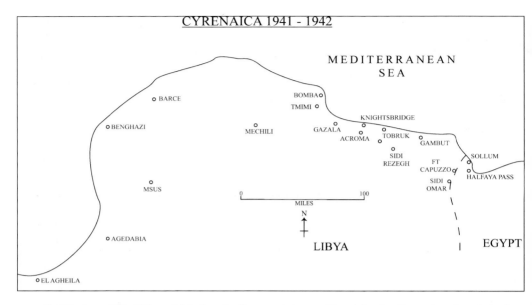

CYRENAICA 1941 - 1942

MEDITERRANEAN SEA

at LG5, then H3, H4 and Mafraq before arriving at Ramleh, the Squadron's original home in 1920, on 16 October for a stay of three days. However the aircraft remained for an extended stay at Habbaniya, only leaving for Lydda on 26 October. By this time the ground party had already moved on, having arrived at LG116, midway between Alexandria and the Libyan border, four days previously. LG116 was just another staging post as the Squadron awaited the departure of 113 Squadron from LG15. Once the latter LG was vacated, 14 Squadron moved into LG15 in the first few days of November.

By November 1941 the situation in the Western Desert had changed in scale if not in geography since 14 Squadron had left four months previously. Although the front line remained just inside the Egyptian border as it had done since the failure of Operation *Battleaxe* in June, both sides had been significantly reinforced. Rommel s Panzergruppe Afrika (upgraded from the original core formation of the Afrika Korps) included two Panzer divisions (15th and the 21st, formerly the 5th Light Division), two infantry divisions and the Italian XXI Corps of four infantry divisions. Under direct Italian control was XX Corps comprising of an armoured division and a motorised infantry division. Auchinleck's land force facing Rommel was the newly-formed Eighth Army commanded by Major General A G Cunningham CB DSO MC[34]. This consisted of XXX Corps (including 7th Armoured Division), XIII Corps (including 2nd New Zealand and 4th Indian Infantry Divisions) and the sizeable Tobruk garrison of 70th Infantry Division, the Polish Independent Carpathian Rifle Brigade and 32nd Army Tank Brigade. In all, there were some 120,000 men on each opposing force.

Allied aircraft in Egypt positioned west of Suez had been reorganised in October under Air Headquarters Western Desert and 14 Sqn was to join 270 Wing (along with other Blenheim squadrons: 8, 45, 55, 84 and the Free French Lorraine Squadron). AHQ Wester Desert was commanded by Air Vice-Marshal A Coningham[35] CB DSO MC DFC AFC. The vulnerability of lone Blenheims was being addressed by either singleton night operations or the use of larger daylight formations for which fighter escort could be provided. Also being addressed were new techniques to improve the hitherto poor liaison with the Army for timely air support.

Operation *Crusader*

As the Eighth Army massed inside Egypt, the targets for 14 Sqn were familiar to the old hands from the earlier part of the year: the same airfields in Cyrenaica and the same front-line forces inside the Libyan border that they had bombed in the summer would be revisited. However, for about half the crews the coming offensive would be their first experience of the Western Desert.

LG15 was only four or five miles north of LG116, situated on the escarpment overlooking the coast and the railway station at Sidi Haneish. Like most of these landing grounds it was merely a tract of cleared and levelled desert. The Officers and Sergeants messes were wooden sheds with tables, chairs and a bar; the other ranks mess was a large marquee and the Ops room a smaller marquee. Tents accommodated two or four men. However, the Squadron's stay at LG15 was only temporary as the forthcoming Allied offensive was planned to push westwards across the Libyan desert with its air support following behind.

The first sorties took place on 9 November when five aircraft[36] launched against storage dumps around Gazala North airstrip and an adjacent fort just west of the airstrip. These attacks were part of an attempt to neutralise Axis air power prior to the ground offensive. Although the raids were largely inconclusive, some hits were noted by two of the attacking aircraft. However, the Luftwaffe was also on the offensive and attacks were being reciprocated on Allied airstrips. LG15 was dive-bombed by two aircraft in the early evening of 10 November and about twenty bombs fell on the airfield. A Blenheim belonging to 113 Squadron was damaged and LAC T H Turner[37] of 14 Squadron's Photographic Section was killed. Damage to the runway and poor weather led to the cancellation of an attack on Gazala South that night. Two nights later, however, in the early hours of 12 November, dumps and repair and maintenance shops near Gazala South were attacked by six aircraft[38]. The bomb load also included five hundred leaflets for each aircraft and incendiaries. Sgt Honig's aircraft crash landed back at LG15 after suffering a hydraulic failure and the collapse of one undercarriage leg.

After pausing of a few days (which included a co-operation exercise with the army and an unsuccessful rendezvous with a fighter escort) the tempo of operations increased on 17 November, the day preceding the opening of the ground offensive. In a change to previous routine, the day's raid started with six aircraft[39] deploying early in the morning to LG110 for a briefing and to meet with their escort of twenty-four Tomahawk fighters. Unfortunately, the day started tragically when one of the aircraft [40] swung on take-off in low visibility and crashed. Although Sgt V C Royal s[41]

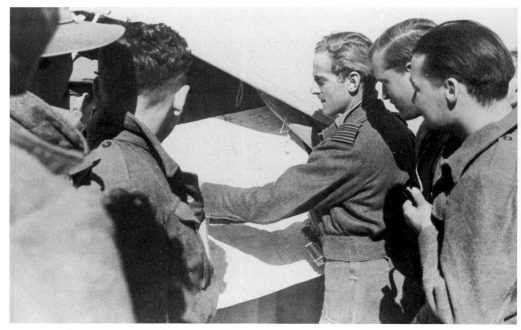

Wg Cdr J K Buchannan DFC briefing crews for a mission in late 1941 or early 1942.

crew escaped with only the air gunner, Sgt C C Murfitt[42], suffering slight burns, the crash destroyed a tent and killed three of the Squadron's aircrew, Flt Sgts R W Chubb[43], B L Jenkins[44] and A L Ellis[45] who were resting inside. The subsequent fire raged furiously, detonating a 250-pound bomb and some of the 40-pound bomb load. A replacement aircraft was dispatched to LG110, bringing the formation strength back up to six but the raid, on the landing ground at Gambut, failed. Wg Cdr Buchanan's aircraft suffered an electrical failure which prevented the release of his bombs: unfortunately these were the mark upon which the other aircraft had been instructed to release their weapons. The formation landed back into its new base, LG75 without having bombed the airfield.

The ground party convoy arrived at LG75 the next day as did the balance of the serviceable aircraft. Four individual sorties were launched in the afternoon to attack the landing ground at Bir el Baheira where a dozen enemy aircraft were reported to be bogged down after heavy rains during the night. The attack, at ten-minute intervals, was conducted using cloud for cover but one of the four Blenheims[46] flown by Plt Off C D Loughlin[47] failed to return. The graves of the three crewmen were later found, dug by the Germans and inscribed 'To Three Brave Airmen'.

That same morning saw the first thrust of Operation *Crusader*. XXX Corps' 7th Armoured Division crossed the border near Fort Maddalena, fifty miles south of the

Axis defensive line which ran from Sidi Omar to the pass at Halfaya and up to the coastal town of Sollum. This heavily armoured force then proceeded northwest towards besieged Tobruk where 70th Division were facing four Italian infantry Divisions (Brescia, Trento, Bologna and Pavia) and the German Afrika Division. Meanwhile the more lightly armoured XIII Corps swung south around Sidi Omar itself, in a manoeuvre to attack the Axis front line strongholds at Bardia, Sollum and Halfaya from the rear.

14 Squadron aircraft were involved with direct support of the advance: on 19 November the Bardia-Tobruk road was attacked and the next day seven aircraft deployed via LG112 with a fighter escort to attack vehicles and tanks in the wadis just north of El Adem. There followed another four days of sorties against Axis vehicles on the El Adem-Acroma road; this was the western half of a road built by the Germans and Italians to bypass the enclave at Tobruk so they could supply their units around Bardia. Intensive operations in various sectors of the battle area continued for each of the subsequent days until 4 December when a sand storm halted operations and provided a respite.

The sorties during *Crusader* would typically last two to three hours, and would comprise up to twelve aircraft from 14 Squadron, each armed with four 250-pound bombs, accompanied by other Blenheims from 45, 84 or the Lorraine Squadrons. This bomber formation would be protected by Hurricane or Tomahawk fighter escorts. On some days, however, individual aircraft were sent out on 'cloud cover' raids using the weather to conceal them from the anti-aircraft defences. Bombing was typically carried out from 6,000 feet or less and the 250-pound bombs were fitted with short rods extending from the nose of each weapon which were designed to make the bomb explode before it buried itself into the soft ground. During this period only two aircraft were reported as being damaged. Sgt Willis recalled that "the vast majority of my operations were in formation and a fair number were at night. So I (as a pilot) seldom saw anything worthwhile as to the target or anything else for that matter during formation raids... the broad conclusion I came to was that while a box of six or nine or, even better, twelve could do considerable damage over the usually dispersed armoured column, the single-bomber attack with four 250-pound bombs was far less certain. In single raids the pilot quickly knew if there had been anything remotely like a hit or miss. My impression was that on our own we seldom hit anything much."

By the eighth day of the offensive the westward thrust had been halted short of Tobruk. The 7th Armoured Division had taken the airfield at Sidi Rezegh (about 15 miles south east of the Tobruk perimeter), then lost it to a counterattack from the 21st Panzer Division. This in turn halted the spirited breakout by the Tobruk garrison, who had pushed out towards the southeast to link up with the advancing 7th Armoured Division. Meanwhile to the east in the XIII Corps area, the 5th New Zealand Brigade advancing from Fort Capuzzo had succeeded in isolating the Axis border strongpoints of Sollum and Halfaya from Bardia; 7th Indian Brigade had also captured Sidi Omar against staunch Italian and German infantry resistance. Having confounded the link-

A Blenheim dropping its bomb load over a target in the Wesern Desert. (M Johnson)

up at Tobruk, Rommel's two Panzer divisions and the Italian Ariete armoured Division had set out south east towards the border at Sidi Omar. 25 November found the 21st Panzer Division pitted against the Indian Division at Sidi Omar while the 15th Panzer Division swung north towards Sidi Azeiz and XIII Corps. It was this day that turned out to be one of the most concentrated days of effort in the history of the Squadron with thiry-two sorties launched in three waves of eleven, eleven and ten aircraft respectively, attacking the 21st Panzer Division column to the south of Sidi Omar. Characteristically, Wg Cdr Buchanan led all three waves. The last wave was re-armed and airborne again just one hour after the second wave landed. In all, the Squadron reported one hundred and twenty 250-pound bombs landing amongst enemy armoured fighting vehicles and their efforts contributed greatly to slowing down the advance of the German force.

Repulsed from Sidi Omar, a much depleted 21st Panzer Division followed the 15th Panzer Division north towards Bardia and Sollum the next day. Meanwhile on 27 November a renewed thrust out of Tobruk established a thin corridor of contact between the besieged garrison and New Zealanders in the Ed Duda area south east of Tobruk. On the same day, to the south west of Tobruk, nine 14 Squadron aircraft led a similar number from 84 Squadron in an attack on enemy motor vehicles on the El Adem-Acroma "bypass" road. A low cloud base forced the leading aircraft down to 2,000 feet, which left the trailing elements stepped-down to a vulnerable 800 feet leaving 84 Squadron to take the brunt of the anti-aircraft fire. One of their aircraft was lost and another badly damaged. However, these attacks kept up the pressure on Axis armour around Tobruk while the success of the breakout hung in the balance.

In the last days of November Rommel turned his armoured Divisions forces westwards away from the border area, back towards the fragile Tobruk corridor. Here the focus of action continued into December. Although the 15th Panzer Division had made little progress at Ed Duda in early December, it had forced the withdrawal of the 2nd New Zealand Division near Sidi Rezegh and Belhamed. Believing the battle for Tobruk to be nearly won, and seeing an opportunity to advance eastwards once again to the Bardia-Sollum area, Rommel sent units including the 15th Panzer Division and Italian armour down the Bardia road and the track to Capuzzo (Trigh Capuzzo), on 2 December. During this time 14 Squadron, along with the other Blenheim units, continued to engage the enemy ground forces. On 1 December the Squadron provided six aircraft for a formation of eighteen Blenheims which picked up a fighter escort at LG 124 and then bombed a mechanised column to the south of Ed Duda. The following day five aircraft attempted to bomb vehicles on the El Adem-Acroma road near Bir El Gubi, but were unsuccessful because of low clouds. A day later, four Blenheims bombed vehicles and armour on the Trigh Capuzzo about 10 miles east of Sidi Rezegh, claiming a number of direct hits. However, on 4 December sandstorms once again swept the area, stopping all flying operations. Flying was to have resumed the next day but operations were brought to a temporary halt by a spectacular, but sadly fatal, accident at LG75. 14 Squadron aircraft were on the ground with engines turning awaiting their turn when for take off, when in rushing to make a rendezvous with fighters, two formations, one from 45 Squadron and one from the Lorraine Squadron, took off simultaneously from opposing ends of the runway. In the desperate effort to avoid each other, two aircraft stalled, crashed and blew up. The debris from the accident closed the airfield and the aircraft on the ground returned to their parking and shut-down, too late to re-plan the raid. It was not until 6 December that 14 Squadron was in action again, this time as part of a Wing formation which attacked a concentration of vehicles near near Bir El Gubi.

By the end of the first week in December Rommel realised that success was just beyond his grasp and he therefore withdrew his forces westwards to Gazala some 30 miles west of Tobruk. Here he established a more tenable line of supply and communications. By the 10 December Tobruk had been relieved, but in turn the Axis strongholds at Bardia, Sollum and Halfaya were now besieged by the British.

Rommel's withdrawal brought some respite for 14 Squadron, with two days of stand-down and a further two days free of operations. However, six aircraft were launched on individual "cloud cover" raids on 9 December. Poor weather prevented all but three of them from finding a target and Sgt H S Grimsey[48] was unable to find the landing ground on his return from attacking Bomba. After running out of fuel he and his crew abandoned the aircraft[49] successfully. As the front line shifted forwards the Squadron needed to use operating bases further to the west: El Adem was used as a forward base on the 12 December. Six aircraft deployed there for briefing and then returned to LG75 after the sortie. During this mission enemy fighters were seen in action for the first time in the offensive, setting the trend for the succeeding sorties. The German fighter force had been recently been augmented by the deployment of all three Gruppe of JG27 (I, II and III/JG27), introducing the more potent Bf109F to the theatre. Two days later eight Blenheims[50] were operating independently, tasked against opportunity targets around Derna; Sgt F W Dennis'[51] aircraft failed to return.

Sandstorms provided another two day pause but on 17 December six aircraft set off for Landing Ground at El Adem. Here they were to be briefed on their target and join the remainder of the Wing formation and the fighter escort. However, during the transit flight one aircraft suffered a seized engine and force landed on a road east of El Adem, while another suffered an engine failure on landing and crashed on the airfield whereupon its 250-pound bomb load exploded. Miraculously none of the crew was hurt in either incident. A third aircraft failed to start leaving only three 14 Squadron aircraft to join the escorted formation which attacked the road east of Derna. This formation was repeatedly attacked by Bf109Fs for three-quarters of an hour and all three aircraft were damaged, although the crews escaped injury.

This last attack coincided with the evacuation of Axis forces from the line at Gazala. Rommel's resupply chain from Italy was under severe pressure from anti-shipping strikes which had prevented over half of the replacement equipment reaching his ports in North Africa. On 17 December a deliberate and cohesive fighting withdrawal of Rommel's forces had begun, moving back towards El Agheila on the western edge of Cyrenaica, the starting point of his first offensive nine months earlier.

Keeping pace with the front line, 14 Squadron moved westwards too. After bombing vehicles 3 miles west of El Mechili on 18 December, six aircraft landed back at Gambut which had, at the last moment, been designated as its new 'home'. Unfortunately supplies hadn't caught up with the plan and the formation discovered a complete lack of fuel at Gambut so they flew back to LG75. Here they met with a similar problem, before finally heading back to Gambut for the night. One aircraft was lost in the process when Plt Off S F Lawson[52], who had only having been on the Squadron for a week, landed his Blenheim[53] heavily enough to collapse the undercarriage. Shortage of fuel again precluded operations the next day though 'normality' was resumed on the 20 December when seven aircraft participated in a raid on Barce airfield and the remainder of the Squadron, "B" Flight, arrived at Gambut.

As an indication of the speed of change across the middle of Cyrenaica, 14 Squadron sorties against Barce on 20 December and Megrun two days later were staged through Gazala 2 and El Mechili respectively, airfields that only recently had been deep behind Axis lines. Christmas 1941 was heartily cheered by the actions of a press officer, Fg Off P H F Tovey[54], whom Fg Off Whittard recalled as a large and jovial character. Although he flew occasionally on operational trips he "took up rather more space than was comfortable in a Blenheim." Tovey went on a forage in his vehicle and returned with a morale-boosting stock of Chianti, leaving an unsolved mystery about where he obtained it. Presumably they were spoils left behind by the Italian divisions.

Benghazi fell to the Allies on Christmas Eve and a few days later the front line stabilised just to the east of Agedabia. However, 14 Squadron's area of interest switched back to Bardia and three waves of six aircraft were launched against the defences and gun emplacements around Bardia on 27 December. The next day five waves each of six aircraft continued the bombardment, and two waves also attacked the Bardia defences on 30 December. However, the Afrika Korps' vehicles near Agedabia had not been forgotten and six aircraft led by 11 Squadron operated through the forward fighter base at Msus to bomb vehicles to the southeast of Agedabia. On the last day of the year seven 14 Squadron aircraft led a formation with the Lorraine Squadron, once again via Msus, for two waves against transports and tanks near Agedabia.

Gambut offered RAF personnel a unique insight into the destruction and detritus of the battlefield. Normally such things would be very distant from an airfield, but inside Libya the Blenheims were on ground which had been fought over twice in the previous year. Around Gambut, until only recently the Afrika Korps HQ, could be seen the aftermath of *Crusader* tank battles littered over the desert. The winter climate did not match the popular image of an African desert: days could certainly be warm and sandstorms or rising dust an ever-present hazard, but conversely on a cloudless night the desert could be cold and near freezing. Vehicles had to be drained overnight to avoid freezing damage and the scarce water had to be saved for the next day. Heavy rains which could turn the airfield into a desolate morass, capable of bogging down vehicles and aircraft, were another source of discomfort: the sleeping accommodation, typically consisting of a shallow slit trench with a tent erected over the top, would fill with water and need bailing out.

LAC R G Dawson[55] recalled that "there was never time for proper latrines to be dug and organised, and the routine was to grab a spade or a trenching tool and wander off into the desert for a few hundred yards, dig a small hole, and fill it in again after use. One evening as dusk was approaching and we were waiting the call from the cookhouse to line up for a meal, a friend of mine and myself decided that we just had time to do the necessary and walked due south for a couple of hundred yards before digging. Whilst occupied with our natural functions one of us noticed a wooden packing case about twenty yards away which had been almost covered by blown sand from the previous day's sandstorm.

"This packing case was something like three feet by two feet by ten inches deep, and although there was lettering in German on the side this had been partly obliterated by the action of the blown sand and in any case we could not read German. The thought that could possibly contain food of some sort was sufficient for us to uncover it and carry it back to camp. When broken open the packing case was found to contain a dozen very large tins (about 8 inches diameter and 10 inches tall) with no identification marks that we could decipher. Still with food in our mind we opened on of these cans with a bayonet only to be greeted with a most awful smell. The cans contained German sauerkraut and was immediately taken away and buried.

"It was only the following day that it became apparent that we had not only been lucky, but also extremely foolish, in picking up this case as during the day there was a large explosion from the other side of the landing ground where a squadron of the Fleet Air Arm was operating and it transpired that a couple of ratings had also found a half-covered packing case, but unfortunately this one had been booby-trapped and they were both killed."

LAC A J Hanson[56] had a similarly cautionary tale about the hazards of exploring a battlefield. "In their haste to leave, the Germans had kindly left some motorbikes behind and a very good friend of mine, LAC Maurice Best[57], and myself 'acquired' one each. We often spent our off-duty time exploring the area around Gambut on our motorbikes. There is an escarpment running through the area, and on one particular occasion we found a quite well-hidden cave in the escarpment. We entered the cave and found that it had been used by a German film unit for working on films, probably propaganda films of German forces in action on the desert and of British and Indian troops captured out in the Desert. We had a good rummage around the cave and left with a few bits and pieces. It was two or three days later that we heard the cave had been discovered by some other people and the place exploded while they were in there. It was, of course, booby trapped. How lucky can you get?"

So ended 1941, with the loose-ends of Operation *Crusader* still dominating tasking for the forthcoming two weeks. Bardia fell to the South Africans on 2 January 1942 (a day on which overnight rain had flooded Gambut LG) leaving the focus on the much fought over Halfaya Pass. The lack of a Luftwaffe threat in the area and minimal anti-aircraft fire altered the tempo of operations: from 5 to 8 January the aircraft tasked against the Pass took off individually operating a constant stream of "milk run" visits upon the isolated Axis troops. On 6 January, the target area was described as "seldom clear of aircraft" until bombing was suspended after midday due to a sandstorm. The number of sorties belied the underlying poor serviceability of the Blenheims, however, on the 7 January when the twenty four sorties which delivered ninety-six 250-pound bombs to Halfaya were undertaken by only six aircraft.

With the imminent capitulation of Sollum (which fell on 12 January) the Axis troops at Halfaya became reliant on sporadic and piecemeal resupply by air during the night. It was discovered that a Ju52 was making pre-dawn drops between 0400 hrs and 0500 hrs, coasting in near Sollum and, after firing a white and green signal cartridge, dropping its supplies from 1,000 feet onto marker flares at Halfaya. On 9 January an overlapping patrol of two aircraft flown by Flt Lt Leon and Sgt G J Webb launched one hour apart to try to catch the drop in progress but bad weather precluded any sightings. The next night Sgt K W Stevenson[58] spotted a circle of flares and, also calling back Sgt T N Archer[59] who had recently departed from the area, bombed the drop-zone at 0430 hrs. Finally Maj Lewis on a solitary patrol on the third night spotted a ring of five flares near the bottom of the pass and proceeded to bomb the mark. Just under an hour later another flare was seen one mile to the northeast of the first and they dropped to 600 feet to strafe the position. The resupply aircraft was spotted but it turned tail and departed on seeing its mission compromised. Halfaya, with its mixed force of Germans and Italians from the Savona Division, surrendered on the 17 January. On the previous day, 270 Wing had been disbanded and 14 Squadron had been transferred into 3 South African Wing.

The Red Headed Lady

The third week in January 1942 heralded the arrival of a visitor who created a stir

A distinguished trio: Major Lewis, Wg Cdr Buchanan and Flt Lt Whittard relaxing after a flight. Both Whittard and Buchanan were awarded the DFC for their service with 14 Squadron, while Lewis won the DSO. Buchannan is holding a bottle of Dawe's Black Horse Ale, a Canadian beer.

throughout the Squadron encampment. The female American journalist Morley-Brooke Lister[60], described as a "tall, slim and athletic Californian with a splendour of red hair,"[61] had been based in the Middle East since 1940 as a correspondent for the magazines *Time, Life* and *PM*. Whilst in Egypt she had also gained her civilian pilot's licence. She had previously visited 211 Squadron in September 1940 and had flown on a short training flight with them. The visit to 14 Squadron was also supposed to be a short one, but when Wg Cdr Buchanan promised to take her along on that afternoon's raid to Halfaya Pass, she relinquished her seat on the aircraft back to Cairo, having apparently "fallen for his charm on the spot." According to Fg Off Whittard, she arrived on 13 January and stayed with the Squadron for twelve days. The Halfaya Pass sortie was a relatively low-risk task that entailed Buchanan leading a formation of four Lorraine Squadron Blenheims. Whittard was the observer on that short fifty-five minute flight for which the Squadron diary lists no gunner – though Glarner records Lister flying in the turret of a Blenheim. It is likely that she also flew on the mid-day raid against Halfaya on 16 January: Sgt Willis, who was flying number two in formation that day, recalled that he flew a couple of trips "formating on her beacon-like auburn head."

Naturally everyone took great interest in the movements of the tall, red-headed lady who was elegantly dressed in a tailored bottle green suit. The domestic arrangements at the camp were modified to accommodate perhaps the only female in Cyrenaica. The medical officer was detailed to the task and he had a tent and toilet erected in front of the Officers' Mess – it gained the nickname 'Kennedy's Folly' – to which Buchanan was allegedly a frequent visitor. Willis recalled lending his camp bed, which he found unpractical in the scraped out hole under his canvas bivouac, and having it returned "squashed flat." Plt Off C A North[62], also living in a hole in the ground, claimed the tent on her departure and it subsequently passed to Plt Off R W Lapthorne[63]. Buchanan's batman maintained that he used to deliver two cups of tea to the CO's tent in the mornings. Miss Lister may have flown on training flights after the sortie to the Halfaya Pass, and it is fairly conclusive that she accompanied Buchanan on the multi-stage sorties to Agedabia via Msus on 22 January, and the hunt for the Italian convoy on the next day. After the Agedabia sortie on which he flew as number two, Sgt Willis was summoned to the CO's tent to be met by Buchanan and Lister standing side-by-side with glasses in their hands. One anecdote has it that a ground crew rigger exploited the novelty of having a female in the cockpit of the Blenheim by quickly closing the canopy to retain the scent of her perfume and then charging the men "two ackers a sniff!"

Eventually her presence on these flights became known to the higher echelons, who decided that she had overstepped her remit. A "strongly worded signal" recalled her quickly to Cairo. Plt Off C K Goodwin[64] wrote that the CO's farewell to her was "in the lounge of Heliopolis airport and the ladies' powder room – we were the only people in the lounge at that time." This probably occurred on 25 January, a day on which almost uniquely Buchanan did not participate in a raid. The affair, as it certainly was, had all the elements of a cinematic script. Lister returned to work for the United States Military North Africa Mission in Cairo.

Rommel's raid into Cyrenaica, January 1942

Although the front line in Western Desert at the start of 1942 looked remarkably similar to the one held a year previously, the strategic context had completely changed. The entry of America into the war and the failure of Hitler's Russian campaign both presented long-term threats to Rommel's force. However in the short term, his supply routes had been secured by the arrival of U-boats in the Mediterranean Sea and the aerial might of Luftflotte II in Italy. Thus by mid-January 1942 Rommel's logistical problems had been resolved and he could take the offensive once more.

At dawn on 21 January 1942 the Afrika Korps advanced with the Italian XX Division and other infantry divisions proceeding along the road from El Aghelia towards Benghazi. The next day Rommel's forces had reached Agedabia and 14

Squadron deployed nine aircraft[65] forward to Msus where they picked up their fighter escort before bombing a motorised column of some five hundred vehicles to the southwest of Agedabia. Unfortunately the bombing was not particularly accurate and although the formation was attacked by both Bf110s and Bf109s there was no damage to the bomber aircraft. On directives from 3 SAAF Wing, the aircraft were re-racked at dusk in order to take two 500-pound bombs, in place of the more usual load of four 250-pound bombs. Nine aircraft plus another seven from 11 Squadron deployed on 23 January via Benina to Berka from where four of them[66] they swept the coast northeast of Benghazi until fading light looking for elements of the Italian Fleet. A convoy of about twenty ships had been reported and although some 11 Squadron aircraft found a battleship the other aircraft in the search failed to find locate the convoy. The next day one aircraft, which had become unserviceable, had to be abandoned at Berka when it seemed that the airfield was about to be overrun by the German advance. On 25 January 14 Squadron dispatched seven aircraft[67] to Mechili from where they operated against a force of about thirty vehicles on the Antelat-Agedabia road, achieving some success with their 250-pound bombs.

Over the next two days amid the misery of the worst sandstorm experienced in the area, followed by heavy rain, the operational elements of the Squadron relocated to Bu Amud. Six aircraft deployed to Mechili to search, with all 3 SAAF Wing's available Blenheims, for advancing columns of enemy vehicles to the south of that airstrip. However the bad weather confounded the search and much later it was realised that movement towards Msus had been a feint. By this time the Germans had reentered Benghazi. The Squadron was now split into two parts; the aircraft were at Bu Amud and the "servicing party" was back at Gambut. Meanwhile, the Eighth

Blenheim Z7627 seen in January 1942. Flt Lt Keck RAAF and his crew were killed in this aircraft on 30 March 1942 when they were shot down into the sea by Hurricanes. (Andrew Thomas)

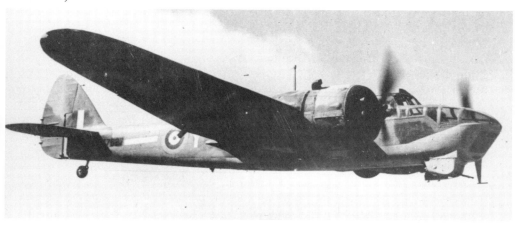

Army fell back to positions thirty miles west of Tobruk, taking up defence of the "Gazala Line" from 6 February. The ground war remained static here for the next four months.

Behind the Gazala Line

Although the army was static, 14 Squadron moved again on 2 February 1942. Leaving a refuelling and rearming party at Gambut, two thirds of the Squadron headed east for LG76, pausing overnight near Halfaya Pass. The rest of the ground crews arrived at LG76 three days later via Sidi Barrani. However over the next two days everyone moved again, this time to LG116 which had been the Squadron's first temporary home when it returned from Iraq.

The advanced landing ground at Gambut was used as a forward operating base for a number of formation raids during early February while the Squadron moved home. These sorties comprised attacks on Axis positions to the west of Gazala, including the airfields at Derna and Martuba, and two fruitless operations were also mounted against reported enemy shipping. According to Maj Lewis[68] "The Derna LG raid [on 8 February] was to catch fighters refuelling. We were to have top cover of twelve Hurricanes, another twelve as medium cover and six Kittyhawks of Killer Caldwell's crowd as close cover. It was a mess, as when the medium cover took off from their 'drome they were jumped by [Bf]109s. Our top cover came down to help them but when the shemozzle was over they couldn't find us so we went over the target with just our six Kittys close cover and got jumped on the way out... I heard that Killer Caldwell[69] was furious about the whole thing." The raid had involved eight 14 Squadron aircraft[70] along with four more Blenheims from 11 Sqn and an escort of Kittyhawks from 112 Squadron. The bombers scored a direct hit on a Bf109 on the ground, but two enemy fighters were able to attack the formation resulting in the loss of one of the Luftwaffe fighters and a defending Kittyhawk. The next day the Germans retaliated with a pre-dawn attack on Gambut with incendiaries and bombs which caused shrapnel damage to four Squadron Blenheims and a Tomahawk although there were no casualties.

A day later Lewis flew the GOC-in-C Eighth Army, Lt-Gen N M Ritchie CBE DSO MC[71] from Gambut to El Adem.

In another reorganisation of the Squadron, and new OC 'C' Flight, commanded by Sqn Ldr A C Mills[72] was formed in mid February. This brought the strength of the Squadron up to thirty-three crews totaling one hundred and four aircrew many of whom were fresh from training. During this time aircraft were rotated between the rear base at LG116 and the forward base at Gambut. Bir El Baheira, close to the front line, was also used as a forward base briefly between from 20 February. Luck ran out, however, on 23 February, when the Squadron ferried the aircraft from Bir El Baheira eastwards to the new semi-permanent home at LG116. On what should have been a low-risk transit flight in "friendly" skies, two of the Blenheims were intercepted by marauding Bf109s[73]. One Blenheim escaped damage, but the other[74] suffered sustained attacks by four of the fighters and was crippled by hits in both of its engines and the flying controls. Sgt Bosworth crash landed the aircraft, with engines on fire, into the desert twenty miles west of Sidi Barrani. Although the aircraft was completely wrecked, the crew survived the crash. Unfortunately the observer Sgt R K Swann[75] was seriously injured with lacerations to the head and he died in hospital the next morning.

Two days later a raid on the airstrip at Martuba (West) turned out badly. Six aircraft departed at ten minute intervals on a moonlit evening for a five hour mission, but very poor visibility made target acquisition nearly impossible: two aircraft bombed the coastal road instead, one the Martuba (East) field and another Martuba (West), while a fifth couldn't drop due to electrical problems. The problems continued as the bombers tried to recover to LG116. "I've never been so lost in my life..." recalled Maj Lewis, "Six of us took off and only Buck got back home. I was just on the point of giving my crew the option of bailing out or crash landing as I intended to do as it was bright moonlight, when I suddenly saw an aircraft with lights on making an approach. I followed him in (it was actually a Hurricane night fighter sent up to intercept us as our IFF wasn't working). I got a red light but kept on going and it suddenly turned to green! It was the first time I'd seen and used a glidepath indicator. I made a clot of myself when someone stuck his head in the cockpit and asked if I knew where I was and I said Mersa Matruh – in fact I'd landed at Idku in the Delta! ...I didn't feel so bad when I got back and found out that I wasn't the only one to get lost." Two other aircraft had landed LG15 and Fuka, leaving two more still unaccounted for.

Ironically the only aircraft[76] to bomb the correct target ran out of fuel and ditched into the sea just off cape of Ras El Kanayis. The Squadron received news that Plt Off F R Brown[77] and his crew had been killed in the ditching but an hour later he rang the Squadron to ask for transport back to base. The confusion didn't end there: two days after the raid a telephone call informed the Squadron that the crew of the final missing aircraft[78] was safe and well but it turned out not to be entirely accurate. The Blenheim, flown by Flt Sgt Willis, had been hit by flak on the way to the target and the crew jettisoned their bombs before turning for home. They made it back across the front line but the aircraft was on fire and had to be abandoned. Willis and his navigator Sgt E Barr[79] parachuted to safety but the Wireless Operator Sgt H P Tew[80] didn't get out.

Despite the operational lull, the toll in men and aircraft continued into March. A formation practice on 3 March left two Blenheims damaged after a mid-air collision forced them to land in the desert some 15 miles from LG116. The downed aircraft were spotted by a Blenheim which had been sent to direct a lorry to the scene of the crashes. A party of engineers was then sent out to repair one aircraft[81] which was considered capable of being flown back to base. Four days later Maj Lewis, without a crew, completed the 20-minute flight from the desert to the landing strip. Although neither crew was injured, this event was an unhappy start to a series of serious accidents in the month.

The very next day a replacement aircraft[82] being delivered from adjacent Qasaba crashed onto LG116 after striking its port wing on the Officers' Mess and ploughing into the ground. The pilot, Fg Off J A Harvie[83], sole occupant of the aircraft was killed instantly. The accident was officially recorded a misjudgment of the approach, but witnesses considered that the aircraft had hit the pole of the Officers' Mess tent while "beating up the camp" and that the disaster had been caused by a total misjudgment by the pilot.

The quiet period lasted a week until on 7 March, just after Buchanan had led a formation of six Blenheims for the benefit of the RAF Film Production Unit, tasking was received for a mission that evening to attack Tmimi satellite airstrip. Instructions were also received to deploy nine aircraft the next morning to Bir El Baheira. That evening's mission saw yet another loss when the first of six aircraft took off late at night. It was a clear night with the prospect of mist later on. The first Blenheim[84] took off in good conditions, but was heard to crash soon afterwards. It caught fire and the bomb load exploded. Rescuers found only the Observer, Sgt W V Howey[85], still alive. The raid was cancelled when a thick fog settled a quarter of an hour later.

Four aircraft eventually took off in the early hours of the 10 March from Bir el Baheira to attack Martuba using 250-pound bombs and illumination flares. Buchanan was late off on this sortie after changing aircraft when his original mount became bogged down on the landing ground. The raid itself was uneventful but later in the day as the aircraft returned to LG116 from Bir El Baheira, one[86] of a formation of three, forced landed in the desert near Sidi Barrani. The remaining two circled the scene and observed the crew emerge unscathed; two days later a Blenheim picked them up from LG75.

The increased Luftwaffe presence in the Mediterranean caused the airfields in Crete to become the focus of attention once again for bombing raids. Candia (Heraklion) airfield on the north coast was targeted by nine 14 Squadron aircraft in the early hours of 15 March. Taking off at fifteen minute intervals, loaded of four 250-pounder bombs, they reported the black-out precautions on the island to be quite poor though area cloud hampered in the target four of the aircraft. Two of the bombs on each aircraft were fitted with time delay pistols causing detonations six to twelve hours after the raid.

Another aircraft was lost the next day during a raid on the Aghelia-Agedabia road. After deploying forward to Bir El Baheira, six Blenheims[87] to crossed the enemy lines in formation intending to route to the south of El Aghelia (at the south-eastern corner of the Gulf of Sirte) before fanning out northwards to attack targets of opportunity on the coastal road. However, that is not quite what happened. Sgt W J MacMichael[88], Flt Sgt Willis' newly posted-in observer, was convinced that Buchanan's navigator Fg Off Goodwin had got his dead-reckoning plot wrong and that they had gone too far west, overshooting the point where they should have split up and fanned-out north. "We had been flying for well over two hours," recalled Willis, "when MacMicheal could no longer, evidently, contain his misgivings as to where Buck's navigator was taking us! Few things were said by the crew in formation (no intercom between aircraft of course) except over the target. So I was alarmed when MacMichael blurted out his doubts, 'I don't know where this lot are going, but by my reckoning they are twenty minutes past the break-up point!' To be twenty minutes west of where you should be

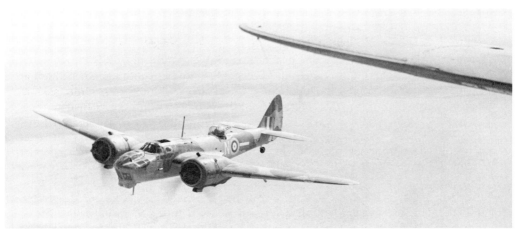

Blenheim Z7631 was flown by Flt Lt Keck on the ill-fated raid against El Aghelia on 16 March 1942. The aircraft served with 14 Squadron until August 1942. (IWM CM 003105)

was tantamount to being forty minutes light on fuel. This was some sort of cock-up but all I could do was make it clear that I was leaving independently, and not because I was in difficulties. So I pulled slightly up and away, gently waggled my wings and headed off due north."

Willis, having fanned-out by himself, spotted the coast road some ten minutes later and identified a supply depot comprising some wooden buildings which they bombed. Then they descended to a hundred feet to allow the gunner, Flt Sgt G P Rylands[89] DFM, to put in a long ten-second burst into four large trucks whose occupants had been seen to have scattered. This they did from a range of less than two hundred yards as they flew past the vehicles before pulling up for the return to Bir El Baheira. Only one other aircraft found the coastal road and bombed it and only one other aircraft, Buchanan's, managed to return to Bir El Baheira. Three sets of bombs were jettisoned into the desert due to fuel shortage and a random track was bombed by another. Sgt Webb landed at Tobruk while Flt Sgt Grimsey and Flt Lt H K Keck made it as far as El Adem after nearly seven hours. For the remaining aircraft piloted by the new flight commander, an epic nine-day walk across the desert was about to start: Sqn Ldr Mills with Sgts R N Ey[90] and J A R Hunt[91] crash-landed behind enemy lines.

En-route to the target, the starboard engine, started losing oil and began to fail. The crew who were on their first operational sortie after completing their training at 70 OTU decided to return to base. Their problems were compounded by the fact that the port engine was not developing enough power to keep the aircraft airborne and despite jettisoning their bomb load into the desert the aircraft kept its inexorable descent towards the ground. When the starboard engine finally seized their fate was sealed. The crew elected for the option of a wheels-down landing on the rocky terrain below. Although the aircraft was wrecked on landing, all three crew members were miraculously unharmed but now they were faced with the dire situation of being stranded in the desert miles inland and miles behind enemy lines.

With provisions consisting of water bottles, a first aid kit, a tin of peaches and a packet of ration biscuits they decided to abandon the aircraft in case it attracted German patrols. After binding their loose-fitting boots tightly with parachute cord to make them more suitable for the long march ahead, and robbing the P6 compass from the aircraft, they set off to walk towards friendly territory east of the Gazala Line.

The first evening was bitterly cold and wet. The following evenings were just bitterly cold. They walked into the coolness of the evening and started in the pre-dawn chill after huddling together for warmth to sleep. The desert yielded little vegetation, just small bushes of 'camelthorn' and their water and biscuits strictly were rationed until, on the fifth day the water ran out. However, the odd items of salvation came their way: they came across a tortoise, which was eaten raw and then they started to find the detritus of war, abandoned vehicles from the four earlier campaigns across Cyrenaica. A tin of Indian curry was discovered and rusty radiator water was drained into Jerry cans which they lugged along like treasure for the rest of the trek. At one point they tried to attract the attention of a passing German patrol, but the Germans apparently did not see them. The water was depleted again and they were running out of hope of survival.

Then on 26 March, the tenth day, they spotted a bowser truck in a depression and upon further investigation, they discovered a well hole complete with a rope and bucket. They had secured a source of water. Some more scouting around produced a tin of rice and with two spare matches they managed to get a fire going. Then salvation arrived: the well at Bir Tengeder was charted on the maps and was constantly being visited by the long range patrols of both armies. Down the track leading to the well came three armoured cars of the long range desert patrol of the Royal Dragoons.

After an adventurous journey back to friendly lines, which included inadvertently driving into a minefield and witnessing an armoured car shoot down an Italian Savoia-Marchetti which paid them unwelcomely close attention, they arrived back at 14 Squadron on 29 March. Here they received a warm reception (a "blow out") in the mess. The crew was then sent for a month's medical leave in Cairo.

During their absence, 17 March saw the start of another cascading series of events which troubled the enemy not one bit but cost the Squadron dearly. Ten aircraft deployed west to Bir El Baheira for an anti-shipping patrol in the afternoon against a convoy reported to be two hundred miles northeast of the Benghazi coast. Eight aircraft[92] got airborne for the patrol but in attempting to join up in formation two of them collided and both crews were killed. It seems that Sgt Good was concentrating on joining up with their lead aircraft and failed to see Flt Sgt R G S Linley's[93] aircraft which was over the airfield with its undercarriage partially retracted at the time. The remaining aircraft had a fruitless search, three of them returning due to fuel shortage with one putting down in the desert twelve miles west of Gambut causing minor damage to the undercarriage.

A similar wastage afflicted the Squadron three days later on another raid against

Candia on Crete. In the moonless small hours of 20 March, five aircraft took off for four-hour sorties but two never made it airborne. The third aircraft[94] to start its take-off run, piloted by Sgt C H Bowling[95], was seen to climb alarmingly quickly whereupon it stalled and crashed into the ground killing the Wireless Operator Sgt P Munyard[96] and fatally injuring the observer Sgt MacMichael who died a few hours later. Bowling, who survived with bad leg bruises, later stated that he realised that he was climbing too steeply so throttled back the engines, resulting in the loss of control. Thirty minutes later another Blenheim[97] took off, but it was seen not to gain any height and, two hundred yards past the end of the runway, it struck an oil drum just beyond the airstrip perimeter. Despite the pilot, Sgt K M Dee[98], applying full power the aircraft sank back onto the ground shearing off propellor blades. The crew this time were extremely fortunate and narrowly escaped the wreckage before one of the bombs exploded, though the observer, Sgt H G Marshall[99], broke his right leg. The last four sorties were cancelled as a result of the crashes and an air raid warning. Of those airborne one returned to base reportedly spun from 10,000 feet to 500 feet and landing with unserviceable instruments. With only two aircraft getting to the cloud-covered target area, the raid achieved no observed success.

Both aircraft involved in the take-off accidents were subject to investigations and the conclusions were the same in both cases. Coincidentally both pilots joined the Squadron in February from 70 OTU (based at Nakaru in Kenya) but their night flying on Blenheims amounted to a mere half-dozen hours under bright moonlit conditions: along with other newly-qualified pilots of the time, their instrument flying experience in the Blenheim was non-existent leading, the Squadron Commander to attribute the crashed to a lack of training in realistically dark conditions. This episode illustrates that, even discounting the threats of combat, crews needed training, proficiency and experience to survive operational flying in the Western Desert. 3 SAAF Wing observed that the "operations formed another chapter in 14 Squadron's history of accidents and misfortunes of the last fortnight." And as Flt Sgt Willis observed, "such losses sap morale, more so than those caused by enemy action."

There was a light-hearted footnote to this tragedy: the fourth aircraft to take off (and one of the two to reach the target) contained both Wg Cdr Buchanan and Maj Lewis. They had spent that evening in the mess celebrating Buchanan's birthday and, fortified by a large quantity of beer, Buchanan decided to add himself to the bombing effort. Unable to dissuade his Squadron Commander from this foolhardy action, Lewis, who himself was also "well oiled" elected to join Buchanan for the sortie. Their accuracy over the target was, however, frustrated by cloud cover and Lewis recalled that a crate of empty beer bottles was also dropped on the theory that the whistling sound as the bottles fell through the air would be a convincing impression of a falling bomb! Lewis understood that Buchanan later "got a rocket from Wing for having a CO and a senior flight commander in the same aircraft on ops."

The remainder of March saw a couple of days of sandstorms but otherwise pleasant weather in which a series of training sorties were flown on the directions of HQ RAF Middle East, to practise overwater navigation and searches. Ten crews were briefed by the Command Navigation Officer to this effect. It was during one of the training sorties over the sea on 30 March that another tragic loss occurred when a flight of three Blenheims was mistakenly attacked by South African Hurricanes near the cape of Ras Alam El Rumb (near Mersa Matruh). One Blenheim[100] flown by Flt Lt Keck was shot down and was last seen striking the water with smoke pouring from the fuselage. The crew was killed.

March had been expensive in aircraft and crew, and none of the losses were the consequence of enemy action. Sadly, April was to continue in much the same vain. After some ineffective sorties during the first week of the month, a series of successful attacks against the Luftwaffe presence on Crete was started on 9 April. Early in the morning, nine aircraft left at fifteen minute intervals for Maleme where seven of them bombed buildings, starting fires on the airfield. Meanwhile one Blenheim attacked the secondary target at Tymbaki, on the south coast. A repeat visit was ordered the next night, but this time the Squadron suffered more casualties within the confines of its own landing ground. The third aircraft[101] to launch, flown by Plt Off B S Slade[102] crashed after it struck telephone wires shortly after take-off, but happily the crew was uninjured. The next aircraft[103], faired worse: just after getting airborne it crashed and burst into flames, killing the pilot Sgt P D Clauson[104] and seriously injuring the other two crewmen. Once again, this accident was probably caused by the aircraft stalling after take-off. On the raid itself, three aircraft started a large fire at Maleme and two others attacked Tymbaki and Candia. All aircraft reported heavy anti-aircraft fire which was aided by two or three searchlights. This short series of attacks on Crete lasted for the next two nights but only four aircraft made it to the targets in the early hours of 11 April and only two on the last night.

One of the aircraft on that final night raid against Crete could not find its way back to LG116 because it could not pick up the radio direction finding (DF) bearings which were usually provided by wireless stations at Matruh and Maaten Bagush (rear HQ for AHQ Western Desert). The aircraft eventually landed near Alexandria. When it returned to base later in the day there was an investigation into the problems experienced by the Wireless Operator with his radios. Wireless technician Cpl E A Meader[105], was responsible for the radio sets in this particular aircraft and when he checked the sets' transmission and reception with stations in Malta and Alexandria he could find no fault. However, Meader recalled that the radio sets[106] fitted in the Squadron's Blenheims were extremely unreliable. Already obsolescent at the outbreak of war and notoriously difficult to operate, these outdated radios were mounted awkwardly in the confined space of the gun turret. Even basic tasks like change frequency bands, were fiddly: plug-in coils had to be swapped, and the many other adjustments that were needed made it difficult to tune the radio accurately, especially so in the confines of the turret on a dark night. Furthermore, atmospheric propagation at different times of the day on these Medium and High Frequency bands made communications unpredictable.

On 12 April four aircraft, each loaded with ninety-six 9-pound anti-tank bombs, also deployed eastwards to Heliopolis to participate in a bombing demonstration. Five days later the aircraft returned after what must have been a welcome break in Cairo. A visit to Heliopolis was described by Fg Off Whittard as an extremely popular duty. Typically crews would go straight to downtown Cairo and book in at the Continental Hotel where they would have a decent haircut and a very welcome hot bath and general clean-up. Once cleaned of desert grime they might proceed to Groppi's for coffee or ice cream. Next would follow drinks and lunch at Tomm's Bar and in the afternoon a visit to either the Heliopolis Sporting Club or the Gezira Club for a swim and afternoon tea. Then they would repair back to the Continental for more drinks and dinner, followed perhaps by a trip to the cinema at about nine o'clock. After this they might finish up with a drink and snack at the National Hotel where eggs and bacon were usually available around midnight.

Back in the Western Desert, the Squadron's attempts to run a training programme for its new crews were frustrated variously by sand storms, requirements to stand-by for operations at Bir El Baheira and finally a request on 17 April from 235 Wing to provide six aircraft for a naval co-operation task. These aircraft were to deploy forward to LG05 near Sidi Barani, but preparation for the task was hampered by dust storms, and all six aircraft landed by mistake at LG121, some ten miles to the east. Only three serviceable aircraft made it to LG05, whereupon two were declared unserviceable. An attempt to bolster the contingent at LG05 was delayed due to doubtful weather the next day, but of the two that eventually departed, one[107] crashed in the dust haze about four miles to the south of LG05. 2nd Lt P J Chapman[108] SAAF, and his Australian crew[109] were killed. The 235 Group task ultimately resulted in five aircraft sweeping for submarines and shipping northwest of Sidi Barrani and Tobruk on 20 April but the searches turned up nothing.

Four days later the Squadron learned that it was to be withdrawn from the Western Desert and the unit's equipment was packed up in readiness to withdraw the remaining deployed aircraft. On 28 April the Squadron was notified that it was to move to El Firdan, on the west bank of the Suez Canal, just north of Ismalia. The loaded lorries were ready to move and the convoy was on the road the next morning heading eastwards via Amirya near Alexandria and a second stop on the road between Cairo and Ismalia before arriving at El Firdan on 1 May. Back at LG116 the few remaining personnel readied the aircraft and rectified those currently unserviceable allowing the Blenheims to fly east in half-dozen strong waves on 2 May and a handful of stragglers to follow a day later.

The stay at El Firdan was to last for the duration of May, however it became clear towards the end of the month that the Squadron would be required to return to the Western Desert. The Squadron started to retrace its step back to the desert on 29 May and was back at LG116 almost exactly a month after it had left it. During the stay at El Firdan, the flying activities comprised a programme of training to practise formation flying and night flying, as well as numerous co-operation exercises with the anti-aircraft gun defences along the canal zone. In contrast with the attrition of the preceding months, the only casualty during this period was when Sgt E S Brown[110] ran off the end of the runway at Kabrit during night flying exercises. On 15 May Wg

Cdr Buchanan DFC* handed command of 14 Squadron to Wg Cdr W S G Maydwell[111] DFC.

Rommel's Second Offensive

Since the end of Operation *Crusader*, the Kriegsmarine and the Luftwaffe had between them gained domination of the central Mediterranean. Allied convoys to Malta and Egypt, had been virtually halted and it was the Allies now who suffered from the problems of a weakened supply chain. Rommel had benefited greatly from this new balance of power and with a reinforced Afrika Korps he was now in a strong enough position to take the offensive once more. On 26 June the Afrika Korps and the Italian XX Corps struck against the southern flank of the Gazala Line near Bir Hacheim.

At first, Rommel's attempt to swing around the south of the defensive line then the thrust north behind it was successfully countered. By 30 June the main Axis striking force, comprising the Afrika Korps plus the Italian Ariete Division, was penned up in an area which became known as "The Cauldron." However, the effort to destroy the Axis forces on the 5 and 6 June ended in complete military disaster for the British.

On the same two days that the army was engaged in a fierce battle, the 14 Squadron diary for LG116 two hundred and fifty miles away records that "nothing of importance occurred" on "an otherwise quiet day." The next evening, 14 Squadron resumed night intruder sorties against the airfields on Crete with attacks by six aircraft[112] on Heraklion and Tymbak that evening. Ten crews were briefed for follow-up raids the following night, but a heavy ground mist meant that only four aircraft managed to get airborne. Of these only Wg Cdr Maydwell[113] achieved any notable success, thanks to flares dropped by Wellingtons over Heraklion. One aircraft[114] was lost on its return to LG116 in another night landing accident: Fg Off D R W Brooks[115] misjudged his height and the aircraft crashed a quarter of a mile south of the airstrip and burst into flames, killing the observer Plt Off C R Cowan[116]. The accident was also attributed to the fatigue of flying on instruments for five hours for an otherwise experienced pilot on his first long night trip and led to the Squadron reviewing their instructions for diverting aircraft in cases of poor landing conditions.

No operations took place from LG116 for the next four nights but in the meantime in the desert south of Gazala, Rommel had defeated the British armour in the battle of Knightsbridge on 12 June and he was advancing towards Tobruk. The British army hastily withdrew eastwards before they were cut off.

Although 14 Squadron crews stood by for night intruder operations from 12 June, they were not tasked on that night; instead the opportunity was taken to provide some more night flying practice for the more inexperienced crews. The following night, two more crews set off for night flying practice, but while they were airborne enemy aircraft were reported in the area: the aerodrome lights were extinguished and the two aircraft were instructed to hold over Mersa Matruh until the "all clear." However, when the enemy aircraft departed, neither Blenheim could be contacted and their whereabouts became a mystery. Meanwhile, five aircraft mounted another raid on Crete. Sgt J H Elliott[117] chanced across Heraklion with all its lights and flarepath illuminated and diving from 10,000 feet to 3,000 feet he bombed the flarepath.

The raid was repeated the following night but this time Sqn Ldr A N Pirie's Blenheim[118] went missing after calling for radio bearings on its way back. Thus by the morning of 15 June three aircraft were missing in the desert within a short flying time from LG116.

Search aircraft were dispatched to try to find the men. News came in of wreckage[119] eight miles south of LG010 and the ground party sent to investigate found it and its all-Australian crew all dead. It was presumed that the inexperienced pilot had become disorientated in the darkness among the searchlights and had flown into the desert at high speed. Better news came from Sgt Elliot who landed to pick up Plt Off H C Ridley[120] and Sgt A Payne at the site of their crash[121]. To add to the drama for the rescued crewmen, Sgt Elliott burst a tyre on take-off in the desert and the undercarriage subsequently collapsed on landing. The missing pilot, Sqn Ldr Pirie[122], started to walk after the crash and found his way home later. The last unaccounted-for aircraft[123] and its crew remained missing and were never found.

Fifteen sorties were directed against Crete over the next four nights coinciding with the Operation *Vigorous* convoy from Egypt to Malta. The convoy which sailed on 12 June but returned to Alexandria four days later after heavy Axis air attacks took its toll on the ships. While these last sorties were underway against Crete, British land forces were pushed from the south of Tobruk and on 18 June the second invasion of Tobruk began. However, the defensive arrangements quickly became untenable and at dawn three days later 19,000 British, 10,500 South African and 2,500 Indian troops surrendered.

The Eighth Army withdrew further eastwards to regroup and defend a line from Mersa Matruh, some one hundred and thirty miles inside the Egyptian border. Abandoning plans of the invasion of Malta, the German High Command authorised Rommel to pursue the Eight Army into Egypt. German forces crossed into Egypt on 23 June and two days later Axis reconnaissance units started probing the defences at Mersa Matruh just thirty miles west of LG116.

The swift advance by Rommel's forces caused chaos for 14 Squadron with counter-order following order throughout the days following the fall of Tobruk. On that day 14 Squadron rejoined 3 SAAF Wing (having been temporarily under AHQ Egypt's direct control since leaving for El Firdan) and immediately received instruction to move forty miles east to LG21. The next day an advanced convoy set off, followed by the main party a little later. As they neared the destination the second convoy found the first convoy returning to LG116 with word that the move had been cancelled. Subsequently, on nearing Maaten Bagush a third instruction to get to LG21 was received. That night the vehicles were left in limbo scattered along the road while the aircraft remained at LG116. The farce was only resolved when Wg Cdr Maydwell went to HQ at Maaten Bagush in person the next day and refused to move any further until he had received written instructions from the Senior Air Staff Officer. The

The 14 Squadron convoy moving the unit's ground equipment to a new Landing Ground. The trailer on the left is the Chance Light. (Ron Page)

original movement instructions had not in fact been originated from the Squadron's new authority, 3 SAAF Wing, but from AHQ Egypt's 234 Wing and a multitude of other authorities. The Squadron moved back to LG116.

On 24 June with Axis forces bearing down rapidly from the west, the chaos continued at LG116. At first instructions were received to standby for day operations, but three hours later the Squadron was told that it would be used instead for night operations. With telephone communications almost non-existent, a dispatch rider was sent to 3 SAAF Wing HQ at Maaten Bagush to get clarification. He returned with instructions that eight aircraft were to launch that evening to attack vehicles on the Tobruk to Bardia road. The aircraft took off at dusk and although bombs were dropped in the specified areas, there was no evidence of enemy troops there and no results could be seen. Just after midnight, and before the main raid landed back at LG116, a German bomber attacked the landing ground. First it dropped flares, then it carried out two bombing runs followed by strafing passes. It lingered too long, however, and a night fighter caught it sending it crashing in flames. Unfortunately the raid had caused casualties: a bomb fragment fatally wounded one of 14 Squadron's ground crew, LAC K Friedl[124].

The next day twelve Bofors guns were in place around LG116, but 14 Squadron's base party started the move back to LG97. Once again the Squadron was told to standby for daylight operations, but once again this instruction was countermanded a few hours later. Nine Blenheims left that evening to attack concentrations of vehicles in the vicinity of LG07 and the following evening another nine bombed vehicles between Sidi Baranni and Mersa Matruh. In both raids the bombing caused a number of fires and post-war analysis[125] reveals that "it was the RAF which was the real British fighting force at this time... the Afrika Korps war diaries contain constant references to the damage done by British airmen and the failure of the Luftwaffe to intervene effectively." Enthusiastic British anti-aircraft fire was directed against one of the Blenheims as it flew at 1,000 feet, but it escaped unscathed. At around the time that the Blenheims were expected to return, an aircraft was spotted over the airstrip. However, as it descended and then opened fire with its cannons it was belatedly identified as a Bf110 which was then engaged by the Bofors gunners.

The Axis attack on Mersa Matruh began late on the same day, 26 June, and although the Germans and Italians were being held back, battlefield communications were extremely bad and in the ensuing uncertainty the British given orders to withdraw. On 29 June columns of both Allied and Axis troops were heading eastwards, towards the last Allied line of defence at El Alamein.

14 Squadron retreated east just ahead of the armies. On 27 June the unit had received instructions to fall back immediately to LG24. In what was by now a practised art, lorries were loaded and any vehicle fluids that would be useful the advancing enemy were poured away. At short notice, the convoy set out, avoiding the main roads by traversing the desert. As soon as it arrived at LG24, it was instructed to continue to LG97 where, on the 28 June, where it joined 12 and 24 Squadrons SAAF. These units were all part of a great concentration of aircraft withdrawing from the approaching threat.

"Soon enough the whole of the front totally collapsed," recalled LAC Dawson, "leaving all squadrons operating in that area in danger of being quickly overrun and their aircraft destroyed. In the absence of any specific instructions from HQ, the CO decided that all our aircraft should take off immediately and fly east until they found a landing-strip that could accommodate them as near as possible to the RAF HQ at Burg-el-Arab.

"All remaining personnel were instructed to destroy everything that could be of use to the enemy, load themselves into the Squadron's trucks (mainly Bedford 3-tonners) with as much water and rations as could be found, and make their way separately (not in convoy) to Burg-el-Arab. It was advised that the coast road should not be used as this was continually under attack by Bf109s and Ju88s, and that a course at least six to eight miles inland would be best. Also, single vehicles were less likely to be attacked than a group.

"This trip eventually took about three days and nights, but as it was impossible to navigate by night we bedded down under the truck and waited for dawn, hoping that we would not be spotted by the enemy. On the second night having found a small depression in the desert in which to bed down, we were awakened by the rumble of tank engines and German voices. On peering carefully over the edge of the depression we found that a whole regiment of Afrika Korps tanks and vehicles, having broken through the defensive positions set up by the 8th Army, was parked about a hundred yards away having a stop for food!

"We were expecting to be challenged any moment or to receive an 88mm shell through the truck, but whether our truck was not seen in the small depression or whether the enemy just assumed it was an abandoned vehicle we shall never know. In the event after about an hour, the whole tank regiment moved on eastward and in the morning we were able to continue with our journey and were lucky enough to avoid any further contact. We did, in fact decide to take a chance on the coast road as it would be so much quicker. This proved to be a good decision as we were not attacked at all, and the only happening of note was that we came across a NAAFI Supply Depot that was being abandoned and we were told to help ourselves to anything we wanted, so the truck was quickly loaded-up with cigarettes, Egyptian beer (awful stuff) and toilet paper, which we had not seen for years!"

Operations resumed on the night of 28 June, when seven aircraft were tasked against the airfield LG121 and vehicles between Sollum and Mersa Matruh. Two aircraft suffered engine problems and returned to base, but the five remaining aircraft dropped their bombs on concentrations of vehicles on the coast road which they could see through gaps in the clouds. Unfortunately the cloud cover meant that the results could not be observed. A similar raid the next night involved only two aircraft and was hampered by haze.

The last day of June the base party was on the move again, this time heading for LG Y, though the operational Flights remained at LG97. Rising sand that afternoon made for poor flying conditions at LG97 and as a Kittyhawk from 2 Squadron SAAF attempted to land, it struck a 14 Squadron Blenheim parked at the edge of the landing ground. The Kittyhawk overturned killing the pilot, 2nd Lt JS Warden[126] and a 14 Squadron ground engineer, Cpl H Gibbons[127], who was working on the Blenheim, died from his injuries half an hour later.

That day leading elements of Rommel's 90th Light Division came upon the defences of El Alamein; in a masterpiece of understatement, the 14 Squadron Operations Diary for 30 June comments "our position is becoming serious."

First Battle of El Alamein

On 1 July 1942 the front line was only just over seventy miles from Alexandria; this was a similar distance to that covered in the rush east from Mersa Matruh. The evacuation of Egypt now seemed a distinct and imminent reality as a general panic, known as "The Flap," took hold along the Nile. Trains and roads were crowded with those trying to flee and headquarters and embassies burned documents. However, despite its proximity to the heart of Egypt, the line at El Alamein was a strong defensive position which, unlike the Gazala Line would not be outflanked. About thirty miles south of the coastline was the Qattara Depression, which stretched far to the south-west. With its high, steeply-sloped escarpment and difficult terrain, it was considered to be impassible for a fighting army. Three defensive 'boxes' in various states of preparation created a tenuous "Alamein Line" southwest from El Alamein station to the Depression. The only prospect for advance for Rommel lay through the narrow end of the funnel created by the Depression's rim and the coast at El Alamein.

Rommel may have expected a victory before the Allies could consolidate their positions, but the weight of the Western Desert Air Force was pitted against his extended transport columns. In his own reports he acknowledged the debilitating effects constant air operations inflicted upon his vehicles and vital supplies.

14 Squadron concentrated on these interdiction raids for most of July, starting in the early hours of 1 July with an attack by three aircraft on vehicles east of Sidi Barrani. There was a similar raid by five aircraft the following night. Later on 2 July Wg Cdr Maydwell led a formation of six aircraft[128] on a daytime raid against a mechanised column which was approaching the 9th Indian Brigade's positions near Naqb Abu Dwei on the edge of the Qattara Depression. Twenty large vehicles were bombed and a number of direct hits were achieved. Early on 4 July five aircraft[129] took off at ten-minute intervals, tasked against airstrips in the Maaten Bagush area which had only recently been their own home. Sgt Russell's aircraft suffered an engine failure as it returned, and after a successful forced landed in the desert the crew[130] walked for three days to safety, earning their "Flying Boot" as new members of "The Late Arrivals Club." Similar sorties took place on the next two nights and another aircraft[131] was lost on 6 July when Sqn Ldr Pirie failed to return from the target area between Mersa Metruh and Fuka. Following a one-day pause, five aircraft carried out attacks on the coastal road west of Sidi Abdel Rahman early on 8 July. On this raid, one Blenheim was held in a cone by three searchlights for several minutes but despite being subjected to heavy anti-aircraft fire, no damage was sustained.

There was no operational flying for the next nine days while the Squadron moved firstly to LG98 on 10 July and then, after a short stay, to LG88. Meanwhile word was received that the Squadron was to relinquish the Blenheim and be "re-equipped with Baltimore aircraft." Shortly afterwards two Baltimores arrived at the LG Y so that crews could familiarise themselves with the new type. However for the time being the Blenheims would continue to be used for operations, which resumed on the evening of the 17 July. For the next week, the Squadron's efforts were focussed on the facilities at Mersa Matruh. On this first evening the target comprised the jetties and port facilities. Four aircraft[132] led by Flt Lt A Watson DFC[133] took off and formed up over LG 88, before heading north to cross the coast and then turning for Mersa Matruh. The formation broke up in the falling darkness and attacked the target singly from the north.

The following evening four aircraft[134] led by Sqn Ldr R H Moore[135] DFC used the same routing to attack a tank repair workshop near Mersa Matruh. The results of this attack were inconclusive and Moore's aircraft crashed short of the airstrip after the engine failed while making its approach to land. Night raids on 19 and 21 July concentrated again on the harbour. According to Sgt R A Yarburgh-Bateson[136] "we were supposed to bomb from about 6,000 feet but some of the aircraft were so decrepit they could not climb to that height with a full bomb and fuel load (four 250-pound and four 25-pound incendiaries) before the target was reached. The whole trip lasted between three and four hours... I well remember the trauma of flying over a peaceful moonlit Mediterranean then turning south for the coast and being met by a sudden upsurge of flak on the run in to the target. The perspex nose of the Blenheim, in which the Observer/Bomb-Aimer sat, offered no sense of protection. We observers used to sit on our tin hats to protect those parts of our anatomy we regarded as the most important!"

On the evening of 22 July 14 Squadron mounted its largest operation for some time: eight aircraft[137] formed up into two boxes of four before following the usual routing over the sea to Mersa Matruh. Over the following ten days twenty-nine sorties were directed against vehicles in the supply chain and aircraft on the forward landing grounds. All these sorties were flown at night with aircraft taking off at, typically, fifteen minute intervals and proceeding to the target singly. On 1 August three aircraft[138] got airborne, and headed for LG18 near Fuka. Flt Lt Watson, in the first aircraft, could not locate the target because of ground mist and so bombed a nearby tented encampment which was not fully blacked-out; however, Sgt H W T Bates'[139] crew spotted the flarepath and bombed the airfield. They also saw another aircraft, probably Sgt A F Ellis', attacking the target at the same time, but the third Blenheim did not return from the mission. In fact Sgt Ellis[140] had been attacked by a Ju88 which damaged the starboard engine. Ellis forced landed the crippled machine about forty miles southeast of Fuka, thereby unwittingly achieving the distinction of being the

Sgt Maurice German was 14 Squadron's last Blenheim Casualty. His foot was severely injured when Blenheim Z9614 was shot down on 1 August 1942 and he was taken to a German medical facility. It is believed that he was lost at sea when the German ship *Nino Bixio* was sunk while transporting Prisoners of War from Africa later in the month. (Christine Dean)

last Blenheim lost by 14 Squadron on operations. Ellis and his observer Sgt H B A Langmaid were uninjured but the third crewman, Sgt M German[141], injured his right foot in the crash. All three were taken prisoner and Sgt German was reported to have been taken to hospital at Fuka, but he was never seen again.

The next day in the dawn hours of 2 August 1942, two Blenheims[142] carried out a repeat attack on the previous night's target at LG18. After delivering their bombs, they crossed out to sea over Burg El Arab and returned to LG88 completing the last sortie that 14 Squadron would mount offensively with the Blenheim.

In the ground war Rommel's advance had ground to a halt and both sides settled into the defensive.

Notes

1 Rodolfo Graziani, 1st Marquess of Neghelli (1882 – 1955), had led Italian forces in Libya in the 1920s and Abyssinia in the 1930s.

2 Field Marshal Sir Archibald Wavell, 1st Earl Wavell GCB, GCSI, GCIE, CMG, MC, PC. (1883 – 1950) had been GOC Palestine and Transjordan in the late 1930s. He later served as Viceroy of India.

3 Generalfeldmarschall Erwin Rommel (1891-1944) took command of the Atlantic Wall defences in France after the North African Campaign. He committed suicide after being implicated in the plot to kill Hitler.

4 Sqn Ldr Geoffery Whittard DFC left the RAF in 1950, but continued to serve in the RAFVR for another ten years.

5 Blenheim Z5863.

6 A Pre-war regular, Donald Francis left the RAF in 1963 to run a village shop in Kent; he subsequently joined the Post Office, retiring in 1985. He founded the 14 Squadron Association in 1983.

7 21-year old Ronald Johnson was from South Tottenham. He was killed in action eleven days later.

8 Plt Off Johnson in T1994.

9 Sgt Taylor in Blenheim T2274.

10 Plt Off Johnson in T2173, Sgt N W Hoskins in Z5979, Sgt Matetich in L8874, Flt Sgt Taylor in T2346, Plt Off Gilmore in V5511. Norman Hoskins aged 23 was from Alexandria, Egypt.

11 OLt Gerhard Homuth claimed two of them, earning him the award of the Knight s Cross for twenty-two victories in air combat. Ofw. Herbert Kowalski claimed another two and Lt. Heinz Schmidt the other.

12 Sqn Ldr Stapleton in Z5593, Fg Off LeCavalier in Z5979 (?), Fg Off Mackenzie in T2338, Flt Lt Buchanan in Z5761, Lt Forrester in V5510 and Sgt Moulton in T2065.

13 Flt Lt Green in Blenheim T2065, Sgt Jeudwine in T2003 and Lt Forrester in V5510.

14 Fg Off LeCavalier in Z5593, Fg Off Mackenzie in T2338 and Sgt Dickson in Z5582.

15 Charles Bury aged 21 from Hagley, Worcestershire.

16 Flt Lt Maurice Fearn DFM, (b 1919) was from Invercargill, New Zealand.

17 Maj Eric Lewis DSO DFC SAAF from Durban later commanded 16 Sqn SAAF.

18 MRAF Lord Tedder (1890-1967) retired from the RAF in 1950 having served as CAS; he later became the Chancellor of Cambridge University.

19 John Willis was shot down and taken Prisoner of War in 1942.

20 The weapon load for each Blenheim on these sorties was 24 x 20lb and 12 x 40lb bombs, contained in 4 Small Bomb Containers (SBCs). Each container occupied the space of a 250lb bomb but itself contained either 6 x 40lb bombs (arranged in two clusters of three) or 12 x 20lb bombs (in three clusters of four). A 4-container load required the removal of the bomb bay doors due to the bulk.

21 Sqn Ldr Stapleton T2064, Lt Lewis Z5882, Fg Off Illsley T1977, Fg Off Buchanan T2236, Plt Off Moulton Z5886, Sgt Willis Z5770.

22 Sqn Ldr Stapleton T2064, Lt Lewis Z5770, Sgt Willis Z5767, Fg Off Buchanan T2236, Plt Off Moulton Z5886, Sgt Warwick T2389, Fg Off Illsley T1977, Sgt A Honig T1877 and Sgt P N Keeley V5444.

23 Flt Lt David Warwick won the DFC while serving with 684 Sqn in 1944. He retired from the RAF in 1954.
24 Born in Perth, Western Australia, Fg Off Amichai "Honk" Honig DFM (1919-43) was Jewish and was brought up in Palestine. He was killed in action flying a Beaufighter with 603 Sqn in Aug 1943.
25 Flt Sgt Percy Keeley was killed in action in Jan 1942 while flying with 113 Sqn in Burma.
26 Field Marshal Sir Claude Auchinleck (1884-1981) was an ex-Indian Army officer. He was C-in-C India from 1943-47 after which he retired to Marrakech.
27 The convoy comprised mostly 3-ton and 15cwt Bedford trucks with bowser trailers for the carriage of water and aviation fuel and a generator trailer (mainly used for charging aircraft and vehicle batteries). The CO s Humber staff car completed the fleet.
28 Harold Parker, aged 44 was from Gainford, County Durham.
29 Originally from South Africa, Wg Cdr Lionel Cookie Leon DSO DFC* (1919-2006) commanded 55 Sqn in 1945 and returned to his native country to farm after the war; however an opponent of apartheid, he moved to Australia in 1974.
30 After the war, Londoner Ray Ball (1919-2007) ran a butchery business, first in London and later in Surrey.
31 Sqn Ldr Buchanan in V5792.
32 Blenheim V5444.
33 Ken Wilson (1916 –) from Melbourne Australia.
34 An artilleryman, who had enjoyed success during the East African campaign of 1941, General Sir Alan Cunningham GCMG KCB DSO MC (1887 – 1983) retired from the Army in 1946.
35 Air Marshal Sir Arthur Coningham KCB KBE DSO MC DFC AFC (1895 – 1948) was known as "Mary," apparently derived from "Maori," reflecting his origins in New Zealand. He was killed in an air accident in1948.
36 Sgt G J Webb in V5925, Plt Off P Goode in Z6436, Flt Lt J D Towlson in V5582, Sqn Ldr A J M Smythe in T2127, Sgt Willis in T2236. Flt Lt Geoffrey Webb was born in 1920 in Sydney. Sqn Ldr Peter Goode, aged 21, from Woodford Halse, Northamptonshire was killed in March 1943. Gp Capt Anthony Smyth OBE DFC (1915-2007) subsequently commanded 11 Squadron. A keen mountaineer he founded the RAF Mountaineering Association. Flt Lt John Towlson resigned his commission in 1942.
37 22-year old Thomas Turner was a married man from Shrewsbury.
38 Plt Off Wilson in Z6436, Wg Cdr Buchanan in Z6044, Sgt Coles in T2241, Plt Off C D Loughlin in V5582, Sgt Honig in V5925 and Plt Off Leon in V5950.
39 Wg Cdr Buchanan in V5573, Maj Lewis in V5582, Sgt Willis in V6183, Sgt Honig in T2064, Sgt H S Grimsey in Z5976, Plt Off Loughlin in Z5943.
40 Blenheim T2241.
41 Vivian Royals was commissioned in 1942 and survived the war.
42 Cyril Murfitt was commissioned in Feb 1944.
43 Robert Chubb aged 22 from Catford, London was an observer.
44 21-year old Brian Jenkins, an Wireless Operator/Air Gunner was from Reading.
45 Arthur Ellis, also a 21-year old WOp/AG was from Loudwater, Buckinghamshire.
46 Wg Cdr Buchanan in Z5976, Sgt Honig in T2064, Maj Lewis in V5582, Plt Off Loughlin in Z9543.
47 Douglas Loughlin (1913-41) was born in Liverpool. A keen sportsman he taught at Grosvenor St John's School for Boys from 1935 until he joined the RAFVR in 1939.
48 Wg Cdr Harry Grimsey OBE DFC AFC (b Stowmarket 1913) retired from the RAF in 1968. His career included flying as a VIP pilot and he was involved in transporting delegates to the Yalta Conference.
49 Blenheim T2064.
50 Wg Cdr Buchanan in V6461, Sgt F W Dennis in Z5860, Maj Lewis in V5582, Plt Off Wilson in V6508, Sgt Webb in Z9584, Sgt Warwick in V5950, Sgt J H Bosworth in Z6443, Sgt Willis in V6183. Fg Off John Bosworth (b 1912) returned to Australia after being injured when he was shot down in Jan 1942.
51 28-year old Frederick Dennis was from Dubbo New South Wales.
52 Shirley Lawson (b 1918) left the Squadron soon afterwards and after repatriation to Australia he left the RAAF and became an agrochemical engineer.
53 V6508.

54 "Bill" Tovey had worked for the Daily Express before the war.

55 Ron Dawson (b Dec 1920, Rugby. Warwickshire). Had been a trainee pilot in 1940 , but a medical problem made him unfit for aircrew duties and he was posted to Middle East in 1941 as an MT Fitter (with 14 Sqn). After the war, founded and ran several highly successful building and industrial property investment companies in the UK, with subsidiary companies in the USA..

56 A keen footballer, Jim Hanson served with 14 Squadron as an engine fitter from 1940 in Port Sudan all through the Middle East war until the Sqn moved to England in Sep 1944.

57 M S Best (d 2005), also an engine fitter, was an exact contemporary of Jim Hanson.

58 Flt Sgt Kenneth Stevenson aged 19 from Birmingham was killed in action in Mar 1942.

59 Terence Archer (b 1914) was from Rockhampton, Queensland.

60 A graduate of the University of California, Morley Lister (b 1913) was born in London and started her journalistic career with the *San Fransisco Call Bulletin*. In the 1960s she was the Art Critic for the *Detroit Free Press*.

61 "De Montmartre à Tripoli"- André Glarner, Editions Musy, Paris 1945.

62 After the war Charles North transferred to the Secretarial Branch of the RAF; he retired from the RAF as a Sqn Ldr in 1968.

63 Rod Lapthorne DFC (1917-1999) joined Australian National Airlines after the war, eventually becoming a senior Training Captain with Ansett Airlines; he joined the Australian Department of Civil Aviation in 1969.

64 Flt Lt Cecil Goodwin DFC (1910-2002) returned to New South Wales after the war.

65 Wg Cdr Buchanan Z7701, Sgt Willis Z7893, Sgt Webb Z9656, Maj Lewis V5657, Sgt Bosworth Z9729, Sgt Archer Z7970, Sqn Ldr Leon Z9576, Sgt J S J Hamilton-Martin V5947, Sgt G W Clarke-Hall V5950. Sqn Ldr John Hamilton-Martin AFC retired from the RAF in 1963. "Wal" Clarke-Hall DFC (1915-2009) from Albany, Western Australia returned to banking after the war.

66 Wg Cdr Buchanan in Z9636, Plt Off Keck in V5657, Plt Off Goode in Z7701 and Maj Lewis in Z7893.

67 Sqn Ldr Leon in Z7893, Sgt Archer in Z7970, Sgt Hamilton-Martin in V5947, Sgt R J Good in T2124, Sgt J H Elliott in V5387, Sgt Stevenson in V5657. Sgt Robert Good (1920-1942) from Glenelg, South Australia was killed in a mid-air collision in March 1942.

68 In Blenheim V5387.

69 Gp Capt Clive Caldwell DSO DFC★ (1910-1994) later served in the Pacific war and was involved in the Morotai Mutiny when he tried to resign from the RAAF in protest over the tasking of its fighter units. He finished the war with 27 confirmed kills and after leaving the RAAF in 1946 he had a successful business carer with a cloth import/export firm.

70 Wg Cdr Buchanan in Z7690, Sgt Webb in Z9729, Plt Off Goode in Z7992, Maj Lewis in V5387, Plt Off H K Keck in Z9576, Sgt Clarke-Hall in Z5886, Sgt R K Francis in Z7893, Sgt Good in Z6443. Harry Keck (1912-42) from Mavern, Victoria W Australia was killed when his Blenheim was shot down by a Hurricane.

71 General Sir Neil Ritchie GBE KCB DSO MC KStJ (1897 – 1983) was later replaced as GOC-inC Eighth Army, but continued a successful military career, ending as C-in-C Far East Land Forces in 1947. After retiring from the army he emigrated to Canada.

72 Wg Cdr Alan Mills retired from the RAF in 1955.

73 Luftwaffe claims show Bf109F pilot Fw. Fritz Gromotka of 6 Staffel JG27 was credited with the only downing of a Blenheim that day, at 1315 hrs west of Sidi Barrani.

74 Blenheim Z9729.

75 21-year old Robert Swann was from Henley Beach, South Australia and had been a watch maker before the war.

76 Blenheim Z6443.

77 Francis Brown (b 1914) was from Perth, Australia.

78 Blenheim V5657.

79 Eric Barr broke his ankle on landing.

80 33-year old Phil Tew was from Morecambe Lancashire.

81 Blenheim V6184.

82 Blenheim Z7893.

83 23-year old John Harvie was from Unley Park, South Australia.

84 V5954 crewed by Sgt K W Stevenson, Sgt W V Howey and Sgt L Johnson. Kenneth Stevenson, aged just 19, was from Bournville, Birmingham; 26-year old Lawson Johnson was from Newcastle-upon-Tyne.

85 22-year old Sgt William Howey from Edmonton, Alberta Canada, died the next day from his injuries.

86 Blenheim T2387.

87 Wg Cdr Buchanan in Z9584, Flt Sgt Willis in V6298, Sgt Webb in Z9656, Sqn Ldr Mills in V5446, Flt Sgt Grimsey in V5960 and Flt Lt Keck in Z7631.

88 Walter MacMichael, aged 31, from Sandy Bay, Tasmania Australia was killed in action two weeks later.

89 Paul Rylands from Westmoreland Cumbria was killed in action at the end of the month; he was 22 years old. His elder brother, Maj H G Rylands of the Royal Lancashire Regiment was killed in action in the Far East in 1945.

90 Reginald "Mick" Ey was from Toorak Gardens, South Australia. He later served with 55 Sqn

91 Flt Sgt Johnnie Hunt aged 27 from Adelaide was killed in action with 55 Sqn in Apr 1943.

92 Wg Cdr Buchanan in Z9584, Sgt T N Archer in Z7970, Plt Off F R Brown in Z7989, Plt Off M C Johnson in Z9722, Sgt G F Highman in Z5893, Sqn Ldr Ferguson in Z7514, Sgt Good in T2124, Flt Sgt R G S Linley in Z7991. Terence Archer (b1914) was from Rockhampton, Queensland, Australia. Francis Brown (b1914) was from Perth, Western Australia. Murray Johnson (b1919) from Propect, South Australia won the DFC a few months later. Gordon Highman, aged 21, from Broadview, South Australia was killed in action three months later.

93 Richard Linley, aged 22, was from Limpsfield, Surrey.

94 Blenheim Z5893.

95 Charles Bowling (b1915) of Currie, Tasmania Australia.

96 Peto Munyard aged 22 was a married man from Como Western Australia.

97 L9418.

98 After serving with 87 Sqn RAAF in the Far East, Wg Cdr Ken Dee DFC transferred to the Administrative Branch of the RAAF after the war.

99 Harold Marshall (b1921) was born in England and emigrated to Australia.

100 Z7627.

101 V6453.

102 Bruce Slade (b1920) was from Adelaide, South Australia.

103 Z9722.

104 21-year old Peter Clauson was born in China, but later lived in Kalgoorlie, Western Australia.

105 Before the war Ted Meader had been a clerk with the Gas Board.

106 type T1083 transmitter and type R1082 receiver sets.

107 Z7963.

108 21-year old Patrick Chapman was from Vereeniging, Transvaal, South Africa.

109 Sgt D W McConville and Sgt R R Richardson; Douglas McConvile, aged 26, was from Williamstown, Victoria, Australia and 20-year old Ray Richardson was from North Fremantle, Western Australia.

110 Eric Brown.

111 Gp Capt "Dick" Maydwell DSO DFC (1913-2006) had originally been commissioned into the Somerset Light Infantry and earned the DFC while serving with 53 Sqn in 1940. After commanding 14 Sqn he went on to command 325 Group, but in 1944 he was involved in a collision with a train and lost his right leg. He retired from the RAF in 1958 and spent his retirement in Somerset using his considerable skills as a marksman culling deer and controlling pigeons. Maydwell also served as a Vice President of the 14 Squadron Association.

112 Plt Of Grimsey in Z7517, Sgt Ellis in T2389, Plt Off Slade in Z6425, Sgt Elliott in Z9795, Plt Off Lapthorne in Z7419 and Sqn Ldt R H Moore DFC in Z9746.

113 In Blenheim Z9795.

114 Z9656.

115 Flt Lt Deryck Brooks, who had joined the RAF in 1939, transferred to the RCAF in 1945

116 Colin Cowan aged 27 from Balhannah, South Australia was an engineering graduate of Adelaide University.

117 Flying a Marauder, Fg Off Joseph Elliott (b 1915) from Perth, Western Australia was to score 14 Squadron's first success with a torpedo the following year.

118 Z9795.

119 Z7517 Sgt Highman, Sgt W D Lynch and Sgt W L Carnie. William Lynch, aged 21, was from Kendra, Queensland, Australia; Wilfred Carnie also 21 was from Barmera, South Australia.

120 Flt Lt Harold Ridley DFC flew as Eric Lewis' navigator on Marauders. After the war he transferred to the Secretarial Branch of the RAF and retired in 1959.

121 Z9795.

122 An exact contemporary of Buchanan, Alexander Pirie joined the RAF in 1937; he ended the war as a Sqn Ldr, but served on in the RAF Reserve as a Flt Lt until 1954. He died in 1996.

123 Z6044 Sgts C M Leaver, H M J Powell and R J Hehir. Cyril Leaver aged 21 was from Taunton, Somerset, Hubert Powell aged 23 was from Alveston, Gloucestershire and 24-year old Robert Hehir was from Ashford, South Australia.

124 LAC Karel Friedl was originally from Czechoslovakia.

125 The North African Campaign 1940-43, Gen Sir William Jackson – Batsford 1975.

126 Before the war, 24-year old J S Warden, from Pretoria, Transvaal, South Africa had been a Chartered Accountant.

127 Henry Gibbons.

128 Wg Cdr Maydwell in Z6184, Plt Off Johnson in Z7841, Plt Off Lapthorne in Z7709, Plt Off Willis in Z7970, Plt Off Grimsey in Z7514, Sgt T G N Russell in T2989.

129 Sgt G C Egebjerg in Z7712, Sgt Clarke-Hall in Z7970, Sgt T C Bullock in Z7514, Sgt C J O'Connor in Z7841, Sgt Russell in T2389. Gunnar Egebjerg (1917-193) was born in California but brought up in Denmark. After serving in the RAFVR he transferred to the USAAF in March 1943. After the war he moved to California. Tom Bullock, from Chetham, Manchester, was killed in action in April 1943. Cornelius "Neil" O'Connor (1921-2000) enjoyed a long post-war career in aviation which included 14 years as an Air Traffic Controller immediately after the war and later flying helicopters in Papua New Guinea.

130 Sgts Russell, F V Dyson and W J Nicholas. All three were killed in action while flying together in May 1943. Thomas Russell, aged 21, was from Melbourne, Victoria, Australia. 29-year old Francis Dyson was from Caulfield, Victoria, Australia and William Nicholas was a 32-year old married man from Tarwin Lower, Victoria, Australia.

131 Z7712.

132 Flt Lt A Watson in Z9710, Plt Off Willis in Z9826, Sgt Bullock in Z6428, Plt Off Johnson in Z5649.

133 Originally a farmer from Surrey, Wg Cdr Anthony Watson DSO DFC later commanded 227 Sqn. While flying Beaufighters, he shot down 6 enemy aircraft being shot down himself in 1943. He retired from the RAF in 1947.

134 Sqn Ldr Moore in Z6428, Sgt Elliott in Z9826, Plt Off Lapthorne in Z7417, Sgt Dee in Z9655, [illegible] V5649.

135 Flt Lt Robert Moore DFC, who had won the DFC while serving with 11 Sqn, resigned from the RAF in 1955.

136 Arthur ("Tony") de Yarburgh-Bateson, the Lord Deramore (1911-2006) served with 14 Squadron on Blenheims Marauders and Wellingtons. After the war he resumed his career as an architect. He was President of the 14 Squadron Association from 1984 to 2001.

137 Lt W A Leach in R3889, Flt Lt Watson in Z9710, Sgt L E Einsaar in Z6184, Plt Off Lapthorne in Z9655, Sgt Bullock in Z5761, Lt K A Richardson in Z9647, Sgt J H F Kelly in Z7514 and Sgt Egebjberg in Z9826. Wally Leach returned to South Africa at the end of the war. Ken Richardson, also from South Africa, became a PoW. John Kelly was commissioned in 1944 and served after the war in the Training Branch of the RAFVR.

138 Flt Lt Watson in Z6184, Sgt H W T Bates in Z9655 and Sgt Ellis in Z9614.

139 From Northumberland, Hugh Bates rejoined his family Lubricants & Fuels business after the war.

140 Alan Ellis was eventually taken via a PoW holding camp (Dulag Luft) to Stalag VIIIB then by the end of 1943 to Stalag Luft III. He had worked for Mobil Oil in Western Australia before enlisting and rejoined the Company on demobilisation.

141 25-year old Maurice German was from Highgate, Middlesex. It seems likely that he perished as a passenger on the Italian prison ship *Nino Bixio* which was torpedoed on 17 Aug 1942.

142 Sgt C C Truman in Z9655 and Sgt R A Barton in Z9651. Carl Truman, aged 33 was from Lane Cove, New South Wales, Australia; Raymond Barton, aged 29, was from Burnside, South Australia. Both of these crews were killed in action in February 1943.

Chapter 8

1942–44
The Marauder Years

Enter the Marauder

14 Squadron was formally withdrawn from the line on 4 August 1942 for conversion to the Marauder. The unit, now comprising only six Blenheims and three Bostons, moved to LG Y, just west of Ismailia, where crews kept themselves current on the Blenheims; the Bostons gave pilots the opportunity to get used to handling an aeroplane with the unfamiliar tricycle undercarriage. Five days later the Squadron moved again, this time to LG 224, twenty miles west of Cairo, where nine brand new Martin B-26 Marauders awaited them. Twice a heavy as a Blenheim, the Marauder was an imposing and intimidating machine, standing twenty feet high on its tricycle undercarriage. It also came with a reputation as a "widow maker". "When I saw my first Marauder," recalled Maj Lewis, "I was scared as I thought I'd never be able to fly such a huge aircraft." The new aircraft required a crew of six, so Marauder crews were formed by the simple expedient of combining two Blenheim crews. The by-product of each amalgamation was one extra navigator who had to be replaced by another air gunner; furthermore one pilot would be the captain while the other was relegated to the role of second pilot. This process caused some angst amonst crews whose loyalty to each other had been forged by shared hardships: even so some, like Sgt Bates' navigator, Sgt J B Dutton[1], volunteered to leave the Squadron early, while they still had some choice about where they went next.

Three USAAF pilots, Lt Col F Garrison Jr[2], Maj J E Welborn and Capt Marrs, and a RAF instructor, Sqn Ldr B G Meharg[3], were seconded to LG 224 to help with the initial conversion. Despite the Marauder's fearsome reputation, Squadron pilots soon found that when treated with respect the aircraft was not unduly difficult to fly. The main handling difference was on the approach, where the Marauder was flown at around 150 mph – considerably faster than the landing speed for a Blenheim. This higher landing speed was indirectly the cause of an unfortunate accident on 20 August when four Egyptian labourers tried to cross the runway in their lorry just ahead of their aircraft[4] as it touched down. The Marauder hit the truck, wrecking both vehicle and aeroplane and killing all four Egyptians, but luckily neither Lt Col Garrison, nor his student Plt Off Willis were injured.

The conversion process caried on over the next few months, but progress was frustratingly slow because of unserviceabilities with the new aircraft. During this period

FK375 "Dominion Revenge" flown by Wg Cdr W S G Maydwell in late July 1942. The aircraft is one of the few which wore the short-lived desert camouflage reflecting the expectation that the aircraft would be used as light bombers. However when the Squadron converted to the maritime role a month or so later the aircraft was repainted in a more appropriate green and grey sheme.

the Squadron moved yet again to Fayed on the western shore of the Great Bitter Lake on the Suez Canal. The first operational sortie by a 14 Squadron Marauder[5] was flown by Lt B W Young[6] on 28 October. The Battle of El Alamein was in full swing, but Young's mission took him not over the battlefield as might have been expected, but out over the Mediterranean to carry out a a weather reconnaissance of Crete. For this eight-hour sortie an extra 1,000 gallon "overload" fuel tank was fitted in the bomb bay, a configuration which would become the standard fit to 14 Squadron's Marauders. Young's task also gave a good indication of the Squadron's future role: the next day the Squadron received news that they had been transferrred to 201 Group, which specialised in maritime operations. During early November a number of maritime reconnaisance sorties were flown. One eventful sortie[7] was flown by Wg Cdr Maydwell's crew on the afternoon of 6 November, and ranged around the Cyclades Islands to the north of Crete. During this patrol Maydwell found five "invasion barges" packed with troops which he strafed. Shortly afterwards came across a Ju52 transport aircraft, but as he manoeuvred to engage it the crew realised that it was a Red Cross aircraft, so they let it go on its way. Later in the patrol they found a pair of merchant ships under the escort of two He115s. As they approached the ships they came under heavy anti-aircraft fire which caused considerable damage to the Marauder, setting fire to the overload fuel tank in the bomb bay and wounding the turret gunner, Sgt W J Nicholas, in the leg. The fire was tackled by the wireless operator, Sgt D G Clarke, using a bottle fire extinguisher; once that was empty, Clarke had to use his bare hands to beat out the last of the flames[8]. Continuing with the mission, Maydwell saw two more ships at anchor in an island bay, and a convoy escorted by five destroyers and seven Ju88s. When the Marauder approached the convoy for a closer look they were

EUBOEA
KHALKIS
IZMIR
TURKEY
AEGEAN
SEA
ATHENS
GREECE
GIOS
GEORGIOUS
KYTHNOS
NAXOS
MELOS
CYCLADES
ISLANDS
TILOS
RHODES
DODECANESE
ISLANDS
SOUDA BAY
MALEME
TYMPAKI
CRETE

EASTERN MEDITERRANEAN AND AEGEAN SEAS 1942 - 1943

0   50   100   150
MILES

N

LIBYA
BENGHAZI
GAMBUT

chased off by two of the Ju88s. The return leg of this eight hour sortie was flown under cover of darkness.

The next day a major strategic event changed the whole face of the war in North Africa: American troops landed on the Morrocan and Algerian coast, opening a "western front" in North Africa. With decisive vistory at El Alemein close at hand it was clear that the Germans would soon be ejected from North Africa, but it was also clear that the battle for control of the Mediterranean would take on a new significance. In Egypt the training continued and it was during a practice bombing sortie on 24 November that tragedy struck. As Fg Off W R Bower's[9] Marauder[10] approached the bombing range at Shallufah, just north of Suez, the tail unit broke off and the aircraft dived into the ground, killing the whole crew.

On 30 November the majority of crews and aircraft were detached to Shallufah for a torpedo dropping course. A handful of crews from "A" Flight continued conversion training for new crews at Fayed while the remaining few continued to fly operational sorties from a detached base at Gambut. These sorties included a number of "offensive shipping searches" designed to interdict the Afrika Korps' martime supply lines. The first bombing attack against shipping was carried out by Fg Off Slade[11] on 6 December, when he engaged an 800 ton schooner off the Libyan coast just east of Tripoli. However, the schooner met Slade's attack with accurate anti-aircraft fire and the bomb-aimer Sgt F W Bayley was hit and wounded just before the bomb release point, causing him to release early and the bombs all fell short.

There was a brief change from maritime work on 11 December when four Marauders[12] bombed the aerodrome and station at Gabes in Tunisia, but the majority of operational work consisted of reconnaissance along the Libyan and Tunisian coast. On 16 December a formation of three Marauders was carrying out an offensive shipping sweep to the west of Benghazi. On the outward leg they had been escorted by a flight of Beaufighters which shot down a Ju52 off Tripoli, but on the return leg the Marauders were alone when they were mistakenly attacked by a formation of nine Malta-based Spitfires. Sgt L A Einsaar's[13] aircraft[14] was so badly damaged by the fighters that he eventually had to forced land in the sea about fifteen miles to the west of Benghazi. The aircraft caught fire as it hit the water and then sank almost immediately, taking with it Sgt R I Ploskin[15], Sgt P F Cockington[16] and Sgt A E Watts[17]. Einsaar, Sgt L R Dixon (the second pilot) Sgt L B Willocks (the gunner) had managed to escape from the wreckage and scrambled aboard the life raft. However, Einsaar then saw the navigator, Sgt T E Exell[18], in difficulty in the water, separated from the dinghy by a sea of flame. Einsaar immediately dived into the water and managed to reach Exell, but the navigator was badly injured and he died in Einsaar's arms shortly afterwards. The survivors were located by an Air Sea Rescue Wellington and picked up by a rescue launch two hours later.

Mines and Torpedoes

Two nights later, six Marauders set off to drop mines into the harbour at Tunis. They set off from Shallufah to Berka, just outside the newly-liberated Benghazi to refuel before five aircraft[19] set out for the long flight to Tunis. Each Marauder carried two 1,200-pound American magnetic mines in one side of the bomb bay with the overload fuel tank on the other side. The mines had to be dropped from below 200 feet. "As it was to be a night mission," recalled Sgt C J O'Connor, "at briefing we all wanted to know how we got to fly under 200 feet without a radar altimeter. The briefing Officer struck chill in our hearts when he said matter-of-factly 'Well, you will make a landfall on the north-east tip of Tunisia at Cape Bon. There are 200 foot cliffs for some miles to the west of Cape Bon, so you let down in the moonlight until you are just below the cliffs.'" On arriving off Cape Bon O'Connor found the cliffs that the briefing officer had mentioned and let down just below their level, noting that the altimeter read minus thirty feet.

"As we ran in on our mine dropping run," continued O'Connor, "I asked Buck [the navigator, Sgt J C Buckland[20]] if he was sure it was Tunis harbour. He did not have to answer, for suddenly, on came the searchlights, and flak from anti-aircraft guns began hammering a Marauder about a quarter of a mile ahead. The pilot pulled up and started weaving, but his evasive actions were to no avail. A shell must have hit his mines or fuel tank, for his aircraft exploded into a large ball of orange flame." In fact O'Connor had just witnessed Plt Off Willis' Marauder flying into the sea, or perhaps hitting a gantry crane as he tried to avoid the anti-aircraft fire[21]. Another pilot, Plt Off Grimsey narrowly missed a ship's mast as he made his attack.

"Buck had opened the bomb bay doors of our aeroplane, ready to drop our mines. Suddenly he yelled 'Pull up!! Gantry cranes ahead!! Mines dropped.' Reacting automatically to Buck's urgent outburst, I climbed steeply to avoid the cranes, then turned for home up the harbour with the knowledge that our job was done. Relief was short-lived, for almost immediately, from the mid-upper gunner came the sharp call of 'Night fighter'. A couple of bursts of tracer fire went past us as I dived the aircraft towards the water. At about 400 feet, the fighter broke off his attack, no doubt thinking that we would plough into the drink. I stopped weaving and levelled out at an altimeter reading of minus fifty feet."

On the return leg, O'Connor attempted to transfer fuel from the overload tank, but the fuel gauges read empty. When Flt Sgt C A Long[22], the second pilot, went back to check the bomb bay, he found that the fuel tank was no longer there – in the heat of the moment, as they narrowly missed the gantry cranes, Buckland had dropped the mines and the fuel tank into Tunis harbour. With little fuel and few options remaining, O'Connor decided to divert to Malta. Arriving there just after an air raid, O'Connor landed in pitch darkness. Fortunately Long had previously flown Spitfires from Malta and knew that the runway was very short; he shouted for O'Connor to apply the brakes, and the aircraft shuddered to a halt just before the sheer drop to the sea at the end of the airstrip. As they taxied clear, the port engine failed through lack of fuel.

Maj Lewis and Capt Young had a slightly easier time on Christmas Eve when, flying via Berka, they dropped mines in daylight off Qarqanna island near Sfax. Christmas Day itself was something of a celebration as the Torpedo Course at Shallufah was finished and the whole Squadron was reunited at Fayed. The Squadron's operations diary recorded "a magnificent spread in all Messes."

Now that crews were qualified to use torpedoes, the weapons were carried regularly on "offensive torpedo reconnaissance" sorties around the Aegean Sea. At first these met with little success. On the afternoon of 3 January Lt L C Jones[23] and Capt Young were operating amongst the Cyclades islands in pooor visibilty under a low cloudbase. As they approached Gios Georgios, about forty miles south of Athens, the pair stumbled across a convoy of five ships escorted by twin-engined fighters. According to Jones "Capt Young then came on the R/T with the order to attack, we turned in fluid formation on an approximate course of 305°. At about 2,000 yards Capt Young who was slightly ahead, broke across to my starboard in front of me. I

Torpedo-carrying FK151 at low level over the sea, flown by Maj E M Lewis SAAF on an armed reconnaissance of the Aegean on 1 February 1943. (Alan Cadell)

continued my attack, dropping my torpedo... I then broke away over the bows to port and [my] tail gunner Sgt A Taylor reported dense clouds of smoke astern. I then turned through 90° to have a look, but owing to visibility could see nothing, visibility being two to five miles." But Jones' torpedo had missed his target and he also lost contact with Young in the murk. Subsequent radio calls from Young's aircraft[24] indicated that he was being attacked by fighters. The Marauder was shot down into the sea with the loss of all the crew except Young, who survived the crash and was taken prisoner.

Nine days later, Maj Lewis and Fg Off Clarke-Hall came upon a small merchant ship to the east of Kythnos. "Both aircraft turned to starboard to attack in fluid formation," reported Clarke-Hall, "I then switched over from R/T to intercom to warn my crew of the impending attack and overlooked switching back to R/T, so missing Maj Lewis' further instructions to discontinue the attack." Lewis had identified the vessel as the *Isora*, a neutral Spanish ship and tried to call off the attack. Unaware of this, Clarke-Hall dropped his torpedo, but fortunately it missed the target. It was not until 20 January that a 14 Squadron Marauder[25] carried out a successful torpedo attack. On that day Plt Off Elliott and Fg Off Grimsey found the *Alfredo* just south of Melos. Elliott "sighted one vessel with one aircraft protection on the starboard bow. I gave instructions over the R/T to attack and both aircraft turned starboard and attacked in fluid formation. The enemy aircraft, an Arado 196 made a head on attack on Fg Off Grimsey making him break off his attack and preventing a drop. The Arado then attacked me and by feinting right then left I managed to pass and resume my attack... the torpedo was seen to run true and straight by my gunners and a hit was made on the vessel in the proximity of the bow... I saw an explosion and the ship heeled over to port side and within one minute half sunk with the screw out of the water. The ship was laden and there was no flak from it."

Two later attacks were less successful: on 23 January Fg Off R W Lapthorne and Flt Sgt O A Phillips[26] dropped their torpedoes against two ships off Tilos island, but

The last moments of the *Alfredo* after she was torpedoed by Fg Off J H Elliott RAAF just south of Melos on 20 January 1943.

saw no results. Eight days later Fg Off Grimsey and Fg Off M C Johnson attacked a large passenger vessel off Melos Island. The ship was escorted by two destroyers and three Ju88s. Once again both torpedoes missed their target, and the Marauders attracted the attention of Ju88s, which gave chase. Grimsey was engaged by two Ju88s for fifteen minutes, during which he carried out violent evasive action at altitudes below 100 feet. The engagement only ended when Grimsey's gunners scored hits on one of the German aircraft and it was seen to turn away with smoke coming from its starboard engine.

Throughout January and early February 14 Squadron's Marauders flew daily maritime reconnaissance sorties, supplemented by frequent anti-submarine patrols and offensive shipping sweeps. These latter were part of a combined, but unco-ordinated, campaign by 201 Group aircraft and RN submarines against axis shipping using the waters of the Aegean. While many ships had to run the gauntlet of submarines and aircraft in the Aegean, others were able to use the well-sheltered route between the eastern coast of Greece and the large island of Euboea. Here the narrow channel, with steep hills on either side, offered a route which was safe from attack by both submarines and aircraft. However this waterway had a narrow choke point at the Euripus Strait near Khalkis, which was an ideal place to lay mines. On 9 January two aircraft[27] loaded with magnetic mines took off from Shallufah bound for the Burgi (Bourtzi) Channel, a few miles south of Khalkis where the waterway narrowed to a half-mile width before opening into the Gulf of Euboea. Plt Off Elliott had to return to Shallufah soon after take-off with engine trouble, but Wg Cdr Maydwell continued alone, threading his way northwards through the Dodecanese islands as far as Psara. From here he turned westwards towards Khalkis to approach the target over Euboea from due east. Once over the straits, the Marauder would be very vulnerable as there was no room to manoevre to avoid anti-aircraft fire. "I had deliberately chosen midday as the time of the strike," recalled Maydwell, "guessing that the Italians would be changing the guard and probably having a siesta. This assumption proved to be correct and the anti-aircraft gunners in the channel were taken unawares and all the shots they fired were way behind us... [the mines] had to be droppd at thirty feet and as slow as possible. We were so low on that operation that my tail gunner got soaked in sea water spray. So much so that the ground crew asked him if he had been swimming!" As they flew homebound they saw a small convoy of four ships to the east of Naxos and were fired on by the escorting destroyers, but no damage was done.

Maydwell set off for the Burgi Channel again on 14 February. This time he was at the lead of three aircraft, but once again his number two dropped out because of unserviceability, leaving Maydwell and Plt Off C P M Phillips[28] to carry on[29]. They followed a similar route to that used on the previous mission; this time, however, the weather was appalling and the aircraft had to negotiate their way round heavy storms, with thick cloud covering hilltops. It was difficult to find the target area in such conditions, but once again the Marauders achieved complete surprise and dropped their mines successfully to the south of Khalkis

The next day two Marauders[30] set off for a routine offensive shipping sweep of the Aegean. Nothing further was heard from Flt Sgt Truman's aircraft, but it was presumed to have been shot down when the formation attacked a merchant vessel in the eastern Aegean. During the engagement Lt Jones' aircraft was badly damaged and one engine failed, but he managed to coax the aeroplane to the Turkish coast and landed at Izmir, where the aircraft and its crew were interned. On the same day the Squadron was informed that they would move from Fayed to Berka III just outside Benghazi: a road journey of over seven hundred miles which would take them from 17 to 23 February to complete.

The Melos Harbour Raid

Despite the risks taken by the Marauder crews, the offensive torpedo sweeps of the Aegean had not been particularly effective: only seven torpedoes were dropped in two months and of these just one had found its target. The problem was that the aircraft had to hunt their quarry in a massive area of sea riven with a myriad of small islands, each of which provided a hiding place for ships. Meanwhile, heavily escorted convoys dashed from the shelter of one island to the next, offering only fleeting and well-defended targets. It was clear that it would be much more effective to attack ships while they were at anchor in one of the many harbours amongst the islands. One of the most important islands in this respect was Melos which boasted a large natural harbour about halfway between Athens and Crete. It was used frequently as a night stop for German ships, whose movements attracted the scrutiny of the Greek resistance group known as Group 5-165. Intelligence from Group 5-165

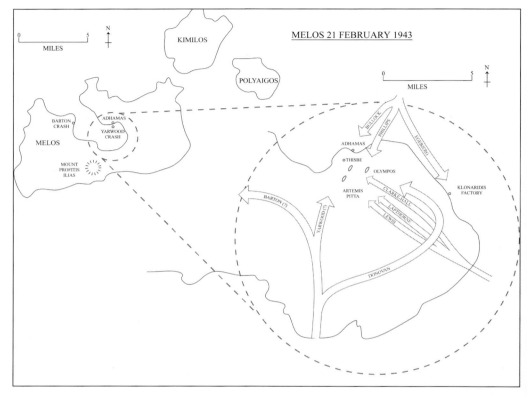

MELOS 21 FEBRUARY 1943

supplemented by a photo-reconnaissance by Plt Off O P Olson[31] of 680 Squadron[32] on 16 February provided 201 Group with enough information to plan an attack on shipping in the harbour.

Late on 19 February Wg Cdr Maydwell received orders to prepare for an attack on Melos two days later. The preliminary briefing was held at 0900 the next day, after which Maj Lewis, who was to lead the mission, carried out a brief formation rehearsal with his crews. Meanwhile Fg Off G Searle[33] of 680 Squadron was tasked to provide photographs of the harbour; unfortunately Searle found much of the harbour area was obscured by cloud so he was unable to confirm the presence of any ships. With no concrete intelligence of the exact number and position of shipping in the harbour, Lewis' plan was for an attack by nine aircraft, three of which would be armed with torpedoes. The remaining six aircraft, armed with 500-pound bombs, would attack any shipping which had not been attacked by the torpedo carriers, or if there was none, they would bomb the harbour and military facilities at Adhamas.

Just after midday on 21 February ten Marauders took off from Shallufah. "We were lined up ready for take-off," recalled Fg Off Lapthorne, "when a crewman left the leader's machine and ran towards us carrying an aircraft escape axe. He explained that the Major had been flying our aircraft the previous day and had forgotten to transfer his lucky axe: would we please exchange? A superstitious lad was our Major."

Disaster almost struck a few minutes later when the fifth aircraft[34] started its take-off run. Sgt O'Connor who was flying the spare aircraft in case one of the others was unserviceable reported that "as we accelerated down the strip carrying a load of four 500-pound delay-fused bombs on one side of the bomb bay, and a tank with 1,000 gallons of fuel on the other side, my second pilot, Carl Long, called the speeds. At 150 mph, I eased the control yoke back, but the aircraft remained firmly on the runway. I applied full back trim. As that made no difference, I decided to abort the take-off. I eased the yoke slightly forward as I went to pull the power off, and the Marauder suddenly leapt into the air... I soon realised that the cables from the control column to the elevators had been reversed. Forward movement was 'up', backward movement into the body was 'down'! After porpoising around the circuit at about 300 feet, we managed to get safely back onto the deck with our cargo of bombs and fuel tanks. When my blood pressure subsided, I discovered that our aircraft had just come out of maintenance and had been rushed onto the flight line with no time to test-fly it."

The remaining strike aircraft headed northwards. "Flying at fifty feet in loose formation," continued Lapthorne, "the nine aircraft crossed the Mediterranean ... to the Kaso Straits at the eastern end of Crete and thence eighty miles north-west to Melos Island. Approaching Melos, the raid, undetected at this stage, broke into three flights: 'A' carrying torpedoes[35] set a north-west course crossing the narrow belt of land separating the harbour from the surrounding sea and dropping to water level in the harbour an hour before dusk... 'B' flight[36] broke left, entering the harbour on a northerly heading to bomb two minutes after 'A' struck. Meanwhile 'C' flight[37] circled right to attack on a southerly heading two minutes after 'B'."

As they breasted the hills into the harbour, Lewis saw two large merchant ships and a smaller coaster in the harbour. Jinking slightly to the left he lined up with the southerly-most ship which was just getting under way. This was the *Artemis Pitta*, which had arrived that morning from Saloniki loaded with drums of petrol and military stores. Fg Off Lapthorne, close on his leader's left side was forced up and over Lewis's aircraft by the jink and he paralleled the line of Lewis' attack on the *Artemis Pitta*. Following the first two aircraft, Plt Off Clarke-Hall aimed for the second merchantman, the *Thisbe*, moored two hunded yards to the right. Although the 1,700-ton *Thisbe* was only slightly larger than the 1,300-ton *Artemis Pitta*, it appeared to the pilots to be a much bigger vessel because it was unladen and was sitting higher in the water. Of the two torpedoes aimed at *Artemis Pitta*, one hit the ship on the stern causing a massive explosion. The ship immediately caught fire and started to sink, spilling damaged petrol drums into the sea which also caught alight, leaving a huge plume of thick black smoke. Lewis' formation had achieved complete surprise and at first there was no defensive fire, but then Clarke-Hall saw "tracer from the ships... whipping past. Release distance of eight hundred yards quickly came up and I fired my torpedo at the larger ship and counted off the five seconds necessary for the piano

Melos 1 – taken by Sgt J T Collyer, the second pilot in Fg Off C P M Phillips' aircraft. The aircraft is heading southsouthwest with Adhamas harbour in the foreground; in the background the shoulder of Mount Profitis Ilias rises to the far right. The smoke pall from *Artemis Pitta* shows clearly and *Thisbe* is visible just in front of it. (Alan Cadell)

Melos 2 – taken a few seconds later, *Thisbe* is now clearly visible in the foreground. The grey smear just above *Thisbe*'s stern is Donovan's Marauder just clearing the superstructure. The large white splash is probably caused by the impact of an aeroplane – possibly Sgt B H Yarwood's Marauder. (Alan Cadell)

wires holding the torpedo tail horizontal to run off, ensuring straight tracking. This was without doubt the longest five seconds of my life... well aware that between the visible tracers was nasty solid stuff we couldn't see." However, Clarke-Hall's torpedo missed its target, possibly because it passed directly underneath the unladen ship. Hugging the water, the three torpedo bombers fled westwards through the narrow channel to the harbour entrance.

While Lewis' torpedo aircraft made their attack Fg Off E Donovan's[38] three bombers hooked round towards the south of the island. Donovan's radio operator Sgt R Slatcher[39] was standing on a ration box so that he could see out of the astrodome where he'd been "waving and making rude gestures to the wireless operators in the other two aircraft, also in their astrodomes." Then the others fell back into a loose line astern formation and the aircraft pulled up over the southern hills just a few seconds after Lewis' Marauders had made their attack. In front of them the smoke pall from the *Artemis Pitta* gave the impression that a number of ships were on fire and it also obscured the *Thisbe* from view. By now the German defences, which included a newly arrived battery of 88mm guns, as well as many 20mm and 37mm guns, were ready and they unleashed a storm of anti-aircraft fire against the three Marauders. As

Melos 3 – this photograph was taken from a German navy vessel, probably in the immediate aftermath of the raid. Looking southwest, it shows the smoke pall from *Artemis Pitta*, with *Thisbe* to the right and the coaster *Olympos* to the left. Mount Profitis Ilias stands clearly in the background. (Dimitri Galon)

Donovan searched for a target "a terrific barrage started hitting me. I pushed the stick forward and got as low as I could on the water and then I spied another ship [the *Thisbe*] still afloat behind the smoke. I did a half circuit of the harbour, being hit continuously and ran in on this remaining ship. I can well remember having to pull back on the stick rather sharply after I had dropped my bombs because I thought I was going to hit the funnel. Bits of metal were flying in the cockpit and the aircraft was actually twice blown virtually out of my hands as I ran in. We got through the harbour entrance and on looking out I saw that the aircraft was very badly damaged." Donovan's bombs overshot the *Thisbe* and landed in the water beyond as the Marauder made its egress. While Donovan threw his aircraft around desperately trying to avoid the ground fire, Slatcher in the astrodome was "thrown about all over the place. Added to this I got a cut above the right eye from the quite alarming amount of flak hitting us and to make it worse the blood from the wound, pouring down my face, temporarily blinded me." Donovan's wingmen were less lucky: both were mortally hit by anti-aircraft fire. Sgt B H Yarwood's[40] Marauder immediately reared up and exploded, crashing into the harbour almost alongside the *Thisbe*, while Flt Sgt Barton's aircraft attempted to escape westwards with its port engine aflame. Barton struggled to gain enough height to allow his crew to escape from the stricken aircraft, but he was unable to do so and the Marauder crashed into the cliffs at the mouth of the harbour.

Coming unexpectedly from the north a moment or so later, just as dusk fell, the last three Marauders led by Plt Off Phillips managed to surprise the defenders so much that subsequent German reports counted only six attacking aircraft. Phillips dropped on the *Olympos*, the 700-ton coaster moored to the southeast of the larger ships, but he did not register any hits. Following him, Plt Off Egebjerg attacked the German depot at the Klonarides factory to the east of Adhamas and Flt Sgt Bullock bombed the harbour installations at Adhamas. All three Marauders made their attacks unscathed.

The surviving aircraft returned to North Africa individually in the darkness. All recovered to Gambut III, except for Bullock who landed at Gianaclis near Alexandria. Donovan's recovery to Gambut was particularly eventful. His task was made slightly easier by Slatcher who had tuned the homing indicator to radio beacon at Gambut, but he was struggling with very a badly-damaged aircraft. As he crossed the Libyan coast, he was engaged by the British anti-aircraft defences and he had to turn back out to sea. Worried now that one or both engines were on the brink of failure, he ordered the crew to abandon the aircraft and then made for Gambut once more. Despite being refused permission to land, he landed anyway; by this stage one engine had failed and the second engine seized as he taxied in. He then discoverd that his crew had ignored his order to abandon the aircraft, such was their faith in his ability to get them safely home.

Algeria

By the late spring of 1943, the Afrika Korps had been beaten back into a small perimeter in northeast Tunisia. Their lines of communication had been considerably shortened to the narrow stretch between Sicily and Cape Bon and the efforts of 14 Squadron's Marauders were now to be concentrated in the Tyrrhenian Sea. Axis forces relied heavily on coastal shipping and transport aircraft to move supplies and troops between the Italian and French ports and the islands of Corsica, Sardinia and Sicily. The Marauders would monitor movements in all the ports and report the positions of any convoys so that they could be attacked by Beaufighter strike aircraft. Maydwell also encouraged his crews to carry out their patrols aggressively, taking the opportunity to engage enemy transport aircraft when possible. The first few weeks of March were taken up with a move to Blida on the Algerian coast, which would place the aircraft much closer to their new operating area. Sixteen Marauders reached Telergma in central Algeria on 2 March and three aircraft flew on to Blida on 10 March. It was a cloudy day and the route to Blida took the aircraft over the Atlas mountains. Plt Off Clarke-Hall managed to stay beneath the cloudbase and find a way through the mountains, but it seems that Flt Lt Goode flew into clouds and had to climb above them. Having cleared the high ground, Goode headed out to sea and started to let down through the clouds. Quite what happened next remains a matter for speculaton, but what is certain is that the Marauder[41] crashed into Algiers harbour, killing all on board. Whether the cause was some unserviceability or handling problem with the aircraft or whether they were shot down by the anti aircraft defences at Algiers, remains unknown. Apart from the loss of an experienced operational crew, the accident also resulted in the loss of the Squadron's Intelligence Officer Flt Lt H M Siewert[42], "A" Flight NCO Flt Sgt W Tatlow[43] and numerous Squadron records which were being transported to the new base. On arriving at Blida Clarke-Hall found the airfield was still under contruction and when he landed the aircraft ran off the end of the unfinished runway. Twelve aircraft managed to land safely at Blida over the next week, but it was clear that that the airfield would be unsuitable for Marauder operations until the runway was completed. Five aircraft therefore detached to Maison Blanche (Algiers) to continue operations.

There was still a need to convert new crews onto the Marauder, so a training flight was established at Shallufah under the command of Fg Off Lapthorne. This element moved up to Blida a few months later where it joined the training echelon of the resident USAAF Marauder Wing.

In the meantime Algeria offered many attractions to Squadron personnel who had endured four years of living in deserts! They were delighted by the opportunity to hike or ski in the mountains. There were also ENSA concerts and other organised entertainment to enjoy in off-duty hours. The organised sport, which had always featured in Squadron life continued, with football featuring highly.

Over the next five months, operating successively from Maison Blanche and Bone in Algeria and then Protville in Tunisia, 14 Squadron's Marauders flew three or four reconnaissance sorties every day. These sorties were flown by single aircraft and typically lasted six or seven hours, flown at low level heights below one hundred feet. As aircraft ranged across the Tyrrhenian Sea and around the islands of Sicily, Sardinia and Corsica they frequently came across enemy shipping and aircraft. It was a very

WESTERN MEDITERRANEAN AND ADRIATIC SEAS
1943 - 1944

hostile operating environment, with the risks of ultra low-level flying magnified by anti-aircraft fire from ships and coastal batteries and by fighters. Although combat losses were not spectacular in number, there was a steady attrition of aircraft[44]. On 12 April Flt Sgt Einsaar did not return from a reconnaissance sortie of the Tyrrhenian Sea, on 25 April Flt Sgt Bullock was lost, followed by Flt Sgt T G N Russell[45] on 9 May, Sgt H E Rawlins[46] on 3 June, Plt Off R K Francis[47] on 28 June and Flt Sgt J D Hunter[48] on 24 July. In nearly all these cases it was suspected that the lone Marauders had been shot down by fighters escorting naval convoys.

The last moments of Einsaar's patrol, as recounted by his navigator for the sortie Fg Off Buckland[49] was perhaps typical of all of these losses. After checking Palermo harbour the aircraft was heading northwards towards Naples. They passed the island of Ustica when "Oscar [Sgt J L Goldsmith[50] GM] called excitedly that fighters were coming at us out of the clouds. Oscar then took command as he and Harry [Sgt L O Harrison[51] DFM] turned their guns in the direction of the enemy planes – two Focke Wulf 190s. Len [Einsaar] pushed the throttles forward and the plane leapt to life.

Oscar called: 'Turn left, turn left' The plane answered easily. Our gunners conserved their fire as the first attack missed. Again they came, and Oscar continued to direct the pilot. Again the guns from both turret and tail barked furiously. Oscar again called out: 'I think I've got one, skipper' Calmly Len replied: 'Good.'

"We were now travelling at 300mph to 350mph. Tracers could be seen passing close by the wings and several shots splintered the fuselage, but it was too early to ascertain if any serious damage had been done. Then we realised that the two fighters had ceased to press the attack-probably getting too far from their base. One could be seen flying as though in trouble, with smoke pouring from the fuselage. At sight of this we gave jubilant cries, but grew quieter as the port engine began to cough. I thought then how true is the well-known description likening the noise to a spanner knocking loosely against the engine casing. Len took trimming action as the engine seized altogether. It was bad as we were then flying only 50 feet above sea level. Len throttled forward the good engine, feathered the port propeller and, with the speed holding, eased the plane up to 500 feet. When we had gained height, Len pulled the jettison cord to release the bomb and extra petrol which would give us a chance of reaching land safely on one engine. Unfortunately, the bomb doors failed to open more than half way. Against orders, I went into the bomb bay, but on opening the door was half blinded and scorched by boiling hydraulic fluid escaping after a hit to the hydraulic system. I covered my face and tried to fight my way in but found it impossible to release the bombs as the bomb release circuit is not properly completed until the doors are fully open. Standing on the six inch ledge with the opening beneath me I tried to knock the bombs off the hook, but it was no use.

"One of the lads hurried me back to the seat, and it became certain that we would have to ditch. We could not reach the height necessary to bale out, and as a Marauder ditching had never been successfully carried out before, our hearts were very low. Speaking to Len over the intercom. I told Len of a nearby island which may or may not be occupied by the Axis. We set course for that island, minute by minute losing what little height we had gained. Len then spoke to the crew in his cool voice: 'Pilot to crew. Pilot to crew. We are making for a small island which may be in enemy hands. See that all escape hatches are open, and jettison the covers. Good luck, everybody.'

"Then Len and the second pilot [Sgt R A Kirkin] chopped through their top cover with an axe. I opened and got rid of my Astro Dome, before Tom [Sgt T P Clowry[52]] and I threw over the heavy Syko machine which we knew would go straight to the bottom, then destroyed the code books. We looked at each other and shook hands, hardly daring to hope that we may come out of the crash alive. 'Good luck,' Our grip tightened on each other's hands, and we added 'Good-bye.' As we got closer and closer to the water I braced myself against the neck and waited. I know I mumbled a prayer. I looked at Len, who, with sweat pouring from his face was trying desperately to hold the plane off as long as possible. He alone of the crew knew what to expect as he had been the sole survivor of another crash.

"Smack! The tail hit the water. Before I was hit with terrific force I heard something smash with a loud report as the fuselage hit the water. For a few seconds only I lost consciousness, but regained it immediately the machine began to sink. I made frantic efforts to rise but something was holding me firmly and dragging me down with the plane. When my mind cleared I realised that it was my safety belt. Quickly undoing it, I floated up and wormed myself through the escape hatch to the top. After breaking the surface I hastily gulped air and swam quickly underwater until I was clear of the burning wreckage and oil which covered a large area about the spot where the plane crashed. In the joy that surged over me when I realised that I had survived the crash I completely forgot the rest of the crew for a short time, anyway. Even now I can clearly recall that glorious feeling which transcended every other factor. I must have been gulping and choking for air, my clothing clinging and soggy, but I didn't notice that."

Unfortunately there were also a number of tragic flying accidents. On 10 May a Marauder took off from Shallufah with Plt Off E W McClelland[53] at the controls[54] for a fighter affiliation exercise. As he circled a few miles west of Abu Seir, awaiting the start of the exercise, the aircraft suddenly dived into the ground, killing all aboard. Subsequent investigation showed that metal fatigue had caused a section of the vertical fin to break off, taking with it the rudder and thereby causing complete loss of control. It is probable that this phenomenon had also been the cause of Bower's accident six months earlier and possibly Goode's crash in March. As a result of this accident, the tailfins of all Marauders were modified and strengthened. More lives were lost on 10 July when another aircraft[55] suffered a starboard engine failure while cruising at low level on a training flight off the Tunisian coast. Unable to climb above fifty feet, the aircraft hit sand dunes as it coasted in near Bou Ficha and caught fire. Flt Sgt J T Collyer[56], a pilot who was flying as a passenger in the nose of the aircraft, survived with only slight injuries when he was thrown through the perspex nose by the impact, but the rest of the crew were either killed on impact or died a few days later from their injuries.

However, the Marauders were also able to inflict much damage on enemy aircraft, including shooting down a number of giant six-engined Me323 transports. The first of these was brought down[57] on 22 May by Sqn Ldr H Law-Wright[58]. At 1055 hrs he found a formation of three Me323s about fifty miles due east of Isola Maddalena (the northeastern tip of Sardinia) and closed for the attack. While Law-Wright positioned the Marauder just ahead and to the side of the enemy aircraft, the turret gunner, Sgt W M Cowie[59], and tail gunner Sgt F E Lovelace[60] raked it with gunfire. "We set some of the starboard engines on fire," reported Law-Wright, "and and within fifteen seconds from the start of the action we saw it crash into the sea." With the number three aircraft despatched, Law-Wright attempted to engage the leader, but this time Cowie's and Lovelace's guns jammed before they could inflict any damage.

In May 1943 a Flight of six American P51 Mustang fighters were attached to the Squadron for an operational trial. These aircraft were flown by RAF pilots from 32 Squadron led by Flt Lt D Blair[61] to determine the suitability of the Mustang for coastal rconnaissance. Flt Lt Blair and Flt Sgt C P Ashworth[62] carried put the first operational Mustang sortie on 29 May and their first aerial success came the next day when Fg

Off H A Crawford[63] and Flt Sgt D Campbell[64] shot down a Ju52 off the eastern coast of Sardinia. Other air-to-air successes included a Fiat RS14 floatplane which was downed the next day by Fg Off J K K Gildner and another RS14 shot down in the Bay of Oristano by Flt Lt Blair on 7 June. The Mustangs flew reconnaisance sorties around the Sardinian coast throughout late May and early June, generally operating in pairs. However, overall the experiment was not a success: the Mustang pilots resented their unglamourous role and the Marauder crews resented the flamboyant fighter pilots. The unhappy marriage was dissolved in mid-June and the Mustangs were returned to the USAAF.

On 10 June 1943 Allied troops landed in Sicily and the interdiction of enemy movements in the Tyrrhenian Sea took on greater importance. On that day 14 Squadron Marauders flew four patrols. In the morning Flt Sgt Bates's Marauder[65] shot down a SM82 and in the afternoon Fg Off Johnson was attacked[66] by eight Bf109s. During this engagement the tailgunner Flt Sgt R D Gilbey shot down two of the enemy fighters into the sea.

The Marauder crews continued with their successes against enemy aircaft which they encountered on their patrols. Wg Cdr Maydwell, who had been an accomplished big game hunter in his pre-war army days, viewed his sorties as a shooting safari. During July his crew was particularly successful, bagging down a three-engined SM82 off Sardinia on 15 July and a four-engined Ju90 at Bastia eight days later. On 30 July they boarded Marauder FK142 for a patrol of the Italian coast. "Just before we took off," recalled Maydwell, "Fg Off J F Kennedy[67], our navigator casually remarked that he had a feeling that today was the day we would get a 'big one.' Remarkably he was proved to be absolutely correct." To the north of Corsica just after midday, they sighted a large formation of fourteen aircraft, and as they neared Cape Corse they came across a straggler. It was a Me323 which Kennedy thought "looked like a block of flats" coming towards them. Maydwell positioned his aircraft ahead and to the left of the lumbering giant so that his guners, Sgt G G Graham[68] in the tail and Flt Sgt C Locker in the turret, could engage it. After a short and almost one-sided exchange of fire, the gunners had shot out three of the Messerschmidt's six engines. The pilot decided that the battle was lost and altered course towards the Corsican coast where he crash-landed in a large cloud of dust[69]. However, aggression did not always pay off, as Fg Off Kennedy found when he flew with Fg Off E L Archer on 26 Aug[70]. Archer attempted to engage a Ju52, but got too close and the Marauder was raked by small arms fire from troops inside the Junkers. The Marauder crashed into the sea with the loss of the tail gunner Sgt A Phethean; the rest of the crew were rescued by the Italian Navy and taken prisoner.

Although shooting down enemy aircraft was a great filip to morale, it was not the Squadron's main role, which remained that of coastal reconnaissance. However, the routine was occasionally broken by special tasking. One such mission was flown on 19 July, when two Mauaders left Protville in the early morning darkness bound for Rome. They were to carry out a weather reconnaissance of the city prior to a major raid on it by a force of over five hundred Allied bombers. Fg Off Donovan took off[71]

A giant Me323 transport aircraft flown by Oberfeldwebel Walter Honig comes under fire from Wg Cdr Maydwell's gunners off Cap Corse on 30 July 1943. (Howard Gibbins)

just after 0300 hrs, followed[72] by Wg Cdr Maydwell half an hour later. Both aircraft headed towards the Italian coast at low level: Donovan's approached Rome from a northerly direction, while Maydwell coasted in near Anzio to the south of the city. Despite some low stratus cloud on the coast, which Donovan was able to fly beneath, the weather conditions over Rome itself were ideal and both aircraft skimmed across the roftops just after sunrise. As he left Rome, Maydwell headed across Lake Bracciano, over-flying a line of Cant floatplanes which his gunners strafed. Later reconnaissance reports showed that three of these aircraft had been destroyed. Donovan's return route took him directly over a shipping convoy which engaged him with accurate anti-aircraft fire, fortunately without hitting the Marauder. He then flew under the main bomber force as it headed towards Rome, causing two of the P-38 escort fighters to peel off to investigate the wake left behind the Marauder as it sped homeward at very low level over the sea.

Italy Capitulates

Wg Cdr Maydwell left 14 Squadron on promotion on 25 August and handed over command to Wg Cdr Law-Wright. The Squadron had been busy throughout the month with reconnaissance patrols, typically flying four or five operational sorties a day. The Marauders were also used to search for downed aircrew and by the end of August the unit had been responsible for locating thirty-two USAAF B17 aircrew who had ditched.

On 8 September Italy capitulated. The following day Allied troops landed at Salerno and the Italian Fleet left Spezia to surrender in Malta. The Fleet comprising

Escorting the Italian Fleet to Malta after Italy's capitulation 9 September 1944. A 14 Squadron Marauder flies past the battleship *Vittorio Venito*. (Gil Graham)

three Littorio-class battleships, accompanied by six cruisers and thirteen destroyers was sighted by Flt Lt O A Phillips to the north of Corsica at 1015 hrs[73] on 9 September. Phillips escorted the Fleet until he was relieved[74] by Flt Sgt N D Freeman[75]; Freeman was relieved in turn by Wg Cdr Law-Wright early in the afternoon. During Law-Wright's ten-and-a-half hour sortie[76], which set an endurance record for a Marauder flight, the crew witnessed the sinking of the battleship *Roma*. As the fleet passed the island of Asinara at the entrance to the Straits of Bonifacio, an unseen German bomber launched a radio-guided bomb. "The first sign of attack we saw was when the ships opened fire," reported Law-Wright. "For a moment we thought they were firing at us and we took violent evasive action. Then we saw the flak burst far above us, obviously aimed at a high flying attack. We saw an enormous explosion on one of the battleships. Creamy white smoke went up about 3,000 or 4,000 feet. The smoke on the battleship subsided and it looked as if it were getting under way again. Throughout the attack the ships had taken excellent evasive action and their ant-aircraft fire was accurate. We flew over the ships and took a look at the damaged one. We arrived just as it was sinking. Under a big column of smoke we saw the stern under water and the bow sticking up. The ship appeared to break in two and folded up with the control tower and keel forming a 'V' as the ship slowly disappeared. We watched rescue operations for five minutes and then turned away towards the rest of the fleet which was regaining formation. At this point we encountered a Junkers 88 reconnaissance aircraft. We got in a good burst and our fire persuaded him to head for home"

Almost a year of hard operations had taken its toll of Marauders and reinforcements were needed. There was a constant stream of replacement aircrew going through the Squadron's Training Flight at Blida, but new aircraft proved more difficult to find. The problem was solved at a local level within the Mediterranean Allied Command with the transfer of a number of "surplus" USAAF B26-B aircraft. This version of the Marauder differed in some details to the B-26A which was already operated by the Squadron, but crews quickly adapted to the differences. Although the USAAF authorities formally transferred the aircraft to the RAF, these Marauders were never given RAF serial numbers, retaining instead their American identities.

With former Italian bases now available for use, 14 Squadron had the opportunity to move further forward to be closer to its operatuonal area. Sqn Ldr Grimsey led a detachment of "A" Flight to Grottaglie, near Taranto, on 1 October. From here Marauders could patrol the Adriatic Sea and range once more into Greek coastal waters and the Ionian Sea. Meanwhile the deficiencies of Protville as an operating base during the winter months were becoming clear: heavy rain at the beginning of the month closed the airfield for a few days and plans were made to move a few miles along the coast to Sidi Amor. The break from operations at least gave the personnel there opportunity to see Gracie Fields in concert in Tunis and to keep occupied with a busy calendar of sports fixtures.

Although Protville was unuseable, operations continued from Grottaglie. Sorties from southern Italy were very much part of co-ordinated operations by Allied forces. On 14 October Flt Sgt Bates reported three separate sightings of camouflaged merchant vessels, including a tanker, in the northern Adriatic. As a result of Bates' reports a naval destroyer sunk one of the vessels and the tanker was captured and towed into port, earning Bates the congratulations of Flag Officer Taranto. Bates also played a vital role in a search and rescue operation a few days later. In the evening of 19 October Fg Off A M Cameron's[77] Marauder[78] failed to return from a reconnaissance mission in the Adriatic Sea and Bates took off[79] early the following morning to search for survivors. At 0747 hrs he found an airman clinging to a petrol tank in the sea just north of Palagruzo island and dropped three type "K" dinghies. After watching the survivor clamber aboard one of them Bates then dropped three tins of water. A Hudson arrived on the scene three hours later and this aircraft was itself relieved at 1300 hrs by a Marauder[80] flown by Flt Sgt F M Spedding[81], who witnessed the arrival of a Walrus rescue aircraft escorted by a Flight of Spitfires half an hour later. The survivor was the second pilot, Sgt H Richie[82] who was able to tell what had happened. Flying at fifty feet over the sea, the aircraft had suffered a failure of the ailerons and started to turn uncontrollably until a wingtip struck the sea and the aircraft crashed. Richie was the only survivor.

On 2 November Sqn Ldr Grimsey led a special mission to the German radar installation on the cliffs to the north of at Durrës on the Albanian coast. This radar site, which was used to direct German fighters from bases in Albania, was a thorn in the side of allied aircraft operating in the Adriatic. Grimsey led[83] twenty-four Spitfires to Durrës, where the fighters strafed the radar buildings, leaving them in flames. Even so, Durrës remained a dangerous place, as Fg Off W R Gellatly[84] discovered two days later when his Marauder[85] was intercepted there by two Bf109s. The same aircraft was in action the following day flown by WO Collyer, who sighted a 5,000 ton merchant vessel in the Gulf of Trieste. Following Collyer's report, six Beaufighters were dispatched to attack the vessel using torpedoes and cannon.

Poor weather in the second week of November brought operations Grottaglie to a halt, although some sorties were flown from nearby Brindisi. Sidi Amor remained open, but the Squadron's last operation from that base was flown on 16 November. The unit had been warned to prepare to move to Corsica and after moving first to Blida, most of the Squadron's vehicles and equipment were loaded into the *Argentina*, a vessel that had been captured, thanks to sighting reports by a 14 Squadron Marauder, earlier in 1943. The remainder was loaded into the *Belgian Seaman*. Although the *Argentina* and *Belgian Seaman* arrived in Corsica at the beginning of December, it would not be until 14 January that the first operational sortie would be flown from the new airfield at Ghisonaccia. In the meantime, operations continued from Blida. Construction work at Ghisonaccia continued through December and the first half of January despite the winter weather. The airfield was to be shared with a Wing of USAAF B25 light bombers and the crews were accommodated in tents among the scrub surrounding the airfield. The one minor luxury allowed to Squadron personnel was the establishment of Messes in three abandoned buildings in the nearby village: reflecting the humour of the day the Sergeant's Mess was called the "Getsum Inn" and the airmen's and officers respectively "Gotsum Inn" and "New Inn"

Operations continued from Grottaglie, including anti-submarine patrols in the Gulf of Taranto during the second week of December. A week later it was Christmas. Unlike previous wartime Christmasses, in 1943 the Squadron was widely scattered, with personnel in Tunisia, Corsica and Southern Italy. With no opportunity to celebrate the ocasion together, each detachment held its own celebrations; unfortunately heavy rain curtailed the football and donkey polo that had been organised in Corsica! Wg Cdr Law-Wright, accompanied by the Squadron Engineering Officer Flt Lt I D H Gibbins[86], spent Christmas with the Grottaglie Flight.

Aircraft Losses

Unfortunately a Marauder[87] was lost just before Christmas. Flt Sgt F R Tuxill[88] and his newly-converted crew took off for a familisrisation sortie in the operational area, but crashed into the sea off the coast of Algeria. Another aircraft[89] went missing shortly after Christmas: in the morning of 28 December Fg Off R W Gilkey[90] and the crew of radioed with the report of sighting of a merchant vessel near Levanto. The aircraft was seen a little later by Fg Off A N Hornby[91] AFM, making his first operational patrol[92] with the Squadron, as the Marauders passed each other heading their seperate ways. Gilkey's aircraft was also seen on the radar at Ajaccio about twenty-five miles to the west but the radar trace disappeared and Gilkey's crew did not return from their mission. It is possible that the Marauder suffered an engine failure as it returned to Corsica. Aircraft losses continued through January and February. Plt Off M C Reid's[93] Marauder[94] failed to return from an operational mission on 1 February. Two days later Plt Off S D Lantinga[95] and his second pilot Plt Off C A Duncan[96] were commended for their exceptional airmanship when their Marauder[97] lost a mainwheel on take-off. The loose wheel hit the aircraft severely damaging the pitot probe, thus depriving the pilots of critical airspeed indications. The navigator Plt Off A S Tait[98] recalled that the pilots "struggled to keep the aircraft in the air with one aileron gone and no airspeed indication. They kept the wing from dipping and went out to sea almost to Bonifacio Straits. Made a very wide flat turn with about five degree boost on one engine and forty-five on the other. They kept fighting all the way in the air, got back to the airfield ... Sabe [Lantinga] dived over the top of three P39s who were about to take off and crash landed, making a beauty of of a landing."

Lantinga wrote off another Marauder on 17 February when he crashed on landing at Bone[99], happily without any casualties. In the week between Lantinga's crashes, there was another Marauder flying accident when Fg Off G A A Croskell[100] was seen to fly into the sea[101] while flying from Grottaglie to Blida. The entire crew perished, including Flt Sgt T C Climpson[102], who had completed his tour of operations and was travelling as a passenger on the first leg of his journey back to England.

Another flying accident which occurred in February shook the entire Squadron. Earlier in the month, Fg Off J E F Wright[103] DFC of the RAF's 2 Film Production Unit had visited Ghisonaccia where he had taken footage for a feature film on the work of the RAF in the Mediterranean theatre. The second part of his filming was to take place at Grottaglie and was to include some air-to-air filming. On the morning of 23 February, two aircraft prepared to take off from Grottaglie: one[104] was scheduled for an operational patrol at 0930 hrs and the "A" Flight Commander, Sqn Ldr H Elsey[105], a popular Canadian, was due to carry out an airtest in the second[106]. Fg Off Wright was on board Elsey's aircraft with his camera. The plan was for Elsey to take off just ahead of the other aircraft and for the two Marauders to fly in formation as the latter headed out for its patrol, while Wright shot the air-to-air sequence. Elsey lifted off from Grottaglie at 0920 hrs and started a wide circuit of the airfield to get into position to film the other Marauder's departure. However, as Elsey turned downwind, the port engine was seen to be cutting. Sgt L A Bulbeck, an airframe fitter, was sitting at the radio operator's position for the airtest. He could see "white smoke pour[ing] from the port engine and power from that side disappeared. I could see that Sqn Ldr Elsey was fighting to lift the port wing but there didn't appear to be enough power to lift it." What Elsey could not have known at this stage was that the port engine's main bearing had failed and the engine had completely seized. Elsey turned back towards the airfield, apparently intending to land immediately, for he lowered the undercarriage. At this the Marauder started to descend rapidly and although the pilot subsequently raised the undercarriage he was unable to regain control of the aircraft which crashed in a ball of flame into a olive grove close to the aerodrome. Bulbeck "felt the first impact of the aircraft hitting the trees. The transmitter, anchored beside me, broke loose and hit me on the head as it went out through the roof and I shot forward and made violent contact the receiver in front of me. By this time I lost all interst in the proceedings; I was vaguely aware of seeing leaves, sky and earth and when I came to I was in between two lanes of burning fuel, still strapped to my seat, but a fair way from the wreckage. A later check showed that all four of the seat tubes above the swivel had broken and the seat and I had finished up thirty feet away." The rest of the Squadron personnel came rushing to rescue survivors. The first on the scene was LAC E G W Hall who rushed into the flaming wreckage and pulled out two bodies[107]. Close on Hall's heels was Sgt H Metcalfe[108], who "seeing a pair of legs protruding from the wreckage... pulled and out came Sqn Ldr Elsey, the top of whose skull had ben sliced off." Elsey and his second pilot Fg Off H D Merkley[109] had been killed on the impact, but Fg Off Wright, Fg Off A C Bowes[110], the navigator, and Fg Off H C Campbell[111], a pilot who was flying as a passenger in the aircraft, survived with severe burns. Sadly, Campbell died that evening.

Spanish Iron Ore

From the beginning of 1944, 14 Squadron was operating as two Flights: "A" Flight at Grottaglie covered the eastern operational area along the Adriatic coast of Italy, Yugoslavia and Albania and the Greek Ionian coast. "B" Flight at Ghisonaccia covered the western area from Barcelona along the Spanish, French and Italian Mediterranean coast to Spezia. The Headquarters, Training and Maintenance Flights remained in North Africa divided between Blida and Bizerta, making command and control of the Squadron challenging. Wg Cdr Law-Wright was kept busy travelling between the various detachments of his scattered unit. This situation was improved at the end of March when the Headquarters and Maintenance Flights moved to Alghero in Sardinia; the Training Flight, commanded by Flt Lt Lapthorne, moved to Telergma, Algeria, where it lodged with the American Bombardment Centre.

After the Allied landings at Anzio in late January, most of the Tyrrhenian Sea was under Allied control, but dspite being pushed back, the German defences were no less ferocious. In the early hours of 21 February Fg Off Hornby's crew appoached Spezia in FK120. From his position in the astrodome, the wireless operator Sgt J W A Lowder[112] could see "five E-boats which opened fire on us with cannon and machine gun.. Green tracer whipped past us as we took violent evasive action. Then the shore batteries opened up at us, all around the sky and the sea the bursts appeared and the blast [shook] us about quite a lot." They received a similar welcome at almost evey port as they covered the coastline all the way to Cape Agde. It was not unusual for the coastal batteries to open fire on the Marauders, the huge shells causing great plumes in the water.

With much of Italy in Allied hands, the Corsica-based Marauders began to concentrate on areas further afield, such as the Spanish coast. Much of the work of "B" Flight through April and March involved tracking ships used for the transport of iron ore from neutral Spain to Germany via France. On 15 March Fg Off Lantinga's crew photographed a vessel sheltering in the secluded harbour of San Feliu de Guixols, about fifty miles northeast of Barcelona. This ship was identified as the *Saumur*, one of a number of German-controlled vessels which were plying a steady trade between Barcelona and Port Vendres. Over the next two months, "B" Flight's Marauders kept a close watch on the Spanish coastal waters north Barcelona, typically flying two patrols in that area each day. On the morning of 29 March Fg Off W C MacDonald[113] set off for a patrol of the Spanish and French coast, but his aircraft never returned. It seems likely that he came across the coaster *Romain* just off Mataro, about fifteen miles northeast of Barcelona and crashed into the sea while he circled the ship, possibly as the result of anti-aircraft fire. A week later Fg Off Hornby's crew found a ship dislaying Red Cross markings, off Toreilles; as the crew watched, a flight of nine Beaufighters approached and attacked the ship. The crew was later told that the ship had actually been carrying iron ore and had been sunk by the Beaufighters with the loss of one of the aircraft; however they were also told to remove all reference to the Beaufighters from their log books.

Then on 13 April the crews at Ghisonaccia were formally briefed by Fg Off P L Bullock on "suspected Spanish German controlled ships" and each crew was given a set of photographs. The three ships of particular interest were the *Saumur*, the *Romain* and the *Astrée*. Although numerous neutral vessels were sighted in the following week, it was not until the morning of 25 April that Flt Lt S J R Yelloly[114] located[115] the *Astrée* which had been beached just off Calella, near Barcelona, after having been damaged by Beaufighters. This sighting was confirmed by Fg Off Hornby that afternoon; both Yelloly and Hornby were subjected to heavy anti-aircraft fire as they approached *Astrée*, which was apparently under repair. The vessel was kept under observation over the next few days, during which time WO W J Adey[116] also spotted[117] the *Romain*, sailing off Mataro. On 28 April WO K A L Mailer[118] reported that *Astrée* was still aground but getting up steam and she managed to free herself sometime later that evening. However, her escape was short-lived for she was sunk by the submarine HMS *Untiring* off Port Vendres just three days later. The *Romain* was more fortunate and evaded destruction until September, when she was scuttled in Port Vendres.

The *Saumur* was located once again by Fg Off Lantinga on 11 May, fifteen miles southwest of Cap Agde. This time she was heavily escorted by three Bf109Gs which immediately attacked the Marauder[119]. According to the navigator, Fg Off Tait, "Sabe [Lantinga,] immediately turned our aircraft towards home, used full revs and boost on the aircraft but could only get a top speed of 260 mph straight and level. These three [Bf109s] certainly were persistent as they made in the vicinity of thirty attacks and seemed to let go with everything they had. Their first attack was by two of them simultaneously from directly behind closing in to about two hundred yards when they fired on us. As they committed themselves to the attack, our rear gunner, Pete[120], gave them both a burst from his gun which forced them back a bit. Alex[121], the Wireless Operator, did a marvellous job as fighter controller giving Sabe very good directions, who in turn threw the aircraft superbly about in very violent evasive action, managing to keep their hits on our aircraft down to a minimum. I sent messages out to the effect that we were being attacked by enemy aircraft.

"During one of their attacks, one burst put a hole in the main gas tank and until the hole self-sealed due to its construction, we lost a good stream of gas. One hit on the aircraft appeared to Sabe that he has lost one engine, but it was only a hit on his rudder control. Immediately, he compensated this by three degrees of rudder trim. The three Messerschmidts lost no time in bringing home their attacks because as the two aircraft in the rear broke off from their attacks, the other one came in from either

Marauder FK145 under repair at Ghisonaccia after being damaged during a sustained attacked off the French coast by Bf109s on 11 May 1944. (Colin Campbell)

side. At one time this third aircraft third aircraft came over top of us, made an attack from the front, then dove down underneath us. The Wireless Operator thought at first that this aircraft had gone in the water as we ourselves were very low.

"Pete, our tail gunner, had about the toughest time of all, as at one stage of the dogfight he had a stoppage of his gun, so he had to let the aircraft come in very freely for attacks. He was always very much pleased to see the bursting shells whistle by either side after Alex gave Sabe instructions to skid either left or right. In the first place these bursts were coming directly for him. When Pete repaired his stoppage, he surprised one of the aircraft when he came in close and gave it a very good burst. This aircraft appeared to be damaged and as the aircraft turned its belly up to turn towards the coast our turret gunner, Ron Eaton[122], secured hits on the aircraft. As this hit aircraft turned towards home black smoke was streaming from it profusely and losing height gradually the boys saw this until it was out of sight. The other two made one more attack each before turning towards home, either because their ammunition was expended, or to go in aid of their comrade who was m trouble.

"The three aircraft were firing 20 or 30mm cannons and machine guns. The attack lasted for about fifteen minutes. It was quite a day for Ron Eaton, as it was his twentieth birthday. At times he didn't know which of the three aircraft to shoot at since they were all so close. The boys could see the pilots in each aircraft and the big German crosses on the kites. Pete, to my mind, was a hero as he has a damaged aircraft or a probable to his credit. It is too bad we couldn't have found out but we were in too much danger, other two damaged.

"After the attack was over and we settled down to normal cruising speed once more & climbed a bit higher than usual, reports from different crew members were passed on to the pilot. One generator was shot away so we flew back on one generator. The big thing that worried the pilot on the way back was that a good sized hole was made in the nacelle, where the port wheel was, so he feared a burst tyre which would be bad for landing. A damaged flap also gave Sabe much concern.

"Soon after we flew over our aerodrome, Sabe selected the undercarriage down so as to inspect the port tyre for holes – it looked okay to all hands. As he selected undercarriage down, there had been a hole in the hydraulic pipeline so we lost the hydraulic fluid through this break and the hydraulic pressure dropped down. There was not enough pressure to put down the nose wheel. We opened the front door and tried to force the front wheel down but to no avail. So Roy[123], our second pilot, used the hydraulic emergency pump which pumped the nose wheel down & locked it into position. Since there was no more hydraulic pressure left, the pilot knew there would be no flaps or brakes to help out in landing, so he instructed us all to prepare for a crash landing. He brought the aircraft in very low, just skimming over the tops of the trees and he did as he aimed to do – landed the aircraft right on the end of the runway as he came in at a speed of 170 mph instead of the usual 130. As the aircraft touched down lightly, the port tyre just flattened down so we did a gradual swing to the left, going off the runway over some rough ground. Sabe managed to save the nose wheel leg at one time when going over this rough ground. There was a big bump ahead, so he lifted up the nose wheel to clear the bump, then let it down again. It was really a swell landing and grand airmanship on Sabe's part – none of us were hurt."

Perhaps this account gives some clue as to the fate of three more Marauders[124] which were lost in the period: Fg Off H E V Budge[125] failed to return from a reconnaissance sortie from Ghisonaccia after being attacked by fighters near Toulon on 19 April, Fg Off A T Smith[126] went missing on 7 May also from Ghisonaccia and Flt Sgt J Ross[127] took off from Alghero two days later for a patrol of the Adriatic Sea. The *Saumur* itself survived only another ten days before it was torpedoed off Port Vendres by the submarine HMS *Upstart*.

Summer 1944

"B" flight moved to join the Squadron Headquarters at Alghero in the last week of May, thus simplifying Wg Cdr Law-Wright's command chain. However Law-Wright himself did not have much opportunity to enjoy the fruits of this improvement, as he handed command of the Squadron to Wg Cdr E Donovan DFC on 8 June. Donovan, who had served with the Squadron the previous year and had participated in the Melos raid was a popoular choice of commander.

Reconnaisance missions continued throughout the summer and included the systematic photographing of the French coast to provide information for the planning of the invasion of Southern France, which everyone knew must come soon. Cape Agde remained a particular "hotspot" for these sorties. On 18 June Fg Off M C Hogg[128] had a narrow escape there when his Marauder[129] was intercepted by two Bf109s which subjected the Marauder to a sustained attack which lasted for eight minutes. The second pilot, Fg Off W C Japp[130], recalled that "Merv Hogg, like all Canadians was always well supplied with chewing-gum and kept a generous supply available on the throttle pedestal. I was not, and never became, a chewing gum addict, but it seemed at the beginning of this episode that it would be beneficial for my somewhat dry mouth and I helped myself to some. It was only after the action that I

Fg Off M C Hogg and W C Japp prepare for a reconnaissance mission over the Mediterranean from Grottaglie in the summer of 1944. (Ian Hogg)

felt that this gum was not very chewable and on removing all three sticks from my mouth I could see that the somewhat metallic wrapping had never been removed!"

After the engagement "an intercom check on the two gunners in the rear brought an okay from the mid-upper but the tail-gunner said he had a head wound. I went back along the catwalk, dodged round the mid-upper's feet, and crawled to the tail. George Senior's[131] face was covered in blood which appeared to be coming from his head. I got a field dressing and started wiping it away but could find no wound. I then noticed a great deal of blood on one of George's hands. It took a few moments to put two and two together, but what had happened was that during the action his gun had jammed and in his desperation to clear it he had, unnoticed, cut his hand on the breech mechanism. Perspiring profusely he had then wiped the sweat from his eyes with the back of the bloody hand. The anti-climax was that finding there was no battle wound we both burst into near uncontrolled laughter, probably emotional relief at surviving a very sticky situation. Eventually I started back to the front of the aircraft looking for fuselage damage as I went. As I was passing Smithy's[132] feet in the mid-upper again I happened to notice a neat hole through the sole of one of his boots. Engine noise made normal communication impossible so to attract his attention I thumped his leg and motioned for him to come down. When he did, I could see another neat hole in the top of the same boot. He seemed puzzled so, sitting him down in the fuselage, I removed both boot and sock. I was confronted with what looked like a miniature RAF roundel on both top and bottom of his foot; a circular red wound in the centre surrounded by a blue bruise. It was apparent that during one of our sharp evasive turns a bullet had gone clean through boot and foot but Smithy hadn't felt a thing! Only after my discovery did he start to feel any pain. Although the hydraulic system had been damaged and there were 76 holes in the aircraft, nothing vital had been hit. Either the enemy pilots were poor shots or our evasive action was exceptionally effective."

Two less fortunate crews were those of Lt M J W Brummer[133] who crashed just off Asinara Island[134] while recovering to Alghero on 26 June and Flt Lt N Cornish[135] whose Marauder[136] went missing during a patrol of the Gulf of Venice on 1 July. Lt Overed, who followed exactly the same course as Cornish seven hours later, could find no trace of Cornish's aircraft. The beginning of July also marked a change in tactics by Allied aircraft in the northern Adriatic Sea. Until then, the reconnaissance Marauders and strike Beaufighters had operated separately, with the Marauders reporting any sightings of potential targets and the Beaufighters then being launched to attack if the target was suitable. Under the new arrangement, the Marauder would make its patrol accompanied by an escort of rocket-armed Beaufighters. However, there was a slight complication, for while the Marauder had an advantage of speed over most German aircraft, the Beaufighter's performance was significantly reduced by the drag caused by the underwing rocket racks, making it more vulnerable to German fighters. The idea was for the Marauder to search along the coast for targets, while the Beaufighters remained at a safe distance out to sea; once the Marauder located a suitable target, the Beaufighters would dash in and attack it and then disappear once more to a safe distance from the coast. On 2 July Flt Lt C Glanville[137] set off[138] for a patrol of the Gulf of Venice to try out this new technique. After checking Pula harbour, Glanville continued along the coast and here he found a heavily laden schooner in the Gulf of Venice. The Beaufighters were called in and sunk the vessel; a little later Glanville found a small coaster, and once again the Beaufighters attacked with cannon fire, severely damaging it. The next day Fg Off Boyes[139] led his Beaufighters to dispatch a tug just off Ravenna and on 5 July Fg Off J B MacDonald[140] found a forty-foot vessel thirty miles southwest of Pula which the Beaufighters strafed.

When aircrews were not flying and groundcrews were not busy servicing the aircraft there was plenty of opportunity for sports. Various swiming galas were held in the sea off the beach at Alghero and football and cricket also featured. In July 14 Squadron's football team beat 458 Squadron three-nil at Alghero and the creicket team, under the captainship of Sqn Ldr Yelloly beat 328 Wing by eight wickets.

Submarines and the *Rex*

Anti-submarine patrols were a frequent and unpopular task, which tended to be allocated to "A" Flight. The unpopularity stemmed from the need to fly at the relatively high altitude of 4,000 feet in order to see a large enough area of sea. This made the aircraft vulnerable to attack by fighters, especially if the patrol area was close to the Albanian coast. For such anti-submarine work, the Marauders were armed with four 250-pound depth charges, each which had to be released individually (rather than being dropped as a "stick") by the pilot.

At the beginning of August "A" Flight was orderd to mount daily anti-submarine patrols to try to catch the U596 which had left Pula harbour on 29 July. On the morning of 5 August Plt Off L N Johnson[141] was on patrol[142] near the Albanian coast just north of Corfu when he spotted two schooners in the harbour at Erikoussa island. Diverting from his patrol he strafed the vessels before resuming his patrol northwards. An hour later, about thirty miles north of Erikoussa he saw a submarine on the surface and raced towards it, descending to his attack height of fifty feet. However, the submarine must have seen him first, for it dived under the surface and was fully submerged by the time Johnston was in position to make an attack. Instead he marked the position with a smoke float and then remained overhead awaiting the arrival of five destroyers which had been dispatched from Taranto on his initial report.

The following day, spurred on by Johnson's sighting, Fg Off J P Robertson[143] took up station[144] just to the west of Corfu. At 0910 hrs something unusual caught his eye: "it was a warm sunny day with a smooth sea surface and a very light haze. Both my Second Pilot, Ivor Duffell[145] and I sighted what appeared to be a smoke flare on the surface, and after telling our gunners to keep it in sight, we proceeded to lose height. Much to our amazement the smoke float appeared to be moving and was producing a small wake. We then realised that it was a periscope and we manoeuvred to attack, but at sea level the haze made it difficult to keep the periscope in sight. The optimum angle of attack on a submarine is diagonally across the track, forward of the conning tower. As we were running in behind the object at 180 knots at attack height, I realized we were paralleling its track, so instinctively I ruddered the aircraft's nose across to cut a diagonal path. As I pressed the release button I realised the aircraft was still skidding, throwing the Depth Charges off target. At the time of attack the tail gunner had been instructed to throw out an aluminium marker. I realized I had only dropped three of the four Depth Charges so circling around with no target now in evidence I chucked the remaining Depth Charge in on a presumed track heading from the marker. Unfortunately there was no evidence that we had made a kill or caused any serious damage."

Once again the Marauder remained on station until naval destroyers arrived, there was no evidence of damage to the submarine. In fact it seems more likely that it was not a periscope, but the newly-fitted schnorkel device that Robertson had seen. The anti-submarine patrols continued for another three days, but the only other sighting was by Fg Off J R Jordan[146] of an oil patch on the water to the southeast of Corfu on 8 August.

One week later Allied forces landed in the South of France, signalling the end of coastal operations in the western Mediterranean. The Adriatic, too, was quietening down, and at the beginning of September Wg Cdr Donovan was told to make preparations for the Squadron to move to Tarquinia, just northwest of Rome, where it would start training in formation flying in preparation for joining the Balkan Air Force as a light bomber squadron. At the same time a "flap" was caused by reports that the German navy was towing the Italian Blue Riband Liner *Rex* towards Trieste harbour in order to blockade the harbour entrance. Heavy thunderstorms reduced visibility in the Gulf of Trieste over the next few days, but in the evening of 6 September[147] Sqn Ldr R Hadingham[148] "had passed the ten-mile wide entrance to the bay of Trieste when Jonah [the navigator Sgt S W Jones[149]] called up from the astrodome and stated that he could see a suspicious looking object at four o'clock. He was quite doubtful about it and afterwards stated that he nearly let it go! We turned into the bay and opened up our engines for full power and speed. The flak at Trieste is notorious. As we approached the long black object, we could se that it was something exceedingly large, but its proximity to the harbour at Trieste and to the shore made it necessary for me to pull away before we were certain. Roy [second pilot Sgt R M White[150]] and Jonah enthusiastically nodded their heads, but I was not at all convinced, for I had only seen a large dark shape against the coast, which was poorly illuminated as the sun was already down. We turned away, passing unpleasantly close to Trieste, and did a wide turn and came in for a second run – bad tactics, because on a second run obviously everyone is ready for you. We approached towards the ship for a second time at full speed, everyone tense, and as we came within about two miles I pulled up from sea level to two hundred feet, and there was no possible doubt – it was *Rex*. A beautiful ship with raked bow and counterstern and two squat raked funnels, exactly as we were told in the briefing. As we passed Roy took the two vital photographs necessary to prove our statements, and immediately I dived back to the sea. As we dived away from the ship, we passed right across the front of Trieste harbour, in which we spotted a large merchant vessel of at least 4,000 tons, and just outside, a destroyer, stationary. And as we turned tail, hardly able to believe that we still had not been fired on, all hell was let loose on us, and we paid for our view of this prize target by experiencing three minutes of pretty hair-raising flak. Dirty black puffs would suddenly appear in the air ahead, to one side or above us, and a sudden kick against the tail told me that they were bursting close behind us as well. The sea all around us was speckled with small and large shrapnel from the fragmentation. All the time, with both engines full out, I was putting the aircraft into every type of dive, climb and turn imagineable. We eventually passed out of the danger area completely unscathed, flushed with excitement."

The next day the search was resumed and Fg Off Lantinga located the ship once more, close into the shore near Koper. Lantinga's crew reported that the ship was stationary with no sign of activity on board but the poor weather conditions precluded any further action. The *Rex* was located for a third time early on 8 September by Fg Off Robertson. "The weather was very murky with visibility less than one mile," recalled Robertson, "and we were lucky to stumble across her. *Rex* was stationary about a few hundred yards off shore when we sighted her as we flew an easterly course towards Trieste. We turned back through 180 degrees to allow the second pilot on my right to take photos of her with the hand held camera from the right hand cockpit window. As briefed, a sighting report in 'clear' (highest priority, not coded) was immediately transmitted. As we completed the turn in the murk we found ourselves right in the middle of the box of two destroyers and two armed merchantmen: they had us covered, and the flak was too close for comfort... We escaped back into the

The Italian Blue Riband liner *Rex* seen in the fading evening light of 6 September 1944 near Trieste by Sqn Ldr Hadingham.

murk and went for Ancona without delay." At Ancona the Beaufighter crews of 272 Squadron were standing by and after Robertson briefed them they set off to attack the *Rex* with rockets. Following behind the Beaufighters, Robertson's task was to photograph the aftermath and assess the damage. There was little doubt about the results of the strike: he found her "listing over with white smoke pouring from her... unfortunately the photos weren't so hot due to the poor light and weather."

Smoke issues from the listing hulk of the *Rex* on 9 September 1944 after the rocket attack by 272 Squadron Beaufighters. The rain streaks across the camera lense bear witness to the appalling weather.

The *Rex* episode was the last major operational event for the Squadron in the Mediterranean theatre, although the unit's last operational Marauder flight[151] was flown by Sqn Ldr Yelloly on 21 September. The significance of this event was marred by an unfortunate and avoidable accident on the same day, when WO F Elliott[152] crashed[153] on take-off from Grottaglie. Lining up in darkness he had not used the full length of the runway and hit a power cable just after he became airborne; the entire crew was killed. The next day the Squadron learned that it was to return to the UK, thus ending twenty-four years of service in the Middle East. The Marauders were returned to the Maintenance Unit and the personnel travelled to Naples where, on 12 October, they boarded the SS *Capetown Castle* for the voyage back to England.

Notes

1 Flt Lt Brian Dutton DFC later flew Wellingtons and Lancasters. He transferred to the Air Traffic Control branch of the RAF after the war and left the service in 1962.

2 Col Flint Garrison Jr (1905-1979) commanded 320th Bombadment Group.

3 Wg Cdr Bryce Meharg OBE AFC★ (1917-2000) retired from the RAF in 1972.

4 Marauder FK157.

5 in Marauder FK121.

6 Bruce Young SAAF was shot down in Jan 1943 and became a PoW.

7 in Marauder FK375.

8 Donald Clarke was awarded the DFM for this action. After the war he transferred to the Fighter Control Branch of the RAF which he left in 1954.

9 William Bower, aged 31, was from Union Point, Manitoba, Canada.

10 Marauder FK122.

11 in Marauder FK159.

12 Fg Off F R Brown FK130, Sgt Egebjerg FK131, Flt Lt Brooks FK371, Sgt Einsaar FK376.

13 Described as "a giant of a man" Fg Off Leonard Einsaar DFM (b 1913) was born in Awaba, New South Wales Before the war he had been a policeman in the tough mining town of Broken Hill, NSW and he represented Australia as a rower in the 1936 Olympic Games. He was shot down in 1943 and after spending a year as a PoW he was discharged from the RAAF in 1945.

14 Marauder FK367.

15 Ralph Ploskin from Birmingham.

16 Aged 21, Percival Cockington was from Woodville, South Australia.

17 Alan Watts, aged 27 was from Sheffield.

18 Tom Exell from Kensington, Victoria, Australia was 21 years old.

19 Plt Off Grimsey FK131, Plt Off Clarke-Hall FK155, Lt Leach FK370, Sgt O'Connor FK133, Plt Off Willis FK366.

20 After the war Sqn Ldr John Buckland retired from the RAAF and returned to farming in Mansfield, Victoria, Australia.

21 By a miracle John Willis survived the crash which killed the rest of his crew, probably because he had undone his harness and forgotten to refasten it. It seems that he was blown through the windscreen by the exlosion and he was found by the Germans floating in the harbour kept afloat by his lifejacket. Willis spent the rest of the war as a Prisoner of War and died in 1999. According to his his wishes, his ashes were scattered into Tunis harbour where his crew had perished 56 years earlier.

22 Flt Lt Carl Long AMICE MIMunE retired from the Airfield Construction Branch of the RAF in 1956.

23 Les Jones returned to South Africa after he was released by the Turks following internment in Ankara in 1943.

24 Marauder FK375.

25 Plt Off Elliott in FK142 accompanied by Fg Off Grimsey in FK159.

26 Flt Lt Owen Phillips from Perth, Western Australia was awarded the DFC in December 1943.

27 Wg Cdr Maydwell FK376, Plt Off Elliott FK139.

28 20-year old Christopher Phillips, from Sussex, died from burns received in a flying accident in July 1943.

29 Wg Cdr Maydwell FK139, Plt Off Phillips FK373.

30 Lt Jones FK143, Flt Sgt Truman FK150.

31 Olaf Olson DFC (1920-1953) was taken PoW in the Far East in 1944. He was killed in the Tangiwai train disaster in NZ.

32 In Spitfire PR Mk IV BS362.

33 In Spitfire PR Mk IV BR432.

34 Marauder FK373.

35 Maj Lewis FK370, Fg Off Lapthorne FK151, Plt Off Clarke-Hall FK142.

36 Fg Off Donovan FK121, Flt Sgt Barton FK377, Sgt Yarwood FK139.

37 Plt Off Phillips FK123, Flt Sgt Egebjerg FK378, Flt Sgt Bullock FK126.

38 Wg Cdr Edmund "Ted" Donovan OBE DFC (1916-1999) retired from the RAF in 1961. He commanded 14 Squadron from 1944-45.

39 Richard Slatcher had previously completed a tour on Whitley bombers.

40 Basil Yarwood was from Hereford.

41 Marauder FK154.

42 Henry Siewert.

43 39-year old Walter Tatlow was from Windsor Ontario, Canada.

44 Flt Sgt Einsaar was in FK378, Flt Sgt Bullock FK137, Flt Sgt Russell FK155, Sgt Rawlins in FK112, Plt Off Francis in FK363 and Flt Sgt Hunter in FK147.

45 Thomas Russell, aged 21, from Melbourne, Victoria, Australia.

46 Henry Rawlins, aged 21, was from Nairobi, Kenya.

47 25-year old Robin "Bob" Francis from Buenos Aires, had been an electrician in Argentina before the war and was reputed to have fought in the Spanish Civil War. He was awarded a DFC posthumously.

48 John Hunter aged 25 (from Albury New South Wales, Australia) and his crew survived ditching after being shot down by two FW190s off Livorno and were captured. After the war Hunter returned to Albury where he ran a hardware store.

49 from *Adriatic Adventure* published by Robertson & Mullens, Melbourne 1945.

50 John Goldsmith aged 22 from Jersey had been awarded the GM in 1941 for attempting to rescue a student pilot who was trapped in the burning wreckage of his aircraft.

51 Leslie Harrison won the DFM in 1942 while serving with 107 Squadron.

52 Tom Clowry (b 1911) was a married man from Newtown, New South Wales, Australia.

53 28-year old Eric McClelland was from Blackley, Manchester.

54 Marauder FK376.

55 Marauder FK152.

56 Sqn Ldr James Collyer retired from the RAF in 1963.

57 in Marauder FK160.

58 34-year old Wg Cdr Hubert Law-Wright DSO DFC from Altrincham, Cheshire, was killed in action in April 1945 while commanding 298 Squadron. He was flying a Halifax III over Norway on a resupply mission for the SOE. He commanded 14 Squadron from August 1943-June 1944.

59 Bill Cowie from Rosetown Saskatchewan, Canada.

60 Floyd Lovelace from Winnipeg, Manitoba Canada.

61 Douglas Blair.

62 A New Zealander, Fg Off Corran Ashworth (1921-1944) was killed in action while flying a Mustang with 65 Sqn over northern France.

63 Flt Lt Harvey Crawford was released from the RCAF in 1946.

64 Like Ashworth, Don Campbell, a Canadian, had previously flown Hurricanes with 253 Sqn.

65 Marauder FK159.

66 Marauder FK133.

67 John Kennedy (d 2005) was shot down and taken PoW a month later.

68 Flt Lt Gil Graham DFM (1917-2009) was subsequently the Gunnery Leader with 614 Squadron. At the end of the war he transferred to the Administrative Branch and on leaving the RAF in 1971 he returned to his native Carlisle where he worked for Northern Gas.

69 Remarkably none of the crew of twelve was badly hurt in this crash. In the 1980s, the pilot Oberfeldwebel Walter Honig (1920-2007), made contact with Dick Maydwell and the two became good friends.

70 in Marauder FK373.

71 in Marauder FK147.

72 in Marauder FK142.

73 in Marauder FK110.

74 in Marauder FK149.

75 Neville Freeman DFC (1917-2008) from Dunedin New Zealand, joined New Zealand's National Airways Corporation after the war and rose to become Senior Pilot.

76 in Marauder FK144.

77 A married man and a Chartered Accountant by profession, 29 year-old Adam Cameron was from Kikcaldy, Fife.

78 Marauder FK127.

79 in Marauder FK121.

80 Marauder FK132.

81 Frank Spedding (b 1919) was from Christchurch, New Zealand.

82 Hugh Richie.

83 in Marauder FK142.

84 Ron Gellatly OBE AFC (1920-1983), a New Zealander, was later Test Pilot for the Fairey Rotodyne project and became Chief Test Pilot for Westland helicopters. His last project was the Lynx.

85 Marauder FK126.

86 Gp Capt Ivor Gibbins MBE who retired from the RAF in 1968 and died in 1985 was remarkable in being a fully qualified pilot. He was the Squadron Engineering Officer throughout the Squadron's Marauder period and frequently test flew the aircraft after servicing.

87 Marauder FK131.

88 Frank Tuxill was from Falmouth, Cornwall.

89 Marauder FK133.

90 A Canadian, Richard Gilkey was 28 years old.

91 Sqn Ldr Arthur "Chuff" Hornby AFM, who died in 1999, retired from the RAF in 1963.

92 in Marauder FK110.

93 25 year old Maurice Reid was from Londonderry.

94 Marauder FK142.

95 Sabe Lantinga from Macleod, Alberta, Canada.

96 Charles Duncan, from Coronach Saskatchewan, died in 1988 aged 69.

97 Marauder FK126.

98 Alfred "Joe" Tait (1918-2002) from New Brunswick had been a teacher before the war. After the war he returned to New Brunswick where he served in the Civil Service. A deeply religious man, he was held in great respect by his colleagues on 14 Squadron.

99 in B26B serial number 117958.

100 Geoffrey Croskell from Surrey was 25 years old.

101 in Marauder FK362.

102 A veteran of the Melos Harbour raid, tail gunner Thomas Climpson was from Eastbourne.

103 "Jimmy" Wright OBE DFC (1922-1993) was blinded in the crash and underwent extensive plastic surgery as one of McIndoe's "Guinea Pig Club". After the war he founded a successful film production company.

104 Marauder FK149.

105 Howard Elsey from British Columbia is commemorated by the naming of Mount Elsey, a 7,558 ft peak near Williams Lake BC.

106 Marauder FK130.

107 For this action Edward Hall was awarded the BEM; after the war he joined Marconi at Chelmsford

and died at the age of 81 in 2000.

108 "Bert" Metcalfe, who died in 1997 had retired to Norfolk.

109 Harry Merkley, from Ottawa, Ontario was 22 years old.

110 Allan Bowes, from Canada.

111 Hudson Campbell, aged 22, was from Winnipeg, Manitoba.

112 A pre-war postman, Joe Lowder ISM (b 1922) rejoined the Post Office after the war, retiring in 1982 as a Superintendent. He served as the Hon Secretary to the 14 Squadron Association from 1986-2002.

113 B-26B Marauder 117780.

114 Stanley Yelloly left the RAF in 1957.

115 in Marauder FK120.

116 24-year old William "Bill" Adey was from Melbourne, Australia.

117 in Marauder FK123 at 1025 hrs on 27 April.

118 Fg Off Kenneth "Bill" Mailer left the RAF in 1955.

119 in Marauder FK145.

120 WO P D Musto from Finchley, London. Musto was commissiioned in June 1944.

121 Flt Sgt A H James from Newport, South Wales.

122 Flt Sgt R Eaton from London.

123 Sgt R J Taylor from Egham, Surrey.

124 Fg Off Budge in FK159, Fg Off A T Smith in FK120 and Flt Sgt J Ross in FK110.

125 Herbert Budge, aged 23, from Hove, Sussex; his aircraft was seen by a USAAF B25 which was returning from a bombing raid on Toulon.

126 Trevor Smith, aged 32, was a married man from Menston near Leeds. This was his first mission with his own crew, having previously been second pilot in Yelloly's crew.

127 John Ross aged 25 from Gateshead.

128 Flt Lt Mervin Hogg aged 24 from Warren, Manitoba, Canada was killed in action in April 1945.

129 Marauder FK123.

130 Bill Japp died in 1999.

131 WO G Senior.

132 22 year-old WO George Smith from Toronto, Canada, was killed in Action in April 1945

133 28-year old Brummer was from Natal, South Africa.

134 in Marauder 118039.

135 Neil Cornish, aged 27, came from Otago, New Zealand.

136 Marauder 118017.

137 Cliff Glanville, from Johannesburg South Africa, ran a mining company after the War.

138 in Marauder HD457.

139 in Marauder HD488.

140 John MacDonald From Nova Scotia, Canada.

141 Lance Johnson from Victoria Australia.

142 In Marauder HD508.

143 John Robertson (1921-2009) from Sydney, Australia.

144 In Marauder HD457.

145 Ivor Duffell (1919-1986) from Melbourne Australia.

146 Richard Jordan (b 1920) from New South Wales, Australia.

147 in Marauder HD478.

148 Ronald Hadingham (1918- 1994) had spent most of the war instructing navigation and was the author of the standard textbook on astro navigation. Married to an American, he emigrated to the USA after the war.

149 Sgt Stanley Jones, described by Hadingham as "very solemn, conscientious fellow who takes his work very seriously," also flew in Hadingham's Wellington crew in 1945.

150 Roy White, described by Hadingham as "tall, youthful and a little naive" was a Wellington captain with 14 Squadron at RAF Chivenor in 1945.

151 Marauder 117977.

152 Frank Elliot aged 24 was from Stalybridge Cheshire.

153 Marauder FK138.

Chapter 9

1944–45
The Wellington

Arrival in England

When the *Capetown Castle* docked in Liverpool on 21 October 1944 it carried a squadron which had already changed much from the unit that had fought throughout the Mediterranean campaign. In Naples, all the ground staff who had not completed their overseas tour had been posted to other units in the Mediterranean theatre. They had been replaced by personnel from other units who had completed their overseas tour, with the result that the Squadron which arrived in England contained only about a tenth of its original ground staff. Many aircrews had also been posted away on completion of their operational tours. This dilution of the "Old Squadron" was exacerbated by an increase from twenty crews to thirty crews.

The changes to the Squadron were not limited to personnel: the new location also brought with it new aircraft and a completely new role. When 14 Squadron regrouped at RAF Chivenor, near Barnstaple in Devon, after three weeks' disembarkation leave, four Wellington Mark XIV aircraft awaited them. These aeroplanes were to be used in the Anti-Submarine role to hunt U-boats in the Western Approaches. The Wellington was a very different machine to the Marauder which the Squadron had flown for the previous two years. The obsolescent airframe had been adapted to house a Mark VIA ASV radar which would be operated by an extra crew member to search for U-boats on the surface. Additionally, mounted in the belly of the aircraft was a hydraulically operated retractable searchlight, the "Leigh Light", which would be used in the final stages of a night time attack on a surfaced U-boat.

Ground training on the new aircraft type started on 22 November and over the following week more aircraft arrived. Flying started on 30 November, but was severely curtailed by poor weather and poor serviceability of the aircraft. The latter improved as the groundcrews became more familiar with their new charges, but the weather would remain a major factor throughout the winter. In pure flying terms the Wellington was a much easier aeroplane to fly than the Marauder, but the pilots missed the practical ergonomics of the American aircraft. Furthermore the rigid discipline of night-time Anti Submarine patrols was in stark contrast to the fluidity of the low-level coastal patrols they had flown in the Marauder. The Wellington crew also had to work very closely as a team: flying on instruments, the pilots relied on the navigator to keep them in the correct patrol area while the radar operator searched

282

Wellington CX-A in the snow, January 1945. Apart from its effect on the flying programme, the cold Devon winter was an unpleasant shock for many of the Squadron personnel who were more used to the Mediterranean climate! (Mark Postlethwaite)

the sea for targets. Once a radar contact was found, the radar operator would take over and provide steering so that the pilots could home onto it for a Leigh Light attack. During the training phase this procedure was practised in an exercise nicknamed "Bathmat" in which a Royal Navy minesweeper was positioned in the Bristol Channel to allow crews to carry out the search and homing profile.

Fg Off Robertson thought the Leigh Light "was a very good weapon, although it made the aircraft somewhat difficult to fly at the low altitude you had to use in the attack. When you got a contact you positioned yourself about seven miles away from it at 1,000 feet and then homed in using instruments with the second pilot in the nose ready to lower the light. You would aim to be at fifty feet at one mile from the contact. Height was measured by a radio altimeter which showed a green light if you were at fifty feet, the optimum height for dropping a depth charge, a red light if you were below that and an amber light if you were above about fifty-five feet. In any swell, and there always seemed to be one in the Atlantic, you got a series of green to red to green to amber to green... then to add to the excitement, when you lowered the light for the final run in ... it hung under the belly of the aircraft and made it longitudinally unstable. The pièce de résistance was the natural tendency for the pilot to lift his head and fly visually to the target. This was fatal: the pilot was blinded by the beam, lost orientation and with an unstable aircraft at fifty feet simply went in."

The English winter weather continued to disrupt training and to make life uncomfortable for Squadron personnel. Severe cold and frost, such as the chill that struck Chivenor on 23 December was keenly felt by those who had spent the last few years in warmer climes! However, a full syllabus of ground training kept everyone busy when there was no flying, and an active sports scene, which included soccer, rugby and hockey, also ensured that no-one was idle.

Christmas of 1944 was the first Christmas celebrated by 14 Squadron in the UK since 1918. In marked contrast to the previous year, it was a day when the whole Unit could be together and the majority of the Squadron's personnel spent the day on camp.

The beginning of the New Year was chiefly memorable for the Squadron's first two flying accidents, one of which was fatal. In the first, on 23 January, Fg Off R W Stewart crashed on take-off. He had attempted to get airborne with full nose-down trim applied and when he ran out of runway he could only stop the aeroplane by raising the undercarriage; the Wellington[1] stopped, but it then caught fire and was burnt out. Happily the crew escaped unscathed but the aircraft was completely written off. The following night, Fg Off C J Campbell[2] was flying on a "Bathmat" exercise just off the island of Lundy. As it manoeuvred in the final stage of a practice attack the aircraft[3] flew into the sea, possibly as a result of the disorientation described by Robertson. Campbell, his navigator Plt Off J M J Rowland[4] and Wireless Operator Sgt L M Lewis[5] were all picked up by the minesweeper, but the rest of the crew died in the crash. Unfortunately Rowland and Lewis both succumbed to exposure and shock and both died shortly afterwards, leaving Campbell as the only survivor. The next day a heavy snowfall closed Chivenor for three days.

The Squadron's first operational sortie in a Wellington[6], a ten hour Anti-Submarine patrol in St George's Channel, was flown by Sqn Ldr Hadingham on the night of 2 February. The second followed three nights later flown by Lt M Overed[7] in the same aeroplane, in high winds over a very rough sea. Over the month the frequency of operations slowly built up so that by March the Squadron was typically flying five operational sorties each night. On the morning of 11 March Fg Off Hornby's crew were on patrol[8] near the Scillies with an unserviceable ASV radar. With no radar, the crew had to resort to keeping a good visual lookout. "At about 0830," recalled the ASV operator, WO Lowder, "we sighted a Liberator of [VPB-]103 Squadron US Navy flying parallel with us on a patrol at eight miles distance. About five miles from Bishop's Rock it turned sharply away, diving. We turned too and saw a surfaced sub sitting nice and pretty. The Liberator dropped its depth charges and as we drew near the sea heaved and swallowed the submarine completely. We turned, opened up both bomb doors, took up action stations and went into the attack. As we drew nearer we saw the sub sinking stern first and the crew milling about in the water. Some were floating lifeless, some wallowed in the waves and some were on collapsible rubber rafts waving like hell, presumably to draw attention to the fact that they were helpless and didn't want another stick of explosives." Seeing the survivors, Hornby broke off the attack and returned to his patrol area. The Squadron's Operations Diary noted ruefully that "it was the worst luck in the world that this crew should have missed what might have proved to be the Squadron's first U-boat through unserviceable equipment." However the crew had at least witnessed the sinking of the U681 by Lt Field's US Navy Liberator.

Two nights later Fg Off Duncan's crew suffered more frustration during their patrol in St George's Channel[9]. They picked up several radar contacts, but each one simply faded from the screen as the aircraft turned to home onto them. The weather that night was foul and two of the five operational missions were cancelled before take off. All three of the aircraft which did launch on patrol were diverted to St Eval because the weather had clamped in at Chivenor, but when they reached St Eval they found the weather there was also below limits and they had to divert once again to the US Navy base at Dunkeswell. Here at least all the crews had compensation for their inconvenience in the form of juicy steaks, thanks to the American caterers! Unfortunately there was no diversion and therefore no steaks for Flt Lt F S Hazelwood's[10] crew when they also suffered the frustrations of intermittent contacts on 17 March[11].

Anti-submarine patrols were a relentless and very unglamourous chore. The fact that most of the Squadron's patrols were completed without incident was a good measure of the strategic success of Coastal Command's anti-submarine campaign.

"Chuff" Hornby's crew who witnessed the dispatch of U681 by a US Navy Liberator on 11 March 1945. L-r: W/O L T Copp, Sgt R Unsworth, Plt Off J W A Lowder, Flt Lt A N Hornby DFM, Flt Sgt K E Williams, Flt Sgt A W Hoyle. (J W A Lowder)

However, each operational sortie represented about ten hours' worth of intense concentration by the crew during a tedious patrol, which was usually carried out in darkness, frequently in very bad weather. Wg Cdr Donovan found that "the intense concentration needed for ten hours' instrument flying was extremely exhausting," while his navigator from Marauder days, Fg Off R A Yarburgh-Bateson, described Anti-Submarine patrols as "singularly boring and unrewarding." The Wireless Operator/Air Gunners felt the pressure too: Fg Off Lowder recorded that "the length of time in the air certainly knocks everyone up … also having to stare into the radar screen … gave [us] headaches." Discomfort of long hours spent being buffeted by turbulence at low level was keenly felt by crews: Yarburgh-Bateson described being "desperately air-sick after five hours of vomiting." By the end of ten hours' misery he "looked like the wreck of the Hesperus."

The patrols could be dangerous, too. The threat of icing was ever present. Ice on the wings could bring an aircraft down by destroying its lifting power, and carburettor icing could lead to engine failure. Anti-ice protection was minimal on the Wellington consisting chiefly of paste which was applied to the wings before take-off. WO E A Beasant's crew had a narrow escape from icing on their second operational patrol on 30 April. They had already had a close shave on their first patrol[12] three days beforehand when they cut short their sortie because of an oil leak; on landing they discovered that one engine was on the verge of failure. At midnight on the last day of April, Beasant finished his patrol and attempted to recover to Chivenor, but he soon

The last Squadron Photograph – 14 Squadron Wellington aircrews at RAF Chivenor, March 1945. (Lord Deramore)

ran into severe icing conditions and was forced down to two hundred feet. However it soon became apparent that there was no way through the weather, even by descending to this low altitude. Beasant turned and flew an hour westwards in an attempt to find a gap. Eventually he was able to climb to 12,000 feet before he could turn back towards Chivenor.

April was a month in which a number of routine patrols were interrupted by engine failures: Flt Lt J G Walker[13] cut short a patrol after losing an engine on 10 April, while exactly a week later Flt Lt D B Eagle[14] sent out an SOS after both engines coughed and started to cut. Happily the problem in the fuel supply line proved to be temporary and Eagle was able to make a safe recovery. WO R M White diverted to St Eval after an engine failure on 21 April and on 25 April Fg Off I S Duffel[15] cut short his last operational sortie thanks to the failure of an engine.

However, two crews had been far less lucky on a day which was one of the most disastrous in the Squadron's history. On the evening of 18 April six crews launched for routine anti-submarine patrols. Lt Overed took off[16] just after 2100 heading for the Western Approaches. Four hours later an SOS call was received from the aircraft, but there was no further response from the crew, despite numerous calls instructing them to give more details of their situation. The aircraft did not return to Chivenor and nothing was found by Fg Off Robertson who was diverted from his patrol to mount a search of Overed's patrol area. After staying on station for as long as he dared, Robertson returned to base with minimum fuel after nearly eleven hours' flying time.

Wellington NB869 at St Merryn after Flt Lt Duncan overran the short runway and hit a bus on 21 April 1945. (FAAM)

Some time later the body of Flt Sgt J J Brophy[17] was washed ashore in northern Spain near Bilbao. Flt Lt M C Hogg[18] had taken off[19] a few minutes earlier than Overed; just before midnight he sent a radio message that he was experiencing a fuel leak and would divert to St Eval. It was a clear night and the aircraft reached St Eval safely. Hogg flew over the airfield before turning to position for an approach onto the southeasterly runway, but disaster struck and the aircraft hit the cliffs a few miles short of the runway, and burst into flames, killing all aboard. A hasty Court of Enquiry was assembled, which found that the most likely cause of the accident was that Hogg had lost control of the aircraft after becoming overcome by fuel fumes.

The loss of two crews led by two popular and long-serving aircraft captains was a severe blow to the Squadron and also a disappointing end to Wg Cdr Donovan's tenure in command of 14 Squadron. Donovan, who had served with the Squadron since 1942, handed command of the Squadron to Wg Cdr G I Pawson[20] on 20 April. Pawson himself was no stranger to the unit, having been flying as a supernumerary pilot during the previous months.

Routine patrols continued but it was clear that the war in Europe was fast coming to an end. There was some excitement aboard Wellington "Q" flown by Flt Lt Hazlewood on 27 April when they were diverted to support two corvettes which reported that they were under attack by a U-boat. Hazlewood remained on station until he reached minimum fuel, but he was unable to locate the U-boat. On 8 May VE Day marked the end of the European war. On that day Flt Lt Walker flew an operational sortie, giving him the distinction of having flown operationally on both the first and last days of the war. In September 1939 he had flown as an air gunner in a Blenheim. Over the next few weeks, the operational flying commitment slowly wound down and the Squadron's Operations Diary recorded an "accent on sport now." RAF Chivenor reverted to peacetime working practices on 26 May, with weekend working suspended. 14 Squadron's last operational sortie of the war was flown on 29 May by Flt Lt C M Gibbs[21] DFC who escorted[22] a convoy into the Irish Sea. Two days later all the aircraft were grounded.

For some weeks there had been much speculation about the Squadron's future, but all became clear on 31 May when 14 Squadron at Chivenor was formally disbanded. The crews were dispersed to 179 Squadron, but on 1 June 1945 the Squadron "number plate" was passed on to 143 Squadron, a Mosquito maritime strike unit at Banff.

Notes

1 HF123.
2 Originally from Hobart, Tasmania, Colin Campbell (1920-2011) was an experienced Marauder pilot. After the War he worked in the insurance industry in Melbourne and later retired to Brisbane.
3 MF450.
4 James Rowland, aged 22 was from Edgware.
5 Leonard Lewis from Machynlleth.
6 NB835.
7 Capt Martin Overed SAAF was killed on 19 April 1945 aged 20. He had previously flown Marauders with 14 Squadron.
8 In Wellington "K".
9 In Wellington HF838.
10 AVM Frederick Hazlewood CB CBE AFC★ (1921-2007) had joined the RAF in 1939 as an Air Gunner. His later career included tours as Commandant CFS and AOC 38 Group.
11 In Wellington HF393.
12 In Wellington NB856.
13 Sqn Ldr John Walker DFC retired from the RAF in 1957.
14 Desmond Eagle (d 1995) had previously flown Marauders with 14 Squadron. He retired from the RAF in 1962.
15 Australian Ivor Duffel (1919-1986) from Moreland, Victoria had flown as second pilot to John Robertson on Marauders. He was de-mobbed in 1945.
16 In Wellington NB858.
17 Aged 22 James Brophy was a married man from Liverpool.
18 24-year old Mervin Hogg, from Warren Manitoba, was an experienced and popular Marauder and Wellington captain.
19 In Wellington NB875.
20 Gilbert Pawson had gained his pilot's licence as a 17-year old schoolboy in 1932 while at school at Haileybury. He joined the RAF in 1934. After the War he transferred to the Administrative and Secretarial Branch of the RAF. He retired in 1960 with the rank of Wg Cdr.
21 A New Zealander, AVM Charles Gibbs CB CBE DFC (b 1921) retired from the RAF in 1976.
22 In Wellington NB821.

Appendix 1

Aircraft Operated by 14 Squadron 1915–45

A/C Type	Serial No	Sqn Code	Date On	Date off	Comments	Crew
BE2c	1757		4 Dec 1915	20 Jan 1916	Engine Failure, ditched in Mersah Matruh harbour	Capt A G Moore, Lt R C Gill - OK
BE2c	2114		6 Jul 1916			
BE2c	2116		6 Apr 1916	18 Jun 1916	Shot down during bombing raid on El Arish airfield	Capt R J Tipton - PoW
BE2c	2118		15 Apr 1916	2 Sep 1916	Forced landing on raid on Maghara - a/c burnt	Capt F F Minchin - rescued
BE2c	2700		25 Apr 1916	5 Oct 1916	to X Air Park (Soc 20/10/16)	
BE2c	2770		16 Nov 1917			
BE2c	2776		10 May 1917			
BE2c	4135		11 Jul 1916	22 Jan 1917	to X Air Park	
BE2c	4137		3 Feb 1917			
BE2c	4139		21 Jun 1916	7 Aug 1916	to X Air Park	
BE2c	4152		28 Jun 1916 29 Mar 1917	27 Jan 1917 9 Sep 1917	to X Air Park to X Air Park	
BE2c	4216		26 Aug 1916	30 Dec 1916		
BE2c	4306		5 Jan 1916		Sennussi campaign	
BE2c	4311		2 Apr 1916	11 Jul 1916	Wrecked, struck off charge	?
BE2c	4312		1 Apr 1916	5 Jun 1916	Transferred to 67 (Aus) Sqn	
BE2c	4314		14 Jan 1916			
BE2c	4315		2 Mar 1916	7 Aug 1916	to X Air Park	
BE2c	4319		27 Jun 1916			
BE2c	4327			2 Feb 1917	to X Air Park	
BE2c	4332		19 Apr 1917	5 Jun 1916 16 Jun 1917	Transferred to 67 (Aus) Sqn to X Air Park	
BE2c	4352		5 Feb 1916			
BE2c	4353		1 Apr 1916	21 Jun 1916	Wrecked on force landing, struck off charge	?
BE2c	4354		26 Jul 1916	20 Oct 1916	struck off charge	
BE2c	4356		2 Jun 1916		Sennussi campaign	
BE2c	4389		18 Jun 1916	29 Jun 1917	to X Air Park	
BE2c	4390		18 Sep 1916	5 Feb 1917	to X Air Park	
BE2c	4391		by Oct 1916	1 Nov 1916	struck off charge	
BE2c	4395		27 Sep 1916 29 Mar 1917	17 Feb 1917 24 Sep 1917	to X Air Park transferred to 20 Reserve Wing	
BE2c	4405		10 Apr 1916	13 Aug 1916	transferred to 21RS Abbassia	
BE2c	4406		24 Dec 1915			
BE2c	4419		23 Apr 1916	3 May 1916	Shot down by rifle fire during recce of El Arish	Lt C W Hill - PoW
BE2c	4432		7 Aug 1916			
BE2c	4435		9 Feb 1916			
BE2c	4442		24 Sep 1916	19 Mar 1917	Transferred to 20 Reserve Wing	
BE2c	4453		5 Jan 1916	19 Sep 1916	struck off charge	
BE2c	4455		29 Jul 1916	23 Aug 1916	struck off charge	
BE2c	4473		by Se 1916	16 Jul 1917	C Flt (Arabian Det) - damaged in storm	
Be2c	4478		20 Sep 1916	16 Jul 1917	C Flt (Arabian Det) - damaged in storm	
BE2c	4481		4 Dec 1916	25 Jan 1917	Engine failure - force landed 2 mile S El Aabash	Lt J M Batting, Lt R C Jenkins - OK
BE2c	4482		18 Feb 1917			
BE2c	4483		4 Apr 1916	30 Apr 1917	C Flt (Arabian Det) Crash landed Wadi Hamdh	Capt F W Stent - OK

APPENDIX 1

A/C Type	Serial No	Sqn Code	Date On	Date off	Comments	Crew
BE2c	4485		3 Feb 1917	9 Apr 1917	struck off charge	
BE2c	4488		20 Sep 1916	16 Jul 1917	C Flt (Arabian Det) - damaged in storm	
BE2c	4507		4 Aug 1916	23 Aug 1916	struck off charge	
BE2c	4517		26 Jul 1916			
BE2c	4520		10 Aug 1916			
BE2c	4521		4 Jun 1916			
BE2c	4522		27 Jun 1916			
BE2c	4527		20 Sep 1916	26 Mar 1917	Engine Failure on take-off	
BE2c	4529		7 Sep 1916	11 Jul 1917	Crashed on take-off at Gayadah	Lt J M Batting - OK
BE2c	4551		16 Jun 1916			
BE2c	4552		2 Jun 1916	13 Sep 1916	Sennussi campaign; struck off charge	
BE2c	4553		22 Apr 1916			
BE2c	4554		2 Oct 1916	1 Nov 1916	to X Air Park	
BE2c	4709		26 Jul 1916			
BE2c	4711		13 Dec 1915	27 Jan 1916	Sideslipped and crashed, Mersah Matruh	Lt G deL Wooldridge, Maj A J Ross - OK
BE2c	4712		2 Dec 1915	14 Jul 1916	Transferred to 21 Reserve Squadron	
BE2c	4717		4 Dec 1915			
BE2c	5413		6 Aug 1916	22 Aug 1916	to X Air Park	
BE2c	5421		8 Jun 1916	7 Aug 1917	C Flt (Arabian Det) transferred to X Air Park	
BE2c	6765		20 Feb 1917			
BE2c	6769		11 Jul 1917	26 Sep 1917	struck off charge	
BE2c	6770		8 Aug 1917	22 Oct 1917	Transfer to 40 Wing	
BE2c	6774		25 Jan 1917	15 Feb 1917	Engine caught fire returning from raid on Beesheba. Forced landing	2Lt A J L Barlow - PoW
BE2c	6775		11 Feb 1917	7 Mar 1917	to X Air Park	
BE2c	6776		23 Mar 1917	6 Apr 1917	to X Air Park	
BE2c	6779		19 Feb 1917 4 Aug 1917	19 May 1917	to X Air Park	
BE2c	6781		4 Aug 1917			
BE2c	6802		5 Jul 1917	7 Jul 1917	Transfer to 67 Squadron	
BE2c	6803		14 Mar 1917	10 Jun 1917	to X Air Park	
BE2c	6824		18 Apr 1917	13 Jul 1917	Crashed on t/o, Belah Nr Gaza, stalled into hangar & fig tree	2 Lt G C Gardiner - OK
BE2c	6825		20 Apr 1917	1 Jun 1917	struck off charge	
BE2c	6827		11 Apr 1917	25 Sep 1917	Crashed on landing Belah, nr Gaza - overshot and hit fig tree	Lt Hale
BE2e	7132		29 Dec 1916 30 Oct 1917	12 Apr 1917	to X Air Park	
BE2e	7149		25 Jan 1917	9 Apr 1917	struck off charge	
BE2e	A1279		22 Nov 1917	20 Mar 1918	to X Air Park	Beer & Thorp??
BE2e	A1323		13 Aug 1917			
BE2e	A1324		1 Dec 1917			
BE2e	A1365		9 Aug 1917	28 Nov 1917	Attacked by enemy aircraft NE Junction Station - observer wounded	2Lt C M Hallett OK; 2Lt A C Roxburgh died of wounds
BE2e	A1375		19 Sep 1917		Crashed	
BE2e	A1377		31 Oct 1917			
BE2e	A1801		18 Oct 1917	31 Oct 1917	transferred to 20(T) Wing	
BE2e	A1802		15 Jun 1917 2 Oct 1917	17 Jul 1917	to X Air Park	
BE2e	A1803		7 Jul 1917	23 Jul 1917	Shot down by AA fire while on Artillery Observation patrol	Capt R N Thomas, 2Lt J W Howells both killed

291

A/C Type	Serial No	Sqn Code	Date On	Date off	Comments	Crew
BE2e	A1806		6 Sep 1917	1 Dec 1917	to X Air Park	
BE2e	A1811		4 Jun 1917	10 Nov 1917	Failed to return from attack on Junction Station	2Lt H L C McConnell MC - PoW died of wounds
BE2e	A1839		13 Jul 1917			
BE2e	A2770		16 Nov 1917			
BE2e	A2772		1 Jun 1917	20 Jul 1917		
BE2e	A2773		18 Aug 1917			
BE2e	A2774		16 Sep 1917	18 Dec 1917	Transferred to 113 Sqn	
BE2e	A2775		31 Mar 1917	17 Jun 1917	to X Air Park	
BE2e	A2776		30 Mar 1917	24 Aug 1917	Transferred to 29 (R) Wing	
BE2e	A3066		2 Aug 1917	3 Jun 1918	[Maharaja of Bikanir] transferred to 142 Sqn	
BE2e	A3092		18 Nov 1917			
BE2e	A3093		16 Oct 1917	17 Feb 1918	[Ashanti No 2] Force Landed	Capt G N Wales, Lt P R Bowen OK
BE2e	A3095		1 Dec 1917	13 Sep 1918	[Changma (North Siam) Britons No 1] transferred to 142 Sqn	
BE2e	A3107		16 Oct 1917	1 Dec 1917	[Nigeria] transferred to X Air Park	
BE2e	A8650		1 Dec 1917			
BE2e	A8658		1 Dec 1917			
BE2e	A8664		1 Dec 1917	18 Dec 1917	Transferred to 113 Sqn	
BE2e	A8685		1 Dec 1917	18 Dec 1917	Transferred to 113 Sqn	
BE2e	A8687		1 Dec 1917	18 Dec 1917	Transferred to 113 Sqn	
BE12a	A566		18 Aug 1917	4 Sep 1917	Transferred to 67 Sqn	
BE12a	A575		28 Sep 1918	9 Oct 1917	Transferred to 40 Wing	
BE12	A6311		28 Sep 1917	11 Dec 1917	To X Flt	
BE12	A6323		13 Aug 1917 6 Oct 1917	31 Aug 1917 28 Oct 1917	to X Air Park Transferred to 67 Squadron	
RE8	A3788		5 Jun 1918	1 Sep 1918	to X Air Park for repair	
RE8	A3796		15 May 1918			
RE8	A3799		2 Dec 1917			
RE8	A3804		15 Oct 1918	19 Nov 1918	to X Air Park	
RE8	A3805		22 Mar 1918	15 May 1918	to X Air Park	
RE8	A3806		4 Apr 1918	10 Nov 1918	to X Air Park	
RE8	A3807		c.1918	30 Jun 1918	Engine fail on take-off near Jerusalem - 142 Sqn crew	Capt S J Palmer & 2Lt A J Cripps - injured
RE8	A3808		10 Nov 1917	11 Dec 1917	Transferred to 67 Sqn	
RE8	A3812		22 Jan 1918	22 Mar 1918	Forced landed Jericho after oil tank was shot through	Capt H I Hanmer & Lt R A Tarleton OK
RE8	A3813		19 Mar 1918	12 Apr 1918	to X Air Park	
RE8	A4405		2 May 1918 27 Oct 1918	19 Nov 1918	to X Air Park	
RE8	A4410		27 Oct 1918	19 Nov 1918	to X Air Park	
RE8	A4411		24 Jan 1918			
RE8	A4431		8 Jul 1918			
RE8	A4432		7 Mar 1918	23 Apr 1918	to X Air Park	
RE8	A4434		23 Jan 1918 22 Sep 1918	13 Apr 1918	to X Air Park	
RE8	A4435		26 Feb 1918	13 Apr 1918	to X Air Park	
RE8	A4437		29 Dec 1917	26 Sep 1918	to X Air Park	
RE8	B5003		8 Oct 1918	19 Nov 1918	to X Air Park	
RE8	B5007		19 Feb 1918	10 Apr 1918	Engine failed on take-off, spun in Junction Station	Lt G J Turner - killed, Lt P L Ward - injured

292

A/C Type	Serial No	Sqn Code	Date On	Date off	Comments	Crew
RE8	B5011		23 Mar 1918	17 Oct 1918	to X Air Park	
RE8	B5050		27 Mar 1918	9 May 1918	to X Air Park	
RE8	B5051		2 Mar 1918	3 May 1918	to X Air Park	
RE8	B5054		27 Mar 1918	30 Sep 1918	to X Air Park	
RE8	B5055		10 Mar 1918	31 Mar 1918	to X Air Park	
RE8	B5056		28 Apr 1918	3 May 1918	Forced landed Jericho after engine was shot through	Capt H A Courtenay, 2Lt T E Gohl OK
RE8	B5057		28 Feb 1918	20 Oct 1918	to X Air Park	
RE8	B5058		1 Apr 1918			
RE8	B5851		1 May 1918	11 Jun 1918	Written Off	
RE8	B5861		20 Feb 1918	9 Apr 1918	to X Air Park	
RE8	B5863		22 Mar 1918			
RE8	B5867		16 Feb 1918	9 Mar 1918	F/L & crashed due engine Failure	Lt D R Mackie, Lt C E V Graham - OK
RE8	B6471		10 Mar 1918	28 Apr 1918	Spun in while repositioning after missed approach	2Lt H S Newman, 2Lt J F Thompson - both injured
RE8	B6472		1 Mar 1918	11 May 1918	to X Air Park	
RE8	B6473		27 Mar 1918	27 May 1918	to X Air Park	
RE8	B6500		5 Mar 1918	15 Apr 1918	to X Air Park	
RE8	B6560		8 May 1918	26 Sep 1918	Transferred to 142 Sqn	
RE8	B6561		9 May 1918	21 Sep 1918	Missing over Wadi Farah - poss hit by friendly bombs	Lt J Webster MC, Sgt Mech E J Purling - killed
RE8	B6579		29 Apr 1918	18 Sep 1918	to X Air Park	
RE8	B6581		25 May 1918			
RE8	B6582		3 May 1918	22 Oct 1918	to X Air Park	
RE8	B6583		22 Apr 1918	17 May 1918	to X Air Park	
RE8	B6584		11 Apr 1918	5 Oct 1918	Transferred to 142 Sqn	
RE8	B6603		26 Apr 1918	30 Aug 1918	Written Off	
RE8	B6604		25 Apr 1918		Transferred to 113 Sqn	
RE8	B6608		27 Apr 1918	19 Jun 1918	to X Air Park	
RE8	B6609		1 May 1918	29 Jul 1918	Missing while attacking enemy anti-aircraft section 136	Capt S L Pettit, Lt J G Williams - both missing PoW
RE8	B6684		18 Sep 1918			
RE8	B6688		18 Sep 1918			
RE8	B6689		14 Sep 1918			
RE8	B6691		8 Oct 1918			
RE8	B6693		31 Aug 1918			
RE8	B6697		31 Aug 1918	23 Oct 1918	to X Air Park	
RE8	B6700		8 Oct 1918			
RE8	B6701		27 Oct 1918			
RE8	B6702		20 Sep 1918			
RE8	B6703		22 Sep 1918			
RE8	B6704		27 Oct 1918			
RE8	B6705		27 Oct 1918			
RE8	B7708		9 Aug 1918	17 Oct 1918	to X Air Park	
RE8	B7709		29 May 1918			
RE8	B7710		4 Jun 1918	15 Sep 1918	Hit by AA fire over Yetma	Capt N A Bolton - OK, 2Lt R C Revelle - killed
RE8	C2752		23 Oct 1918	19 Nov 1918	to X Air Depot	
RE8	C5101		18 Sep 1918	19 Nov 1918	[Gold Coast No 16] to X Air Depot	
RE8	C5102		27 Oct 1918	19 Nov 1918	[Sheffield] to X Air Depot	
RE8	D4705		27 Oct 1918	19 Nov 1918	to X Air Depot	

A/C Type	Serial No	Sqn Code	Date On	Date off	Comments	Crew
RE8	D4709		27 Oct 1918	19 Nov 1918	to X Air Depot	
RE8	D6782		28 May 1918			
RE8	D6808		13 May 1918			
Bristol Scout C	4684		28 Jul 1916	10 Aug 1916	to X Air Park	
Bristol Scout C	4685		5 Oct 1916	16 Nov 1916	to X Air Park	
Bristol Scout C	4686		7 Jan 1917	15 Jan 1917	to X Air Park	
Bristol Scout C	4689		1 Aug 1916	8 Oct 1916	to X Air Park	
Bristol Scout C	4693			24 Oct 1916	to X Air Park for repair	
Bristol Scout C	4694		2 Aug 1916			
Bristol Scout C	5318		19 Apr 1916	10 Aug 1916	to X Air Park	
Bristol Scout C	5324		19 Oct 1916	16 Dec 1916	to X Air Park	
Bristol Scout D	5601		8 Nov 1916	19 Jan 1917	to X Air Park - poss crashed 9 Jan 17	poss Lt W E L Seward
Bristol Scout D	7031		11 Dec 1916	1 Feb 1917	to X Air Park	
Bristol Scout D	7032		13 Apr 1917	17 Jun 1917	to X Air Park	
Bristol Scout D	A1760		20 Apr 1917	6 Jul 1917	to X Air Park	
Bristol Scout D	A1761		17 Apr 1917	1 Jun 1917	to X Air Park	
Bristol Scout D	A1764		17 Apr 1917	7 Aug 1917	transferred to 111 Sqn	
Bristol M1B	A5139		22 Jul 1917	3 Aug 1917	Crashed	2Lt M C Crerar - killed
Bristol M1B	A5140		5 Jul 1917	7 Aug 1917	transferred to 111 Sqn	
Bristol M1B	A5141		7 Jun 1917	1 Jul 1917	to X Air Park	
De Havilland 1a	4607		25 Jul 1916	29 Sep 1916	to X Air Park for repairs (Soc 1/11/16)	
De Havilland 1a	4608		24 Jul 1916	5 Mar 1917	Shot down by enemy aircraft while on recce mission	2Lt E A Floyer, 2Lt C V Palmer - both PoW
De Havilland 1a	4609		29 Jun 1916	1 Nov 1916	SoC	{Shot down EA nr Romani -First allied claim in theatre}
De Havilland 1a	4610		28 Jul 1916	23 Aug 1916	struck off charge	
De Havilland 2	A2623		22 May 1917	7 Aug 1917	Transferred to 111 Sqn	
De Havilland 2	A2628		15 May 1917	7 Aug 1917	Crashed	2Lt R A Davey - killed
De Havilland 2	A2629		15 May 1917	1 Jul 1917	To X Air Park	
De Havilland 2	A4779		4 Oct 1917	1 Dec 1917	Transferred to X Flt	
De Havilland 2	A4788		28 Jun 1917	7 Aug 1917	Transferred to 111 Sqn	
Martinsyde G100	7472		5 Oct 1916	16 Oct 1916	Transferred to 67 Sqn	
Martinsyde G100	7473		15 Sep 1916	1 Jul 1917	to X Air Park	
Martinsyde G100	7474		1 Sep 1916	2 Dec 1916	Attacked over Gaza by 2x Fokker + Aviatik, force landed nr Rafa	Capt F F Minchin - OK
Martinsyde G100	7476		7 Dec 1916	16 Jan 1917	Bombing raid on Beersheba, pilot's goggles blown off by shrapnel, crashed on landing	Lt A J L Barlow - OK
Martinsyde G100	7489		6 Jan 1917	9 Jan 1917	Shot down by 3 enemy aircraft 5 miles W Beersheba, crashed in sea	Lt S G Kingsley - OK
Martinsyde G100	7490		18 Jan 1917	15 May 1917	to X Air Park	
Martinsyde G100	A1576		1 Feb 1917	26 Feb 1917	to X Air Park	
Martinsyde G102	A1577		25 Jan 1917	19 Mar 1917	Force landed and caught fire	2Lt H Kirby - injured
Martinsyde G102	A1582		9 Mar 1917	19 Apr 1917	Broke up in mid-air during air combat	Capt F H V Bevan - killed
Martinsyde G102	A1589		12 Mar 1917	28 Mar 1917	Shot down by hostile a/c over Gaza, ditched in sea	Lt G C Dell-Clarke - OK

APPENDIX 1

A/C Type	Serial No	Sqn Code	Date On	Date off	Comments	Crew
Martinsyde G102	A1590		17 Mar 1917	24 Mar 1917	Shot down by AA Fire - ditched in Sea 4 miles N Ashkelon	Lt W E L Seward - OK
Martinsyde G102	A1591		25 Mar 1917	19 Jun 1917	to X Air Park	
Martinsyde G102	A1593		23 Apr 1917	24 May 1917	[Mount Lofty, South Australia] Transferred to 67 Sqn	
Nieuport 17	B1584		22 Mar 1918	18 Sep 1918	to X Air Park	
Nieuport 23	B1545		22 Mar 1918	11 May 1918	to X Air Park	
Nieuport 23	B1637		6 Jul 1918	2 Aug 1918	to X Air Park	
Nieuport 23	B1645		30 Jul 1918	16 Oct 1918	Transferred to 20 Wing ARS	
Nieuport 23	B3554		22 Mar 1918	15 May 1918	to X Air Park	
Nieuport 23	B3580		30 Jul 1918	19 Oct 1918	Transferred to 5 FS Heliopolis	
Nieuport 23bis	B3593		12 Jul 1918	16 Oct 1918	Transferred to 20 Wing ARS	
Nieuport 23bis	B3591			16 Oct 1918	Transferred to 20 Wing ARS	
Nieuport 23	B3644		25 Jun 1918	19 Oct 1918	Transferred to 20 Wing ARS	
Vickers FB 19 Mk2	A5231		3 Jun 1917	7 Aug 1917	Transferred to 111 Sqn	
Vickers FB 19 Mk2	A5232		2 Jun 1917	22 Jun 1917	to X Air Park	
Vickers FB 19 Mk2	A5234		22 Jun 1917	7 Aug 1917	Transferred to 111 Sqn	
Bristol F2b Fighter	B1147		12 Feb 1920			
Bristol F2b Fighter	B1198	●	23 Feb 1922	Apr 1922	Crashed into hangar Ramleh	
Bristol F2b Fighter	C764		30 Jan 1925	Nov 1925		
Bristol F2b Fighter	C802	♥	Nov 1924	1925		
Bristol F2b Fighter	C981					
Bristol F2b Fighter	C1049	♥	3 May 1923	21 Dec 1923	Engine failed while flying Damascus-Ramleh, forced landed in lava country	Fg Off S D Culley, AC1 Dannatt
Bristol F2b Fighter	CR4651		22 Apr 1924	5 Sep 1924	Crashed into hangar Ramleh	
Bristol F2b Fighter	D7815			29 Apr 1925		
Bristol F2b Fighter	D7839		1922			
Bristol F2b Fighter	D7924		4 Feb 1920			
Bristol F2b Fighter	D8058	chequer	Oct 1924 Dec 1926	15 Jun 1925 Jan 1928		
Bristol F2b Fighter	E2288	\	1 Feb 1920	18 Apr 1921	Forced landed and crashed after petrol tube broke and throttle jammed note - appears in Kidd logbook 30/8/1921	Plt Off J C Bulteel & Plt Off B W T Hare both unhurt
Bristol F2b Fighter	E2290			22 Feb 1920	EF, FL Kilo 99, u/c torn off	
Bristol F2b Fighter	E2293		1 Feb 1920	14 Jun 1920	Missing Ramleh to Ismailia, flew off course, Force landed in Sinai Desert, 30 miles W Nekhl, Palestine	Fg Off N Fitzgerald-Eager NZ died of exposure & AC1 PWJ Thackery killed
Bristol F2b Fighter	F4285		27 May 1925			
Bristol F2b Fighter	F4349		May 1925	Nov 1925		
Bristol F2b Fighter	F4459	♦	Jul 1923	3 Sep 1923	Crashed on turn, Abu Sueir	
Bristol F2b Fighter	F4488		1919			
Bristol F2b Fighter	F4502		by Nov 1924	17 Jan 1925	Crashed - error of judgement by pilot	Fg Off RRH Bruce - killed, LAC A Sutton - injured
Bristol F2b Fighter	F4512		Dec 1923	Oct 1925		
Bristol F2b Fighter	FR4583		Jan 1925	Oct 1925		
Bristol F2b Fighter	FR4600		Nov 1925			

A/C Type	Serial No	Sqn Code	Date On	Date off	Comments	Crew
Bristol F2b Fighter	F4612	●	Feb 1922	May 1923	Crashed	
Bristol F2b Fighter	F4651		1922			
Bristol F2b Fighter	F4702		1 Feb 1926			
Bristol F2b Fighter	F4709		Feb 1922			
Bristol F2b Fighter	F4710		by Aug 1922			
Bristol F2b Fighter	F4712	★	Aug 1924	Oct 1925		
Bristol F2b Fighter	F4889		1921			
Bristol F2b Fighter	F4910	chequer	Jul 1922	Mar 1923	U/c collapsed landing, 9 Feb 1923 (repaired)	
Bristol F2b Fighter	F4912		1922			
Bristol F2b Fighter	F4919		May 1922	Oct 1922		
Bristol F2b Fighter	FR4920	♦	1923			
Bristol F2b Fighter	F4927		Nov 1921	May 1922		
Bristol F2b Fighter	F4939	chequer	Nov 1924			
Bristol F2b Fighter	H1451			14 Feb 1922	Transferred to 208 Sqn	
Bristol F2b Fighter	H1465		Jul 1922			
Bristol F2b Fighter	H1467		Feb 1922	25 May 1922	Crashed	
Bristol F2b Fighter	H1491		Mar 1921	Jun 1922		
Bristol F2b Fighter	H1502	♠	Oct 1922	Jul 1923		
Bristol F2b Fighter	H1504			30 Sep 1921	Engine failed on take-off, LG1 Jerusalem	Fg Off W Elliott DFC & Mr Vernon both injured
Bristol F2b Fighter	H1526	\	Apr 1921	Jun 1921		
Bristol F2b Fighter	H1533	chequer		14 Apr 1921	Engine failed, stalled, crashed, Ramleh	Fg Of P J Cox killed & Fg Off C Pilkington seriously injured
Bristol F2b Fighter	H1534			26 Feb 1921	Stalled on landing, Ramleh	Fg Off A Jerrard VC, AC1 G Reeve, both uninjured
Bristol F2b Fighter	H1564		by Feb 1922			
Bristol F2b Fighter	H1609	♦	1 Apr 1925			
Bristol F2b Fighter	H1628		Sep 1922	Dec 1923		
Bristol F2b Fighter	H1646		Jul 1922	Sep 1922		
Bristol F2b Fighter	H1649		1922			
Bristol F2b Fighter	H1651		2 Nov 1922		Rebuilt as HR1651	
Bristol F2b Fighter	HR1651	chequer	Jul 1922	Aug 1923		
Bristol F2b Fighter	H1653		Feb 1922	3 Feb 1922	Overturned landing, Jerusalem	Flt Lt C D Pyne, Fg Off Jarvis - OK
Bristol F2b Fighter	H1654		1921			
Bristol F2b Fighter	H1661			30 Sep 1921	Flew into bank on edge of aerodrome, LG1 Jerusalem	
Bristol F2b Fighter	H1664		May 1922	Nov 1922		
Bristol F2b Fighter	H1672		Nov 1921			
Bristol F2b Fighter	H1676			26 Aug 1921	Engine failed, forced landed, LGl Jerusalem	
Bristol F2b Fighter	H1677		Jun 1922	Mar 1923		
Bristol F2b Fighter	H1681		Oct 1921	Dec 1922		
Bristol F2b Fighter	H1684		29 Jan 1923	Dec 1923		
Bristol F2b Fighter	J6589		19 Dec 1922	Jan 1923		
Bristol F2b Fighter	J6592		Jul 1923			
Bristol F2b Fighter	J6593		Jul 1923 May 1925	May 1924 Jan 1926	Crashed on landing Beersheba 9 Sep 1923, returned to Ramleh by road	
Bristol F2b Fighter	J6602		Dec 1923	29 Apr 1925		
Bristol F2b Fighter	J6606			2 Oct 1924	Ballast shifted, spun in from 300ft, Heliopolis	Fg Off C Bousfield killed
Bristol F2b Fighter	J6618		Nov 1924			
Bristol F2b Fighter	J6619	\	May 1923	3 Oct 1923	Force landing after engine failed between Lydd & Ramleh	Fg Off R R H Bruce & Flt Lt V R Gibbs both unhurt

APPENDIX 1

A/C Type	Serial No	Sqn Code	Date On	Date off	Comments	Crew
Bristol F2b Fighter	J6633			Dec 1929	Broke V-strut landing Ramleh	
Bristol F2b Fighter	JR6635		20 Jun 1925			
Bristol F2b Fighter	J6648	♥	May 1924			
Bristol F2b Fighter	JR6726		17 Jul 1925			
Bristol F2b Fighter	J6767					
Bristol F2b Fighter	J6798		by Jan 1925			
De Havilland 9A	E827	B3	Jul 1926	Jul 1927		
De Havilland 9A	E829		22 Jun 1926			
De Havilland 9A	ER850		Dec 1927	Apr 1928		
De Havilland 9A	E865		May 1928	Oct 1928	Crashed	
De Havilland 9A	E870		May 1928	May 1928	Overturned Burka, burnt on site	Gp Capt L W B Rees VC -OK
De Havilland 9A	E877		by Sep 1923		To UK	
De Havilland 9A	E941		Sep 1923			
De Havilland 9A	ER959		Jul 1928	May 1929		
De Havilland 9A	E8596		Jul 1928		Crashed	
De Havilland 9A	E8675		Jan 1928	Oct 1928		
De Havilland 9A	E8681		Nov 1925	Aug 1926		
De Havilland 9A	E8688		Oct 1929			
De Havilland 9A	E8713		Sep 1923	Oct 1928	To 30 Sqn	
De Havilland 9A	E8744	A	16 Nov 1925	4 Feb 1927	Crashed on nose	
De Havilland 9A	E9922		May 1928	Apr 1930		
De Havilland 9A	E9937		Feb 1925			
De Havilland 9A	H44	B	Feb 1922			
De Havilland 9A	H85		27 Jun 1924	30 Dec 1924	Undershot, struck railway and overturned, Ramleh	Fg Off F C T Rowe slightly injured & LAC G Harding unhurt
De Havilland 9A	H144		Aug 1929	Sep 1929		
De Havilland 9A	H151			26 Jun 1924	Spun in, caught fire & burnt out at LG 'D'	Fg Off R C Creamer DFC & LAC F C Perrin both killed
De Havilland 9A	H163		Sep 1925			
De Havilland 9A	H3453	♦	12 Nov 1925			
De Havilland 9A	H3519		Jan 1927	Jul 1927	To 47 Sqn	
De Havilland 9A	HR3542		Oct 1926	Jul 1928		
De Havilland 9A	H3570		Aug 1929	Sep 1929		
De Havilland 9A	H3635		Nov 1926	Jul 1927		
De Havilland 9A	J6966		Sep 1927	Oct 1928		
De Havilland 9A	J7012		Jun 1927	Dec 1928		
De Havilland 9A	J7022		Feb 1926	Jul 1926		
De Havilland 9A	JR7024	swastika	4 Oct 1926	1928	Overturned and wrecked	Fg Off P deC Festing-Smith
De Havilland 9A	JR7035		Oct 1928	May 1930		
De Havilland 9A	J7067		May 1928	Nov 1929		
De Havilland 9A	J7068		May 1928	Jun 1929		
De Havilland 9A	J7070		10 Jun 1926	Sep 1927		
De Havilland 9A	JR7084	N		1933		
De Havilland 9A	J7086		Oct 1929	Oct 1929	Crashed	
De Havilland 9A	J7092		Sep 1926	Dec 1926	Rebuilt as JR7092 to 4FTS	
De Havilland 9A	J7094		Apr 1926		To 47 Sqn	
De Havilland 9A	JR7101		Sep 1925	Oct 1925	To 55 Sqn	
De Havilland 9A	J7104		May 1928	Apr 1929		

A/C Type	Serial No	Sqn Code	Date On	Date off	Comments	Crew
De Havilland 9A	J7106		May 1925	Aug 1925	To 4FTS Abu Sueir	
De Havilland 9A	J7108			17 Apr 1926	Crashed during dual instruction at Amman	Sqn Ldr H A Tweedie OBE AFC& Flt Lt S H Wallage MC both killed
De Havilland 9A	J7115			Aug 1924	To 84 Sqn	
De Havilland 9A	J7116		Jul 1929	Nov 1929	To 4 FTS Abu Sueir	
De Havilland 9A	J7126		Jul 1925	Aug 1925		
De Havilland 9A	J7251		4 Feb 1927	Jun 1927		
De Havilland 9A	J7252		22 Mar 1928			
De Havilland 9A	J7253				To 84 Sqn	
De Havilland 9A	J7254		Aug 1929	Feb 1930	Crashed	
De Havilland 9A	J7257		Jul 1926	Feb 1927	AD Aboukir	
De Havilland 9A	J7303		Aug 1926	Apr 1927		
De Havilland 9A	J7320		24 Jun 1925	Sep 1925	To 55 Sqn	
De Havilland 9A	J7327		May 1928	May 1929		
De Havilland 9A	J7337		14 Sept 1926 May 1927	13 Feb1927 7 July 1928	Crashed Nablus, repaired. To AD Aboukir	
De Havilland 9A	J7615		Oct 1928	Jan 1929		
De Havilland 9A	J7818		26 Aug 1929	12 Sep 1929	From 4 FTS During Palestine Disturbances	
De Havilland 9A	J7823		May 1928	May 1929		
De Havilland 9A	J7825		Oct 1928	Mar 1930	Crashed into building while landing Amman	
De Havilland 9A	J7826		Feb 1927	Apr 1927	To 84 Sqn	
De Havilland 9A	JR7827		May 1928	May 1929		
De Havilland 9A	J7829		Mar 1927 8 Nov 1929	Oct 1927		
De Havilland 9A	J7831	O	May 1927	1928	To 45 Sqn	
De Havilland 9A	JR7832		1 Mar 1930	1 Jun 1930		
De Havilland 9A	J7833		May 1928	31 Aug 1928	Stalled on take off, dived in and burnt out	Sgt V R Saunders, LAC F W Fletcher - killed
De Havilland 9A	J7834		Jun 1927	Sep 1927		
De Havilland 9A	J7839		Mar 1928		To 84 Sqn	
De Havilland 9A	J7840		Apr 1926	Jul 1926	To 45 Sqn	
De Havilland 9A	J7841		Apr 1926	Sep 1926	To 45 Sqn	
De Havilland 9A	J7844		16 Jul 1926	Nov 1927		
De Havilland 9A	J7845		27 Jan 1927			
De Havilland 9A	J7846		29 May 1926	28 Feb 1927	Overturned in soft ground on force landing	Fg Off D Macfadyen, LAC Hirst - OK
De Havilland 9A	J7871		Jun 1926	25 May 1927	Crashed into Met hut, Amman	
De Havilland 9A	JR7873		Apr 1928	Jun 1928		
De Havilland 9A	J7874		Jun 1927	Dec 1927	To 45 Sqn	
De Havilland 9A	J7889		Jun 1927	Dec 1927		
De Havilland 9A	JR8098		May 1929	Oct 1929	To 4 FTS Abu Seir	
De Havilland 9A	J8099					
De Havilland 9A	J8101		Oct 1928	Feb 1930	Crashed	
De Havilland 9A	J8112		May 1928	Dec 1929		
De Havilland 9A	J8140		Dec 1928	25 Mar 1929	Engine Failure 15 Miles SE Ba'ir Wells	
De Havilland 9A	J8141		May 1928	27 Sep 1929	Crash & burnt Kolundia	no injuries
De Havilland 9A	J8156			1929	Crashed	
De Havilland 9A	J8172					
De Havilland 9A	J8187		26 Aug 1929	12 Sep 1929	From 4 FTS During Palestine Disturbances	
De Havilland 9A	J8190					

APPENDIX 1

A/C Type	Serial No	Sqn Code	Date On	Date off	Comments	Crew
De Havilland 9A	JR8197		Oct 1929	1930	To 4 FTS Abu Seir	
De Havilland 9A	JR8203		26 Aug 1929	12 Sep 1929	From 4 FTS During Palestine Disturbances	
Avro Andover	J7262		27 Aug 1927	1 Mar 1928	For trials - returned to UK after evaluation	
Fairey IIIF Mk IVM	J9064			Jul 1931	Crashed on Landing, Amman	
Fairey IIIF Mk IVM	J9140			Jul 1931	Damaged while taxying	
Fairey IIIF Mk IVM	J9642					
Fairey IIIF Mk IVM	JR9645	O		19 Aug 1932	Undershot landing area, Aqaba	Sgt Hayes OK, LAC Robinson dislocated shoulder
Fairey IIIF Mk IVM	J9654		Aug 1929	10 Aug 1931	Collided with stationary aicraft while taxying, Amman	Plt Off R M Smith
Fairey IIIF Mk IVM	J9657			1932		
Fairey IIIF Mk IVM	J9659		Feb 1930	Aug 1931		
Fairey IIIF Mk IVM	J9660		Nov 1929	Feb 1931		
Fairey IIIF Mk IVM	J9661		Aug 1929	29 Apr 1932	Dual controls. Crashed while practising forced landing	Sgt R W McCheyne OK
Fairey IIIF Mk IVM	J9670		Feb 1931	Aug 1932		
Fairey IIIF Mk IVM	J9792		Oct 1930	Apr 1931	Crashed	Sgt Neal, Sgt Howe slight injuries
Fairey IIIF Mk IVM	J9793	R	Sep 1930		Crashed rebuilt as JR9793	
Fairey IIIF Mk IVM	JR9793		Jun 1930	Dec 1932		
Fairey IIIF Mk IVM	J9794	N	Feb 1930	Jul 1930	Crashed rebuilt as Gordon JR9794	
Fairey IIIF Mk IVM	J9795		Feb 1930	May 1930	Accident	
Fairey IIIF Mk IVM	J9801		Jun 1930	24 Oct 1931	Damaged during forced landing 8 miles S Wadi Rum	
Fairey IIIF Mk IVM	J9803		Apr 1930	Jun 1932		
Fairey IIIF Mk IVM	J9804		Apr 1930	Feb 1932		
Fairey IIIF Mk IVM	J9805	G	Apr 1930			
Fairey IIIF Mk IVM	J9806		Apr 1930	Mar 1932		
Fairey IIIF Mk IVM	J9808					
Fairey IIIF Mk IVM	J9810					
Fairey IIIF Mk IVM	J9811		Apr 1930			
Fairey IIIF Mk IVM	J9812		Apr 1930			
Fairey IIIF Mk IVM	J9813		Apr 1930			
Fairey IIIF Mk IVM	J9814			23 May 1932	While returning from depot, spun in from steep LH turn 2 miles N Gaza. Aircraft subsequently rebuilt as JR9814	F/O E V N Bramley (pilot) LAC Moore killed, LAC L C Menet - OK
Fairey IIIF Mk IVM	J9818		Jun 1930	Apr 1931		
Fairey IIIF Mk IVM	J9819		Jan 1931	Mar 1932		
Fairey IIIF Mk IVM	J8926	L	Jun 1931	Jun 1932		
Fairey IIIF Mk IVM	J9829	M		Aug 1932	Rebuilt as a Gordon	
Fairey IIIF Mk IVM	J9830		Jan 1932	Apr 1932		
Fairey IIIF Mk IVM	K1158					
Fairey IIIF Mk IVB	K1702					
Fairey IIIF Mk IVB	K1703	1	23 Dec 1931	30 Mar 1932	East African Cruise	
Fairey IIIF Mk IVB	K1704	2	23 Dec 1931	30 Mar 1932	East African Cruise	
Fairey IIIF Mk IVB	K1705	3	23 Dec 1931	30 Mar 1932	East African Cruise	
Fairey IIIF Mk IVB	K1713	4	23 Dec 1931	30 Mar 1932	East African Cruise	
Fairey IIIF MkI	SR1143		Aug 1929		Dual controls	
Fairey IIIF MkI	SR1175					
Fairey IIIF MkI	S1178		Nov 1929	Dec 1930	Crashed Amman	

A/C Type	Serial No	Sqn Code	Date On	Date off	Comments	Crew
Fairey IIIF MkI	S1181	N3				
Fairey IIIF MkI	S1183	N1	Nov 1929	4 Dec 1930	Crashed while taking off in hilly ground north of Ma'an	no injuries
Fairey IIIF MkI	S1191					
Fairey IIIF MkI	S1192		Nov 1929	1930		
Fairey IIIF MkI	S1193		Aug 1929			
Fairey IIIF MkI	S1197		Nov 1929	27 Oct 1930	Olio and bottom longerons damaged in landing accident	
Fairey IIIF MkI	S1199		Aug 1930	Dec 1931		
Fairey IIIF MkI	S1204		Apr 1930	20 Aug 1930	Force landed & crashed	
Gordon Mk I	JR9642					
Gordon Mk I	JR9794		Jul 1936	21 Jul 1936	Ran into ditch while taxying, Jericho	Sgt H J Sooley
Gordon Mk I	JR9801	K				
Gordon Mk I	JR9803			7 Aug 1936	Damaged beyond repair	
Gordon Mk I	JR9808			21 Jan 1937	Tail struck ground during landing at Kolundia	Fg Off M A Aylmer
Gordon Mk I	JR9811		Apr 1935			
Gordon Mk I	JR9829		Aug 1936	17 Aug 1936	Struck boulder taxying after landing Jisr el Mejamie	Plt Off J C M Lunn
Gordon Mk I	K1158					AC Stocks killed
Gordon Mk I	K1159			14 May 1937	Struck off charge - beyond economical repair	
Gordon Mk I	K1713		9 Jun 1931	14 Mar 1936	Struck off charge - beyond economical repair	
Gordon Mk I	KR1715	M	9 Jun 1931			
Gordon Mk I	KR2604	P	2 May 1932	7 May 1937	Engine cut after take-off Amman, crash landed	Fg Off R M Fenwick-Wilson - injured
Gordon Mk I	K2606		12 May 1932	9 Sep 1936	Undershot landing at night and overturned, Jisr el Mejamie LG during night ops - Palestine disturbances	Sgt R H Payne - injured
Gordon Mk I	K2607					
Gordon Mk I	K2608		12 May 1932			
Gordon Mk I	K2609		19 May 1932			
Gordon Mk I	K2610		9 Jun 1932	30 Jan 1937	To 2ASU	
Gordon Mk I	K2611		6 Jun 1932			
Gordon Mk I	K2612		9 Jun 1932	11 Dec 1936	Transferred to 35 Sqn	
Gordon Mk I	KR2613		Aug 1932	10 Aug 1937	Engine cut on take off Temelah LG, hit railway embankment	Sgt C R K Brooks
Gordon Mk I	K2614		Jan 1933	21 Dec 1936	Transferred to 207 Sqn	
Gordon Mk I	K2615		Dec 1932	Jun 1933		
Gordon Mk I	K2616	G	9 Jun 1932	25 Oct 1934	Collided with K2706 in formation	Sgt F C W Rogers
Gordon Mk I	K2618			26 Mar 1937	Collided with K2741 in formation	Sgt F N Heapey
Gordon Mk I	K2620		by Jun 1936			
Gordon Mk I	K2621	E	5 Jul 1932	1938?	Crashed, Wadi Rumm	Sgt R G Morison
Gordon Mk I	K2622			30 Jan 1937	Landed in bad ground at Wadi Halfa, Sudan	Sgt R G Morison
Gordon Mk I	K2623	P		6 Feb 1937	Transferred to Iraq	
Gordon Mk I	K2627		10 Oct 1935	10 Feb 1936	Crashed	
Gordon Mk I	K2630		22 Jul 1932		Transferred to 3 Sqn	
Gordon Mk I	K2631	H				
Gordon Mk I	K2632	K	22 Jul 1932	16 Mar 1937	Struck off charge	
Gordon Mk I	K2633		22 Jul 1932		Sold to New Zealand	
Gordon Mk I	K2635	N		29 Dec 1937	Undershot flarepath at night & landed short, Amman	P/O D C Stapleton
Gordon Mk I	K2636	E	9 Aug 1932	16 Feb 1933	Collided with K2621 after landing at Ma'an	P/O G W Heather

300

APPENDIX 1

A/C Type	Serial No	Sqn Code	Date On	Date off	Comments	Crew
Gordon Mk I	K2637	M	by Feb 1937		Transferred to Iraq	
Gordon Mk I	K2638	C	9 Aug 1932			
Gordon Mk I	K2639	B			Crashed	
Gordon Mk I	K2640		9 Jun 1932	by Aug 1938	Transferred to Ramleh	
Gordon Mk I	K2641		9 Aug 1932	15 Dec 1936	Transferred to 207 Sqn	
Gordon Mk I	K2642		9 Aug 1932	25 Jan 1936	Crashed	
Gordon Mk I	K2643		9 Aug 1932	7 Jun 1936		
Gordon Mk I	K2645		9 Aug 1932	6 Feb 1937	Transferred to Iraq	
Gordon Mk I	K2647	D	3 Sep 1932			
Gordon Mk I	K2706		24 Jan 1933	25 Oct 1934	In collision with K2616 in formation	Flt Lt R W M Clark
Gordon Mk I	K2722	L	4 Jan 1935	2 Sep 1937	Hit boulder on landing, u/c collapsed, Rosh Pinna	Sgt R G Morrison
Gordon Mk I	K2724	A	4 Jan 1935	2 Jun 1937	Flew into ground in circuit Beisan	Plt Off C G S Robinson
Gordon Mk I	K2725	G	4 Jan 1935	18 Jul 1939	Struck off charge - beyond economical repair	
Gordon Mk I	K2738	C	20 Jan 1936		Sold to Egypt	
Gordon Mk I	K2739		30 Jan 1936	by Oct 1937	To Amman Stn Flt	
Gordon Mk I	K2741	A	30 Jan 1936	26 Mar 1937	Collided with K2618 and crashed near Amman	Flt Lt M A Aylmer - OK, AC1 R Walker killed
Gordon Mk I	K2742	R	20 Jan 1936		Sold to New Zealand	
Gordon Mk I	K2744	P				
Gordon Mk II	K3986	M	11 Sep 1935			
Gordon Mk II	K3987					
Gordon Mk II	K3992	F	20 Jan 1936	24 May 1938		
Gordon Mk II	K3993	L	20 Jan 1936			
Gordon Mk II	K3994		20 Jan 1936			
Gordon Mk I	SR1178	O	1 Jul 1934		Crashed Amman	
Gordon Mk I	SR1197			18 Oct 1935	Collided with other aircraft on the ground, Amman	Plt Off F J O Lashbrey
Wellesley Mk I	K7713		7 Jul 1940	1940	Transferred to 47 Sqn	
Wellesley Mk I	K7715		19 Sep 1940	1940	Transferred to 47 Sqn	
Wellesley Mk I	K7722		14 Jun 1940	1940	Transferred to 47 Sqn	
Wellesley Mk I	K7723		11 Jun 1940	1940	Transferred to 47 Sqn	
Wellesley Mk I	K7724		2 Sep 1940			
Wellesley Mk I	K7725		11 Jun 1940	1940	Transferred to 47 Sqn	
Wellesley Mk I	K7726		19 Jun 1940			
Wellesley Mk I	K7731		10 Sep 1940	1940	Transferred to 223 Sqn	
Wellesley Mk I	K7735		25 Jul 1940			
Wellesley Mk I	K7739		30 Jun 1940	1940	Transferred to 47 Sqn	
Wellesley Mk I	K7741		11 Jun 1940			
Wellesley Mk I	K7743		7 Jun 1939	14 Jun 1940	Took off 1500hrs, for single-seat dive bombing attack on Massawa airfield. Shot down by CR42	Plt Off R P B H Plunkett missing
Wellesley Mk I	K7749	BF-X	8 Jun 1938	21 Jul 1939	Engine cut, undercarriage collapsed in heavy landing at night , Beersheba	Plt Off M MacKenzie
Wellesley Mk I	K7751		6 Jul 1939	28 Sep 1939	Engine fail at 500't, belly landed 3nm N of Ismailia	Plt Off M MacKenzie
Wellesley Mk I	K7752			27 Mar 1940	Engine cut on take off, hit windsock mast, Aboukir	Flt Lt D C Stapleton AFC, Sgt J A Burcher, Sgt D Farrell OK
Wellesley Mk I	K7755			9 Sep 1940	Engine failed during air test - belly landed Port Sudan	Fg Off T G Rhodes
Wellesley Mk I	K7757		21 Jul 1938	15 Aug 1940	Stalled on landing at Port Sudan due to uneven fuel in wing tanks	Plt Off D M Illsley
Wellesley Mk I	K7758		19 Aug 1938			
Wellesley Mk I	K7759		1 Jul 1938	1940	Transferred to 47 Sqn	

A/C Type	Serial No	Sqn Code	Date On	Date off	Comments	Crew
Wellesley Mk I	K7763		5 Sep 1940	10 Sep 1940	Took off 1115hrs to bomb Kassala. Shot down by 2 x CR42 at 1350 hrs	Plt Off J A Ferguson PoW, Plt Off J Lynch, Sgt T Conway - both killed
Wellesley Mk I	K7764		1 Jul 1938	15 Sep 1940	U/c collapsed on landing, Port Sudan	Plt Off B J Hyde
Wellesley Mk I	K7765		27 Jul 1938	1940	Transferred to 47 Sqn	
Wellesley Mk I	K7767		6 Jul 1940	31 Nov 1940	(A/c hit by AA fire bombing Harmil Island on 22 Aug 1940)	(Plt Off R J Willitts OK, Sgt A H W Matthews killed - 22 Aug 1940)
Wellesley Mk I	K7768		2 Sep 1938	23 Apr 1939	Transferred to 47 Sqn	
Wellesley Mk I	K7769		19 Aug 1938			
Wellesley Mk II	K7770	LY-L	28 Apr 1939	22 Apr 1940	Bounced on landing - crash landed, Amman	Plt Off R J Willitts
Wellesley Mk I	K7773		6 Jun 1940	1940	Transferred to 47 Sqn	
Wellesley Mk I	K7774			1940	Transferred to 223 Sqn	
Wellesley Mk I	K7775			1940	Transferred to 47 Sqn	
Wellesley Mk I	K8529		15 Aug 1940	26 Nov 1940	Transferred to 47 Sqn	
Wellesley Mk I	K8531		27 Aug 1940			
Wellesley Mk I	K8533		2 Sep 1938	15 Aug 1939	Undershot landing, u/c torn off at Amman	Plt Off M MacKenzie
Wellesley Mk I	K8539	R	19 Oct 1940			
Wellesley Mk I	L2622		27 Jun 1940			
Wellesley Mk I	L2626			23 Dec 1938	Inadvertently retracted u/c after landing, Amman	Plt Off J E Gorringe-Smith
Wellesley Mk I	L2631		2 Sep 1940			
Wellesley Mk I	L2643			5 Aug 1938	Wing broke off during air-to-ground firing at Zerka ranges	Sgt R H Sweeting, AC1 W H Crofts - both killed
Wellesley Mk I	L2644	P	20 Jan 1938	28 Oct 1938	Landed downhill, overran runway and hit bank, Amman	Sgt J A Burcher
Wellesley Mk I	L2645		3 Feb 1938	14 Jan 1939	Overshot landing at Ramleh	Plt Off J V Berggren
Wellesley Mk I	L2646	A	3 Feb 1938	3 Jul 1939	Flew into hills Madeba - hills too steep for aircraft performance	Plt Off D A R Elliott
Wellesley Mk II	L2647		11 Jun 1940	3 Oct 1940	Overshot and hit railway cutting while landing at Port Sudan	Sgt J R Taylor
Wellesley Mk I	L2648			19 Apr 1939	Misjudged landing, bounced & crashed, Amman	Plt Off J C G McNab
Wellesley Mk I	L2649		20 Jan 1938			
Wellesley Mk I	L2650		3 Feb 1938		Transferred to 45 Sqn	
Wellesley Mk I	L2651		3 Feb 1938			
Wellesley Mk I	L2652	J/O	3 Feb 1938	3 Jul 1940	Took off 1030 hrs, shot down by CR42 while on recce flt over Dekemhare	Fg Off S G Soderholm, Sgt B L Trayhurn, Flt Sgt J C Dawson missing
Wellesley Mk I	L2653	B	3 Feb 1938	19 Aug 1938	Ran off runway at Azrak, u/c collapsed	Plt Off R R Helsby
Wellesley Mk I	L2654	(BF-)F	12 Feb 1938	1940	Transferred to 223 Sqn	
Wellesley Mk I	L2655	V	12 Feb 1938	13 Feb 1939	Flew into hills in poor weather 3 miles S Wadi Sir	Plt Off L S Bullwinkle, Sgt C J Chick, LAC D J Segrave - killed
Wellesley Mk I	L2656		12 Feb 1938	24 Nov 1939	Engine failed during night landing, Summit Sudan - belly landed	Sgt V C Durant
Wellesley Mk I	L2657		12 Feb 1938			
Wellesley Mk I	L2658		12 Feb 1938	14 Sep 1940	Hit fence on take off from Port Sudan, jettisoned bombs & crash landed	Sgt J A Burcher, Sgt Butler, Cpl W J McConnell - OK
Wellesley Mk I	L2659		12 Feb 1938			
Wellesley Mk I	L2661			27 May 1940	Engine failed - force landed	Plt Off D M Illsley
Wellesley Mk I	L2663	S	1938	11 Oct 1938	U/c collapsed on landing, Amman	Plt Off L S Bullwinkle, Cpl W J McConnell
Wellesley Mk I	L2664			27 Mar 1938	Starboard u/c collapsed while taxying for take off	Plt Off J C G McNab
Wellesley Mk I	L2665	R		11 Jul 1938	Overran runway at night, u/c collapsed - Amman	Plt Off M H T Cook
Wellesley Mk I	L2670	BF-L		21 Jul 1939	Hit ditch landing at night at Beersheba to assist crew of K7749	Plt Off J B LeCavalier - injured
Wellesley Mk I	L2676	D	24 Jun 1940	4 Aug 1940	Hydraulic system damaged & pilot wounded by AA fire over Massawa, belly landing at base	Sgt L A J Patey (injured) LAC Greaves, LAC Martin
Wellesley Mk I	L2689		17 Jun 1940	1 Sep 1940	Took off 0625 hrs for photo recce mission over Harmil Island. Shot down by 3 CR42s	Sgt H N Norris, Sgt B M D'Arcy - PoW, LAC C D Lampard - died of wounds

APPENDIX 1

A/C Type	Serial No	Sqn Code	Date On	Date off	Comments	Crew
Wellesley Mk I	L2691		12 Jul 1940			
Wellesley Mk I	L2693			11 Jul 1939	Heavy landing, Amman bounced but u/c collapsed on second landing	Plt Off J V Berggren
Wellesley Mk I	L2697	(BF-)U	23 Jul 1938	29 Mar 1939	Brakes failed, ran into barbed wire fence, Ma'an	Plt Off R A Green
Wellesley Mk I	L2701			22 May 1940	Heavy landing Port Sudan, u/c collapsed	Sgt L A J Patey
Wellesley Mk I	L2703	B or E	1938	19 Aug 1940	Took off 1030hrs for convoy patrol. Engine failed, ditched near HMS Kimberley at 1653 hrs	Sgt J A Burcher, Sgt G E Dickson, Sgt D Farrell - OK
Wellesley Mk I	L2706	W		24 Mar 1939	Stalled. Heavy landing Helwan	Plt Off A C Godfrey
Wellesley Mk I	L2707	S	14 Aug 1938	6 Sep 1940	U/c collapsed during night landing at Port Sudan	Fg Off T G Rhodes - OK
Wellesley Mk I	L2708	W	11 Jun 1940	16 Sep 1940	U/c collapsed during night landing at Port Sudan	Sgt B T Hopkins - OK
Wellesley Mk I	L2710			1940	Transferred to 47 Sqn	
Blenheim Mk IV	L8874		3 Jan 1941	21 May 1941	Shot down by Me109E during raid on MT Tobruk/Capuzzo road	Sgt J F Matetich, Sgt A A Sutton, Sgt H Jones - killed
Blenheim Mk IV	L9307		4 May 1941	11 May 1941	Crashed on landing at Aboukir after raid on Derna airfield	Sgt G Dickson, Sgt Richie OK, Sgt E Cotton injured
Blenheim Mk IV	L9418		20 Mar 1942	20 Mar 1942	Struck oil drums on night take off from LG116 for raid on Crete, crashed	Sgt K M Dee, Sgt H G Marshall, Sgt J L H du Boulay all RAAF injured
Blenheim Mk IV	N3557		16 Mar 1941		(Transferred to Free French Jan 1941?)	
Blenheim Mk IV	N3581			30 Jan 1942	Crash landed in sand storm nr Bu Amud - 14 Sqn??	Plt Off E Christiansen, Sgt B Pierse, Sgt R Hilditch - OK
Blenheim Mk IV	N3582		19 Dec 1940			
Blenheim Mk IV	R2770		9 Apr 1940	4 Dec 1940	Took off 0430hrs for photo recce Eritrea, shot down by CR42 over Ginda	Fg Off T G Rhodes, Sgt M E F Hitchin, Sgt S C Lewis - killed
Blenheim Mk IV	R2827		28 Aug 1941			
Blenheim Mk IV	R3593		30 Oct 1940	26 Nov 1940	Took off 0450hrs to bomb Nefesit. Damaged by CR42s over Gulf of Zula crash landed 13km north Massawa. Crew rescued by Sqn Ldr D C Stapleton	Fg Off M McKenzie, Sgt M E F Hitchin, Sgt K Ball DFM OK
Blenheim Mk IV	R3733		17 Jun 1941			
Blenheim Mk IV	R3883	R?	22 Jul 1942	26 Aug 1942	Transfer to MU on re-equipment	
Blenheim Mk IV	R3899		19 Sep 1940 14 Mar 1942			
Blenheim Mk IV	T1817		20 Dec 1940		(Fighter version) Transferred to Free French Jan 1941	
Blenheim Mk IV	T1818		13 Dec 1940	8 Feb 1941	Shot down by flak over Asmara	Plt Off P E Renniker, Plt Off H C R Turney, Sgt F G Roy, Plt Off T H Scorror - killed
Blenheim Mk IV	T1819		12 Dec 1940		Transferred to Free French Jan 1941	
Blenheim Mk IV	T1822		14 Dec 1940		Transferred to Free French Jan 1941	
Blenheim Mk IV	T1823		11 Dec 1940		(Fighter version)	
Blenheim Mk IV	T1856		16 Dec 1940	Jul 1942		
Blenheim Mk IV	T1857		2 Dec 1940			
Blenheim Mk IV	T1868		20 Dec 1940	21 Jan 1941	Landed in soft ground at Port Sudan on return from sortie over Eritrea, u/c collapsed	Sgt W Martin, Sgt A Hams, Sgt K Bamber - OK
Blenheim Mk IV	T1877		20 Oct 1940	9 July 1941	Sank into soft sand on landing at Bir El Abd	Flt Lt D M Illsley
Blenheim Mk IV	T1994	LY-G	26 Nov 1940			
Blenheim Mk IV	T2003		1 May 1941	25 May 1941	Shot down by Me109s while attacking Maleme airfield, Crete	Sgt H P Jeudwine, Sgt H Young, Sgt N B Lake - killed
Blenheim Mk IV	T2061			20 Sep 1940	Hit by AA fire over Massawa - port engine failed, force landed	Flt Lt N G Birks, Sgt J P Gillespy, Sgt J LB Cheyne - PoW
Blenheim Mk IV	T2064	A	17 Jun 1941	9 Dec 1941	Lost & ran out of fuel on return from raid on Bomba	Sgt H S Grimsey, Plt Off L Spiller, Sgt B Martell - abandoned OK
Blenheim Mk IV	T2065		11 Nov 1940	25 May 1941	Shot down by Me109s while attacking Maleme Airfield Crete	Flt Lt R A Green, Plt Off A D Browne, Sgt N P Wilson - killed
Blenheim Mk IV	T2115		13 Dec 1940	4 Feb 1941	Took off Port Sudan for raid on Keren-Asmara Road, attacked by Hurricanes & crash landed at Port Sudan	Fg Off M MacKenzie, Sgt D Farrell, Sgt W J McConnell - OK

A/C Type	Serial No	Sqn Code	Date On	Date off	Comments	Crew
Blenheim Mk IV	T2127	K	4 Nov 1941	22 Dec 1941	Engine failed on take off at Gambut, wing hit ground & aircraft crashed	Plt Off P Goode, Plt Off C Hargreaves, Fg Off E P Burdon DFC - OK
Blenheim Mk IV	T2167		9 Nov 1940	14 Dec 1940	Took off 1420 hrs Port Sudan - missing from attack on Zula airfield. Radio message received at 2135 hrs	Sgt B T Hopkins, Sgt J C Hall, Sgt R F Murray - missing
Blenheim Mk IV	T2172			11 Oct 1940	Took off 0825 hrs Port Sudan, engine failed, swung and hit dyke	Flt Lt G D Hill
Blenheim Mk IV	T2173			21 May 1941	Shot down by Me109E during raid on MT Tobruk/Capuzzo road	Plt Off R F Johnson, Sgt M C Fuller, Flt Sgt A M Morrison - killed
Blenheim Mk IV	T2175		21 May 1941		Transferred to 55 Sqn May 1941	
Blenheim Mk IV	T2179		21 Jan 1941		Transferred to 45 Sqn May 1941	
Blenheim Mk IV	T2181		9 Jan 1941	12 Jan 1941	RTB from raid on Asmara with engine failure, damaged in ground collision	Sgt G Dickson, Sgt Cotton, Sgt Edley - OK
Blenheim Mk IV	T2185		29 Nov 1940			
Blenheim Mk IV	T2236	O	17 Jun 1941			
Blenheim Mk IV	T2241		27 Aug 1941	17 Nov 1941	Swung on take off in low visibility at LG15 & hit tent aircraft burnt out	Sgt V C Royals, Plt Off G McKenny, Sgt C C Murfitt OK, but 3 occupants of tent killed
Blenheim Mk IV	T2249		21 May 1941			
Blenheim Mk IV	T2274		1 Mar 1941	10 May 1941	Shot down by CR42s near Sollum	F/Sgt J Taylor, Sgt J Parker, Sgt R Hall - OK
Blenheim Mk IV	T2338		4 May 1941	27 May 1941	Abandoned after becoming lost on return from raid on Maleme airfield	Flt Lt M Mackenzie - missing, Sgt M B Fearn, Sgt W J McConnell rescued by army after 5 days in desert
Blenheim Mk IV	T2346		4 May 1941	21 May 1941	Shot down by Me109E during raid on MT Tobruk/Capuzzo road	Flt Sgt J R Taylor, Sgt J A A Parker, Sgt F A Culham - killed
Blenheim Mk IV	T2387	Y	26 Aug 1941	10 Mar 1942	Force landed in desert on return to LG99 - crew safe	?
Blenheim Mk IV	T2389	E	4 May 1941	4 Jul 1942	Force landed in Desert 80 miles W Wadi Natrum after engine failure on return from attack on Ma'aten Bagush airfield	Sgt T G N Russell, Sgt F V Dyson, Sgt W J Nicholas - OK walked through desert for 3 days
Blenheim Mk IV	T2426		9 Apr 1942			
Blenheim Mk IV	T2428			26 Nov 1941	Tyre burst on landing at LG75, aircraft tipped over	crew OK
Blenheim Mk IV	V5387	G	26 Jan 1942	1 Jul 1942	To MU on re-equipment	
Blenheim Mk IV	V5444		17 Jun 1941	25 Aug 1941	Leaflet raid on Teheran. Engine cut due to lean fuel mixture ran into wall during forced landing Kirkuk	Sqn Ldr D M Illsley DFC, Sgt J H Hibbert, Plt Off E P Burdon DFC - OK
Blenheim Mk IV	V5446	M	22 Feb 1942	16 Mar 1942	Force landed in desert behind enemy lines after starboard engine failed while returning from a bombing raid west of Benghazi	Sqn Ldr A C Mills, Sgt R N Ey RAAF, Sgt J A R Hunt - OK rescued by army after 9 days
Blenheim Mk IV	V5510			25 May 1941	Shot down by Me109s over Souda Bay while attacking Maleme airfield	Lt S R E Forrester, Sgt W A J Fretwell, F/Sgt R F Hall - killed
Blenheim Mk IV	V5511		3 May 1941	21 May 1941	Shot down by Me109E during raid on MT Tobruk/Capuzzo road	Plt Off R G Gilmore, Sgt K J Wilkie, Sgt T K Riley - killed
Blenheim Mk IV	V5573	Z	17 Nov 1941	25 Nov 1941	Tyre burst on landing & u/c collapsed after raid on Sidi Omar	Maj E M Lewis SAAF, Sgt Johnson, Sgt Cooke - OK
Blenheim Mk IV	V5582	R	27 May 1941	12 Jun 1942	Stalled on landing at LG116 u/c collapsed	
Blenheim Mk IV	V5593		25 May 1941	27 May 1941	Crashed in desert after raid on Maleme airfield	Fg Off J B Le Cavalier, Sgt C P A Bury killed, Sgt Page - bailed out OK
Blenheim Mk IV	V5642		15 May 1941			
Blenheim Mk IV	V5649	B	14 Jul 1942		To MU on re-equipment	
Blenheim Mk IV	V5657	O	22 Jan 1942	25 Feb 1942	Damaged by flak over Martuba, caught fire near Bir Hachim and abandoned	Flt Sgt J T Willis DFM OK, Sgt E Barr injured, Sgt H P Tew killed
Blenheim Mk IV	V5770		10 Jun 1941			
Blenheim Mk IV	V5792			19 Aug 1941	Stalled in finals turn, u/c collapsed on heavy landing, Habbaniya	Sqn Ldr J K Buchanan - OK
Blenheim Mk IV	V5925		25 Aug 1941	12 Nov 1941	Crash landed at base after raid on Gazala south, due hydraulic failure	Sgt A Honig, Sgt Brown, Sgt Ford - OK
Blenheim Mk IV	V5947	M	19 Nov 1941	28 Jan 1942	Prop failure - crashed on take off at Mechili for raid on Msus	Sgt R G S Linley, Sgt A J B Humphries, Sgt T G Smail - OK
Blenheim Mk IV	V5949		26 Jun 1942			

APPENDIX 1

A/C Type	Serial No	Sqn Code	Date On	Date off	Comments	Crew
Blenheim Mk IV	V5950	V/M	9 Jun 1941	2 Apr 1942	Engine failed on t/o LG116, u/c raised to stop	Sgt G W Clarke-Hall, Sgt W Bethune, Sgt E G Clarke - OK
Blenheim Mk IV	V5954		7 Mar 1941	7 Mar 1942	Took off at night from LG116 to bomb Tmimi. Flew into ground in haze & exploded	Flt Sgt K W Stevenson, Flt Sgt W V Howey RCAF, Sgt L Johnson - killed
Blenheim Mk IV	V6015	D	19 Nov 1941		Transferred to 162 Sqn May 1942	
Blenheim Mk IV	V6021	V		9 Jul 1942	Crashed on night take off Abu Sueir	Plt Off B K Armstrong, Fg Off J Maurin-Bonnemain, killed, Plt Off R M McCawley - injured
Blenheim Mk IV	V6183	U	27 Aug 1941	17 Dec 1941	Belly landed at El Adem after engine seized & prop detached	Flt Lt H K Keck, Plt Off L Farrow, Sgt M German - OK
Blenheim Mk IV	V6184		17 Jun 1941	3 Mar 1942	Collided with Z7908 during formation practice near LG116 crash landed, repaired & passed on to Groupe Lorraine	?
Blenheim Mk IV	V6231	L	28 Aug 1941	18 Dec 1942	Transferred to 45 Sqn	
Blenheim Mk IV	V6298	Q	10 Mar 1942			
Blenheim Mk IV	V6453		9 Apr 1942	10 Apr 1942	Hit wires on night take off at LG116 to bomb Maleme airfield	Plt Off B S Slade, Plt Off G W Allingame, Sgt G A Lindschau all RAAF - OK
Blenheim Mk IV	V6461	B	20 Nov 1941	17 Dec 1941	Both engines failed while turning finals at El Adem	Sgt T N Archer, Sgt Brown, Sgt Guy - OK
Blenheim Mk IV	V6508	P	27 Nov 1941	18 Dec 1941	Heavy landing at Gambut - u/c collapsed	Plt Off S F Lawson, Plt Off C K Goodwin, Sgt B Alexander - OK
Blenheim Mk IV	Z5761	J	3 May 1941			
Blenheim Mk IV	Z5767		1 Mar 1941			
Blenheim Mk IV	Z5770		3 May 1941	28 Jul 1941	Heavy landing at Nicosia - u/c collapsed	Sgt A Honig & crew OK
Blenheim Mk IV	Z5860	O/G?	24 Nov 1941	14 Dec 1941	Shot down during raid on MT on Derna/Bardia road	Sgt F W Dennis, Flt Sgt W R Campbell, Sgt J A Redfern - killed
Blenheim Mk IV	Z5863		15 Apr 1941	15 Apr 1941	Failed to return from recce of Halfaya & Sollum	Plt Off I Ormiston, Sgt A H L Fraser killed, Sgt E Smith - PoW
Blenheim Mk IV	Z5882	R	17 Jun 1941			
Blenheim Mk IV	Z5886	S	9 May 1941	18 Mar 1942	Struck oil drum on t/o LG116, landed with u/c partly retracted	crew injured
Blenheim Mk IV	Z5893	Q/W	23 Nov 1941	19 Mar 1942	Stalled and crashed after night t/o at LG116 for raid on Crete	Sgt C H Bowling injured, Sgt P Munyard killed, Sgt W J MacMichael died of injuries
Blenheim Mk IV	Z5976		17 Nov 1941			
Blenheim Mk IV	Z5979		3 May 1941	21 May 1941	Shot down by Me109E during raid on MT Tobruk/Capuzzo road	Sgt N W Hoskins, Flt Sgt H W Easton, Sgt W Calver - killed
Blenheim Mk IV	Z6044	X /JK	25 Aug 1941	13 Jun 1942	Missing from night flying practice - became lost after flare path extinguished at LG10 due air raid in progress	Sgt C M Leaver, Flt Sgt H M J Powell, Sgt R J Hehir - missing
Blenheim Mk IV	Z6157		8 Apr 1942			
Blenheim Mk IV	Z6184		17 Jun 1942		V6184??	
Blenheim Mk IV	Z6425	B	20 Apr 1942	15 Jun 1942	Landed with burst tyre - u/c collapsed	Sgt J H Elliott, Sgt C Davies, Sgt C Simmons, P/O H C Ridley, Sgt A Payne (latter 2 rescued from Z9795) - OK
Blenheim Mk IV	Z6428		20 Apr 1942	18 Jul 1942	Engine failed while returning to LG88 after raid on Matruh, crash landed short of flare path	Sqn Ldr R H Moore DFC, Flt Sgt L Bradford, Sgt A J Tucker - OK
Blenheim Mk IV	Z6436	F/V	9 Nov 1941	26 May 1942	Crashed and nosed over at Kabrit - written off	Sgt E S Brown - OK
Blenheim Mk IV	Z6443	C	25 Aug 1941	25 Feb 1942	Ditched off Ras-el-Kanayis after running out of fuel on return from bombing Rubah airfield	Plt Off F R Brown, Sgt C B Young - OK, Sgt R W Danks - injured
Blenheim Mk IV	Z7047	JL	4 Aug 1942	1 Aug 1942	To MU on re-equipment	
Blenheim Mk IV	Z7298		3 Jul 1942	1 Jul 1942	To MU on re-equipment	
Blenheim Mk IV	Z7373	O	19 Mar 1942	9 Aug 1942	To 108 MU on re-equipment	
Blenheim Mk IV	Z7414		8 Apr 1942			
Blenheim Mk IV	Z7417	JL	1 Apr 1942			
Blenheim Mk IV	Z7419	Z	7 Jun 1942	8 Jun 1942	Hit sand hill while beating up sqn bathing party nr Ma'aten Bagush	Sgt J Burt, F/Sgt L L Bernthal - OK
Blenheim Mk IV	Z7485		24 Jun 1942	30 Jun 1942	Hit by Kittyhawk AK753 while parked	Cpl H Gibbons working on aircraft killed
Blenheim Mk IV	Z7514		14 Mar 1942	4 Oct 1942	Ferry flt to 103 MU heavy landing at Luxor	Plt Off C Thomas - OK

305

A/C Type	Serial No	Sqn Code	Date On	Date off	Comments	Crew
Blenheim Mk IV	Z7515		10 Apr 1942			
Blenheim Mk IV	Z7516		19 Jun 1942	19 Jun 1942	Engine failure on take off from LG116 for night intruder sortie over Crete	Plt Off B S Slade, Plt Off G W Allingame, Sgt G A Lindschau - OK
Blenheim Mk IV	Z7517	Z	11 Apr 1942	13 Jun 1942	Missing from night flying practice - became lost after flare path extinguished at LG10 due air raid in progress	Sgt G F Highman, Sgt W D Lynch, Sgt W L Carnie - killed
Blenheim Mk IV	Z7518		16 Jun 1942			
Blenheim Mk IV	Z7591		21 Jul 1942			
Blenheim Mk IV	Z7627	Y		30 Mar 1942	Shot down into the sea by Hurricanes	Flt Lt H K Keck RAAF, Flt Sgt J H Hibbert, Flt Sgt G P Rylands - killed
Blenheim Mk IV	Z7631	N	10 Mar 1942	15 Aug 1942	To 108 MU on re-equipment	
Blenheim Mk IV	Z7690	N	27 Jan 1942			
Blenheim Mk IV	Z7701	Z	18 Dec 1941			
Blenheim Mk IV	Z7709	JM	8 Jun 1942			
Blenheim Mk IV	Z7712		4 Jul 1942	6 Jul 1942	Crash landed after damage during attack on MT near Fuka	Sqn Ldr A N Pirie, Sgt J Beckett - OK, Sgt W J Bartholomew killed
Blenheim Mk IV	Z7789	RT	18 Jul 1942	18 Jul 1942	To MU on re-equipment	
Blenheim Mk IV	Z7798		16 Jun 1942			
Blenheim Mk IV	Z7841	K	15 Jun 1942	27 Aug 1942	To 108 MU on re-equipment	
Blenheim Mk IV	Z7893	U	8 Jan 1942	4 Mar 1942	Hit Officers' Mess tent during beat up of LG116 & crashed	Fg Off J A Harvie - killed
Blenheim Mk IV	Z7908	L	22 Feb 1942	3 Mar 1942	Collided with V6184 during formation practice near LG116 crash landed	Sqn Ldr L E Leon injured, Flt Sgt J H Hibbert, F/Sgt G P Rylands - OK
Blenheim Mk IV	Z7917		5 Jul 1942			
Blenheim Mk IV	Z7952		21 Jul 1942			
Blenheim Mk IV	Z7963		18 Apr 1942	18 Apr 1942	Crashed while attempting force landing in haze near Sidi Barani	2Lt P J Chapman, Sgt D W McConville, Sgt R R Richardson - killed
Blenheim Mk IV	Z7970	P	8 Jan 1942			
Blenheim Mk IV	Z7989	R	25 Feb 1942	25 Jul 1942		
Blenheim Mk IV	Z7991			17 Mar 1942	Collided with T2124 while forming up over LG140 for shipping strike crashed near Bir-el-Baheira	Flt Sgt R G S Linley, Sgt A J B Humphries, Sgt T G Smail RAAF - killed
Blenheim Mk IV	Z7992	K	4 Feb 1942		To MU on re-equipment	
Blenheim Mk IV	Z8936		3 Aug 1942		To MU on re-equipment	
Blenheim Mk IV	Z9543		17 Nov 1941	18 Nov 1941	Failed to return from raid on Bir El Baheira	Fg Off C D Loughlin, Plt Off E D Main, Fg Off A Franks - missing
Blenheim Mk IV	Z9576	E	18 Nov 1941			
Blenheim Mk IV	Z9584	H	22 Nov 1941			
Blenheim Mk IV	Z9614		1 Aug 1942	1 Aug 1942	Shot down near Fuka	Plt Off A F Ellis, Sgt H B A Langmaid, Sgt M German - injured PoW
Blenheim Mk IV	Z9647		22 Jul 1942			
Blenheim Mk IV	Z9651		1 Aug 1942			
Blenheim Mk IV	Z9655	D	18 Jul 1942	22 Jul 1942	Damaged by flak, u/c collapsed on landing at LG 88	Fg Off R W Lapthorne wounded, Plt Off D L Jones, Plt Off G M King - OK
Blenheim Mk IV	Z9656	J	29 Nov 1941	9 Jun 1942	Crashed in mist near LG116 on return from night intruder sortie over Crete	Fg Off D R W Brooks, Plt Off W E Hickman - injured, Fg Off C R Cowan - killed
Blenheim Mk IV	Z9710		8 Jul 1942			
Blenheim Mk IV	Z9720	Q	18 Jul 1942			
Blenheim Mk IV	Z9722	J	10 Mar 1942	10 Apr 1942	Side-slipped into ground on night t/o LG116 to bomb Maleme airfield	Sgt P D Clauson killed, Sgt C O Thorn, Sgt C R Grandfield - injured
Blenheim Mk IV	Z9729	A	22 Jan 1942	24 Feb 1942	Damaged by 4 Me109s while en route Baheira to LG116, crash landed in the desert	Sgt J H Bosworth, Sgt A Hoyle, Sgt E Curtis (pax) - OK, Sgt R K Swann died of injuries
Blenheim Mk IV	Z9746		7 Jun 1942	12 Jun 1942	Crashed on landing during night circuit flying	Flt Sgt T C Bullock, Plt Off C A North, Sgt J L Mouatt - OK

306

APPENDIX 1

A/C Type	Serial No	Sqn Code	Date On	Date off	Comments	Crew
Blenheim Mk IV	Z9795		10 Mar 1942	15 Jun 1942	Crash landed in desert after return from raid on Crete - no lights at LG10 due air raid in progress	Sqn Ldr A N Pirie, Plt Off H Ridley, Sgt A Payne - all OK
Blenheim Mk IV	Z9817	AB	1 Jul 1942	2 Jul 1942	To MU on re-equipment	
Blenheim Mk IV	Z9826		5 Jul 1942		To MU on re-equipment	
Marauder I	FK109	W	22 Jun 1944	13 Sep 1944	Tyre burst on take off at Alghero; landed wheels up	Plt Off A R Herschell, Flt Sgt F J Harris, Flt Sgt R Ashdown, WO J K Gasteen, Flt Sgt H A O'Donnell, Flt Sgt K G Robertson - OK
Marauder I	FK110	E	13 Mar 1943	9 May 1944	Took off Grottaglie 0858 hrs for recce mission of W Greece & Albania. Presumed shot down by anti-aircraft fire in Adriatic Sea	Sgt J Ross, Sgt W M Green, Flt Sgt A Woods, Flt Sgt E J Ryan, Flt Sgt T Mackrell, Flt Sgt H G Andrews - all missing
Marauder I	FK111	V/TV	15 Aug 1943	21 Apr 1944	Ditched after take-off at Bone. This aicraft was used by Training Flight	?
Marauder I	FK112	L	1 Sep 1942	3 Jun 1943	Took off 0858 hrs and reported that it had sighted a convoy at 1306 hrs E of Sardinia. Convoy protected by 3 fighters, aircraft presumed shot down	Sgt H E Rawlins, Sgt W L Lumsden, Flt Sgt L J Austen, Flt Sgt H E Burton, Flt Sgt J K Nuttal, Flt Sgt E Liddle, - all missing
Marauder I	FK117	C	5 Sep 1942	18 Mar 1943	Crashed at 1505 hrs while practising single-engine circuits at Fayid, Egypt	Sgt C H Fletcher. Sgt P F Lynch - OK, Acting Flt engineer LAC J I Lewis killed
Marauder I	FK118	N/[TE]	7 Oct 1942	21 May 1944	Damaged beyond repair in accident - no further details. This aircraft was used by training Flight	Lt M Overed
Marauder I	FK120	X	18 Oct 1942	7 May 1944	Took off Ghisonaccia 0905 hrs for recce mission	Fg Off A T Smith, Fg Off F J Dell, Flt Sgt O P Lawson, Sgt R E Addis, Flt Sgt W W Rice, Flt Sgt S McLennaghan - all missing
Marauder I	FK121	Y	2 Sep 1942	21 Sep 1944	Transferred to MU	n/a
Marauder I	FK122	P	12 Sep 1942	24 Nov 1942	Tailplane broke off while manoeuvring on the bombing range at Shallufa - aircraft crashed	Fg Off W R Bower, WO D L Rawson, Plt Off P M Willis, Sgt H G Williams Sgt E Cookson - all killed
Marauder I	FK123	J	6 Sep 1942	21 Sep 1944	Transferred to MU	n/a
Marauder I	FK124	Z	9 Apr 1944	13 Sep 1944	Took off in darkness at 0550 hrs at Alghero in wrong direction for night take-offs and flew into a hill shortly after becoming airborne	Fg Off M T Holmes, Plt Off P M Todd, Sgt C S Keefe, Sgt W G H Ellis, Sgt M Irwin, WO W H Scourfield - all killed
Marauder I	FK126	P	21 Sep 1942	3 Feb 1944	Mainwheel broke off and damaged port aileron and pitot head on take-off at Ghisonaccia for airtest; aircraft destroyed during subsequent landing	Plt Off S R Lantinga, Plt Off C A Duncan, Flt Sgt A H James, WO R H Mahood, Flt Sgt PD Musto- all OK
Marauder I	FK127	K	29 Aug 1943	19 Oct 1943	Took off from Grottaglie at 1345 hrs. Crashed in Adriatic at 42.46N 16.26E after aileron failure which caused uncontrollable turn to starboard. Wingtip hit sea	Fg Off A M Cameron, Fg Off G Ingram, Flt Sgt D G Williams, Flt Sgt C V Proud Sgt A I Leslie - killed, Sgt Ritchie, 2nd pilot, rescued by ASR
Marauder I	FK128	B	1 Sep 1943	27 Sep 1943	Took off from Protville for shipping recce at 1030 hrs. Attacked by 2 x Arado 196 at 1411 and 2 x Me109 at 1414 hrs. Crashed on landing at Protville due to damage sustained to undercarriage	Flt Sgt F M Spedding, Sgt P J Boyes, Sgt J Stephenson, Fg Off E W Hills, Sgt W I Pollock all OK
Marauder I	FK130	F	26 Sep 1942	23 Feb 1944	Took off Grottaglie for airtest & film detail 0920 hrs. Port engine failed, aircraft crashed and burnt out	Sqn Ldr H Elsey, Fg Off H D Merkley, Fg Off H C Campbell - all killed, Fg Off A C Bowes, Fg Off J E F Wright DFC (Film Unit) Sgt L A Bulbeck - all injured
Marauder I	FK131	E	8 Oct 1942	15 Dec 1943	Missing from low-level navex – crashed into the sea 15 miles off the coast of Algeria near Cap Bengut	Flt Sgt F R Tuxil, Sgt G F Simpkin, Fg Off W H Davies, Flt Sgt S G Thomas, WO W D Kearney,WO G L Ready - all missing
Marauder I	FK132	S	1 Sep 1943	21 Sep 1944	Transferred to MU	n/a
Marauder I	FK133	A	28 Feb 1943	28 Dec 1943	Took off from Blida at 0800 hrs for recce mission. Levant, last position report 48N 08.30E at 1337 hrs [50km WNW Ajaccio]	Fg Off R W Gilkey, Sgt H E Bryce-Jeffrey, WO R A Billings, Flt Sgt A B Tuttle, WO C Toupin, Flt Sgt D A Thompson - all missing

A/C Type	Serial No	Sqn Code	Date On	Date off	Comments	Crew
Marauder I	FK134	P	29 Apr 1943	5 Jun 1943	Tyre burst on landing, swung & broke back, Blida	Flt Sgt N D Freeman, Flt Sgt R O B Fagan, Flt Sgt A A Jones, Flt Sgt E W Pearce, Flt Sgt H G Hardy, Sgt C V Proud - all OK
Marauder I	FK135	P	24 Apr 1944	21 Sep 1944	Transferred to MU	n/a
Marauder I	FK138	X	5 Jun 1944	21 Sep 1944	Used only 3/4 of available runway at Grottaglie at 0405 hrs struck power cables beyond airfield after take-off and crashed	WO F Elliot, Sgt A K Stewart, Sgt J M Kahle, Sgt R Heller, Flt Sgt H Bates, Flt Sgt C M Taylor - all killed
Marauder I	FK139	M	1 Oct 1942	21 Feb 1943	Shot down by anti-aircraft fire during raid on Milos harbour	Sgt B H Yarwood, Sgt H Walker, Flt Sgt E T H Maclean, Flt Sgt R C Davie, Sgt F Gotheridge, Sgt W J E Glenn - all killed
Marauder I	FK141		8 Jul 1943	8 Jul 1943	Aircraft being ferried to unit from Egypt to Protville. Swung on landing at intermediate stop at Castel Benito, u/c collapsed and aircraft burnt out	Plt Off A J Dolan, Sgt D B Eagle, Sgt E V H Weatherley, Sgt R M Parrack - injured, Sgt D D Harris, Flt Sgt R Lodge, Capt F W Bayliss killed
Marauder I	FK142	R	23 Sep 1942	1 Feb 1944	["**Dominion Triumph**"] Took off 0920 hrs from Ghisonaccia for recce mission Cape Corse - did not return	Flt Sgt M C Reid, Flt Sgt J T Brown, WO A Western, Flt Sgt T N Gilchrist, Flt Sgt W H Carr, Flt Sgt P Daley - all missing
Marauder I	FK143	R	23 Sep 1942	15 Feb 1943	["**Quephelani**"] Engine failure while attacking enemy ship during armed torpedo recce mission from Shallufah - aircraft force landed in Turkey & interned	Lt L C Jones, Flt Sgt J H F Kelly, WO H A Dube, Flt Sgt B J Mack, Sgt J B Ackland, Sgt A Taylor - all safe, interned
Marauder I	FK144	M	18 Feb 1943	21 Sep 1944	Transferred to MU	n/a
Marauder I	FK145	N	21 Oct 1942	21 Sep 1944	Transferred to MU	n/a
Marauder I	FK147	B	1 May 1943	24 Jul 1943	Took off Protville 1147 hrs for shipping recce of Elba, Corsica and Spezia. Ditched after engine damaged by 2 x FW190 off Leghorn	Flt Sgt J D Hunter, Flt Sgt L A John, Flt Sgt R Egan, Flt Sgt L Murphy, Flt Sgt M F Stephens, Sgt R V Jackson - all safe PoW
Marauder I	FK149	D	5 Jan 1943	21 Sep 1944	["**Dominion Thunderer**"] Transferred to MU	n/a
Marauder I	FK150		18 Sep 1942	15 Feb 1943	Took off 1045 hrs Shallufa, with FK143 for recce mission, Aegean. Last communication at 1630 hrs	Plt Off C C Truman, Flt Sgt J I Thompson, Fg Off B T Connell, Flt Sgt R E H Hope, Flt Sgt K Firth, Flt Sgt W J Semple all missing
Marauder I	FK151	O	4 Dec 1942	21 Sep 1944	Transferred to MU	n/a
Marauder I	FK152	S	11 Mar 1943	10 Jul 1943	T/o from Protville to carry out air firing practice over sea. Starboard engine failed and a/c force landed at Bou Ficha at 1030 hrs, aircraft burned out	Fg Off C P M Phillips, Fg Off E J Bertuch, Flt Sgt F V Parker, Sgt E T E Jones, Sgt D M M Rice, killed; Flt Sgt F H Mason injured; Sgt J T Collyer safe
Marauder I	FK153	Q/P	3 Sep 1942	21 Sep 1944	Transferred to MU	n/a
Marauder I	FK154	K	2 Sep 1942	10 Mar 1943	Took off Telergma for transit to Blida at 1000 hrs, but crashed into Bay of Algiers at 1130 hrs. Poss shot down by friendly fire from defences of Algiers harbour while descending below cloud	Sqn Ldr P Goode, Flt Sgt H D Clapson, Flt Lt N T G Beacham, Sgt V Brown, Sgt C V Walkinshaw, Sgt L W Hunt, Fg Off HM Siewert (Sqn Int O), Flt Sgt W Tatlow (NCO ic "A" Flt) LAC D V Bullen - all killed
Marauder I	FK155	V	8 Oct 1942	9 May 1943	Took off Bone 0510 hrs for recce mission over Tyrhennian Sea - shot down	Flt Sgt T G N Russell, Flt Sgt P Fennell, WO F V Dyson, Flt Sgt W J Nicholas, Sgt J W Armstrong, Sgt W H Ayton - all missing
Marauder I	FK156	C	1 Jul 1943	21 Sep 1944	Transferred to MU	n/a
Marauder I	FK157		9 Aug 1942	20 Aug 1942	While landing at LG224 (Cairo West) a truck pulled out in front of aircraft, struck u/c causing aircraft to crash	Lt Col F Garrison & Plt Off J T Willis OK, 4 Egyptians in truck killed
Marauder I	FK159	B/W	27 Oct 1942	19 Apr 1944	Took off Ghisonaccia 0620 hrs for recce mission - shot down by fighters	Fg Off H E V Budge, Fg Off O H M Hall, WO D K Schroder, WO B J MacKinnon, WO J M Power, WO A Hutton - all missing
Marauder I	FK160	P/H	30 Oct 1942	26 May 1943	Starboard mainwheel collapsed on landing, Bone	Flt Sgt H E Rawlins, Sgt W L Lumsden, Flt Sgt L J Austen, Flt Sgt E E Burton, Flt Sgt J H Nuttal, Flt Sgt J Liddle, - all OK
Marauder IA	FK362	H	6 Apr 1943	8 Feb 1944	Took off Grottaglie at 0930 hrs for transit flt to Blida - crashed into the sea en-route	Fg Off G A A Croskell, Sgt K S Milford, Fg Off J H Irwin, Sgt A J Sims, Flt Sgt P Ellenbogen, Flt Sgt J E J B G Lussier, Sgt T C Climpson - all missing

A/C Type	Serial No	Sqn Code	Date On	Date off	Comments	Crew
Marauder IA	FK363	G	12 Dec 1942	27 Jun 1943	Took off Bone 0800 hrs for recce of Corsica & Sardinia - did not return	Plt Off R K Francis DFC, Flt Sgt R G Miles, Fg Off E S Murphy, Flt Sgt I D Carnie, Flt Sgt S G Jellis, Flt Sgt D W Sloggett - all missing
Marauder IA	FK364	B	21 Feb 1943	24 Apr 1943	Took off Bone for recce mission. Engaged by FW190 - port engine failed, starboard engine failed while landing at Tingley, Algeria	Fg Off B S Slade, Fg Off J M MacDonald, Flt Sgt G A Lindschau, Sgt H S Mutch, Sgt F E Lovelace - all OK, Flt Sgt E F Beddell (2nd pilot) died
Marauder IA	FK365	U	28 Feb 1943	21 Sep 1944	Transferred to MU	n/a
Marauder IA	FK366	S	7 Sep 1942	20 Dec 1942	Took off Berka for minelaying operation in Tunis harbour Exploded after being hit by anti-aircraft fire	Plt Off J T Willis DFM - PoW, Sgt S H Porteous, Plt Off R W Barr, Plt Off P B Martell, Sgt F Barrett, Sgt H F Ford - all missing
Marauder IA	FK367	J	6 Sep 1942	16 Dec 1942	T/o Berka 0950 hrs for offensive sweep of Tripolitanian coast. Shot down by 9 Malta based Spitfires 15miles off Benghazi	Sgt L A Einsaar, Sgt L R Dixon, Sgt L B Willcocks - OK, Sgt T E Exell, Sgt R I Ploskin, Sgt P F Cockington, Sgt A E Watts - killed
Marauder IA	FK370	Z/L	11 Sep 1942	3 Dec 1943	["*Dominion Upholder*"] Nosewheel collapsed air test during run-up at Blida, engine caught fire	Flt Lt I D H Gibbins - OK
Marauder IA	FK371	A	6 Sep 1942	25 Apr 1943	Took off Blida for recce mission, Tyrrhenian Sea. Did not return	Flt Sgt T C Bullock, WO F L Trovillo, Plt Off J L Mouatt, Sgt C Warburton, Fg Off D G Bentham, Flt Sgt J S Patman - all missing
Marauder IA	FK373	S	21 Feb 1943	26 Aug 1943	Took off Protville 0712 hrs for recce of Sardinia & Corsica - shot down by Ju52	Fg Off E L Archer, Flt Sgt A R Smith, Fg Off J F Kennedy, Flt Sgt G A Linschau, Sgt J T Jones - all PoW; Sgt A Phethean killed
Marauder IA	FK374		20 Jul 1943	20 Jul 1943	Took off Shallufa for delivery flt to Protville. Ran out of fuel & force landed in the Western Desert 20 miles from Tarhuna, Libya	Fg Off D F Thomas, Fg Off G A A Croskell OK No further details
Marauder IA	FK375	D	22 Sep 1942	3 Jan 1943	["*Dominion Revenge*"] Took off Shallufa 0942 hrs on torpedo armed recce in Aegian Sea. Attacked convoy at 1415 hrs off Aghios Giorgios Is - probably shot down by escorting Me 110	Capt B W Young - PoW, Sgt E A Meadwell, Plt Off J E Foley-Brickley, Plt Off K J Bennett, Flt Sgt D T Ray, Sgt S Hunt - all killed
Marauder IA	FK376	H	7 Sep 1942	10 May 1943	Took off Shallufa for fighter affiliation training flt. Tail broke off at 0930 while circling Abu Sueir airfield, a/c crashed 2m SW Abu Sueir	Plt Off E W McClelland, Sgt G B Wooten, Sgt A Williams, Sgt L C W Finlayson, Sgt E E Blumfield, Sgt R C Quinney, Cpl W F Cooke - all killed
Marauder IA	FK377	Y	8 Oct 1942	21 Feb 1943	Shot down by anti-aircraft fire during raid on Milos harbour	Sgt R A Barton, Flt Sgt N A MacMillan, Plt Off R H Annells, Sgt G Arnold, Sgt F J Armstrong, Sgt R F Bell - all killed
Marauder IA	FK378	G	8 Oct 1942	12 Apr 1943	Took off Blida 0800 hrs for recce mission in Tyrrhenian Sea. Attacked by 2 x FW190, damage caused port engine to fail. Ditched near Island of Ustica, nr Trapani	WO L A Einsaar DFM, Sgt R A Kirkin, Fg Off J C Buckland, Sgt T P Clowry, Sgt L O Harrison DFM - all PoW; Sgt J L Goldsmith GM killed
B26B	117761	Q			["Boomerang"] USAAF - used for training at Telergma	
B26B	117765	C			USAAF - used for training at Telergma	
B26B	117776	V	17 Dec 1943		["Most Likely"] transferred from USAAF to RAF, used for training at Telergma	
B26B	117780	T	27 Sep 1943	29 Mar 1944	Transferred from USAAF. Crashed into sea while investigating German ship off Mataro, Spain.	Fg Off W C Macdonald, Fg Off J W Lewis, Flt Sgt C M Peedom, Flt Sgt R Lanham, Flt Sgt M T Woods, Flt Sgt F R Lamond - all killed
B26B	117796		9 Sep 1943		["Twin Engined Queenie"] Transferred from USAAF to RAF, used for training at Telergma	
B26B	117825	B	19 Sep 1943		Transferred from USAAF to RAF, used for training at Telergma	
B26B	117831				Used for training at Telergma, USAAF inventory crashed, 3 Jun 1944	
B26B-2-MA	117877	P			["*Mary Lou*"] USAAF - used for training at Telergma (written off 11 Sep 1944)	
B26B-2-MA	117897	V	25 Sep 1943		["*Birmingham Blitzkreig IV*"] Transferred from USAAF to RAF	
B26B-2-MA	117900				USAAF (crashed 27 Feb 1944)	

A/C Type	Serial No	Sqn Code	Date On	Date off	Comments	Crew
B26B-3-MA	117958	B	26 Sep 1943	17 Feb 1944	["*Cap'n Blood II*"]Transferred from USAAF to RAF. Crashed on landing at Bone	Plt Off S R Lantinga, Plt Off C A Duncan, Plt Off A S Tait, Flt Sgt A H James, WO R H Mahood, Flt Sgt P D Musto- all OK
B26B-4-MA	117977	R	25 Sep 1943		Transferred from USAAF	
B26B-3-MA	117978	Q	26 Sep 1943		["*Flak Eater*"] Transferred from USAAF to RAF	
B26B-3-MA	118017	G	18 Sep 1943	1 Jul 1944	["*Devil's Playmate*"] Transferred from USAAF to RAF. Took off Grottaglie 0515 hrs for a recce of the Gulf of Venice & Ancona. Did not return	Flt Lt N Cornish, Fg Off K Davis, Flt Lt J D Phillips, Plt Off J E F Wall, WO W W McKeown, Flt Sgt A Finn - all killed
B26B-4-MA	118031	TM	18 Sep 1943		Transferred from USAAF to RAF, used for training at Telergma	
B26B-4-MA	118037	A	18 Sep 1943		Transferred from USAAF to RAF	
B26B-4-MA	118039	Z	31 Aug 1943	26 Aug 1944	Transferred from USAAF to RAF. Took off Alghero 1052 hrs. Crashed into the sea half mile W Asinara Isle off NW tip Sardinia on recovery to Alghero after patrol.	Lt M J W Brummer (SAAF), Flt Sgt A Allsop, Flt Sgt D Flack, Sgt J O Heath, Sgt D Martin, WO D Edwards - all killed
B26B-4-MA	118041	B	31 Aug 1943		["*Daisy June II*"] Transferred from USAAF to RAF	
B26B-4-MA	118046				USAAF - used for training at Telergma (written off 17 Sep 1944)	
B26B-4-MA	118197				USAAF - used for training at Telergma (writen off 17 Sep 1944)	
Marauder II	FB503	F	1 Jun 1944	21 Sep 1944	Transferred to MU	
Marauder III	HD457	B	30 Jun 1944	21 Sep 1944	Transferred to MU	n/a
Marauder III	HD468	H	30 Jun 1944	19 Sep 1944	Tyre burst on take-off at Ciampino - u/c collapsed	Wg Cdr E Donovan DFC, Fg Off W G Notman, Plt Off J W Halkett DFM, Plt Off C R Butler-Mason, WO R D Pocock, Sgt J G Hopwood - all OK
Marauder III	HD470	T	25 May 1944	21 Sep 1944	Transferred to MU	n/a
Marauder III	HD487	E	30 Jun 1944	21 Sep 1944	Transferred to MU	n/a
Marauder III	HD488	A	1 Jun 1944	21 Sep 1944	Transferred to MU	n/a
Marauder III	HD489	F	25 May 1944	21 Sep 1944	Transferred to MU	n/a
Marauder III	HD491		30 Jun 1944	21 Sep 1944	Transferred to MU	n/a
Marauder III	HD498	E	30 Jun 1944	21 Sep 1944	Transferred to MU	n/a
Marauder III	HD503		30 May 1944	21 Sep 1944	Transferred to MU	n/a
Marauder III	HD508	C	25 May 1944	21 Sep 1944	Transferred to MU	n/a
Marauder III	HD538		30 Jun 1944	21 Sep 1944	Transferred to MU	n/a
Marauder III	HD548	S	22 May 1944	5 Aug 1944	Swung on take-off at Foggia and collided with USAAF Liberator	Flt Sgt P J Boyes, Sgt M C W James, WO J M J Rowland, Sgt J Stevenson, Sgt W L Pollock, Flt Sgt J P McGlyn - OK
Marauder III	HD595	G	29 Jun 1944			
Marauder III	HD596		30 Jun 1944			
Marauder III	HD598	D	30 Jun 1944	21 Sep 1944	Transferred to MU	n/a
P51-2 Mustang	137364		28 Apr 1943	16 Jun 1943		
P51-2 Mustang	137368		17 May 1943	16 Jun 1943		
P51-2 Mustang	137369		29 Apr 1943	16 Jun 1943		
P51-2 Mustang	137370		13 May 1943	16 Jun 1943		
P51-2 Mustang	137414		28 Apr 1943	16 Jun 1943		
P51-2 Mustang	137429		6 May 1943	16 Jun 1943		
Boston MkIII	Z2183		Jul 1942	Jul 1942	used for conversion training	
Boston MkIII	Z2259		Jul 1942	Jul 1942	used for conversion training	
Boston MkIII	Z2278		Jul 1942	Jul 1942	used for conversion training	
Boston MkIII	AL759		Jul 1942	Jul 1942	used for conversion training	
Boston MkIII	AL717		Jul 1942	Jul 1942	used for conversion training	

APPENDIX 1

A/C Type	Serial No	Sqn Code	Date On	Date off	Comments	Crew
Walrus	L2214		22 Jun 1940			
Wellington GR XIV	HF123	CX-M	25 Oct 1944	24 Jan 1945	Attempted to take-off with full nose down trim; failed to get airborne and raised u/c to stop. Caught fire & burnt out	Fg Off R W Stewart, Flt Sgt J E Hardie, Fg Off S Hastewell, Flt Sgt C B Lloyd, Flt Sgt S Hibbard, Flt Sgt J G Hopwood - OK
Wellington GR XIV	HF196	CX-M	22 Jan 1945	26 Mar 1945	Cat B	
Wellington GR XIV	HF197	CX-Y	20 Nov 1944	14 Dec 1944	Take off power was applied with full forward stick against brakes (as per Marauder) - aircraft tipped onto nose	Fg Off J P Robertson & crew - OK
Wellington GR XIV	HF312	CX-H	11 Feb 1945	6 Apr 1945	Cat B	
Wellington GR XIV	HF386	CX-F	2 Dec 1944	25 May 1945	Cat AC	
Wellington GR XIV	HF387	CX-D	25 Nov 1944	14 Mar 1945	Cat B	
Wellington GR XIV	HF393	CX-B	25 Nov 1944	25 May 1945	Struck off charge	
Wellington GR XIV	HF415	CX-Q	20 Nov 1944	26 Jan 1945	To SE Trg Unit	
Wellington GR XIV	HZ770	CX-N	1 Jan 1945	23 Feb 1945	Cat B	
Wellington GR XIV	MF386					
Wellington GR XIV	MF450	CX-C	21 Nov 1944	24 Jan 1945	Crashed into sea North of Lundy Island at 0230hrs during night training with RN minesweeper. Radar Altimeter was u/s	Fg Off C J Campbell - OK, Flt Sgt R J Taylor, Fg Off J M J Rowland, Sgt E Baxter, Sgt E Christon, Sgt L M Lewis, killed
Wellington GR XIV	MF727	CX-E	22 Apr 1945	16 Jun 1945	Doncaster	
Wellington GR XIV	MP752	CX-G	15 Dec 1944	7 Jun 1945	Struck off charge	
Wellington GR XIV	NB801	O			172 Sqn aircraft	
Wellington GR XIV	NB821	D			407 Sqn aircraft	
Wellington GR XIV	NB825	CX-T/L	15 Jan 1945	16 Jun 1945	Doncaster	
Wellington GR XIV	NB828		14 Jan 1945	26 Mar 1945	To 78 MU	
Wellington GR XIV	NB835	CX-P	30 Jan 1945	13 Feb 1945	Bounced on take-off, damaging u/c jettisoned practice bombs and fuel & belly landed	Flt Sgt R M White, Sgt W G Johns, Flt Sgt E D Sykes, Flt Sgt J C Cornwell, Flt Sgt T E Bullas, Flt Sgt F Rowley - OK
Wellington GR XIV	NB836	CX-N	3 Mar 1945	17 Jun 1945	Doncaster	
Wellington GR XIV	NB838	CX-T/J	8 Jan 1945	16 Jun 1945	Doncaster	
Wellington GR XIV	NB841	CX-C	30 Jan 1945	16 Jun 1945	Doncaster	
Wellington GR XIV	NB856	CX-X	8 Jan 1945	16 Jun 1945		
Wellington GR XIV	NB858	CX-V	22 Jan 1945	19 Apr 1945	Missing from Anti Submarine patrol SW Approaches, took off 2103 hrs, SOS call 4 hrs later	Lt M Overed, Flt Sgt E N Rowland, Flt Sgt H J Ryan, Sgt M J Gillane Sgt J R Gee, Flt Sgt J J Brophy - all killed
Wellington GR XIV	NB869	CX-A	21 Nov 1944	21 Apr 1945	Landed on short runway at St Merryn, overran & hit bus	Flt Lt C A Duncan, Plt Off C J Jennings, Plt Off J Inglis, Flt Sgt R Morely, Plt Off K G Robertson, Plt Off G B Dorington - OK
Wellington GR XIV	NB875	CX-Q	17 Mar 1945	21 Apr 1945	Engine failed - flapless landing at St Eval - struck off charge	WO R M White, Flt Sgt WG Johns, Flt Sgt E D Sykes, Flt Sgt J C Cornwell, Flt Sgt T E Bullas, Flt Sgt F Rowley - OK
Wellington GR XIV	NB909	CX-K	10 Jan 1945	17 Jun 1945	8 MU	
Wellington GR XIV	NC419	CX-M	20 Feb 1945	19 Apr 1945	Crashed into cliffs at Trenance Point 4 miles NNE Newquay at 0005hrs after Anti Submarine Patrol. Pilot reported fuel leak	Flt Lt M C Hogg, Fg Off G S Smith, Flt Lt L A Jackson, Flt Sgt E E Pearson, Flt Sgt R D Speak, Flt Sgt L C Barker - all killed
Wellington GR XIV	NC776	CX-B				

Abbreviations used:

ASR	Air Sea Rescue	MU	Maintenance Unit
LG	Landing Ground	RTB	Return(ing) To Base
MT	Motorised Transport	U/c	Undercarriage

With grateful acknowledgement to Ray Sturtivant and Pel Temple for their research which provided the basis for this list.

Appendix 2

14 Squadron Aircraft Markings 1915–45

BE2 series & Martynsides (1915-1917)
Initially these aircraft were finished in a straw-coloured dope, which was well-suited to operating in desert conditions, however. Roundels were worn on the sides of the fuselage immediately aft of the cockpit and a blue/white/red striped flash was painted on the rudder; the aircraft serial number was stencilled in black on the tailfin. When the unit moved into Palestine in late 1916 aircraft were finished in a darker khaki green and the roundels were outlined in white. No unit markings were applied.

RE8 (1918)
All RE8 aircraft were finished in the standard army khaki, with pale brown undersides. National markings comprised roundels, outlined in white, worn on the sides of the aircraft and the blue/white/red striped rudder flash. The serial number stencilled in black outlined in white on the tailfin. No unit markings were applied.

Bristol Fighter (1920-25)
Initially (approximately 1920-23) the Bristol Fighters were finished in the standard khaki green with the Squadron badge painted on the sides of the fuselage in lieu of a roundel. Aircraft serial numbers were stencilled in white on the rear of the fuselage sides just ahead of the tailplane. Tailfins were painted as chequerboards or with other symbols (eg a diagonal bar) and the rudder was painted with blue/white/red striped rudder flash.

From about 1923 onwards the aircraft were finished in a silver dope and the roundel was painted on the fuselage sides. Squadron badge was painted in the front of the radiator grille. Again tailfins were marked with chequerboards, bars, stars and playing card symbols. It is not clear at present whether these markings were individual for each aeroplane (most likely) or whether they represented (for example) different Flights. Serial numbers were stencilled in black on the rear fuselage ahead of the tailplane and in some aircraft repeated on the rudder flash.

DH9A (1925-30)
DH9As were painted overall in silver, with serial numbers in black at the rear fuselage and repeated on the rudder flash. Some aircraft also had letters or symbols on the fuselage aft of the roundel. Initially aircraft had the Squadron badge painted on the radiator grille (as per the Bristol Fighter) but this was later (c. 1927) changed to a plaque mounted on the port side of the nose beneath the exhaust pipe.

Fairey IIIF (1930-32)
Fairey IIIF aircraft were painted silver overall, with black upper fuselage surfaces, outlined in blue trim, to reduce glare. An individual aircraft letter was painted on tailfin in black and repeated in white on the rear decking. The tail flash was coloured red/white/blue – a reversal of the colours used on the DH9A. The Squadron badge was metal plaque mounted on the port side of the nose.

Fairey Gordon (1932-38)
Fairey Gordons were painted silver overall, with black upper fuselage surfaces outlined with a blue trim. Individual aircraft letters were painted in black on the tailfin, and most aircraft did not carry a fin flash. The aircraft serial number, which was stencilled in black (outlined in white) on the aft fuselage, was then repeated on the fin. From c.1937 tailfins were painted Red A

Flight, Yellow B Flight, Blue C Flight, and in these case the individual letter was painted in white on a red or blue background, or black against a yellow background.

Wellesley (1938-41)
Initially the Wellesleys were finished in standard "Temperate Land" scheme of Dark Earth/Dark Green disruptive camouflage with black undersides. Squadron crest (i.e. "approved" pattern winged plate) was painted on the tailfin, and individual aircraft letters were in white aft of the fuselage roundel. All the roundels were coloured red/white/blue/yellow. No fin flash was carried, and the aircraft serial number was stencilled in black on aft fuselage and on the fin, and also in large white letters/figures on the undersides of wings.

From April 1939 the Squadron code letters "BF" in light grey were worn aft of the fuselage roundel with the aircraft individual letter forward of the roundel between the rear cockpit and the triangular fuselage window; the roundels were "toned down" to red/blue and a tan distemper was painted over the dark green of the camouflage to give a "desert" scheme.

From late 1939 the tan distemper was removed and the aircraft returned to standard temperate land scheme with red/white/blue/yellow roundels on the fuselage; the Squadron code letters were changed to "LY" and the Squadron crest was removed from the tailfins. By late 1940 the aircraft at Port Sudan would have looked very tatty with faded, worn and patched-up paint.

Blenheim (1940-42)
The first Blenheims were delivered to the Squadron in Port Sudan in standard Temperate Land scheme with Squadron code letters "LY" as per the Wellesley.

From April/May 1941 in the Western Desert, 14 Squadron Blenheims were finished in standard Desert Scheme of "Dark Earth/Middle Stone" disruptive camouflage with azure undersides. The aircraft serial number was stencilled in black on the rear fuselage sides. Aircraft individual code letter was in light grey ahead of the roundel and there were no Squadron code letters

From early 1942, on return to the Western Desert, the aircraft individual code letters were painted in white ahead of the roundel and instead of Squadron code letters, there was a white bar behind the roundel (this apparently because aircraft were frequently swapped between units). Once again these aircraft would have looked very worn-out.

Marauder (1942-44)
In the expectation that the Squadron would continue in the light bomber role, the first few (probably the first nine or so) Marauders were finished in the standard desert camouflage, with individual aircraft letters painted in black on the sides of the fuselage directly under the dorsal turret. Other aircraft retained the USAAF Olive Drab on upper surfaces and Neutral Grey under surfaces.

However, when the Unit changed role in October 1942 to torpedo bombing and maritime reconnaissance the desert camouflaged aircraft were then repainted in the standard Temperate Sea scheme of Dark Slate Grey/Extra Dark Sea Grey disruptive camouflage. Aircraft letters were painted either in in black or white under the turret. Again, those aircraft which were still painted in the USAAF scheme, including all replacement aircraft, retained that scheme. Most aircraft would have looked very tatty due to wearing of the paint.

By October 1943 all aircraft were in the USAAF-style Olive Drab with grey under-surfaces, with individual aircraft letters painted in red.

Wellington (1944-45)
The Wellington aircraft were finished in standard Coastal Command Temperate Sea camouflage scheme comprising white underside and sides, with Extra Dark Sea Grey on the upper fuselage and wing surfaces. The squadron code letters "CX" were painted ahead of the roundel in red, with individual aircraft letters painted on the opposite side of the roundel.

14 Squadron History References

National Archives Files:

Air1/1269/204/9/85	Shoreham Correspondence Mar 1913-Oct 1915
Air1/1269/204/9/90	Move of 14 & 15 Squadrons
Air1/1660/294/97/4	14 Sqn Various Reports Apr-Oct 1915
Air1/1660/294/97/5	14 Sqn Daily Routine Orders May-Sep 1915
Air1/1660/294/97/6	14 Sqn W/T Correspondence Apr-Sep 1915
Air1/1660/294/97/8	14 Sqn Misc Returns and Reports Sep – Nov 1915
Air1/1660/294/97/11	14 Sqn Returns of A/C on Charge May – Sep 1915
Air1/1753/204/141/4-5	5 Wing War Diary Dec 1915 – Jan 1916
Air1/1754/204/141/7-13	5 Wing War Diary Feb – Jun 1916
Air1/1755/204/141/14-19	5 Wing War Diary Jul- Oct 1916
Air1/1756	5 Wing War Diary Nov 1916
Air1/2186/209/17/3-4	5 Wing War Diary War Diary Oct 1916
Air1/2186/209/17/7-8	5 Wing War Diary Dec 1916
Air1/2188/209/17/13	5 Wing War Diary Mar 1916
Air1/2189/209/17/14-15	5 Wing War Diary Apr, Jul 1916
Air1/2120/207/72/6A & B	Resumé of Operations – 5 Wg RFC/RAF
Air1/449/15/307/1	Supplementary report Col Salmond
Air1/2188/209/17/10	5 Wing War Diary Jan 1917
Air1/1757/204/141/24	5 Wing War Diary Feb 1917
Air1/2336/226/2/33	5 Wing War Diary Mar 1917
Air1/2336/226/2/34 & 35	5 Wing War Diary Apr 1917
Air1/2336/226/2/36	5 Wing War Diary May 1917
Air1/1758/204/141/31	5 Wing War Diary Jun 1917
Air1/1758/204/141/33	5 Wing War Diary Jul 1917
Air1/1758/204/141/35	5 Wing War Diary Aug 1917
Air1/1758/204/141/37	5 Wing War Diary Sep 1917
Air1/2186/209/17/2	5 Wing War Diary Sep 1917
Air1/2190/17/21	5 Wing War Diary Oct 1917
Air 1/1759/204/141/41	5 Wing War Diary Nov 1917
Air1/2191/209/17/28	5 Wing War Diary Dec 1917
Air1/1662/204/97/28	"C" Flight 14 Squadron Bombing Reports
Air1/2120/207/72/6A & B	Resumé of Operations – 5 Wg RFC/RAF
Air1/1759/204/141/45	5 Wing War Diary Jan 1918
Air1/2332/226/2/2	5 Wing War Diary Feb 1918
Air1/1760/204/141/9	5 Wing War Diary Mar 1918
Air1/1760/204/141/51	5 Wing War Diary Apr 1918
Air1/2332/226/2/6	5 Wing War Diary Apr 1918
Air1/1760/204/141/53	5 Wing War Diary May 1918

Air1/1760/204/141/54	5 Wing War Diary Jun 1918
Air1/1761/204/141/55	5 Wing War Diary Jul 1918
Air1/2334/226/2/14	5 Wing War Diary Aug 1918
Air1/2334/226/2/15	5 Wing War Diary Sep 1918
Air1/2334/226/2/18	5 Wing War Diary Oct 1918
Air1/1641/204/94/17-21	HQ Middle East War Diary Oct-Dec 1918
Air1/1661/204/97/16	14 Squadron Bombing Reports
Air1/2120/207/72/6A & B	Resumé of Operations – 5 Wg RFC/RAF
Air1/2267/209/70/37	HQ Middle East – Various Returns
Air1/2390/228/11/127	War Experiences – D Colyer
Air1/1131/204/5/2178	Disbandment of Units
Air 2/1519	Report on Flight to East Africa 1932
Air 2/2319	Unit Badge 14 (B) Squadron
Air 2/7276	Middle East Command: Allotment of Replacement Aircraft 1940-41
Air 5/203	Operations in Transjordania and Palestine
Air 5/1233	Palestine & Transjordan Landing Grounds
Air 5/1237	Middle East Monthly Summaries 1927-29
Air 5/1238	Middle East Monthly Summaries 1930-32
Air 5/1239	Middle East Monthly Summaries 1921-24
Air 5/1240	Middle East Monthly Summaries 1925-26
Air 5/1241	Middle East Monthly Summaries 1933-36
Air 5/1242	Middle East Monthly Summaries 1937-39
Air 5/1243	Operations Palestine 1920-30
Air 5/1244	Operations Palestine 1930-40
Air 5/1245	Palestine Monthly Summaries 1924-30
Air 5/1246	Palestine Monthly Summaries 1931-33
Air 5/1247	Palestine Monthly Summaries 1934-37
Air 5/1248	Palestine Monthly Summaries 1938-39
Air 9/19	Palestine and Transjordan 1921-36
Air 23/799	Amman-Ramadi Air Route
Air 23/6452	14 Squadron Reconnaissance Reports 1940
Air 23/6453	14 Squadron Bombing Reports 1940
Air 23/6454	14 Squadron Bombing Reports 1940
Air 23/6455	14 Squadron Bombing Reports 1940
Air 23/7213	MACAF – Camouflage of Aircraft
Air 23/7074	Photo Interpretation Kyklades
Air 23/7429	Shallufah
Air 27/191-197	History of 14 Squadron & 14 Squadron Operations Record Book
Air 27/865	History of 111 Squadron
Air 29/205	Middle East Interpretation Unit Feb 1943
Air 69/18	Royal Air Force Operations in Palestine during the Arab Rebellion 1936-1939
Air 69/130	Post War History of Palestine & Transjordan, 1936
Air69/202	The Sinai & Palestine Campaign 1914-16

Log Books:
Flt Lt R L R Atcherley – RAF Museum   Flt Lt C P Ashworth (via Vincent Ashworth)

Fg Off H W T Bates (via T Bates)

Sqn Ldr J C Buckland
Deacon logbook – RAF Museum

Sqn Ldr I D H Gibbins (via H Gibbins)
Flt Lt C B Greet – RAF Museum

Fg Off J W A Lowder
AM Sir Douglas Macfadyen (via
AM I Macfadyen)
Sgt F V Parker (via A Parker)

AM Sir John Slessor Logbook –
RAF Museum

Flt Sgt T C Bullock (via M
Bullock)
Flt Lt G W Clarke-Hall
Maj J E Dixon-Spain – Imperial
War Museum
Flt Lt G G Graham
Sqn Ldr E G Hopcraft – RAF
Museum
Maj E M Lewis SAAF
W/O C J O'Connor
(via P O'Connor)
Sqn Ldr H E P Wigglesworth –
RAF Museum
Flt Lt A S Tait (via Linda M
Aiton)

Memoirs:
Maj J E Dixon Spain – journal kindly provided by M O'Connor
Sqn Ldr H I Hanmer – memoir and lecture notes kindly provided by Prof D
Gavish
Lt T Henderson – memoir kindly provided by R Bragger
Sgt C R King – memoir Imperial War Museum 10868
Maj E M Lewis SAAF
Lt H L Lascelles journal Imperial War Museum 3417
Gp Capt WSG Maydwell (Mediterranean Safari)
Neil O'Connor DFC – As it Happened provided by Patrick O'Connor
AM Sir Anthony Selway Memoir – RAF Museum B687
Sgt Walter Showell – diary kindly provided by Mike Lofthouse
AM Sir Ralph Sorley Memoir – RAF Museum MF 10030/1
AVM Sir Thomas Traill – Imperial War Museum 6028

Books:
Adriatic Adventure, Sqn Ldr John Buckland RAAF – Robertson & Mullens 1945
Aircraft of the RAF, Owen Thetford – Putnam 1979
Aircraft Camouflage & Markings 1907-1954, Bruce Robertson – Harleyford 1961
Allenby – Sir Archibald Wavell, Harrap & Co 1940
Australians at War in the Air, Ross A Pearson – Kangaroo Press 1995
B-26 Marauder, WarbirdTech Vol 29, Frederick A Johnsen – Specialty Press/Airlife 2000
Bless "Em All... Some Episodes of my Wartime Service Life 1940-45, E A Meader – E A Meader
1994
A Brief History of the Royal Flying Corps in World War 1 – Ralph Barker, Constable &
Robinson 2002
The Bristol Blenheim A Complete History, Graham Warner – Crecy 2005
The British Airman, Roger A Freeman – Arms & Armour Presss 1989
British Military Aircraft Serias, Bruce Robertson – Ian Allen 1971
The DH9/DH9A File, Ray Sturtivant & Gordon Page – Air Britain 1999
Fairey IIIF Interwar Military Workhorse, Phillip Jarrett – Ad Hoc Publications 2009
For Our Tomorrow He Gave His Today, Vincent A Ashworth – Vincent A Ashworth 2009
Forgotten Soldiers of the First World War, David R Wodward – Tempus 2007

Jump For It!, Gerald Bowman – Evans Brothers Limited 1955
De Montmartre à Tripoli, André Glarner – Editions Musy, Paris 1945
The North African Campaign 1940-43, Gen Sir William Jackson – Batsford 1975
Not Your Average Joe, Linda M Aiton -Linda M Aiton 2003
On a Hillside in Mataro, Peter Dawson – Peter Dawson 1997
RAF Lists 1920-1945 – HMSO
Reports of the Commission of Inquiry into the Palestine Disturbances in May 1921 – HMSO
Roots of the Israeli Air Force 1913-48 Ambar, Eyal & Cohen – Israeli Defence Force/Air Force Air Force History Branch, trans E Makevit
The Royal Air Force An Encyclopaedia of the Inter-War Years Vol I, Wg Cdr IM Philpott – Pen & Sword 2005
The Royal Air Force An Encyclopaedia of the Inter-War Years Vol II, Wg Cdr IM Philpott – Pen & Sword 2008
Seven Pillars of Wisdom, T E Lawrence, – Jonathan Cape 1926
The Spook and the Commandant, Gp Capt C Hill – William Kimber 1975
Spreading My Wings, The Wartime Story of Ronald Hadingham, Evan Hadingham – Blue Caribou Press 2011
Squadrons of the RAF, Wg Cdr J Jefford – Airlife 2001
The Story of the Arab Legion, Brig John Bagot Glubb – Hodder & Stoughton 1948
Winged Promises, Vincent Orange et Al – RAF Benevolent Fund 1996
Wings Over the Desert, Desmond Seward – Haynes 2009
A World Away, Cecil Manson – Pigeon Press 1981
The War in the Air Vol 5, H A Jones – Clarendon 1935
Years of Combat, Lord Douglas of Kirtleside – The Quality Book Club 1963

Miscellaneous Documents:

Aircraft Accident Cards – RAF Museum
Aircraft Movement Cards – RAF Museum
FA Bates – assorted papers kindly provided by M O'Connor
Bundes Archiv Files pertaining to Melos Harbour Feb 1943 – kindly provided by Nicholas Vasilatos & Dimitris Galon
Barcelona Harbour Records March 1944 – kindly provided by P Argila, FPAC
FF Minchin – research papers for biography of Minchin kindly provided by M Partridge

Correspondence:

C Campbell, R Dawson, The Lord Deramore, D Francis, R Froom, G G Graham, J Hanson, P Henry, N Hooker, J W A Lowder, W S G Maydwell, R Page, J Robertson, R Slatcher, D C Stapleton

Periodicals:

Cross & Cockade, Vol 19 No 2 "Henry George Crow" – G Stuart Leslie,
Cross & Cockade, Vol 21 N0 1 "Skies Over the Holy Land" – Peter F G Wright
Cross & Cockade, Vol 24 No 1 "CO in the Sideshows – the Flying Career of Maj FA Bates" – Raymond Vann
Cross & Cockade, Vol 34 No 2 "Lawrence's Air Force" – Peter FG Wright & Roger Bragger
Cross & Cockade, Vol 37 No2 "A British Hydroplane on the Dead Sea" – Dr Dov Gavish
The Geographical Journal, Vol 102 No2 "Journey to Kilwa" – Agnes Horsefield,
History Today, Vol 58 (6) Jun 2008 "Policing Palestine" – James Barker

Over the Front, Vol 13 No 1 "Wings Over Sinai & Palestine" – Dieter H Gröschel & Jürgen Ladek

Flight, various via website – see below

The London Gazette, various via website – see below

Websites:

Air of Authority   http:www.rafweb.org

Commonwealth War Graves Commission http:www.cwgc.org

London Gazette http:london-gazette.co.uk

Flight Magazine Archive http:flightglobal.com

Index

INDEX